Impeccable Solomon?

Impeccable Solomon?

A Study of Solomon's Faults in Chronicles

YONG HO JEON

PICKWICK *Publications* · Eugene, Oregon

IMPECCABLE SOLOMON?
A Study of Solomon's Faults in Chronicles

Pickwick Publications
An Imprint of Wipf and Stock Publishers
199 W. 8th Ave., Suite 3
Eugene, OR 97401

www.wipfandstock.com

ISBN 13: 978-1-4982-6227-9

Cataloging-in-Publication data:

Jeon, Yong Ho.

    Impeccable Solomon? : a study of Solomon's faults in Chronicles / Yong Ho Jeon.

    xviii + 314 p. ; 23 cm. Includes bibliographical references and index.

    ISBN 13: 978-1-4982-6227-9

    1. Bible. O.T. Chronicles—Criticism, interpretation, etc.. 2. Solomon, King of Israel. I. Title.

BS1345.2 J254 2012

Manufactured in the U.S.A.

To my Risen Lord, who is coming

Contents

Preface

SOLOMON IS DEPICTED, BOTH in Kings and Chronicles, as one who achieves the grand and conspicuous task of building the Jerusalem temple. But a substantial difference between the two historical works is apparent in their portrayal of Solomon. Solomon in Kings is depicted as one who committed serious idolatry and was even the ultimate cause of the king-dom division that was punishment from God. In contrast to that, Solomon in Chronicles is interpreted by most scholars as flawless, mainly because Solomon's idolatry and his killing of political enemies are omitted. They believe that in Chronicles Solomon is depicted only as the honourable temple builder, and therefore that the Chronicler's account contradicts that of Kings.

This dissertation attempts to observe Solomon's faults in the account of his reign in Chronicles. The attempt is to challenge the near consen-sus view that Solomon is portrayed as impeccable in Chronicles. Some of the questions that stimulated me to pursue this exploration were: Did the Chronicler really intend to whitewash Solomon against the general knowledge of Solomon's tragic fall, which was apparently presupposed in the post-exile era (Neh 13:26)? Is it reasonable for us to think that the Chronicler believed that he could present Solomon as impeccable against the old tradition? Could the Chronicler really expect to replace the old tradition with his new presentation of an impeccable Solomon?

The present near consensus view of the impeccable Solomon seems to be a citadel that is established on several solid foundations or sub-structures that also are accepted as near consensus views. For example, most commentators agree that King Abijah is portrayed as a good king in Chronicles, in stark contrast to Kings where Abijah is portrayed as a typical bad king. The view of good King Abijah in Chronicles implies that the portrayal of Solomon too can be radically changed in Chronicles from that of Kings. Furthermore, the view strongly supports the suggestion that Solomon is presented as flawless because Solomon's responsibility for the kingdom division is removed in good King Abijah's speech in Chronicles. This view is connected to another near consensus that most speeches in Chronicles actually reflect the theological stance of the Chronicler himself.

Serious challenges have not yet been made to those "substructure consensuses" of the impeccable Solomon view. However, the following kind of questions may be raised. Do the major speeches in Chronicles really reflect the Chronicler's view? Is Abijah really portrayed as a good king in Chronicles? Is Abijah's speech approved by the author? To challenge the consensus view of the impeccable Solomon involves reconsidering several substructures that are generally accepted in the study of Chronicles. It means a radical criticism of the present understanding of Chronicles. This study raises these questions and argues against those near consensus views that support the view of the impeccable Solomon in Chronicles. With additional observations and analysis of literary and theological features of Chronicles, our study will eventually show that Solomon is not presented as impeccable in Chronicles. Throughout the study, the present understanding of Chronicles will be rectified and deepened.

One of the important implications of this study is the relationship between parts of the Bible as canon. It is about how the later traditions treated the previous ones. This study will also show how much the biblical authors sensitively and delicately lead their readers to receive the messages of their works through their literary techniques. Finding contradictions between an old tradition and a new one could be the result of the ignorance or overlooking of the delicacy with which the biblical authors composed their writings.

This dissertation describes its methodology as a "reader-sensitive approach" in order to emphasize the sense that the text is designed to guide its reader sensitively to convey effectively its meaning, message, and intention. The "reader-sensitive approach" can be seen as a subcategory of "reader-response criticism," excluding the possibility of an overly reader-centred reading such as a deconstructionist reading.

In our methodology, which we call a "reader-sensitive approach," it is presumed that the author of Chronicles tried to exploit the reader's pre-understanding or prior-knowledge to achieve his own purpose (or to solve his dilemma). It is agreed by most commentators on the work that there are not a few occasions that betray that the author of Chronicles presumed his reader's prior-knowledge of the old tradition (mostly the Pentateuch and Samuel-Kings). Nevertheless, the reader's pre-understanding or prior-knowledge has not been considered seriously as an element that contributes to the meaning of the text, especially as intended by the author.

The reader's reading process is another important factor in the "reader-sensitive approach." We presuppose that both the authors of Kings and Chronicles composed their works so that the reader's reading process and prior knowledge are exploited to maximize the effect of their messages.

The attempt to challenge the impeccable Solomon view requires several preliminary steps. These include (1) a reconsideration of the portrayal of Abijah in Chronicles and his speech, (2) identification of the frequent appearance, as two of its literary features, of (a) increased complexity of Kings' portrayal and (b) the allusion technique in Chronicles, (3) observation of the close relationship between Chronicles and Deuteronomy (or the Pentateuch), (4) a new interpretation of the Solomon narrative in Kings. In order to get a new interpretation of the Solomon narrative in Kings, this book applies the same "reader-sensitive approach" to that narrative. The application results in finding the nature of Solomon's flaws in Kings as part of the reader's (of Chronicles) prior-knowledge, and it also shows the effectiveness and merit of the "reader-sensitive approach."

Acknowledgments

THIS WORK IS A slight revision of a doctoral dissertation submitted to the University of Bristol, UK, in August 2008. Translations of the Bible are mainly from the NRSV, but where indicated I have used my own translations.

I would like to express my thanks to my teachers. My supervisor, Revd Dr Ernest Lucas, gave me many useful comments on my initial drafts, continuously encouraging me while allowing me my own writing strategy. My external supervisor, Dr Gordon McConville, also gave me important comments on my initial writing, as well as encouragement. Revd Dr Philip Jenson, my tutor during my first year in Trinity College Bristol, encouraged mc to keep studying. While his comments were given a few years before this study began, some of them proved very useful for it. Dr John Bimson gave me very perceptive comments on my study of Solomon in Kings. Revd Dr John Nolland, through his lectures on "reader-response criticism" in my MA course, strengthened my conviction of the suitability of the "reader-sensitive approach" for the present work.

Besides providing an ideal academic environment, Trinity College Bristol has also provided me with good support from other staff members, especially the Librarian Miss Susan Brown. My special thanks go to Mrs Clare Wenham whose help with English style and editorial matters was enormous.

Funding was provided, during my study and the revision process, by Nae-Soo-Dong Church and Bong-Dong Central Church. I give huge thanks for their love, prayer, and financial support, especially to Revd Seong In Hong and Revd Jin Hyun Kim. Also, I would like to give thanks to the Korean Church in general, in which my Lord has nurtured me, and where I received the first motivation for this study.

Acknowledgments

My sincere thanks go to my wife Hi-Seon who took care of me and home, including helping my ministry in Reading Korean Church enormously, allowing me to concentrate my time and energy on the present work. Without her dedication, I could not have undertaken this study.

I would like to thank the Tyndale Bulletin for permission to reuse material from my article "The Retroactive Re-evaluation Technique with Pharaoh's Daughter and the Nature of Solomon's Corruption in 1 Kings 1–12," *Tyndale Bulletin* 62.1 (2011) 15–40.

Lastly and most significantly, I have to acknowledge that God has guided and helped me through all those people in his providence, providing me with the necessary resources, and more importantly, with the strength to ponder the Bible.

Abbreviations

SOURCE ABBREVIATIONS

AB	The Anchor Bible
AbOTC	Abingdon Old Testament Commentaries
AJSL	*American Journal of Semitic Languages and Literature*
Ant	Antiquities of the Jews (Josephus)
ApOTC	Apollos Old Testament Commentary
ATD	Das Alte Testament Deutsch
BASOR	*Bulletin of the American Schools of Oriental Research*
BCOT	Biblical Commentary on the Old Testament
BDB	Brown, F., S. R. Driver, and C. A. Briggs. A Hebrew and English Lexicon of the Old Testament (Oxford, 1907)
BibInt	*Biblical Interpretation*
BLS	Bible and Literature Series
BST	The Bible Speaks Today
BZAW	Beihefte zur Zeitschrift für die alttestamentliche Wissenschaft
CBC	Cambridge Bible Commentary
CBSC	Cambridge Bible for Schools and Colleges
CC	Communicator's Commentary
CBQ	*Catholic Biblical Quarterly*
ConBOT	Coniectanea biblica: Old Testament Series
COTTV	Commentary on the Old Testament in Ten Volumes
CRBS	*Critical Review: Biblical Studies*
CTM	Concordia Theological Monthly
DSB	Daily Study Bible

EncJud	*Encyclopaedia Judaica (Jerusalem, 1971)*
EOT	Exploring the Old Testament
ExpTim	*Expository Times*
FRLANT	Forschungen zur Religion und Literatur des Alten und Neuen Testaments
FFF	*Foundation and Facets Forum*
FOTL	Forms of the Old Testament Literature
FT	*Faith and Thought*
FTS	Freiburger theologische Studien
HAT	Handbuch zum Alten Testament
HCOT	Historical Commentary on the Old Testament
HH	Hermeneia Hermeneia. A Critical and Historical Commentary on the Bible
HSM	Harvard Semitic Monographs
HTR	*Harvard Theological Review*
HUCA	*Hebrew Union College Annual*
ICC	International Critical Commentary
IDB	Interpreter's Dictionary of the Bible (Nashville, 1962)
Int	Interpretation: A Bible Commentary for Teaching and Preaching
JBL	*Journal of Biblical Literature*
JBQ	*Jewish Bible Quarterly*
JANES	*Journal of the Ancient Near Eastern Society*
JETS	*Journal of the Evangelical Theological Society*
JSOT	*Journal for the Study of the Old Testament*
JSOTSup	Journal for the Study of the Old Testament: Supplement Series
JSS	*Journal of Semitic Studies*
TJ	*Trinity Journal*
LS	Louvain Studies
LTQ	*Lexington Theological Quarterly*
NAC	New American Commentary
NBC	New Bible Commentary
NCBC	New Century Bible Commentary
NES	Near Eastern Studies
NIBC	New International Biblical Commentary
NICNT	New International Commentary on the New Testament
OBS	Oxford Bible Series
OBT	Overtures to Biblical Theology

OTG	Old Testament Guide
OTL	Old Testament Library
PC	Pulpit Commentary
PEGLMBS	*Proceedings of the Eastern Great Lakes and Midwest Biblical Society*
RNBC	Readings: A New Biblical Commentary
RTP	*Revue de théologie et de philosophie*
SBB	Soncino Books of the Bible
SBLDS	Society of Biblical Literature Dissertation Series
SHBOT	Studies in the Historical Books of the Old Testament
Shofar	*Shofar: An Interdisciplinary Journal of Jewish Studies*
TBC	Torch Bible Commentaries
TDOT	Theological Dictionary of the Old Testament (Grand Rapid: Eerdmans, 1974–)
TOTC	Tyndale Old Testament Commentaries
TJ	*Trinity Journal*
TynBul	*Tyndale Bulletin*
VT	*Vetus Testamentum*
WBC	Word Biblical Commentary
WeBC	Westminster Bible Companion
WMANT	Wissenschaftliche Monographien zum Alten und Neuen Testament
WTJ	*Westminster Theological Journal*
WWSup	Word & World Supplement Series
ZAW	*Zeitschrift für die alttestamentliche Wissenschaft*

GENERAL ABBREVIATIONS

ch	chapter
chs	chapters
Ev	English version
n.	footnote
LXX	Septuagint
NT	New Testament
OT	Old Testament
x	times
//	parallel passage

BIBLICAL BOOKS

Gen	Genesis
Exod	Exodus
Lev	Leviticus
Num	Numbers
Deut	Deuteronomy
Josh	Joshua
Judg	Judge
Sam	Samuel
Kgs	Kings
Chr	Chronicles
Ezra	Ezra
Neh	Nehemiah
Ps (*pl.* Pss)	Psalm(s)
Prov	Proverbs
Isa	Isaiah
Ezek	Ezekiel
Hos	Hosea
Hag	Haggai
Matt	Matthew
Luke	Luke
Acts	Acts of the Apostles

BIBLE VERSIONS

AV	Authorized Version (King James Version)
NIV	New International Bible
NRSV	New Revised Standard Bible
RV	Revised Version

1

Introduction

1. THE "IMPECCABLE SOLOMON" INTERPRETATION AND QUESTIONS RAISED ABOUT IT

THE IDEA THAT SOLOMON is idealized in Chronicles has a long history. It has long been recognized that Solomon's faults, which appear in Kings, do not appear in the Chronicler's portrayal of the king, and that the omission is intended to idealize Solomon.[1] On the other hand, Solomon in Chronicles suffered scholarly neglect, in contrast to David in Chronicles, who has received abundant attention in relation to the purpose of Chronicles.[2] A distinct change within these trends has been perceived in the last few decades.[3] Modern biblical scholarship interpreted Solomon in Chronicles as being under the shadow of David, at best as a mere follower of his father David.[4] He then began to receive significant attention from scholars such

1. E.g., Wellhausen, *Prolegomena*, 182, 187; Cultis and Madsen, *Chronicles*, 313; Rudolph, *Chronikbücher*, 135, 225–26; Mosis, *Untersuchungen*, 162–68; Braun, "Solomonic Apologetic"; Braun, *1 Chronicles*, xxxii–xxxv; Japhet, *I & II Chronicles*, 48.

2. E.g., von Rad, *Geschichtsbild*, 119–36; Im, *Davidbild*.

3. Braun, "Solomonic Apologetic," 504. Braun explains briefly the major changes of the discussion on Solomon in Chronicles over several decades.

4. E.g., North thinks that the Chronicler treats Solomon disgracefully. "By a double pun on the name Solomon . . . David reduces to mere nominalism the fitness of his son to take responsibility for the building" (North, "The Chronicler," 412).

as Rudolph.[5] Eventually Solomon in Chronicles was promoted, by later commentators like A. Caquot, Braun, Mosis, and Dillard, into the position of ideal king who was, in some senses, of an even higher status than his father David.[6]

A brief summary of arguments of Braun and Mosis will suffice here. Braun observes that David and Solomon have an equal status in Chronicles, in three respects. Firstly, Solomon is presented as a divinely chosen king just like David (1 Chr 17:11; 22:7–10; 28:6). Secondly, Solomon's kingship is presented as enjoying all Israel's "unanimous" assent and support just as David's had been (1 Chr 29:22b–25a). Thirdly, Solomon is presented as a king dedicated to the cult, more specifically to the Jerusalem temple and its functionaries, just like his father David (e.g., 2 Chr 8:12–16).[7]

However, Braun goes beyond simply seeing David and Solomon as equal. He thinks that Solomon appears to "surpass" David at least in two points. Firstly, the Chronicler presents Solomon as impeccable through providing an apologetic for Solomon against the king's presentation in Kings, by omitting the content of 1 Kgs 11, which describes Solomon's apostasy. Additionally, Solomon's worship in a high place in his early reign is vindicated by additional material which tells us that the tabernacle of Moses was there. According to Braun, moreover, Solomon obeys God perfectly without a single failure. Secondly, Solomon appears to "surpass" David as the chosen one to build the temple, from which David is disqualified. Therefore, for Braun, Solomon is presented in Chronicles as in

---

5. Rudolph, *Chronikbücher*, 225–26. Rudolph concludes that "Wie bei David ist auch bei Solomo die messianische Erwartung, wenn überhaupt, nur schwach angedeutet (s. 6 16 f. 42 7 18)" ['As with David, the messianic expectation is also generally present in Solomon, but without strong emphasis': my translation] (ibid., 226).

6. Braun, *1 Chronicles*, "it should be noted that the Chronicler does not present to us a blameless David. His responsibility for the abortive census, for example, is magnified in Chronicles (1 Chr 21). Above all, his rejection as the temple builder is specifically charged to the fact that he has shed much blood (1 Chr 22:8) and is a man of war (28:3)" (ibid., xxxiii), "No indication is given that any part of Solomon's reign was characterized by anything other than complete obedience and service to Yahweh" (ibid., xxxiv); Caquot, "Messianisme." Caquot thinks that Solomon in Chronicles is presented as "an impeccable king;" Mosis, *Untersuchungen*; Dillard, "The Chronicler's Solomon," "Solomon is even more idealized than David in Chronicles . . ." (ibid., 292). Dillard's view seems to be inevitable to him for he sees David's transgression in his order of a census, and God's rejection of David as the temple builder while he cannot see any fault of Solomon; Mosis suggests that David is presented as better than Saul, and Solomon better than David (Mosis, *Untersuchungen*).

7. Braun, "Solomonic Apologetic," 507–11.

certain ways *superior* to David, who is portrayed as having some flaws and as being rejected by God as the temple builder.[8]

Nevertheless, Braun believes that the Chronicler intended to present the work of David and Solomon as "a single unit centering in the erection of the temple."[9] He cites three occasions that explicitly show this paralleling of David and Solomon. Firstly, David and Solomon are mentioned together in 2 Chr 7:10 in the context of the dedicatory feast of the temple, while in its Kings only David is mentioned. Secondly, David and Solomon are mentioned together again in 2 Chr 11:17, as a standard for Rehoboam, the subsequent king. Lastly, the two kings' names are mentioned side by side in 2 Chr 35:3–4, as instruction-givers for the Jerusalem cult.[10] Hence, Braun proposes that Solomon's status is presented as fundamentally the same as David's in Chronicles.

Therefore, Braun's argument for Solomon's superiority to David, as the chosen temple builder and impeccable king, does not necessarily mean that David is inferior to Solomon. For example, he admits that, in the matter of the founding of the dynasty, "David's pre-eminence" is observed.[11] Rather, his intention is to correct the "imbalance" in the discussion of Chronicles, which had usually put its focus on the significance and pre-eminence of David, overlooking the significance of Solomon.[12]

While Braun proposes a moderate view of Solomon's superiority over David in that the two kings have *basically* equal status, Mosis proposes a bolder view that Solomon is *fundamentally superior* to David. His view of Solomon's superiority is derived from his observation of three patterns in the king's portrayal in Chronicles: he observes three paradigms of kings in Chronicles, of which Saul, David, and Solomon provide respective archetypes. According to Mosis, Saul represents the exilic state through disobedience to God, and David represents a recovery state from an exilic situation through repentance and obedience to God, while Solomon represents the ideal state in which God's blessing is fully enjoyed in the kingdom.[13] Kings after Solomon are regarded as following either Saul or David, but no king fits the paradigm of Solomon.[14] For Mosis, Solomon is

8. Ibid., 512–14.

9. Ibid., 514.

10. Ibid., 514–15.

11. Ibid., 515.

12. Ibid., 504, 512.

13. Mosis, *Untersuchungen*, 164–69.

14. Ibid., 203. "Dabei ist beachtenswert, daß sich kein Abschnitt finden läßt,

in fact the archetype of the coming messianic king. In tune with this, the wealth and glory of Solomon are nothing but the projection of messianic splendor. Likewise, the Gentile nations' abundant tribute to Solomonic Israel is also a projection of the messianic era.[15]

We will refute, in subsequent sections, Braun's argument that Solomon is presented as impeccable in Chronicles, but here we can briefly refute Mosis' view of Solomon's superiority over David as providing the best paradigm. Firstly, and fundamentally, it is questionable whether his three paradigms provide overall convincing frameworks. While his observation of the contrast between Saul and David concerning their attitude toward the ark is convincing, his distinction between David and Solomon as separate paradigms is not: the parallel which apparently appears between David's reign and Solomon's does undermine Mosis' view. If the unity between David's reign and Solomon's in relation to the temple building, as Braun suggests, is accepted, Mosis' view cannot be strongly maintained. Additionally, it is observed that while Hezekiah is explicitly compared to David (2 Chr 29:2), at the same time the portrayal of Hezekiah's reign follows that of Solomon, as Williamson convincingly shows.[16]

Furthermore, it is in fact observed that the evaluations of some kings refer neither to David nor to Saul in Chronicles. There are subsequent kings who are evaluated as not as good as David, but are still regarded as not as bad as Saul. For example, while for an evaluation of the good king, Jehoshaphat, David is mentioned as an archetype (2 Chr 17:3), but for an "average quality king," Jotham, David is not mentioned at all. In fact, the Chronicler presents several kings as "average quality," who are neither as good as David, nor as bad as Saul. This phenomenon does not fit into Mosis' simplistic framework of kings in Chronicles.

In a recent eclectic suggestion proposed by Japhet,[17] Solomon is regarded as having equal status with David, constituting a golden period

---

der der in Salomo dargestellten Heilszeit entspricht. Auch die „guten" Könige nach Solomo hält der Chr in deutlicher Distanz zum salomonischen Ideal." ['Additionally it is noteworthy that no passage has been found which corresponds to the golden era represented by Solomon. Also, the 'good' kings coming after Solomon are found by the Chronicler to fall short of the Solomonic ideal': my translation]

15. Ibid., 155–61, 163.

16. Williamson, *Israel*, 119–25.

17. Japhet, *Ideology*, 488–89. Japhet changed her position on Solomon in Chronicles from an ideal king to a king who constitutes a golden age of monarchy together with his father David even though he himself is "far from" being an ideal king. "As individual characters, neither David nor Solomon is idealized in the book of Chronicles, but when the two figures are united by one central idea, their period becomes

of Israelite monarchs, while "as individual characters, neither David nor Solomon is idealized in the book of Chronicles."[18] Nevertheless, she insists that every flaw of Solomon, which is obvious in Kings, has been omitted to whitewash the king who ruled in the golden age of Israel after his father King David. When Japhet states that it can hardly be said that Solomon is idealized in Chronicles, it means no less than that his achievement is dependent upon his father's preparation. While insisting that Solomon is not idealized as an individual character, she does not, in fact, point out any specific passage that is intended to reveal Solomon's flaws. Moreover, she willingly accepts substantial passages as showing Solomon's greatness and blessing.[19] In that sense, Japhet still holds to the interpretation that Solomon in Chronicles is a "flawless" or impeccable king.[20]

However, recently Kelly has challenged this long sustained view or consensus and insists that the presentation of Solomon in Chronicles is far from an idealization, but that in many points in Chronicles Solomon's flaws are hinted at or alluded to. For example, he points out that "Criticism from the *Vorlage* [i.e., Kings][21] of Solomon's rule is also retained in 2 Chronicles

---

the golden era of Israelite history." For Japhet's previous view, see Japhet, "Chronicles, Book of": "The point of departure for the history of David and Solomon is the desire to fashion an image without blemish, whereas in the era of the kings of Judah no effort is made to describe an ideal picture" (ibid., 527). However, many scholars still think that both kings are presented as ideal in Chronicles. For example, Braun thinks that "both kings . . . in complete loyalty and devotion to Yahweh" (Braun, *1 Chronicles*, xxxv.); Wilcock insists on his interpretation on 2 Chr 1:14–17 that David's victory over war and Solomon's peaceful trade shows the two aspects of ideal kingship (Wilcock, *Chronicles*, 127); "With the exceptions of David and Solomon, even the best Judahite kings had been guilty of crimes that brought punishment from Yahweh" (Trotter, "Reading, Readers-Saul's Death," 310); Duke also thinks both kings are idealized (Duke, "Rhetorical Approach," 120–21).

18. Japhet, *Ideology*, 489.

19. Ibid., 478–89.

20. Ibid., 488.

21. [my insertion] The term "*Vorlage*" means, "an original version of a manuscript or a book from which a copy is produced," according to the *Oxford Advanced Learner's Dictionary*. However, in the biblical study, the term seems to be used in a rather wider and vague sense, i.e., "underlying source" or "basis," etc. This thesis also will use the term in that conventional sense.

There have been two views of the *Vorlage* of Chronicles. One is the view which regards the so-called Deuteronomistic history as the *Vorlage* of Chronicles, which is the majority view at the moment (For example, McKenzie, *The Chronicler's Use of the Deuteronomistic History*). The other view, which had been a majority view until 200 years ago, and was restated by G. Auld recently, is that Chronicles has a common source with Samuel-Kings (so-called "Book of Two Houses"), and consequently the major part of Deuteronomistic history (i.e., Samuel-Kings) is not regarded as the

10:4, 10, 11, 14," and maintains that negative source material for Solomon's evaluation[22] was not omitted in order to idealize him but simply to focus on another theme.[23] To examine Kelly's point, Throntveit checks royal speeches in Chronicles, and observes that this study does not provide any clear or direct answer to this issue. He also observes that it is evident that the royal speeches in Chronicles have a strong tendency to emphasize God's initiative in giving his mercy and blessing to Solomon in spite of Solomon's weakness.[24] Throntveit concludes, agreeing with Selman[25] at this point, that Chronicles shows that God himself shows his mercy according to his sovereign good will, despite human "weakness."[26] Neither Throntveit nor Selman points to any concrete passage in Chronicles that shows Solomon's weakness or flaws, except the passages that describe the situation after his death (i.e., 2 Chr 10).[27] However, when we consider that the Solomon account consists of a comparatively large amount of material, we can guess that the author might have left some hints to allude to "Solomon's weakness" within the scope of the account of his reign.

Vorlage of Chronicles (Auld, *Privilege*). This study will take the former view as its assumption for some basic reasons. That is, firstly, we have never had such literature except the texts of Kings in the Septuagint and the Massoretic text. Secondly, it should be pointed out that even if the so-called common source material had existed, it would be impossible to reconstruct the so-called common source, for, if the authors of Kings and Chronicles, respectively, omitted some part of the common source, there is no way for us to know it (contra Auld). This point does not directly refute the common source theory. Nevertheless, the point implies that it is not easy to produce a reliable conclusion from the common source theory. The probable view that the *Vorlage* of Chronicles is not exactly the same as the present Samuel-Kings in Massoretic text (Lemke ("The Synoptic Problem") and Mckenzie) does not seem to affect our study, for our discussion will not be involved with such minute details of the text and such minor variations will not affect our discussion significantly.

22. "In his concluding note to this section the writer refers to the rest of Solomon's acts 'from first to last,' which are recorded in 'the words of Nathan the prophet and in the prophecy of Ahijah the Shilonite and the visions of Iddo the seer concerning Jeroboam the son of Neba' (2 Chron. 9.29b, no parallel)" (Kelly, *Retribution and Eschatology*, 90–91). Kelly maintains that, "mention of Ahijah implies that the Chronicler's readers will be familiar with the account of Solomon's apostasy (cf. 1 Kgs 11.29–30)."

23. Kelly, "Messianic Elements," 257–58; Kelly, *Retribution and Eschatology*, 90–91.

24. Throntveit, "Idealization of Solomon-Royal Speeches."

25. Selman, *1 Chronicles*, 251.

26. Throntveit, "Idealization of Solomon in Royal Speeches," 425–27; Throntveit, *When Kings Speak*, 75; "the contrast between the power and might of Yahweh and the weakness and dependence of his people."

27. Selman, *2 Chronicles*, 359. Selman observes that Ahijah's prophecy, and the Israelites' complaint allude to Solomon's wrong doings.

Kelly's challenge seems to be on firm ground, once we accept that the author of Chronicles is a skilful writer who designed every part of his writing or material in order to produce a coherent whole picture. If we take into account the subtlety and artistry of the Chronicler, which had previously been ignored[28] but has now been recognized in recent studies of Chronicles,[29] it is probable that the Chronicler used subtler devices than have usually been expected, in order to present Solomon in line with the description of 2 Chr 10. It seems that the prevailing idealized Solomon interpretation in Chronicles has suppressed the proper observation or reading of the Solomon account in Chronicles.

A new trend in the understanding of the nature of Chronicles also requires a fresh approach to the Solomon account. Even a scholar like Braun, who thinks that the Chronicler was "building upon Samuel-Kings and interpreting, supplementing, and deleting,"[30] holds that "in contrast to his usual method of dealing with his *Vorlage*, his (the Chronicler's) account of Solomon's reign amounts to a virtual rewriting of that history."[31] However, in his recent study of Abijah in Chronicles, Deboys convincingly proved that the Chronicler had not tried to rewrite Abijah's story in opposition to the one in Kings, but only tried to supplement the story of Abijah in Kings by including previously unmentioned aspects of Abijah's reign.[32] In other words, in his view, the Chronicler did not try to subvert the Deuteronomistic presentation, but supplemented it. This suggestion is significant because the portrayal of Abijah in Chronicles has usually been regarded as a conspicuous example of the Chronicler's rewriting of some

28. Japhet, "Chronicles and Ezra-Nehemiah," 307; "the general evaluation of Chronicles and Ezra-Nehemiah as compilations, of inferior artistic merit, and the difficulty of their peculiar idiom, have not encouraged research."

29. Many recent studies have revealed the exquisiteness of the artistry of Chronicles, for example, Dillard, "The Chronicler's Solomon"; Duke, *The Persuasive Appeal*; Williamson, "Accession of Solomon"; Braun, "Solomon the Chosen Temple Builder." In contrast to previous low evaluation of the Chronicler's literary skill, recent scholars evaluate the literary quality of Chronicles highly. For example, Braun, *1 Chronicles*, "considerable literary skill" (ibid., xxiii); Selman, *1 Chronicles*, "The books of Chronicles are clearly a carefully crafted work of literature. The author is equally skilled, however, in integrating into the patterns already described a large number of external sources, taken partly from other sections of the Bible and partly from extrabiblical documents" (ibid., 34).

30. Braun, *1 Chronicles*, xxiii.

31. Ibid., xxxiv.

32. Deboys, "Portrayal of Abijah." An older case of this view is seen in Albright, "The Date and Personality of the Chronicler," 120. "The Chronicler's method in redaction the Book of Kings was to supplement, not to rewrite."

of the depictions in Kings. If this is the case, and it can be applied to other passages including the Solomon account, we have reason to reconsider the view of an idealized Solomon in Chronicles, for his presentation in the Deuteronomistic history obviously contains very negative elements. In tune with this trend, a scholar like Kelly does not think that the Chronicler tried to rewrite the previous tradition of Solomon.[33]

It is true that some scholars such as Knoppers still try to prove that the Chronicler tried to rewrite Israelite history, even nullifying the previous tradition.[34] In Kings, the whole responsibility for the division of the kingdom plainly falls upon Solomon. In Knoppers' view, however, in Chronicles, the whole responsibility for the division of the kingdom falls upon Jeroboam, a villain. Knoppers' interpretation is in a sense inevitable, for he thinks that Solomon is idealized in Chronicles,[35] and consequently the responsibility for the division of the kingdom cannot be placed on Solomon's shoulders any more, but on someone else. His interpretation is not convincing, but raises many questions. For example, in order to insist on his argument, he has to avoid confronting the significant passages (i.e., 2 Chr 10:4, 10, 11, 14; 2 Chr 10:15).

Another important question in interpreting Chronicles is whether it is possible that the author of Chronicles believed that his writing would be accepted by his readers, even though he was suggesting such a different, or even contradictory, presentation from his *Vorlage* or his reader's prior knowledge, as some interpreters assume. Scholars like Payne answer in the negative.[36] Payne argues that the Chronicler, who presupposed the reader's prior knowledge of the first historical work in so many places, could not have expected his work to supplant this old tradition. His argument has merit, for it is evident that in many places in Chronicles the author seems to assume the reader's prior knowledge of the omitted tradition which appears in Samuel-Kings, as many scholars agree.[37]

33. Kelly, *Retribution and Eschatology*, 91. "The Chronicler does not contradict his *Vorlage*, but rather concentrates on its essential meaning for his community."

34. Knoppers, "Rehoboam in Chronicles." Additionally, Sugimoto, through two exemplary cases (1 Chr 18–20 for omission case, and 2 Chr 17–20 for addition case), takes a similar stance that the Chronicles is "structurally independent from the text of Samuel-Kings," which means that the Chronicler used the text of Samuel-Kings as simple source material, for his own independent work. According to him, Chronicles "as a whole is not intended as 'exegesis' or 'revision' of the Samuel-Kings text" (Sugimoto, "Chronicles as Independent Literature").

35. Knoppers, "Rehoboam in Chronicles," 429–30.

36. Payne, "The Purpose and Methods of the Chronicler."

37. For example, Childs, *Introduction*, 646–67; Whybray, *The Good Life*, 114–15.

Another important problem for the interpretation of Solomon in Chronicles concerns the chaotic state of the interpretation of Solomon in Kings. This is evident when we observe that even the starting point of Solomon's corruption is regarded quite differently by scholars, although recent studies incline to the view that Solomon's corruption is observed from the early stage of his reign.[38] That means that the nature of Solomon's corruption in Kings is not yet fully or clearly understood by many interpreters. Most commentators, on the account of Solomon in Chronicles, regard the Solomon account in Kings as its *Vorlage*,[39] and that the Chronicler presumes the reader's prior knowledge of the omitted material in his writing.[40] The confusion in the interpretation of Solomon in Kings therefore means that the interpretations of Solomon in Chronicles were built upon a vulnerable foundation. For example, it is clear that many of Chronicles' Solomon think that the material of chapters 1–2, and 11 in 1 Kings, has been omitted in Chronicles to present Solomon in an idealized way.[41] This view is totally dependent upon the assumption that Solomon's flaws appear only in chapters 1–2 and 11 in 1 Kings.[42] However, recent studies of the Solomon account in Kings show that many other parts of the Solomon account are intended to show negative aspects of his reign.[43]

Selman, *1 Chronicles*, 35; Selman maintains that a reason for the omitting of the alleged Solomon's faults, in Chronicles, is due to the reader's prior knowledge. "One of the reasons for omitting this material is that the reader is expected to have a working knowledge of much of Samuel and Kings." For a concrete example of this view, Williamson, *1 and 2 Chronicles*, 239.

38. Kang, *The Persuasive Portrayal*; Seibert, *Subversive Scribes*. This will be discussed later.

39. E.g., Japhet, "Chronicles, Book of," 525. Japhet thinks that the Chronicler relied more heavily upon the source in Kings, in his writing of Solomon's reign, than of David's reign, while she believes that the Chronicler "disregards the weak points of Solomon's reign"; Jones, *1 & 2 Chronicles*, 68; Braun, *1 Chronicles*, xxiii; Tuell, *First and Second Chronicles*, 5; Selman, *1 Chronicles*, 35, 72.

40. E.g., Childs, *Introduction*, 646–47; Selman, *1 Chronicles*, 35.

41. E.g., Japhet, "Chronicles, Book of," 525. Japhet's understanding of the Solomon account in Kings is similar to Jobling's: "Chronicles disregards the weak points of Solomon's reign and omits both the struggles for the crown at the beginning of it and the religious deviations, the sins, and the failings at the end (1 Kings 11:1–40)"; Williamson, *1 and 2 Chronicles*, 192; Selman, *1 Chronicles*, 35. Selman also seems to regard the same passage as the one that shows Solomon's only faults, while he does not think that Solomon in Chronicles is portrayed as flawless.

42. Jobling, "'Forced Labor': Solomon's Golden Age," 60. Jobling thinks that only 2:12–46 and ch. 11 are the negative presentation of the Solomon in Kings.

43. E.g., Parker, Frisch, and Brettler agree that Solomon's corruption appears from ch. 9 in Kings, while they have different views on details. Parker, "Repetition"; Frisch,

As a whole, the recent studies of the Solomon account in Kings recognize that the account is subtler and more complicated than had previously been recognized. However, these new insights into and understandings of the Solomon account in Kings have not yet been exploited by interpreters of the Solomon account in Chronicles. This fact also requires a new approach to the Solomon account in Chronicles.

2. JUSTIFICATION OF THE ATTEMPT TO APPLY A READER-SENSITIVE APPROACH[44] TO THE SOLOMON ACCOUNT IN CHRONICLES[45]

This book defines its methodology as "a reader-sensitive approach," and it means that the author of the biblical text was very much aware of his

---

"The Narrative of Solomon's Reign"; Brettler, "The Structure of 1 Kings 1–11." On the other hand, some other scholars like McConville and Bimson think that Solomon's corruption appears from very early chapters of the account like chapter 2 or 3. Bimson, "1 and 2 Kings"; McConville, "Narrative and Meaning." Two recent monographs of the narrative show the same view. Kang, *The Persuasive Portrayal*; Seibert, *Subversive Scribes*.

44. As regards the designation of the methodology of the present study, this study will use the term "reader-sensitive approach" rather than "reader-response approach," in order to avoid the impression that the reader can understand a text in a way that the author did not originally intend. While the concept of the "reader-sensitive approach" is included in the concept of the "reader-response approach" in its wide sense, I will choose to use "reader-sensitive" to articulate the implication of the methodology of the present study. The "reader-sensitive approach" presupposes that although the reader's role in forming the sense of the text is great, the ideal reader's reading is guided by the literary technique or strategy employed by the author, as the author intends. In other words, our "reader-sensitive" is opposite to the deconstructionist view in the spectrum of "reader-centered approach" in a wide sense. For various stances in the reader-response approach, see Tate, *Biblical Interpretation*, 214–30.

As for the supposed reader or ideal reader of the Solomon account in the present study, we suppose that the post-exilic restoration community in Jerusalem is the first reader (cf. 2 Chr 36:22–23 and the evidence of the genealogies in 1 Chr 3). However, the present study does not necessarily suppose that the account or Chronicles as a whole was intended only for the first reader. Our basic view is that a history work is not written only for the author's contemporaries, but also next generations whom the author thinks will need the same lessons of history. The issue of the first reader will be treated when we discuss the setting and purpose of the composition of Chronicles in chapter 4.

45. The present study can not provide an outline or analysis of the Solomon account as a whole, due to the limit of space. Rather the study will focus on Solomon's faults. Nevertheless, when an attempt to reconstruct the reader's reading experience is made, the other parts of the account are considered to some extent in chapter 7.

reader; in other words, he was reader-sensitive. The author considered the prior knowledge and reading process of his reader, and even tried to exploit them, through his literary technique.

An application of this approach to the Solomon account in Chronicles[46] is worth attempting when we consider the following three points. Firstly, while the reader's prior knowledge of the old tradition or *Vorlage*, which is frequently presumed by the author, is agreed by most interpreters to be a conspicuous feature of Chronicles, a reader-sensitive approach, which takes into account the reader's prior knowledge in interpretation (in order to detect the intended meaning of the text), has not been applied to Chronicles and especially the Solomon account.

Among the advanced analyses of the Solomon account in Chronicles are several structural analyses of the account that shed much light on the understanding of it.[47] These structural or literary analyses of the account have not observed or detected any weakness or flaw of Solomon within the text of Solomon's reign. Duke's recent attempt to interpret Chronicles with a rhetorical approach does not detect any flaw in Solomon in the account. Duke's attempt is noteworthy as a substantial and comprehensive interpretative attempt at applying a literary or rhetorical approach to Chronicles.[48] Duke's methodology, adopted from Aristotle's rhetorical theory, is aware of the "reader's will" as a part of its approach. However, Duke does not pay attention to the supposed reader's prior knowledge that might affect his or her interpretation of the Solomon account.[49] It means that a more straightforward and full-scale reader-sensitive approach has not yet been applied to the Solomon account.

---

46. The present form of the text, as it is in the Massoretic text, is the object of this exploration, while the text of the Septuagint does not vary the main issues of our discussion except for dating of the composition of Chronicles.

47. E.g., Dillard, "The Chronicler's Solomon," 299–300; Duke, *The Persuasive Appeal*, 65; Kelly, *Retribution and Eschatology*, 87–88; Selman, *2 Chronicles*, 285–86; 233.

48. Duke, *The Persuasive Appeal*; Duke, "The Ethical Appeal of the Chronicler," 33–51.

49. Ibid., 63–66, 102. Duke proposed a slightly modified structural analysis of the Solomon account, from Dillard's structural analysis (ibid., 64–65). Duke's understanding of the Solomon portrayal is not different from the conventional idealized and impeccable Solomon view, while he is aware of the importance of the reader's role as he states that "he [the Chronicler] *invites his audience to evaluate* each of his portraits of the generations of their past and *to understand* why things happened as they did" [my reference and emphasis] (Duke, "Model for a Theology of Biblical Historical Narratives," 76).

Secondly, some interpretations of the Solomon narrative in Kings stimulate a "reader-sensitive" approach. It is interesting that not a few interpreters notice the relevance of the reader-sensitive approach to the Solomon narrative in Kings. However, they apply the method to the narrative only partially or accidentally (or even unconsciously).[50] When it is considered that both a reliable interpretation of the Solomon narrative in Kings as the *Vorlage* and the reader's prior knowledge are preliminary requirements for the interpretation of the Solomon account in Chronicles, it is worth attempting an interpretation of the Solomon narrative with a reader-sensitive approach, which will be used for the interpretation of the Solomon account in Chronicles as well. Moreover, as the new insights into and understandings of the narrative recently obtained in the study of the Solomon narrative in Kings have not been fully applied to the interpretation of the account in Chronicles, this is another reason to try a reader-sensitive approach to the Solomon narrative, accommodating newly discovered insights into the narrative.

As shown so far, the reader-sensitive approach, which pays prime attention to the reader's contribution to forming the meaning of a text, has not been substantially applied yet to either account.[51] Hence, it is worthwhile to apply the reader-sensitive approach consistently to both the Solomon narrative in Kings and the Solomon account in Chronicles. Through the application of it to the Solomon narrative in Kings first, two significant results will be sought: (1) The relevance and effectiveness of the reader-sensitive approach will be examined in its application to the Solomon narrative in Kings. (2) This interpretation may then provide us with a new understanding of what the supposed reader's prior knowledge is like in the interpretation of the Solomon account in Chronicles.

Thirdly and finally, given that 2 Chr 10 shows implicit criticism of Solomon's reign, as Kelly proposes, the present study expects that the reader-sensitive approach should produce a new interpretation of Solomon in

---

50. For example, Nelson, First and Second Kings, 66–67, "Suddenly, all the glittering gold of Solomon's reign takes on a grimmer aspect, tarnished by the remembered word of Deuteronomy 17:17 . . ."; Bimson, "1 and 2 Kings," 343, "When we read it in the light of later events it is hard to avoid the conclusion that . . ." ; Provan, 1 and 2 Kings, 4–5, "They have produced a text that is intended to make sense as it is read cumulatively from beginning to end . . ."

51. We will name the account in Kings "the Solomon narrative" as many scholars have named it, while we will name the account in Chronicles "the Solomon account." It is primarily for convenience of clear distinction, while it is admitted that also from the judgment that the account has even less dramatic element to be named "narrative." However, when we should refer to both, we will call them "accounts" for convenience.

Chronicles, against the prevailing view. The reader-sensitive approach as our methodology will be briefly explained as follows.

3. THE METHODOLOGY OF THE PRESENT STUDY: A READER-SENSITIVE APPROACH, THE RESULT OF WHICH IS SUPPORTED BY THEOLOGICAL AND LITERARY OBSERVATION

The "reader-sensitive" approach is, in a sense, a well-recognized method in biblical study, although it is usually known by other designations. The first two paragraphs under the title "Reader-Response-Criticism" by Margaret Davies are sufficient to define the nature of our approach.

> Reading is a dangerous activity. It can change our perspective, stir our emotions, and provoke us to action. In other words, reading elicits a response. This happens because *the reception of literature is not passive but active and constructive. We try to make sense of the text.* The text itself is impotent until we realize its potential meaning, and while we are engaged with it, we may be influenced by our interpretation.
>
> Recently, some literary critics have turned their attention away from author and towards *the reader who comprehends the text, who deciphers words and sentences, relates parts to the whole, selects and organizes, anticipates and modifies expectations, and creates meaning.* Reading is a co-operative endeavor. *Through its literary conventions and strategies, the text presents a puzzle, which the reader must solve to gain understanding.* The reader is drawn into the adventure not only by what the text spells out but also by what it withholds. *To understand literature, the reader must begin to fill in the gaps, to infer what is not given, at least provisionally, until what is unclear at first is clarified by what follows.* This creation of meaning may change the reader in the process, because *literature in the Bible does not simply tell us about the spirit of a past age or its social conditions, but allows us to experience them* [emphasis mine].[52]

Furthermore, the role of the pre-understanding of the reader must be considered as another important interpretative key in making sense of a text, as Randolph Tate states:

---

52. Davies, "Reader-Response," 578.

> Every reader approaches a text under the guidance of a perspec-
> tive. Any text is read, perceived, and interpreted within a preex-
> istent structure of reality. All understanding and interpretation
> proceed from a prior understanding or a system of making
> sense of reality. . . . I am always being affected by my present ho-
> rizon of understanding, a horizon within which and from which
> all things are intelligible to me. Without this horizon of under-
> standing, this world of *preunderstanding*, discovering meaning
> would be simply impossible. Without a preunderstanding, un-
> derstanding is impossible [Tate's emphasis].
>
> A reader may approach a text without presupposing the
> results of reading, but the same *reader will never engage a text
> without some preunderstanding*. . . . Readers always wear tinted
> glasses and make sense of a text according to the particular
> shade of the lenses [emphasis mine].[53]

The term "pre-understanding" usually tends to indicate a general
hermeneutical concept, i.e., the whole epistemological pre-knowledge
through which all new information can be perceived by the subject. It
may include, for example, the reader's sociological pre-knowledge, which
could affect his or her perception of the new information.[54] In that sense
it is impossible to reconstruct the reader's pre-understanding as a whole.
However, in this study, we will consider a specific part of the reader's pre-
understanding, which we can reconstruct. It is the reader's prior knowledge and understanding of existing texts.

In our reader-sensitive approach, we will focus on the two major elements: (1) the reader's reading process which is a central idea of Davies'
description of "reader-response criticism" and is crucial to constituting
the meaning of the text through the reader's mind,[55] and (2) the reader's
prior knowledge with which the reader perceives the text as Tate states.[56]

---

53. Tate, *Biblical Interpretation*, 187–88.

54. For example, Robbins considers the reader's specific expectation in a specific
social context as a key-element to interpret the Gospel of Mark. According to him, the
reader's expectation (or pre-understanding) is closely related to the rhetorical strategy
of the Gospel of Mark. He labels his methodology "socio-rhetorical analysis." See,
Robbins, *Jesus the Teacher*.

55. For example, Clines' interpretation shows the possibility of this approach. See
Clines, "The Ancestor in Danger," 67–84.

56. Tate put the reader's pre-understanding in the first place among his discussion
of elements of the reader response criticism (Tate, *Biblical Interpretation*, 187–88).

Through the combination of these two elements, we will reconstruct the reader's reading experience.[57]

This study intends neither to establish a comprehensive view of the Chronicler's literary technique or strategy in terms of a reader-sensitive approach, nor to apply the reader-sensitive approach to the whole work.[58] Rather, the present study will try to provide a new interpretation of Solomon's faults in Chronicles through a reader-sensitive approach. In the process, a reader-sensitive interpretation of the Solomon narrative in Kings will also be produced, as a preliminary step. The interpretations will be confirmed by the observation of the literary features and (or) theological stance of the works (or the Hebrew Bible when necessary).

The contents of this book are as follows. In chapter 2, we will examine whether the alleged textual grounds of "impeccable Solomon" are tenable. An alleged dilemma is pointed out, which is not reconcilable with "impeccable Solomon" in Chronicles. Additionally, a crucial ground of the "impeccable Solomon view," the description of the division of the kingdom in Abijah's speech where the responsibility for the division is allegedly moved from Solomon to Jeroboam, is refuted. In chapter 3, a new interpretation of the Solomon narrative in Kings will be examined, as a preliminary step to a proper reading of the Solomon account in Chronicles, using the reader-sensitive approach. In the following three chapters, 4, 5, and 6, the features of Chronicles which are a background to our understanding of the account will be examined. The nature and purpose of the work (chapter 4) and the literary features (chapter 5), and the theological stance of the Chronicles in relation to the Deuteronomic law (chapter 6) will be proposed as bases for our interpretation of the Solomon account in Chronicles. Finally, in chapter 7, a new interpretation of the Solomon account in Chronicles will be proposed using a reader-sensitive approach. It will be examined whether the new interpretation is in tune with the nature (and purpose), and with the literary and theological features of the work as a whole and whether it is supported by them. Then in the concluding chapter a summary of the study and a few implications will be provided.

57. Except for the short introduction of the methodology (i.e., reader-sensitive approach) of the present work here, the appropriate explanations which are required for the interpretations of specific cases, will be provided in necessary points.

58. The present study will not provide a comprehensive application of the reader-sensitive approach to the Solomon account for practical reasons. (1) The present study challenges near consensus views and consequently uses the space to refute the views. (2) The interpretation of the Solomon account, focusing on Solomon's faults in Chronicles occupies no little space.

2

The Problem of an
Idealized Solomon in
Chronicles and its Dilemma

1. THE INTERPRETATIVE PROBLEM OF SOLOMON IDEALIZED IN CHRONICLES

THE LONG SUSTAINED TREND which sees an idealized Solomon in Chronicles has greatly influenced the interpretation of the account. The grounds for this interpretation can be summarized as follows.

1. The observation that the Solomon account and the David account in Chronicles constitute a single unit of Israel's golden age (cf. parallelism: 1 Chr 21:26 and 2 Chr 7:1[1]; 1 Chr 22:12 and 2 Chr 1:10; 1 Chr 29:12 and 2 Chr 1:11–12; 1 Chr 22:3–4 and 2 Chr 1:18–2:1 [ET 2:1–2] / Unity: 2 Chr 7:10; 2 Chr 11:17, etc.)[2] leads many interpreters

---

1. Jarick, *1 Chronicles*, 136.

2. Williamson, *1 and 2 Chronicles*: "single episode" (27), "the unity of the reigns of David and Solomon" (192); Braun, *1 Chronicles*, xxxv: "in a very similar fashion," "parallel," "complementary." Braun thinks that 1 Chr 22, 28, 29 especially unites the two kings' accounts; Japhet, *Ideology*, 488: "creates some sort of parity between David and Solomon, as far as he is concerned, the two reigns constitute one period"; Dillard, *2 Chronicles*, 1–5; Dillard, "The Chronicler's Solomon," 292. Dillard thinks that both kings are idealized, but especially Solomon is more idealized. von Rad, *Old Testament*

to the conclusion that Solomon is consciously idealized. This is because the other in the pair, David, has long been regarded as being portrayed as the ideal king of Israel.[3] It is plain throughout the book that David is the standard or canon for the following kings (e.g., 2 Chr 17:3;[4] 28:1; 34:2).

2. The most basic argument of those "idealized Solomon" interpretations is that the passages dealing with the faults and transgressions of Solomon which appear in Samuel-Kings, most conspicuously 1 Kgs 1–2 (power struggle) and 11:1–40 (intermarriage, apostasy and following disasters), appear to be omitted in Chronicles.[5] This is usually pointed out alongside the case of the idealized David, accounts of whose severe transgressions of adultery and murder in Samuel are omitted in Chronicles.[6]

3. As the flipside of the previous point, some additional passages that portray Solomon in a positive light also seem to support the "idealized Solomon" interpretation. Firstly, the presentation of Solomon in Chronicles follows some previous significant and admirable figures in the biblical tradition, like David, Joshua, and Bezalel.[7] Secondly,

---

Theology, I, 350–51; Braun, *1 Chronicles*, xxxiii, Braun thinks that the detrimental elements to David are omitted (outlaw life, Bathsheba, inability in his old days); Jones, *1&2 Chronicles*, 46. Williamson also argues that the fact that the description of the succession of David and Solomon in Chronicles is modeled on the succession pattern of Moses and Joshua supports the unity of the reign of David and Solomon, for Moses and Joshua in Deuteronomy and Joshua is presented as a unified reign. See Williamson, "Accession of Solomon," 356–57.

3. E.g., von Rad, *Geschichtsbild*; Im, *Davidbild*.

4. "The earlier way of father David" (in an alternative reading).

5. McKenzie, *The Chronicler's Use of the Deuteronomistic History*, 84, 86; Burns, "Solomon's Egyptian Horses and Exotic Wives," 32. Burns thinks that Solomon was "a hero-king from a golden age" to the Chronicler and the Chronicler omitted "all reference detrimental to him (Solomon)"; Japhet, "Chronicles, Book of," 526–27. Japhet thinks that the difference between the presentation of David-Solomon and following kings is caused by the fact that the Chronicler was very selective of the material of David and Solomon *in order to idealize them*, while the author did not try to idealize any other following kings and consequently simply summarized or paraphrased the source material (italics mine).

6. E.g., Braun, *1 Chronicles*, xxxiii. Braun enumerates "his outlaw days, his adultery with Bathsheba and the ensuing murder of Uriah, and the physical weakness of his latter days" as the omitted passages, which result in an "idealized David" presentation.

7. Dillard, "The Chronicler's Solomon." Apart from the omitting of the detrimental passage, Dillard also numerates the cases of the presentation in Chronicles in which Solomon is portrayed as the second David, the second Joshua, and the second Bezalel.

Solomon's accession is described in a more secure and welcomed mood than in Kings (1 Chr 22:9–10; 28:6, 7, 10; 29:22–25. Cf. 1 Kgs 1–2).[8] Thirdly, Solomon is described as having an important role in the cultus, which does not appear in Kings (cf. 2 Chr 35:4).

4. The fundamental cause of the division of the Israel kingdom does not seem to be presented as Solomon's sin of apostasy.[9] Especially in Abijah's speech the responsibility for the division seems to be placed on Jeroboam, but not on Solomon (2 Chr 13:6–7).[10] The presupposition of this argument is that most speeches in Chronicles are regarded as reflecting precisely the Chronicler's own view.[11]

5. Solomon performed a special task, in obedience to God, in his building of the temple.[12] It should also be noted that as the temple builder, Solomon seems to be described as having even better qualities than David (1 Chr 22:8–9).

6. Solomon is presented as a standard for kings of the Israelite kingdom together with David, in 2 Chr 11:17.

7. The stark contrast between the presentations of some kings, such as David, Rehoboam, Abijah, and Manasseh in Kings and Chronicles, has been recognized.[13] This point does not directly support the "idealized Solomon" interpretation, but seems to suggest a possibility of it, in contrast to the presentation of Solomon in Kings, which shows his transgression, the presentation of him in Chronicles is totally different.

Braun points out that the people's glad acceptance of him is added (1 Chr 12:39–41 [ET 12:38–40]) (Braun, *1 Chronicles*, xxxiii).

8. Braun, *1 Chronicles*, xxxiv.

9. Dillard, *2 Chronicles*, 107–8; Braun, "Solomonic Apologetic," 512; Braun, "Toward the North," 62.

10. Knoppers, "Rehoboam in Chronicles."

11. E.g., Drive, "Speeches in Chronicles," 255; von Rad, "Levitical Sermon"; Williamson, *1 and 2 Chronicles*, 251–53; Braun, *1 Chronicles*, xxiii; Braun, "Toward the North," 62. Deboys provides the list of scholars who have this view. See Deboys, "Portrayal of Abijah," 57 n.34. Throntveit also conveniently provides a list of studies on speeches in Chronicles (Throntveit, "Idealization of Solomon," 414 n. 13).

12. Williamson, *1 and 2 Chronicles*, 192, 236; Selman, *1 Chronicles*, 50.

13. E.g., Dillard thinks that the presentation of David, Solomon in Chronicles "contrast[s] sharply" with that in Kings (Dillard, "The Chronicler's Solomon," 289).

The points above are not a thorough list,[14] but cover the major grounds of the interpretation of an idealized Solomon. The multiplicity of the points seems most to persuade interpreters to conclude that the presentation of Solomon is intended to be read as "an idealized king" and also a "flawless king." However, it is possible to refute every point above, as follows.

1. It is very clear that King David is not presented as flawless in Chronicles,[15] even though to some extent his presentation has an aspect of an idealized king.[16] David's cultic failure in his first attempt of carrying the ark to Jerusalem (1 Chr 13:1–13), and his sinful census, which causes God's punishment, costing seventy thousand Israelites' lives (1 Chr 21:1–14), plainly show his faults.[17] Therefore, Solomon's being on a parity with David in the Israelite golden age cannot guarantee his being flawless. In fact, Solomon's being such can rather imply his imperfection.[18]

14. For example, for some commentators such as Braun, Solomon's lengthy reign of forty years is accepted as a signal which indicates Solomon's "complete loyalty and devotion to Yahweh" and "God's blessing" upon it. Braun, *1 Chronicles*, xxxv.

15. Ibid. Even Braun, who maintains David and Solomon are idealized, has to admit that "it is surprising that the Chronicler does not explicitly say that David or Solomon were perfect in Yahweh's service" (xxxl); "the Chronicler does not present us a blameless David" (xxxiii).

16. Ibid., xxxiii.

17. It is noteworthy that David's transgression is magnified in 1 Chr 21, being compared to its *Vorlage*, 2 Sam 24. In 2 Sam 24 God causes David to order the census, while in 1 Chr 21 Satan is the tempter. That means that David is described as having more responsibility in 1 Chr 21. This point can be easily overlooked by some commentators, for they concentrate on other issues like the identity of Satan, apologetic motive of Chronicler who substitutes God by with Satan. Nevertheless other commentators cannot overlook that David's fault is magnified in 1 Chr 21 (ibid., xxxiii; Selman, *1 Chronicles*, 201; von Rad, *Old Testament Theology, I*, 350; Kaiser, *Introduction to the Old Testament*, 177). Selman also points out that David's ensuing repentance is magnified in Chronicles (*1 Chronicles*, 206). Additionally, Selman also suggests that by addition and changes, the Chronicler's description of David's sin and his repentance has a "striking resemblance" to "that of David's murder and adultery in 2 Samuel 11–12 (201). This issue will be discussed in a later chapter, which will treat the Chronicler's allusion technique. The variation of 1 Chr 17:3 "earlier ways of his father David" can be understood in this light.

18. Selman, *1 Chronicles*, 50, 62. Selman thinks that neither David nor Solomon is presented as "spotless" in Chronicles. "David as a 'spotless holy king who delivers solemn orations,' or Solomon as 'completely without fault in his relationship with Yahweh' but these . . . assessments correspond neither with reality nor with the Chronicler's text" (62).

2. The omission of the material from the *Vorlage* does not aim to idealize Solomon, but to concentrate the focus upon a specific theme, i.e., cultic matters or temple building.[19] It is plain that not only negative materials but also positive materials are omitted altogether to avoid distraction from the issue of temple building.[20] For example, the account of Solomon's wise judgement (1 Kgs 3:16–28) is omitted in Chronicles. If the Chronicler's aim had been to idealize Solomon, the account should have been retained in Chronicles.[21] Or, the omission possibly betrays that the author simply presupposed his reader's prior knowledge of the matter.[22] Moreover, some commentators' understanding of the presentation of Solomon in Kings might be preventing them from noticing some negative elements present in the account in Chronicles.

3. The positive additional material does not guarantee that Solomon is portrayed as flawless. Firstly, the additional material of a more secure and welcomed accession than in Samuel-Kings is true not only of Solomon's case (1 Chr 22:9–10; 28:6, 7, 10; 29:22–25. Cf. 1 Kgs 1–2) but also of David's (1 Chr 11:3b; 12:39–41 [ET 12:38–40]), and it is plain that the material does not guarantee a flawless David in Chronicles. Then why should we think that it should be so in Solomon's case? The Chronicler's additional and consequently different presentation can be simply explained as his trying to emphasize the glorious aspects of a united monarchy in the more positive description of those accessions. Secondly, while it is true that the presentation of

19. Kelly, "Messianic Elements," 258; Selman, *1 Chronicles*, 49–50. Through structural analyses of the Solomon account in Chronicles, there is a consensus that "the narrative centers on the construction and dedication of the temple," which shows that the focus of the narrative is the temple matter (Williamson, *Israel*, 65; Dillard, *2 Chronicles*, 5–7; De Vries, *1 and 2 Chronicles*, 233; Duke, *The Persuasive Appeal*, 65; Selman, *2 Chronicles*, 285–86; Kelly, *Retribution and Eschatology*, 87–88).

20. Throntveit, "Idealization of Solomon in Royal Speeches," 426; Kelly, *Retribution and Eschatology*, 90. "Rather it is the Chronicler's means of concentrating on what he sees as the lasting significance of Solomon's reign, the fulfillment of the Davidic covenant through the building of the temple and the establishment of the Davidic dynasty"; Dillard, *2 Chronicles*, 2. It is interesting that even Dillard who sees an idealized Solomon in Chronicles admits that the omission could have a different explanation apart from "idealization."

21. For other examples, Solomon's love for God, walking in the statutes of his father David (1 Kgs 3:3a), God's special favoritism for Solomon in his giving the name "Jedidiah" (2 Sam 12:25).

22. Selman, *1 Chronicles*, 35. "One of the reasons for omitting this material is that the reader is expected to have a working knowledge of much of Samuel and Kings . . ."

Solomon following significant biblical figures throws a positive light upon Solomon, that presentation does not necessarily mean that Solomon is portrayed as flawless. The presentation of Solomon in Chronicles which recalls some figures in biblical tradition is mainly intended to show the continuity between two occasions, and explain the function of Solomon in those occasions. Moreover it should be pointed out that those figures which are alluded to as the models of Solomon were not presented as flawless in the biblical tradition. Thirdly, the cultic role of Solomon cannot guarantee his flawlessness either, for David is presented as having faults in spite of his massive cultic role.

4. The view that Abijah's speech as a whole reflects precisely the Chronicler's own view should be reconsidered. Any ordinary reader cannot only detect the untruth or exaggeration of Abijah's speech, but also explain why it is so. Abijah's assertion that Rehoboam was young and weak and so could not resist the northerners' rebellion (2 Chr 13:7) evidently contrasts with the previous passage, which shows his harsh response to the northern representatives (2 Chr 10:1–14) and his attempt to recover northern territory with military power (2 Chr 11:1), which could be stopped only by God's intervention (11:2–4).[23] Abijah's speech certainly includes some theological elements which can be wholly accepted as reflecting the author's own view that the Davidic dynasty and the Jerusalem temple have authentic authority over Israel.[24] However, the plain fact that Abijah's speech is very political

23. This point was well detected by old commentators. Keil points out that Abijah's description of Rehoboam as "soft hearted" "does not conform to the state of the case as narrated" in ch. 10. He observes that "on the contrary, he was hard and defiant" (Keil, *I & II Chronicles*, 351–52). Keil explains that "Abijah wishes to justify his father as much as possible in his speech, and shifts all the guilt of the rebellion of the ten tribes from the house of David on to Jeroboam and his worthless following" (352). Zöckler follows Keil's view that Abijah is justifying his father unfairly, stating that "Abijah relates in this his speech the events in the revolt . . . in a very inexact way (Rehoboam did not show himself 'weak of heart' on that occasion, but rather hard and daring of heart, etc.)." (Zöckler, "Chronicles," 200). Selman is an exceptional as a recent commentator who shows a similar view to this one.

24. Abijah's speech has been explored as a part of comprehensive studies of so-called Royal speech or oration. While the two theological themes in the speech have enjoyed the intense interest of scholars, Abijah's description of the division situation has not received due careful attention. For example, Mason, *Preaching the tradition*, 38–43; Throntveit, *When Kings Speak*, 36–38. While the importance of the two themes, is unanimously accepted by scholars, opinion of the relationship between the two institutions is divided largely into two different views. One is the view that the

seems to have been overlooked. Exaggeration and subtle distortion of real facts for the speaker's interest is not an unexpected thing in such a political situation, as Selman rightly points out.[25] The view that Abijah's speech reveals the author's position that the responsibility for the division of the kingdom lies not upon Solomon but mainly upon Jeroboam (in order to exculpate Solomon),[26] assumes that the Chronicler was employing only a simple style. However, it is now well acknowledged that the Chronicler is not a simple writer, but one who uses subtlety.[27] The view that sees all the speeches in Chronicles as delivering precisely the author's perspective is not applicable, at least to this case. (A detailed discussion of Abijah's speech and his account will follow in a later part of this chapter.)

5. That Solomon is used as a standard or canon for other kings (2 Chr 11:17) does not guarantee that Solomon is portrayed as a flawless king. First of all, it should be pointed out that David, who is more frequently mentioned as a standard to evaluate following kings, is not presented as flawless, while Solomon is described as a standard for other kings only once. The unique occasion can be explained as being related to the situation, just after the David-Solomon reign. Through David and Solomon's reign the temple has been established, so the two kings' common outlook, i.e. devout commitment toward the God of Israel in temple building, is the reason why they are presented as a standard for the king who follows them. That Solomon is presented as a standard together with David also makes it more possible that he is not presented as flawless, for David is not presented as

---

two institutions are everlasting ones, expecting the restoration of Davidic dynasty (either messianic or royalist view) (von Rad, Williamson, Japhet, etc). The other is the view that the Davidic dynasty is assimilated into the cultic or temple institution, being satisfied with the present "priestly theocracy" under Persian authority (Plöger, Riley, Mason, etc).

25. Selman, 2 Chronicles, 380. Selman observes that "Abijah's defence of his father Rehoboam (v. 7) seems somewhat exaggerated in view of chapter 10, though the political device of presenting the facts in the best possible light is familiar enough!"

26. In this sense, Mason even maintains that the speech of Abijah "might be described as exegesis of the Kings account of the division of the kingdom" (Mason, Preaching the tradition, 42). Mason's assertion is not convincing, for not only the Kings account but also even the Chronicler's presentation of the division situation is plainly contradictory to Abijah's description of it.

27. Deboys, "Portrayal of Abijah." "Chronicler is a more sophisticated and less rigid theologian than often allowed" (59). However, I do not agree with Deboys in his acceptance of Abijah's speech as a whole, as representing the Chronicler's view.

flawless, while he is more frequently mentioned as the standard king throughout the book (i.e., 2 Chr 17:3; 28:1; 29:2; 34:2). Moreover, it should be noted that even some good kings, who are portrayed as committing wrong in their latter days, are presented as the standard for their sons. (2 Chr 20:32; 21:12;[28] 27:2). If Solomon was portrayed as flawless, as some commentators claim, then he should have been presented as the standard for following kings, instead of David, for then Solomon alone would be flawless in Chronicles. But it is not the case. It is most likely that Solomon is mentioned in 2 Chr 11:17 as the standard of cultic faithfulness, but not moral or religious fidelity. The immediately previous passage (2 Chr 11:13–16), which is about cultic matters, may support this point. It is noteworthy that other occasions where Solomon is presented as a good example or directions-giver (2 Chr 30:26; along with David, 35:4) are about only cultic matters.

6. Building the temple does not guarantee Solomon to be a flawless king. It is true that in some aspects Solomon has more suitable qualifications than David as a temple builder (1 Chr 22:8–10). However, it is also true that the role of David in temple building is more substantial, and Solomon is a mere follower or executor of what David has prepared and done (1 Chr 17:1; 22:5; 23–26 (especially 23:6; 25:1); 28:2; 28:11–29:9 (especially 28:11–12, 19; 29:2–5; 2 Chr 6:7–8)). Again it should be pointed out that David is not presented here as flawless. Moreover, the motive for selecting the temple place is nothing but David's serious transgression, which costs seventy thousand Israelites' lives (1 Chr 21:14). Deep involvement in temple building does not itself guarantee a builder's flawlessness.

7. The view which sees a contrast in the presentations of certain kings between Kings and Chronicles should be carefully reconsidered. As Deboys' study shows, Chronicles often emphasizes some aspects which have not been mentioned in the *Vorlage* without denying the previous account in the *Vorlage*.[29] The Chronicler's presentation of Israelite kings is not as simple as it appears at first sight. For example,

---

28. For Jehoram, Jehoshaphat (his father) and Asa (grandfather) together are proposed as his standard (2 Chr 21:12) while they are not flawless. In this light, it is not special remarkable that David (Rehoboam's grandfather) and Solomon (his father) who are not flawless are together proposed as a standard for Rehoboam (2 Chr 11:17).

29. Deboys, "Portrayal of Abijah," 59–60. Deboys summarizes the tendency as "yes, but . . . "

even though the presentation of Abijah seems to be quite opposite to that in Kings, i.e. very favorable to him, there is "not one word to say in Abijah's favor" in Chronicles.[30] More significantly, the religious purge in the first decade of the reign of Asa (2 Chr 13:23—14:4 [ET 14:1–5]),[31] the son of Abijah, implies the idolatrous practice done during Abijah's reign, as its *Vorlage* evidently testifies (1 Kgs 15:12b). Furthermore, in Manasseh's case, although it is true that very positive material is added in his presentation, no positive evaluation appears in his account, while his great transgression is not omitted. All these indicate a greater possibility that Solomon in Chronicles is not presented in a totally different light from its *Vorlage*.[32]

As we have seen so far, none of the points that are regarded as supporting grounds for the interpretation of "idealized and flawless Solomon," is completely tenable, when each of them is examined. Moreover, the following additional points reveal that the Chronicler did not intend to idealize Solomon or portray him as flawless.

1. Most importantly and plainly, not only is Solomon's tyranny revealed in 2 Chr 10:4, 11, 14, but also Solomon's sin of idolatry is evidently implied in the mention of Ahijah's prophecy (2 Chr 9:29; 10:15) and God's intervention to confirm the division of the kingdom as punishment for Solomon's sin (2 Chr 10:15; 11:4), as Kelly points out.[33] If we presume that the Chronicler would not have included content from the *Vorlage* which is contradictory to his intention,[34] the inclusion of

---

30. Ibid., 50.

31. Asa also removes his mother Maacah from being queen mother because of her idolatry of Asherah (2 Chr 15:16), which seems to happen between the fifteenth year and thirteenth year of his reign (cf. 2 Chr 15:10; 15:19).

32. Kelly maintains that "the Chronicler is not really concerned to conceal or deny Solomon's failings," and also points out that "it is now generally recognized that 2 Chron. 1.1 contains an allusion to 1 Kgs 1–2, while 2 Chron. 8.2 (Solomon's receipt of cities from Hiram) does not contradict 1 Kgs 9.10–14 (cf. Williamson, *1 and 2 Chronicles*, 193, 228)" (Kelly, *Retribution and Eschatology*, 90–91).

33. Ibid., 90–91; Kelly, "Messianic Elements," 258. W. M. Schniedewind also thinks that "Although Chronicles excludes the prophecy of Ahijah from its narrative, it is likely that the reference to "the prophecy of Ahijah the Shilohite" in Solomon's source reference is an allusion to the prophecy given in the Deuteronomistic History." He also proposes that "Chronicles probably reflects Ahijah's prophecy in Shemaiah's statement to Rehoboam that the division of the kingdom was from YHWH (cf. 2 Chron. 11.4)" (Schniedewind, *The Word of God*, 222).

34. Japhet, "Chronicles, Book of," 529. "He (the Chronicler) indeed transfers large sections of his sources into his book literally, and where the sources conform with his purpose, or at least do not contradict it, he transfers them with only slight change,

these passages must mean that he did not intend to present a flawless Solomon. Even those commentators who maintain that Solomon is idealized and portrayed as flawless in Chronicles admit that the reader's knowledge of the *Vorlage* is presumed in those passages.[35]

The majority interpretation of Solomon's reign in Chronicles, which sees a flawless Solomon there, faces an unsolvable "theological dilemma" in this passage, as Japhet acknowledges honestly.[36] Many scholars have tried to solve this dilemma, proposing various interpretative suggestions.[37] The commentators tend to avoid explaining the problematic passages by focusing only on the historical critical issues involved or simply not making any comment on them.[38]

2. In Chronicles, every king is described as having some fault. Even Josiah, who is presented as the perfect and flawless king in Kings, is not portrayed as flawless in Chronicles (2 Chr 35:22). Solomon's confession that "there is no one who does not sin" in his prayer at the temple dedication ceremony in the *Vorlage* (1 Kgs 8:46, cf. 2 Chr 6:36) seems to be better illustrated in Chronicles with additional and supplementary information (for Asa, 2 Chr 16:7–12; for Jehoshaphat, 2 Chr 20:37; for Joash, 2 Chr 24:17–27; for Amaziah, 2 Chr 25:14–16, 20, 27; for Uzziah, 2 Chr 26:16–23; for Hezekiah, 2 Chr 32:25). This seems to fit one of the major themes in Chronicles,

---

chiefly linguistic."

35. Dillard, *2 Chronicles*, 85–86, 87, 88–89. "The author presumes his reader's familiarity with the parallel history at 1 Kgs 11:26–40; as part of his idealizing the reign of Solomon, the writer does not mention any details regarding Jeroboam, apart from his name in a source he acknowledges (9:29)" (85–86); "The Chronicler again presumes the reader's familiarity with the parallel history (1 Kgs 11:29–33). Since he has presented Solomon as blameless, the Chronicler would hardly include the information that the schism itself was attributable to Solomon's sins" (87). Dillard asserts that to present Solomon's reign as "blameless," the author attributes the schism of the kingdom not to Solomon, but to Jeroboam and Rehoboam (89); Williamson, *1 and 2 Chronicles*, 239. Williamson who supports perfect Solomon presentation in Chronicles acknowledges that the knowledge of 1 Kgs 11:26–40 and 11:29–39 is presupposed in 2 Chr 10:2 and 10:15 respectively, however, he does not provide any explanation of how this passage can go with the blameless Solomon presentation.

36. Japhet, *I & II Chronicles*, 657.

37. For example, Williamson, *1 and 2 Chronicles*; Johnstone, *1 Chronicles 1–2 Chronicles 9*; Knoppers, "Rehoboam in Chronicles."

38. E.g., Dillard avoids the explanation how this aspect can be compatible with "blameless Solomon" presentation by taking historical criticism on the problematic verses. (*2 Chronicles*, 86, 87); A similar way is observed in Williamson's treatment of the passage. See Williamson, *1 and 2 Chronicles*, 236–40.

transgression and atonement, which Johnstone observes.[39] Additionally, the seventy years' land sabbatical, which appears at the end of the book, confirms this, for the 490 years that is implied by seventy sabbatical years means the whole monarchy period.[40] By mentioning this, the Chronicler reveals that land sabbatical law has never been kept throughout the whole monarchy period, and thus God's law has never been thoroughly kept in the kingdom (cf. Lev 26:34–35).[41]

3. Surprisingly and significantly, the Chronicler does not give Solomon any positive assessment in the account. Even a scholar who maintains that Solomon is idealized in Chronicles is surprised by this fact.[42] If the author really intended to idealize Solomon, a praising comment would naturally be expected. The accounts of the reigns of those good kings, like Asa, Jehoshaphat, Uzziah, Hezekiah, and Josiah, all include some positive evaluations (Asa, 2 Chr 14:1 [ET 14:2]; Jehoshaphat, 17:3–4; 20:32; Uzziah, 26:4; Hezekiah, 29:2; Josiah, 34:2). Even less eminent kings have positive evaluations (2 Chr 24:2; 25:2; 27:2). In the case of David, the high evaluation is mentioned by God himself (2 Chr 7:17). It is noteworthy and significant that the evaluation is absent not only in Solomon's case but also in

39. Johnstone, "Guilt and Atonement."

40. Williamson, *1 and 2 Chronicles*, 418. "to the beginning of David's reign gives a total of 474 years. If some allowance is made for the uncertain length of Saul's reign (cf. 1 Sam. 13:1), it will be seen that the figures could coincide almost exactly"; McConville, *Chronicles*, 270; Wilcock, *Chronicles*, 287. De Vries, however, calculates that total years "for all the kings since Saul equals 457 years," so he regards the number of the years as more or less symbolic (De Vries, "The land's Sabbath in 2 Chr 36:21," 101). Most recently, Jarick discusses this issue and concludes that "But in any event, we can say that the period of the monarchy, whether calculated down to the last Sabbath or merely approximating the desired parameters, looks to be the period of sabbathlessness . . . " (*2 Chronicles*, 192–95).

41. De Vries, "The Land's Sabbath in 2 Chr 36:21." "To be placed at the very end of Chr's book implies that this cryptic statement yields the symbolical meaning of the entire book" (96). "The land is seen as making up for the sabbath years which it previously failed to "enjoy"— and for which it was now rendering recompense—i.e., the time of all the previous sabbath years since Israel's first settling in the land" (100). De Vries thinks that the verse is the last verse of the original work of the Chronicler, regarding the present last two verses (2 Chr 36: 22–23) as an additional one by a later editor. We do not agree with this view, while we think that disagreement with De Vries' view does not make any difference to the significance of the verse in its location in the end of the book any way.

42. Braun, *1 Chronicles*, xl. "it is surprising that the Chronicler does not explicitly say that David or Solomon were perfect in Yahweh's service."

Abijah's case, whose transgression in the *Vorlage* is subtly implied in Chronicles.

A conceptual confusion is also involved with the present issue. That is, does idealization mean flawlessness or not? There is a need for conceptual clarification of "idealization" in terms of the presentation of David and Solomon, for scholars generally use the term "idealization" without a precise definition. According to different definitions, "idealization" can or cannot be compatible with having "flaws." In the case of David, idealization must be compatible with "faults," for David's transgressions appear plainly in the text (1 Chr 13; 15:13; 21), so observations such as Braun's that David is idealized in Chronicles, while not presented as blameless, seem to be inevitable.[43] However, in Solomon's case, the term "idealization," when used by scholars, is generally used to mean thoroughly "flawless' or "blameless,"[44] while others maintain that Solomon's "weakness" is plain, even though it is mentioned only in the passage following his death, concluding that "the Chronicler does not actually idealize Solomon."[45] The former view is not tenable as we have seen so far, and the latter view stimulates us to investigate the description of Solomon's reign, to detect more allusions to his weaknesses and faults.

2. THE SO-CALLED THEOLOGICAL DILEMMA IN 2 CHRONICLES 10 AND THE PLACE OF THE RESPONSIBILITY FOR THE DIVISION OF THE KINGDOM

The Chronicler's presentation has been seen as rather simplistic. For example, the fact that the Chronicler did not treat the history of the northern kingdom had led interpreters to conclude that the Chronicler did not

43. E.g., See Braun, *1 Chronicles*, xxxiii. Braun's concept of "idealization" is ambiguous, when he states that "significant passages from Samuel-Kings which might be considered unfavorable to David . . . are absent in Chronicles, resulting in an idealized account. . . . While there is some truth to this picture, it should be noted that the Chronicler does not present to us a blameless David."

44. E.g., Dillard's comment on 2 Chr 10:15 is typical, where he self-contradictorily explains that "The Chronicler again presumes the reader's familiarity with the parallel history (1 Kgs 11:29–33). Since he has presented Solomon as blameless, the Chronicler would hardly include the information that the schism itself was attributable to Solomon's sins" (Dillard, *2 Chronicles*, 87). Japhet's position is exceptional for she observes that Solomon is not idealized, but flawless in Chronicles.

45. Kelly, "Messianic Elements," 260.

have any interest in the northerners. However, a close reading does not allow this, as Williamson has well demonstrated.[46] Likewise, although the absence of any explicitly negative element or evaluation of Solomon has led interpreters to conclude that Solomon is presented as flawless in the narrative, with a new approach the "simplistic" view may turn out to be inadequate.

It is necessary to recall here why the majority of scholars see Solomon as being presented as flawless in Chronicles. A characteristic of this consensus is the emphasis on the temple building as the main task of Solomon as a king. For example, Williamson and Dillard both see the centrality of the temple building in their literary structure analyses of the narrative structure, although they disagree in details.[47] For most scholars, that Solomon accomplishes his main task of the temple building is a principal ground for regarding Solomon as presented as idealized and flawless in Chronicles.[48]

The view that Solomon is presented as flawless seems to be strengthened by the interpreters' tendency to see the meaning of other materials in the narrative in relation to the temple building.[49] Since most of the narrative is about the temple building, and Solomon is the successful builder of the temple, so the narrative could not present Solomon as having any flaws or faults. For example, McKenzie not only insists that Solomon's wealth and prosperity in 2 Chr 1 are presented as the preparatory sources for the following temple building,[50] as most interpreters think,[51] but also alleges that Solomon's wealth and fame which appear after the temple building are presented as a reward from God for his accomplishment of the great task.[52] The logic of the flawless Solomon view can be summed up as follows. (1) The temple building is, without doubt, the positive thing *par excellence*.

46. Williamson, *Israel*, 87–140.

47. Dillard, "The Chronicler's Solomon," 299–300; Dillard, *2 Chronicles*, 5–6; Williamson, *1 and 2 Chronicles*, 192. For the comparison of the two analyses, see Jones, *1&2 Chronicles*, 44–45.

48. For McKenzie, Solomon is even superior to David, for he is the actual temple builder. "If anything, he is David's superior, since he is the actual builder of the temple." McKenzie, *1–2 Chronicles*, 227.

49. For example, ibid., 227. "The Chronicler's account of Solomon is really about the temple."

50. Ibid., 230–31. McKenzie believes that the structure of 2 Chr 1–9 makes clear that Solomon's incomparability in wealth, wisdom, fame all serves the temple.

51. For example, Williamson and Dillard.

52. McKenzie, *1–2 Chronicles*, 255, 256, 259.

(2) Most of the narrative is related to the temple building in this or that way. (3) Therefore, the whole narrative is presented as a positive description. (4) Consequently, Solomon's reign should be regarded as presented as flawless.

However, the logic of this view cannot be sustained. Firstly, it is evident that the whole account of Solomon cannot be put under the single theme of the temple building, although temple building is the most conspicuous and dominant theme of the Solomon account. Some commentators overemphasize the dominance of the theme of the temple building in the narrative beyond the textual presentation. For example, the wisdom of Solomon in 2 Chr 1 is regarded by most commentators as a preparing element for the temple building.[53] However, such an interpretation ignores the plain description of the text. While Solomon's wisdom influences the building project, for which Huram praises God (2 Chr 2:11 [ET 2:12]),[54] nevertheless, the text states his wisdom has been asked and given for him to "judge" (שׁפט) his people (2 Chr 1:9–10). Although the famous episode of his judgment between two harlots in the *Vorlage* is omitted in Chronicles, his wisdom is given by God for the judgment of the numerous people who are like the dust of the earth (2 Chr 1:9–10).[55] Another example is the description of Solomon's conquering of Hamath-zobah in 2 Chr 8:3. Although it is emphasized that Solomon is a man of peace, as the proper qualification of the temple builder in Chronicles, this additional material does not seem to be well matched with the main theme of the temple building. Rather the material has something that might undermine the image of Solomon as a man of peace as the qualification for the temple building, producing a more complex presentation of Solomon, as will be shown in chapter 5.[56] Therefore to understand every part of the narrative

---

53. For example, Williamson, *1 and 2 Chronicles*, 192–93, 195. "In his view, rather, the primary purpose of the gift of wisdom, and hence the best example of its exercise, was to equip Solomon for the task of temple-building"; McKenzie, *1–2 Chronicles*, 231–32. "That is, he wants wisdom in order to lead the people in building the temple."

54. Williamson thinks that 2:11 [ET 2:12] is a case that confirms that the true expression of the wisdom is temple building (Williamson, *1 and 2 Chronicles*, 192).

55. Contra McKenzie. "The purpose and demonstration of Solomon's wisdom in Chronicles is not clever legal judgments but the building of the temple" (McKenzie, *1–2 Chronicles*, 230).

56. Japhet accounts for the passage as the Chronicler's attempt to equate Solomon to David. That is, while the Chronicler added to the portrayal of David temple building matter, which is mainly of Solomon's, he also added an account of conquest to the portrayal of Solomon, which is mainly of David (Japhet, *Ideology*, 488).

in relation to the single theme of the temple building risks ignoring the complexity and subtlety the narrative might contain.[57]

Secondly, even in the task of the temple building, Solomon's role is reduced in Chronicles, in comparison with that of others, mainly of David. David's role is emphasized in terms of contribution to the temple building, in contrast to the *Vorlage*, as Japhet rightly observes.[58] Thus the organization of the building workers (2 Chr 2:16–17 [ET 2:17–18]; 1 Chr 22:2) does not appear in its *Vorlage* (1 Kgs 5:29–30 [ET 5:15–16]; 9:21; 5:27 [ET 5:13]) but is attributed to David in Chronicles. Further, in the collection of the building material, the contribution of David is emphasized and Solomon's role is reduced to "only to replenish the supply" in Chronicles (1 Chr 22:2, 4, 14; 29:2–5), while in its *Vorlage*, David's contribution to this field does not appear except for his dedicated treasure which is stored in the treasuries of the temple (1 Kgs 7:51).[59] David's contribution to the building project also appears in his preparing Israelite craftsmen in Chronicles, who work with an expert from Tyre (2 Chr 2:6 [ET 2:7], cf. 1 Chr 22:15, the name of the expert is, according to 1 Kgs 7:13–14, Hiram). The Israelite craftsmen whom David prepared do not appear in the *Vorlage*. Further, as for the expert's engagement for the building project, the contribution of Huram (Hiram in Kings), King of Tyre appears in Chronicles (2 Chr 2:12–13 [ET 2:13–14]), while only Solomon is involved in this matter in its *Vorlage* (1 Kgs 7:13–14).[60] It means that even the description of the temple building, which is the main task done by Solomon in Chronicles, does not aim to idealize Solomon. On the other hand, Solomon's instituting temple worship is added in Chronicles (2 Chr 8:14). However, considering the above points, it is unlikely that the addition aims to idealize Solomon. Significantly, in the passage which describes Solomon's instituting the temple worship, Solomon is not called by the honorable title "man of God," while

57. See also, 1 Chr 28:6–7; 2 Chr 9:8 for another example of a wider portrayal of Solomon than the temple builder.

58. Japhet, *Ideology*, 485–88. This is a partial reason for Japhet to think that Solomon is not presented as idealized, although flawless, in Chronicles.

59. Besides, of the preparation of material for the temple building project, Japhet rightly points out that David's contribution is brought into a relief in 1 Chr 18:8, where it is clearly stated that a great amount of bronze that is David's spoils is used in order to make temple vessels, while the parallel passage in the *Vorlage* only states the fact that David took such an amount of bronze from a specific region (ibid., 487–88). However, Japhet's observation that 1 Chr 18:8 is contradictory to 1 Kgs 7:46, which is repeated in 2 Chr 4:17, is not plausible, for 1 Kgs 7:46 simply described the place where the vessels are moulded from the bronze wherever the bronze is originally acquired.

60. Ibid., 486–87.

his father David, who prepared the institution, is given such a title (2 Chr 8:14).[61]

Thirdly, the blessing upon Solomon is not described as a reward,[62] but as God's unconditional blessing or grace, whether or not it is according to his promise to David (1 Chr 17:11–14). 1 Chr 29:25 and 2 Chr 1:1 plainly show that God's blessing upon Solomon precedes any of his merits or good work. This is one of the cases against the view that retribution theology dominates the account.

God's promise that he will not take away his grace from David's son, even when the son commits sin (1 Chr 17:11–14), should be considered significant in the reading of the Solomon narrative, for Solomon must be the first and prime beneficiary of the promise before anyone else. Further, even God's asking for Solomon's wish after Solomon's offering of a thousand burnt offerings (2 Chr 1:6–7), should itself be regarded as a conspicuous example of grace rather than an appropriate reward for Solomon's seeking God,[63] for God does not offer such a thing to other pious kings. It is plain that God has the initiative on that occasion. It might also be noteworthy that "It pleased the Lord that Solomon had asked this" in 1 Kgs 3:10 is omitted in Chronicler's account. All of these points indicate that Solomon's prosperity is based upon God's grace rather than on his own merits or good work, while it is undeniable that his accomplishment of temple building is still a great achievement. That his prosperity is based upon God's unconditional blessing upon him again might imply that his prosperity and blessing may co-exist with his faults and flaws.

Fourthly, the overall structure of the narrative also suggests a negative outlook. According to Dillard, the Solomon account has a chiastic structure, and reflects "the author's pivotal interest" in its central item.[64] The central piece of the account (2 Chr 7:1–10) is of cult (i.e. the temple dedication ceremony). It means that temple cult is the author's most important concern.[65] However, it should not be ignored that the pieces immediately adjoining the central piece are about human sinfulness: Solomon's asking

---

61. The honorable title "man of God" is used in Chronicles for only four persons: Moses (1 Chr 23:14; 2 Chr 30:16), David (2 Chr 8:14), the prophet Shemaiah (2 Chr 11:2), and an anonymous prophet (2 Chr 25:7, 9).

62. Contra McKenzie (McKenzie, *1–2 Chronicles*, 231, 255, 256, 259).

63. Contra McKenzie. "the reward for his obedience and righteous request" (ibid., 231).

64. Dillard, "The Chronicler's Solomon," 300; Dillard, *2 Chronicles*, 1987, 5.

65. Dillard, "The Chronicler's Solomon," 300, "Even a cursory examination of this outline of the reign of Solomon shows the centrality of the cult in this narrative."

for forgiveness in the future (2 Chr 6:22–39), including for himself in that instance (2 Chr 6:21 cf. 6:36), and God's solemn warning of transgression and devastating punishment in the future (2 Chr 7:11–22). This implies that human sinfulness, including Solomon's, provides a foil for the temple cult, the central concern.

Finally, the most decisive material that suggests a negative presentation of Solomon is the reference to his heavy burden upon Israel admitted by his successor, the mention of the fulfilment of Ahijah's prophecy, and the prophetic word of Shemaiah the man of God (2 Chr 11:4). These passages strongly imply or presume the reader's prior awareness of Solomon's misdeeds in its *Vorlage*,[66] and consequently cannot go with the view of flawless Solomon, as has been mentioned already in chapter 1, where some additional suggesting the possibility of a negative evaluation of Solomon have been mentioned.

The "theological dilemma" admitted by Japhet (1989)[67] has raised a variety of interpretations over the responsibility for the division of the kingdom in view of 2 Chr 10:15.[68] Most scholars who think that Solomon in Chronicles is presented as flawless consequently put the responsibility for the division of the kingdom upon someone else.

Williamson's view (1982) of the division of the kingdom is not exactly an attempt to solve this dilemma.[69] Rather, his concern is to harmonize two seemingly irreconcilable elements, i.e. the legitimacy of the northerners' grievances, which seems to be approved by the fact that there is no explicit criticism of their request in the text,[70] and the rebellious element of the

---

66. Williamson, *1 and 2 Chronicles*, 239; Dillard, *2 Chronicles*, 85–88; Curtis and Madsen, *Chronicles*, 363.

67. Japhet, *Ideology*, 657; McKenzie also acknowledges the problem which arises from 2 Chr 10:15. He seems to think he cannot provide a full explanation as is revealed in his using of reserved or confined expressions like "the tension between these two explanations is partially assuaged if we adopt the view that . . ." (McKenzie, *1–2 Chronicles*, 263); Knoppers also acknowledges the problem that, in Chronicles presentation of Solomon with its very positive light, the responsibility of the division of the kingdom should not be placed upon Solomon (Knoppers, "Rehoboam in Chronicles," 430). However, he believes that the Chronicler clearly moved the responsibility of the division from Solomon's shoulder to Jeroboam's."

68. Knoppers recognizes "the disagreement among biblical critics concerning the precise perspective the Chronicler exhibits toward the major figures and pivotal events of this era" (Knoppers, "Rehoboam in Chronicles," 423–24).

69. Williamson, *1 and 2 Chronicles*, 237–40, 251–53. However, it turns out that it could not persuade even Japhet who is very supportive of him in many other issues in the Chronicles study (Japhet, *I & II Chronicles*, 657).

70. Williamson, *1 and 2 Chronicles*, 236.

northern tribes, which is condemned in Abijah's speech, which he regards as the Chronicler's own view.[71] Williamson tries to solve this dilemma by distinguishing the initial division from the sustained state of division after Rehoboam's rule. In his view, the initial division is legitimate, for it happened in an abnormal situation. However, the *ongoing independence* of the northern tribes, after the abnormal situation is over, is blameworthy. When the abnormal situation had ceased, according to Williamson, the northern tribes should have come back under the God-established Davidic rule, but they did not. Only the northern tribes' sustaining the division situation after Rehoboam's reign is problematic (Williamson applies immediate retribution theology here, and contends that each generation is treated by God according to their own doings).[72]

Suggesting this interpretation, Williamson proposes that the responsibility for the initial division should be put upon Rehoboam's young subjects who forced (rather than advised) him to respond harshly to the northern party, on the basis of his interpretation of 2 Chr 13:7. He follows Josephus's view (*Ant.* 8.277) in his peculiar interpretation of the verse, basically accepting Abijah's speech as the Chronicler's own sermon (the problem of this speech will be treated in the following section),[73] while he thinks that heavier responsibility is laid upon Rehoboam in

---

71. Ibid., 251–53. Williamson thinks that Abijah's speech "should be regarded primarily as a thinly-veiled comment by the author" (251).

72. Ibid., 237, 251: "with the accession of the true Davidide Abijah normality has been restored, since the Chronicler regards each generation as being directly responsible to God for its actions without reference back to previous circumstances. This implies that on the political level there is now no reason why the northerners should not call off their rebellion" (251). Welch shows a similar view to Williamson in that there is no blame of the Jeroboam or northerners for the initial division but the sustained division is blameworthy. However, Welch's view is different from Williamson's in thinking that God allows the initial division for Rehoboam is a "unworthy scion," laying the responsibility for the division mainly upon Rehoboam (Welch, *Post-Exilic Judaism*, 190). Knoppers mistakenly thinks that Williamson, following Welch's view, puts the blame for the division upon Rehoboam, "the villain" (Knoppers, "Rehoboam in Chronicles," 424). In fact, Williamson puts the real blame for the initial division upon Reboboam's young advisors (Williamson, *1 and 2 Chronicles*, 253), while he does not exculpate Rehoboam (238).

73. In his earlier interpretation in his *Israel*, Williamson approved the conventional interpretation of 2 Chr 13:7, which puts the responsibility of the division upon Jeroboam, as a possible alternative interpretation (Williamson, *Israel*, 122). However, in his later commentary he seems to approve only his peculiar interpretation, which puts the real blame upon Rehoboam's young subjects (Williamson, *1 and 2 Chronicles*, 252–53).

this event than in its *Vorlage*.[74] According to Williamson, Jeroboam too bears "much of the responsibility" in both the initial division and the sustained division state.[75]

However, Williamson's account has some debatable features. Regarding the precise place of the responsibility for the division, Williamson's view is not quite clear, and even self-contradictory. On one hand, he maintains that there is no condemnation of the northerners at the event of the initial division,[76] for their grievances are legitimate; on the other hand, he puts no little responsibility upon Jeroboam who represents the northerners and their cause.[77] That is, Williamson maintains that Jeroboam, as leader of the northerners, bears some responsibility for the initial division, even though the cause of the northerners for the initial division is legitimate. Moreover, Williamson, on one hand, emphasizes the significance of the Chronicler's attributing the division to God's will,[78] so he thinks

74. "[B]ecause the Chronicler omitted the material from 1 Kg. which was critical of Solomon, Rehoboam becomes personally more responsibility for the division in this account" (Williamson, *1 and 2 Chronicles*, 238)

75. "There is no doubt that the Chronicler wished Jeroboam to carry much of the responsibility on the northern side not only for the initial division of the monarchy in this chapter, but also for its continuation later (cf. 13:5ff)" (ibid., 238).

76. "This (the need of repentance of the Northerners) is not so much because of the initial division, for which they are nowhere condemned, and which is regarded as due to God's will, as because of their continued independence after their legitimate grievances could be regarded as settled" (ibid., 237).

77. "There is no doubt that the Chronicler wished Jeroboam to carry much of the responsibility on the northern side not only for the initial division of the monarchy in this chapter, but also for its continuation later (cf. 13:5ff)" (ibid., 238). Knoppers' understanding of Williamson's view does not seem to be precise at this point, i.e., Knoppers sees that Williamson put the responsibility for the initial division upon Rehoboam, "Williamson, then, sees Rehoboam as the villain most responsible for the secession" (Knoppers, "Rehoboam in Chronicles," 424). In fact, Williamson puts the heaviest responsibility upon Rehoboam's young subjects (Williamson, *1 and 2 Chronicles*, 253), while it is true that Williamson sees Rehoboam's responsibility for the initial division become heavier in Chronicles than in Kings for criticism of Solomon disappears in Chronicles (Williamson, *1 and 2 Chronicles*, 238).

78. On his comment of "brought about by God" in 2 Chr 10:15, Williamson maintains that "the importance of the Chronicler's retention of this phrase should not be underestimated" and "he (the Chronicler) does not regard the rebellion by the northerners as reprehensible" (Williamson, *1 and 2 Chronicles*, 239). Knoppers' misunderstanding of Williamson's view on the place of the responsibility for the initial division, seems to be caused by his confusion of Williamson's view and Welch's, on the basis of the observation that the latter two scholars have the same view in that the initial division is valid. (Knoppers, "Rehoboam in Chronicles," 424). Knoppers seems to have missed page 253 of Williamson's commentary, where Williamson put the most serious responsibility for the division upon Rehoboam's young subjects.

that the northerners are exculpated by the Chronicler on the matter of the initial division, but on the other hand he attributes the responsibility for the initial division to Rehoboam (more than in its *Vorlage*), Jeroboam, and most seriously Rehoboam's young advisors.

Williamson seems to suppose that God could allow even the division of the kingdom for the reason of some "abnormality"[79] in his chosen Davidic monarch. That implies that in each generation the kingdom could be divided if there were some abnormal state of affairs, and should be reunited in the next generation even after the secession party has established its own monarch according to God's own will or allowance. This seems unlikely. Relying heavily upon Abijah's interpretation of the secession situation in his speech in 2 Chr 13,[80] Williamson seems to regard Rehoboam's weakness (2 Chr 13:7) or the whole situation as abnormal.[81] It is very unlikely, however, that the Chronicler saw God as one who considers a new king's weakness as a serious abnormality, which could result in and justify the division of the kingdom. If the "abnormality" means the whole situation that required the meeting between Rehoboam and the northerners, then Solomon cannot avoid responsibility for the division anyway, as the fundamental cause of that situation. Moreover, since the first three years, at least, of Rehoboam's reign are presented as positive, i.e., as a period of faithfulness to God, this undermines Williamson's view of an abnormal situation as the fundamental excuse for the northerners' secession.[82]

79. Williamson, *1 and 2 Chronicles*, 253. Williamson states "Thus whereas some explanation of Rehoboam's weakness is provided (v 7) so that the period of the division is regarded as *abnormal*, yet with the accession of the true Davidide Abijah *normality* has been restored, since the Chronicler regards each generation as being directly responsible to God . . ." [my emphasis] (251).

80. Williamson's interpretation of description of the secession situation in Abijah's speech in 2 Chr 13, is not accepted by most interpreters. See Knoppers, "Rehoboam in Chronicles," 437–38 (n. 48); Dillard, *2 Chronicles*, 107–8.

81. "Advantage was taken of Rehoboam's weakness (7b), but this was clearly seen as an exceptional circumstance. The Davidic king would normally have been expected to be able to withstand such pressure. . . . Once again, attention is drawn to the abnormality in the situation at Rehoboam's accession, but now, . . . that unique situation has returned to normality" (Williamson, *Israel*, 112–13). "[T]he period of the division is regarded as abnormal, yet with the accession of the true Davidide Abijah normality has been restored . . ." (Williamson, *1 and 2 Chronicles*, 251). "The abnormality of the division is further underlined by the fact that the Davidic king at that time was young and irresolute" (Williamson, *1 and 2 Chronicles*, 253).

82. Knoppers, "Rehoboam in Chronicles," 433 n. 40. "Even if this period of fidelity begins after the rupture (Williamson, 1 and 2 Chronicles, 237–45), the claim of Welch (and Williamson) that it would do the North no good to associate with Rehoboam because of his abandoning Torah is misleading. Rehoboam and his people 'walk in the

Lastly, Williamson's insistence that in the days of Abijah the northern tribes should come back to Davidic rule, as the abnormality of Rehoboam's day is over, contradicts his observation that in 2 Chr 10:15 the reader's prior knowledge of 1 Kgs 11:29–39 is presupposed.[83] In 1 Kgs 11:29–39, God's appointing Jeroboam as the ten tribes' legitimate ruler, as punishment for Solomon's apostasy, is plainly described. If the reader's prior knowledge of Solomon's sin as a legitimate foundation of the Jeroboam's northern kingdom as dynasty is admitted, it is not likely that the reader can conclude that the northern kingdom is criticized as illegitimate in Abijah's day.

McConville (1984) points out that the text blames neither the northern tribes and Jeroboam, nor Rehoboam, concerning the division, but attributes the cause to the will of God, which is "inscrutable" in Chronicles, for the work omits the details about the cause which appear in its *Vorlage*.[84] However, it is very unlikely that the division of the kingdom should have no explicable reason. Since one of Chronicles' features is its eagerness to explicate the hidden cause of historical events (e.g, compare 1 Kgs 22:49 [ET 22:48] to 2 Chr 20:36–37),[85] McConville's suggestion loses its persuasive power.

Following the interpretations of Williamson and McConville, Dillard and Knoppers put the responsibility for the division more plainly upon Jeroboam's shoulders. Dillard (1987), refuting Williamson's interpretation of 2 Chr 13:7,[86] thinks that the responsibility for the division falls upon both Jeroboam who had a "lust for power" and Rehoboam who acted with "folly," while relatively heavier responsibility falls upon Jeroboam on the basis of 2 Chr 13:7.[87] Knoppers (1990) also puts the responsibility for divi-

---

way of David and Solomon' for three years and only then abandon the Torah (2 Chr 11:17; 12:1–2)."

83. Williamson, *1 and 2 Chronicles*, 239.

84. McConville, *Chronicles*, 151–53. "Ultimately, therefore, Chr. is content to leave the reason for the division in the inscrutable mind of God" (153).

85. For another example, the Chronicler's explanation of the cause of the pious king Josiah's sudden death (2 Chr 35:22b).

86. Dillard, *2 Chronicles*, 107–8. Knoppers also provides a criticism of Williamson's interpretation (Knoppers, "Rehoboam in Chronicles," 437–38). Dillard analyzes that Williamson's peculiar interpretation was caused by his excessive zeal to read the text in favor of the Northern tribes (108).

87. Dillard, *2 Chronicles*, 89, 108. "Having eliminated the blame for the schism in connection with Solomon's sin (1 Kgs 11), where will the Chronicler assign the blame? Certainly Rehoboam bears some of the onus (2 Chr 10), but the full weight of reproof is assigned to Jeroboam and his congeners" (108).

sion upon Jeroboam, regarding Rehoboam as a victim.[88] Knoppers points out that at least the first three years of Rehoboam's reign, in which the division occurred, are described positively in the account, and the secession of the northern tribes led by Jeroboam has no justification.

In recent interpretations, the major responsibility for the division falls upon Rehohoam's shoulders. In Johnstone's view (1997), Rehoboam's departing from Jerusalem, the God-chosen city, in order to meet the rebellious party is the most problematic factor in the process of the division[89] (this interpretation is based on Johnstone's view of Zion theology in Chronicles),[90] while the impudent request of the northern tribes, i.e., to bargain the relationship between the God-given Davidic king and themselves, is not acceptable. Most recently, McKenzie (2004) again puts the major responsibility for the initial division upon Rehoboam, for a different reason from Johnstone's.[91] According to McKenzie, the northern tribes did not intend to rebel, but only wanted to lighten their heavy burden. Only Rehoboam's harsh response "leads them to secede" and God "does not condone Rehoboam's response."[92]

88. Knoppers, "Rehoboam in Chronicles." "The Chronicler does not exonerate Rehoboam; nevertheless, he does seem to place the blame for the division upon Jeroboam" (439).

89. Johnstone, *2 Chronicles 10–36*, 24–25. "C's presentation is, then, that Rehoboam should never have left Jerusalem to go to Shechem (Compare other disastrous departures from Jerusalem, 2 Chron. 18.2; 22.5; 35.20; and see 2 Chron. 16.2; 25.1/; 28.16; 32.31). By going there he shows himself inadequate, and having got there he shows himself inept" (25). McKenzie also observes the problem of the king's going to Shechem to be made king, however, for McKenzie the king's departing Jerusalem itself is not the king's fault, while it "does not bode well for the future of the kingdom" in contrast with the cases of David (1 Chr 11:1) and Solomon (1 Chr 28–29), where the people came to the kings (McKenzie, *1–2 Chronicles*, 261).

90. Johnstone, *1 Chronicles 1–2 Chronicles 9*, 15. "In his study of the fifteen subsequent reigns from Rehoboam to Josiah and the sequel (2 Chron. 10–36), C undertakes an exhaustive exploration of the potentiality of the sacramental theology of the royal house of David, with its messianism and related Zion theology (for example, in 2 Chron. 13.12, cf. Isa. 7.14; 2 Chron. 20.20, cf. Isa. 7.9), to express and to realize Israel's destiny among the nations of the world."

91. McKenzie distinguishes the responsibility for the initial division and sustained division after that as Williamson does, with a different detailed explanation. His view is that "the initial schism was divine punishment for Rehoboam's arrogance but that the continued separation of Israel and especially the religious and cultic measures taken to support the separation are sin" (McKenzie, *1–2 Chronicles*, 263).

92. Ibid., 262. "It is only his attitude toward them that leads them to secede." However, in other places (261, 269), McKenzie plays down the tone concerning Rehoboam's responsibility for the division. "The division of the kingdom at the beginning of Rehoboam's reign had to be at least partly his fault, since it could not be blamed

The variety of interpretations concerning the responsibility for the division, as outlined above,[93] shows how difficult it is to put the responsibility upon someone for a particular reason, with the exception of Solomon whose possible responsibility is generally ignored. Four problems should be pointed out here about the interpretations above. Firstly, strangely enough, the mention of Solomon's heavy yoke upon the Israelites (2 Chr 10:4–14), which is not only complained of by the northern party (10:4), but also admitted by Solomon's successor (10:14),[94] has not been treated directly or has been neglected by the commentators,[95] although the passage evidently suggests Solomon's wrongdoing.[96] Secondly, a satisfactory explanation of 2 Chr 10:15 has not yet been proposed. For example, Johnstone does not treat the verse squarely.[97] Williamson and

---

on Solomon" (261), 'since the division of the kingdom in the Chronicler's view was at least partly the result of Rehoboam's arrogance . . ." (269).

93. Knoppers acknowledges "the profound disagreement among biblical critics concerning the Chronicler's view of this critical period . . ." (Knoppers, "Rehoboam in Chronicles," 423–24, 430).

94. Solomon's heavy yoke is implicitly or indirectly acknowledged also in the advice of Rehoboam's old and young subjects (2 Chr 10:7; 10:10–11).

95. For example, Williamson, *1 and 2 Chronicles*, 239; Dillard, *2 Chronicles*, 86. Knoppers does not even include the passage in his discussion of the place of the responsibility for the division (Knoppers, "Rehoboam in Chronicles"). Johnstone thinks that it is "incidentally" that "Rehoboam is made to concede the rightness of the people's complaints" (25), maintaining that Solomon is exculpated of enslavement (24), and it is confirmed by Rehoboam's remark in 2 Chr 10:14 (26) (Johnstone, *2 Chronicles 10–36*, 24–26).

96. Commentators seem to acknowledge that Solomon's heavy yoke is revealed here. For example, Williamson thinks that there is "allusion" to "passages in Kings not included in the Chronicler's portrayal of Solomon" here (Williamson, *1 and 2 Chronicles*, 239). McConville states that "the request by the people under Jeroboam is not comprehensible unless the Israelites themselves had somehow suffered from the heavy demands placed by Solomon upon those within his borders, even if in principle the oppressive measures were only directed against foreigners . . ." (McConville, *Chronicles*, 151). Dillard even acknowledges that "the biblical text alludes to the sociopolitical ills that attended the splendor of the Solomonic empire; the hated corvée and heavy taxation are undoubted factors that fanned the dissatisfaction in the North" (Dillard, *2 Chronicles*, 88) and "Certainly the chapter shows an awareness of the social and political ills left from Solomon's reign" (89). Dillard believes that Solomon's not imposing forced labor upon Israelites in Kings (1 Kgs 9:15, 20–22) and Chronicles (2 Chr 2:16–17 [ET 2:17–18]; 8:7–10) only means "instances of the practice," maintaining that texts (cf. 2 Chr 10:4, 18; 1 Kgs 15:22 // 2 Chr 16:6; Jer 22:13–14) support the existence of the heavy yoke (86). However, most of those commentators somehow do not link it to the issue of whether Solomon is presented as flawless or not.

97. Johnstone, *2 Chronicles 10–36*, 27. Johnstone does not explain why it should be Ahijah's prophecy which is to be fulfilled here.

Dillard do acknowledge, on the crucial passage, 2 Chr 10:2, 4, 15, that the reader's knowledge of the omitted contents is presupposed.[98] Yet this has no weight in their interpretation. Thirdly, most commentators neglect the significance of 2 Chr 11:1–4, God's word through Shemaiah the man of God, which is another allusion to Solomon's faults.[99] Fourthly, if Abijah's interpretation of the division situation in 2 Chr 13:7 exactly reflects the Chronicler's own view, the responsibility for the division should fall upon Jeroboam (and his party).[100] However, Abijah's explanation of the division is contradicted by the previous passage on the division itself,[101] while Abijah's interpretation contradicts 2 Chr 10:15, where it is plainly stated that God himself caused the division of the kingdom to fulfill Ahijah's prophecy.

The solution to the dilemma exists only in giving up the old belief that Solomon is presented as flawless in Chronicles, acknowledging the reader's prior knowledge as an intended interpretative factor, and applying this to the interpretation of the passage. The view that Solomon is

---

98. Williamson, *1 and 2 Chronicles*, 237, 239. Williamson thinks that the mention of the prophecy of Ahijah the Shilonite (2 Chr 9:29) "presupposes that the Chronicler's readers will refer even to those parts of the earlier work which the Chronicler has omitted for ideological reasons" (237). Furthermore, he believes that in the passages of Jeroboam's being in Egypt in 2 Chr 10:2, the fulfillment of Ahijah's prophecy in 2 Chr 10:15 presupposes the knowledge of 1 Kgs 11:26–40, and 1 Kgs 11:29–39 respectively (239); Dillard likewise thinks that, in the latter two passages in Chronicles, "the Chronicler presumes the reader's familiarity with the parallel history" at 1 Kgs 11:26–40 and 11:29–33 respectively (Dillard, *2 Chronicles*, 85–86, 87); Also, Curtis and Madsen, *Chronicles*, 367. McKenzie also acknowledges the possibility of the reader's prior knowledge of the Ahijah's oracle in 1 Kgs 11 cautiously with another possibility (McKenzie, *1–2 Chronicles*, 263). On the same passages, Knoppers criticizes Williamson in that "Williamson seems to think that the Chronicler's selections from his *Vorlage* have identical meanings to their use in his *Vorlage* (Knoppers, "Rehoboam in Chronicles," 431). Knoppers seems to be sensitive to the implication of admitting the reader's prior knowledge of the contents of its *Vorlage*, while Williamson does not. It is also noteworthy that Williamson thinks that Solomon's "heavy burden" upon his people in 2 Chr 10:4 has "the allusions to passages in Kings" which is "not included in the Chronicler's portrayal of Solomon."

99. For example, McKenzie does not ask why God gave such a command, while he regards the passage as providing the reason for Rehoboam's following prosperity (McKenzie, *1–2 Chronicles*, 264).

100. With a few exceptions. For example, Williamson's and Johnstone's peculiar interpretations.

101. Curtis and Madsen, *Chronicles*, 375. It is interesting that Curtis, on the one hand, thinks that Abijah's description of the division situation in 2 Chr 13:7 is contradictory to the previous passage of the division situation itself, but on the other hand, believes that Abijah's speech reflects the Chronicler's position (375–76).

presented as flawless in Chronicles is possible only when it is supposed that the Chronicler was a clumsy writer. However, it is more likely that the reader is expected to be reminded of Solomon's apostasy and God's follow-ing sentence, as the ultimate cause of the kingdom division, through the reminders of it included by the Chronicler. Furthermore, it is plain in the text that Solomon's oppression of the Israelites, although it is described in-directly, provides a cause on a political level of the division, along with his son's stupidity. In view of this, much of the responsibility for the division of the kingdom falls upon Solomon's shoulders, in Chronicles as in Kings.

In sum, it is reasonable to conclude that Solomon in Chronicles is by no means presented as flawless.

3. RECONSIDERATION OF THE DESCRIPTION OF THE DIVISION SITUATION IN ABIJAH'S SPEECH

The reason why the significance of 2 Chr 10 regarding the division of the kingdom has been overlooked, and that the content of it is regarded as a "dilemma," seems to be twofold. Firstly, the concept of an idealized or impeccable Solomon has been too dominant in the interpretation. Sec-ondly, the account of the division of the kingdom in the speech of Abi-jah, the successor of Rehoboam (2 Chr 13:6–7), has been construed as the Chronicler's own view of the situation, as a so-called "royal speech" or "royal address."[102] Although von Rad's original proposal that speeches

102. The view that speeches in Chronicles exactly reflect the theological perspec-tive of the Chronicler himself has been proposed by Driver (1895), von Rad (1934), and Plöger (1957), and followed by Japhet, Dillard, and Williamson, etc. For a brief survey, see Japhet, *I & II Chronicles*, 36. However, Selman supports the stance taken in this study.

Since von Rad initially drew scholarly attention to the addresses in Chronicles (von Rad, "Levitical Sermon"), speeches or addresses in Chronicles have become a subject of scholarly discussion, although von Rad's own proposal has been challenged since by Mathias (Mathias, "Levitische Predigt").

In fact, von Rad's attempt to see the author's theological stance through the sermons of the narrative figure has its model in Köhler's view that speeches of major figures in the Deuteronomistic history are the Deuteronomist's sermon, as he confesses (von Rad, "Levitical Sermon," 267). Von Rad adopts Köhler's view into the Chronicler's his-tory (for him it is Chronicles and Ezra-Nehemiah), suggesting that study of the sample speeches indicates that the author of the speeches (and therefore the author of the whole work) is a second temple Levite. Noth also has a similar view on the speeches in the so-called Deuteronomistic history).

While von Rad treats only five of the addresses in Chronicles to show his point, Throntveit proposes all the royal speeches in Chronicles (1987); further Mason pro-poses a comprehensive study of all addresses (including priest address, prophetic

in Chronicles are "Levitical sermons" has been criticized, his assumption that speeches in the work reflect the author's own theology is generally accepted. Most commentators seem to accept that Abijah's speech is described "as exegesis of the Kings account of the division of the kingdoms," as Mason observes.[103] Moreover, some scholars propose that Abijah's speech is programmatic. For Plöger, Abijah's speech and Hezekiah's announcement are both calls to the northern kingdom or people to return to the authentic Davidic dynasty and Jerusalem cult.[104] Throntveit, accepting Plöger's view, adds that Abijah's speech (2 Chr 13:4b–12) and Hezekiah's announcement (2 Chr 30:6b–9) mark distinctive periods of the kingdom.[105] In the period between the two speeches, Israel is presented as a divided kingdom, whereas in the periods before Abijah's speech and after Hezekiah's announcement, Israel is presented as a united kingdom.[106] To sum

---

address, etc.) with other post-exilic addresses in other biblical works (Mason, *Preaching the tradition*; Mason, "Some Echoes of the Preaching"), which mainly aims to criticize von Rad's view (134) (Throntveit, too. 135). However, although von Rad's initial proposal has been severely criticized, the basic form-critical approach to the addresses in Chronicles has continued. Von Rad does not treat Abijah's speech in his article, but for the following scholars, Abijah's speech becomes a very significant speech which occupies a crucial point in the whole structure of the Chronicles.

Seemingly positive presentation of Abijah in Chronicles, which is regarded by many as a contrast to the presentation of Abijah in Kings, can be another factor which is related to the issue. In Chronicles' study, victory over enemies and having many children, building project, a large army, etc have been regarded as a sign of God's approval of a Judean king as God's blessing, and the account of Abijah includes some elements of them, i.e., his victory over the Israelite army (2 Chr 13:2b–19) and many wives and children (2 Chr 13:21). However, the problematic nature of his victory over the Israelite army, and the nature of his blessing will be discussed in the following section in this chapter (also in chapter 5). The present study does not see Abijah presented positively in the account.

Mason prefers the term address to speech, for he thinks that "to call them 'sermons' begs the question of their form, for some of them are too short to be that." According to him, "address" is more appropriate English vocabulary for the case (Mason, *Preaching the tradition*, 2–3). However, the present study will use the term "speech" according to convention.

103. Mason, *Preaching the Tradition*, 42.

104. Plöger, "Reden und Gebete."

105. Throntveit, *When Kings Speak*, 115–18.

106. To support his view, Throntveit points out that the presentation of Hezekiah's reign has parallel elements of both David and Solomon, the kings of the united kingdom. However, it is doubtful that the intention of Abijah's speech is really to call the northern people to return to the Davidic dynasty, for it is plain that Abijah's speech is delivered to the northern army in order to deter them from waging the battle, not in order to call them to return to the Davidic dynasty.

up, Abijah's speech has been construed as reflecting the Chronicler's own stance and theology.

The first point, that Solomon is presented as impeccable in Chronicles, has been disputed in the previous sections to some extent, and will be contested throughout the book. As for the second point, because 2 Chr 10 clearly shows the process of the division of the kingdom, Abijah's speech cannot be construed as a fully authorized comment by the author. This is so even though most scholars believe that it is precisely the Chronicler's view. Rather, Abijah's speech should be understood as a mixture of a popular theology and exaggerated political propaganda. Additional consideration can be proposed as follows.

Many speeches in Chronicles have been studied in terms of a "rhetorical strategy" of the author, as special instruments through which the Chronicler expresses his own ideology and view.[107] Von Rad's original assertion that the speeches in Chronicles are in fact sermons of Levitical personnel for the post-exile community has been challenged. Nevertheless, his original assertion that the speeches are an instrument of the author's own theology has been accepted by most scholars without reservation. Form-critical approaches to the addresses since von Rad seem to have excluded any doubt of the truthfulness of the content of the speeches. Further, since the significance of Abijah's speech for the overall structure of the whole Chronicles has been proposed by scholars like Throntveit and Williamson,[108] the scholarly atmosphere has precluded any attempt to question whether the speech really reflects the "reality" of the book or the author's own outlook.[109] It is tempting to construe Abijah's speech as one of the royal speeches that reflect the author's view or theology precisely. Moreover, the two themes of Abijah's speech (the legitimacy of the Davidic dynasty, and the Jerusalem cult) are the twin themes that are highlighted throughout the work. Additionally, it is understandable that Abijah's victory over the northern tribes and his ensuing prosperity are construed as God's approval (or favor) of the king.[110] However, the near-consensus

---

107. It is interesting to observe here the combination (conflation) of form criticism and rhetorical criticism. In the emerging era of rhetorical criticism Muilenburg proposes rhetorical criticism as being about to lead biblical study beyond the limitation of form criticism (Muilenburg, "Form Criticism and Beyond").

108. Williamson's view is basically no different from the view that most speeches in Chronicles reflect the author's stance. He construes the speech as "a thinly-veiled comment by the author" (Williamson, 1 and 2 Chronicles, 251).

109. Selman is the exception (Selman, 2 Chronicles, 380).

110. Hence, G. Jones even thinks that Abijah is presented as the best king (Jones,

interpretation of Abijah's speech and the account seems to be heavily affected deductively by the view that Chronicler put his own theology and outlook in the mouths of major figures, rather than being the result of objectively evaluating it as it is in context.[111]

3.1 The Significance of the Disparity of the Text (2 Chr 10) and Abijah's Speech (2 Chr 13)

Abijah's speech should be construed according to the basic consideration that, in the reader's prior knowledge through the first history, he is a bad king. Moreover, the content of his speech does not fit the facts of the division of the kingdom presented in 2 Chr 10.[112] Here, Kissling's observation is very relevant to reading the account of Abijah:

> The words which a narrator puts in the mouths of characters may or may not represent the point of view of the narrator. Further, a character's speech and/or actions may or may not have the narrator's approval, morally or ideologically. When a character's speech and/or actions always represent the narrator's point of view and always have the narrator's moral and ideological approval, that character is said to be a thoroughly reliable character. When a character's speech and/or actions do not convey the narrator's point of view and therefore do not have the

---

1&2 Chronicles, 54).

111. Muilenburg's statement is relevant in this regard. He, while basically acknowledging the merits and contribution of form criticism, states that form criticism has the tendency to "lay such stress upon the typical and representative that the individual, personal, and unique features of the particular pericope are all but lost to view; . . . form criticism by its very nature is bound to generalize because it is concerned with what is common to all the representatives of a genre, and therefore applies an external measure to the individual periscopes. . . . The passage must be read and heard precisely as it is spoken" (Muilenburg, "Form Criticism and Beyond," 5).

112. According to Williamson, Caquot is the first one who sees that Abijah's speech does not reflect the view of Chronicler. Caquot, suggesting the "realized theocracy" in the post-exilic temple community, does not believe in the eternal nature of the Davidic dynasty, and observes that the statement of God's giving the kingship over Israel to David and his descendants forever by a covenant of salt (2 Chr 13:15), does not reflect the Chronicler's stance but only Abijah's own legitimacy over against the northern kingdom (Caquot, "Messianisme," 119) (Williamson, "Eschatology," 146). Williamson shows his peculiar understanding of Abijah's speech in terms of the division situation in his work (Williamson, *Israel*, 111–15, 122; Williamson, *1 and 2 Chronicles*, 252–53).

narrator's moral or ideological approval, the character is said to be unreliable in that particular instance.[113]

In light of this, Abijah appears as an unreliable character, for his statement on the division (2 Chr 13:7) does not reflect the author's understanding of the division presented in 2 Chr 10. The division was not caused by Rehoboam's being young and irresolute as Abijah describes it (2 Chr 13:7b), but by God's will (2 Chr 10:15; 11:4). Further, far from Abijah's statement, Rehoboam was neither young, nor irresolute; in fact he was forty-one years old (2 Chr 12:13),[114] chose the hard line (2 Chr 10:13–14), and was resolute enough to start a war to regain the northern tribes (2 Chr 11:1).[115] However, parts of his speech, other than that on the division, do reflect objective and approved reality: his description of the distorted religious practices of the northern Israel kingdom (2 Chr 13:8–9), and the comparatively better or privileged condition of the southern Judean kingdom in terms of religion (2 Chr 13:8, 10–11), is true.

This point is strengthened by the account of the battle that occurs after the speech. In the early stages of the battle, Abijah's Judahite army is put in danger.[116] This is not usually the case when a God-favored king fights against his enemy in Chronicles. The God-favored king usually defeats the enemy army from the start of the battle, even when the enemy has

113. Kissling, *Reliable Characters*, 20.

114. It is admitted that although he was not young at forty-one, "young" can be used to mean the new king's inexperience in his job (cf. the case of Solomon in 1 Chr 22:5; 29:1. Also, refer to 2 Chr 10:8. Williamson points out that the almost identical terms "young and irresolute" (נַעַר וְרַךְ) were used of Solomon at 1 Chr 22:5 and 29:1 (Williamson, *1 and 2 Chronicles*, 253); Barker proposes the possibility that "young" means here "of blamable ignorance, inexperience, and instability" (Barker, *2 Chronicles*, 153), although he thinks that Abijah's age of forty-one years is too old (Barker, *2 Chronicles*, 121)).

115. Selman regards Abijah's statement that Rehoboam was "young and irresolute" is the right expression as meaning being "inexperienced and weak-willed"; however, he thinks that Rehoboam, being forty-one years old, was "fully responsible for his folly," and consequently, "Abijah's defence of his father Rehoboam (v 7) seems somewhat exaggerated in view of chapter 10," although it is understandable as an embellished political statement (Selman, *2 Chronicles*, 380). Keil also points out the discrepancy. "This representation does not conform to the state of the case as narrated in chap. x. Rehoboam did not appear soft-hearted and compliant in the negotiation with the rebellious tribes . . ." Keil, like Selman thinks that "Abijah wishes to justify his father as much as possible in his speech . . ." (Keil, *1&2 Chronicles*, 351–52). Hooker seems to be aware of the contrast between 2 Chr 10:1–19 ("rash and arrogant") and 2 Chr 13:7 ("young and irresolute"), but does not attempt to question the truthfulness of Abijah's description (Hooker, *First and Second Chronicles*, 181).

116. Deboys does not pay attention to this point.

overwhelmingly superior numbers and superior war devices (e.g., 2 Chr 14:7–11 [ET 14:8–12]; 2 Chr 20:1–23).[117] Moreover, the portrayal of Abijah contrasts with those of the succeeding two kings in their battles. Asa and Jehoshaphat themselves pray before their battles against enormous enemy armies, asking for God's help (2 Chr 14:10 [ET 14:11]; 20:3–12), and the battles are won by the Judahite army from the start, while Abijah's prayer or cry to the Lord is not mentioned even when the Judahite army is put in danger in the first stage of the battle. In Abijah's battle, only when the Judahite army cries to the Lord and the priests blow the horns according to Num 10:9, does the battle situation begin to change with the intervention of God (2 Chr 13:14–17). It is noteworthy that in the narrator's explanation of the cause of the victory, Abijah is not mentioned, but only the men of Judah's trust in their ancestors' God (2 Chr 13:18).[118]

In this additional light, it appears that the description of the danger to the Abijah's army, in the early stage of the battle, is intended to hint at or allude to God's disapproval of Abijah and his speech (or more precisely, some part of it) as well. Hence, it is concluded that the victory of the Judahite army is won by God's favor to David rather than Abijah (as well as the Judahite army's trust in God and their prayer), as the *Vorlage* plainly states in the comparatively substantial portion (15:4–5) within the short account of the reign of Abijah (1 Kgs 15:1–8[119]).

As Deboys points out, the fact that in the early reign of the following king Asa, the cleansing of the foreign altars, the high places, pillars, the sacred poles, and the incense altars (2 Chr 14:2, 4 [ET 14:3, 5]) strongly hints at Abijah's religious laxity in the reader's prior knowledge (1 Kgs

---

117. In the cases in Deuteronomy and Judges, immediate victory over the enemy is guaranteed, whether or not the enemy is superior to Israel in number or in war devices. Dt 20:1; 28:7 "The Lord will cause your enemies who rise against you to be defeated before you; they shall come out against you one way, and flee before you seven ways"; Judg 4: 15 (cf. 4:3); 6:21–22 (6:5); 11:32–33; etc.

118. "Thus the Israelites were subdued at that time, and the people of Judah prevailed, because they relied on the Lord, the God of their ancestors" (2 Chr 13:18). Deboys also observes it; however, he suggests that Abijah's speech and people's prayer should be regarded as one set (Deboys, "Portrayal of Abijah," 51). However, his comparing Abijah's case to Hezekiah's case in 2 Kgs 18 and 2 Chr 31 is not relevant, for Hezekiah's case is not of a battle situation.

119. It should be admitted that the description of God's favor to David occupies a substantial part (1 Kgs 15:4–5, thirty-five Hebrew words) of the short account (1 Kgs 15:1–8, 113 Hebrew words) of Abijah (Abijam)'s reign in Kings.

15:3;[120] cf. 1 Kgs 14:23–24[121]), while in his speech he shows pride in the Judahite kingdom's comparative cultic purity over the northern kingdom. His pride presents him as a hypocrite rather than a faithful Judahite king. Nevertheless, the eventual victory of the army of the Judahite kingdom, and Abijah's prosperity, confirm the *Vorlage*'s view that he is favored by God, owing to David. The Judahite king received God's blessing in spite of his faults or shortcomings, which is described as follows.[122]

> Nevertheless for David's sake the Lord his God gave him a lamp in Jerusalem, setting up his son after him, and establishing Jerusalem; because David did what was right in the sight of the Lord, and did not turn aside from anything that he commanded him all the days of his life, except in the matter of Uriah the Hittite.
>
> (1 Kgs 15:4–5)[123]

While some point out that the negative evaluation of the king in the *Vorlage* is omitted in Chronicles, it is significant that there is no positive evaluation of Abijah's reign. The same applies to Solomon. It is significant that the two kings who enjoyed David's merit more than any other kings, and received God's abundant blessing in spite of their faults, do not have any evaluation comment in the generally expected place, i.e., at the end of the account of a king in Chronicle. Possibly the omission of the evaluation statement implies that the king cannot be praised, although he enjoyed God's blessing thanks to others than himself. The only other case is of

---

120. "He [Abijah] committed all the sins that his father [Rehoboam] did before him; his heart was not true to he Lord his God, like the heart of his father David."

121. Idolatry practices done in Rehoboam's day are described as follows, "For they also built for themselves high places, pillars, and sacred poles on every high hill and under every green tree; there were also male temple prostitutes in the land. They committed all the abominations of the nations that the Lord drove out before the people of Israel."

122. Selman states the point well. "A number of David's descendants are treated more positively than in Kings, not because the Chronicler is any more lenient but because he sees in their lives explicit evidence of God's kindness to the undeserving" (Selman, *1 Chronicles*, 62–63).

123. The Chronicler's presentation of the war can be construed as an illustration of the following verse, "The war begun between Rehoboam and Jeroboam continued all the days of his life" (1 Kgs 15:6) in the first historiography. Although it is not retained in Abijah's case, God's kindness toward undeserving Davidic descendents, in spite of their evil, appears in the case of the wicked Jehoram (2 Chr 21:7) with a clear explanation of it (i.e. for the sake of the God's covenant with David). The present study will generally follow NRSV translation for biblical quotation, but when it is necessary my own translation will be provided.

Jehoahaz (2 Chr 36:1–4), which does not have significance, for it is extremely short.

In fact no laudable merit of Abijah's own is described in the account. His speech that does not reflect the whole truth, and the prosperity that he enjoys does not necessarily guarantee that he is viewed as a good king. Hence, the description of the prosperity he enjoys should be construed as showing God's grace as a supplement to the comment of God's abundant grace upon David's descendant(s), for David's sake, which is stated in the *Vorlage*.[124] Abijah's producing many children (2 Chr 13:21) is nothing but a concrete case of God's blessing of successors (1 Kgs 15:4 "Nevertheless . . . setting up his son after him") upon an undeserving descendant of David owing to David.

That the Chronicler's portrayal of Abijah is not a deviation from that of its *Vorlage*, is supported by the observation that even some parts of Abijah's speech "recall" the Kings' description, as Mason observes.[125] That is, in Abijah's speech, "you . . . have with you the golden calves that Jeroboam made as gods for you" (2 Chr 13:8b) reflects "the king . . . made two calves of gold . . . He said to the people, '. . . Here are your gods, O Israel . . .'" (1 Kgs 12:28).[126] Further, "Whoever comes to be consecrated with a young bull or seven rams becomes a priest of what are no gods" (2 Chr 13:9b)

---

124. It is interesting to observe that the account of the king Jehoram, who is evaluated negatively (i.e., "He walked in the ways of the kings of Israel, as the house of Ahab had done, for the daughter of Ahab was his wife. He did what was evil in the sight of the Lord" (2 Kgs 8:18) but enjoys God's favor owing to David (8:19), shows a similar battle case to Abijah's. Jehoram and his army had been surrounded by enemy army but were relieved from the danger (2 Kgs 8:20–21 // 2 Chr 21:7). It is significant that the battle account follows the comment that Jehoram received God's favor in spite of his evil, for the virtue of David (i.e., "Yet the Lord would not destroy Judah, for the sake of his servant David, since he had promised to give a lamp to him and to his descendants forever" (2 Kgs 8:19 / 2 Chr 21:8). That is, it is plain from the context that Jehoram, the bad king, and his army were delivered from their enemy through God's grace given owing to David. It is noteworthy that the two elements "for the sake of David" and "God's promise to give a lamp" are mentioned in both the Abijah account and the Jehoram account in Kings, while other cases do not retain the two elements even when they describe God's favor given upon David's descendant owing to David (1 Kgs 11:34; 2 Kgs 19:34). In this light, Abijah and his army's deliverance from the northern army, and further their defeat of the northern army in 2 Chr 13, can be construed as a concrete case of God's favor given to David's descendent owing to David, in spite of the faults of its beneficiary as described in the *Vorlage*.

125. Mason, *Preaching the Tradition*, 41–42.

126. There is mention of "the calves" in Chronicles (2 Chr 11:13) along with "the goat-demons." However, it is weak as a basis for Abijah's description, while Kings' description shows direct echoes.

reflects "any who wanted to be priests he [Jeroboam] consecrated for the high places" (1 Kgs 13:33).[127]

As for Abijah's pride in the cultic superiority of Judahite kingdom, even in the *Vorlage,* where Abijah is presented as a wicked king, his devotion to the temple cult is hinted at to some extent. That is, "He [Asa] brought into the house of the Lord the votive gifts of his father [Abijah] and his own votive gifts—silver, gold, and utensils" (1 Kgs 15:15; cf. 2 Chr 14:12 [ET 14:13]). The significance of this verse in regards to Abijah's pride in his kingdom's cultic affairs has been neglected. The verse implies that Abijah has good reason to think of himself as faithful to the Jerusalem temple and God, although it is plain that worshiping other deities was practiced or allowed during his reign (1 Kgs 15:12–13; 2 Chr 14:2, 4 [ET 14:3, 5]). Probably, while Abijah ignored the demand of exclusive faithfulness toward God, he believed that he was a faithful Davidic king who did not desert God. He seems to think of himself as a faithful king who expresses laudable devotion in his preparation of votive gifts to the God of Israel. Abijah's proud speech of cultic superiority over the northern kingdom, has its ground on that, at least partially.

Lastly, it can be pointed out that both the contents and themes of the description of Abijah's reign in Kings and Chronicles, are common. They are about nothing but Abijah's war against Jeroboam (1 Kgs 15:7 / 2 Chr 13:2b–19), and his undeserving favor from God, owing to his ancestor David (1 Kgs 15:3–5 / 2 Chr 13:21).

3.2 Williamson's Attempt to Harmonize Abijah's Speech with 2 Chr 10 and a Refutation of It

While Japhet who is aware of the "sharp contrast" between 2 Chr 13:6 and 2 Chr 10:15; 11:4,[128] dismisses the significance of the contrast as "the lack of historiographical and theological continuity, . . . an inherent feature of the Chronicler's work,"[129] Williamson notices the problem of 2 Chr 13:7, that the usual interpretation or understanding of the verse is not reconcilable with the previous situation of the division described in 2

---

127. In Chronicles, it is simply that "Jeroboam and his sons had prevented them [the Levites] from serving as priests of the Lord, and had appointed his own priests for high places . . ." (2 Chr 11:14b–15).

128. Japhet, *I & II Chronicles*, 689, 691–92.

129. Ibid., 689.

Chr 10:1—11:4.[130] It seems that in order to maintain the view that Abijah's speech is one of the royal speeches which reflect precisely the Chronicler's ideology,[131] Williamson interprets the problematic verse in his own way so that the meaning of the verse may not be contradictory to the previous situation described in 2 Chr 10:1—11:4. According to him, those who opposed (or "persuaded" as Williamson prefers[132]) Rehoboam (2 Chr 13:7) were not meant, by Abijah, to be the representatives of the northern tribes, but Rehoboam's young subjects who advised him to respond harshly to the northern representatives.[133] In line with this view, Williamson construes "his master" in 2 Chr 13:6 as a reference to Rehoboam rather than Solomon, and "around him" in the ensuing verse, as a reference to Rehoboam again rather than to Jeroboam.[134]

However, Williamson's attempt to harmonize 2 Chr 13:7a with the division situation previously described (10:1ff) can be refuted as follows (and consequently, cannot secure the view which assumes that there is no flaw in the speeches as the Chronicler's propaganda). Firstly, the overall tone of Abijah's speech is to blame the northerners,[135] and in the context it seems unlikely that Abijah is blaming Rehoboam's young subjects in order

130. Williamson observes a contradiction in Welch's interpretations of 2 Chr 10 and 2 Chr 13 where Welch accepts that the division has "good reasons" (2 Chr 10) and that "fundamental sin lay in the rebellion of Israel against . . . Davidic dynasty" (2 Chr 13) (Williamson, *Israel*, 98; Welch, *Post Exilic*, 189 91).

131. Williamson's view is basically no different from the view that most speeches in Chronicles reflect the author's stance. He construes the speech as "a thinly-veiled comment by the author" (Williamson, *1 and 2 Chronicles*, 251).

132. Ibid., 252–53.

133. Contra Williamson. Williamson asserts that the "certain worthless scoundrels" (13:7) cannot be northern representatives, for he thinks that "all Israel" at 10:3 should be much greater entity (ibid., 252). However, it is apparent that "all Israel" at 10:3 should not be interpreted literally.

134. Ibid. However, most commentators construe the third person singular as Solomon, Rehoboam, respectively. For example, see Selman, *2 Chronicles*, 380. Williamson also quotes Josephus's writing (*Ant.* 8:277) to support his interpretation; however, Josephus's rewriting should be regarded as no more than his own interpretation. Williamson's view of the passage is supportive to his understanding that the Chronicler has an inclusive and positive attitude towards northern Israel, in that the Chronicler does not criticize the northern party but Rehoboam and his young subjects. However, as Dillard rightly observes, "Condemnation of the Northern Kingdom is the overarching feature of the immediate context: Jeroboam's rebellion, resisting the kingdom of God, the illegitimate cult . . ." (Dillard, *2 Chronicles*, 108).

135. In contrast to Williamson's view, Curtis thinks that "here the fault is laid entirely on the representatives of Israel" (Curtis and Madsen, *Chronicles*, 375). Also Dillard, *2 Chronicles*, 108.

to defend his father. Williamson maintains that Abijah put "the blame for what has happened on him (Jeroboam) alone, thereby making the way back for them (the northerners) very much easier."[136] However, it is plain that Abijah's rebuke is mainly towards the northerners (אַתֶּם (v. 8), הִדַּחְתֶּם (v. 9), etc: second person plural). It is noteworthy that it is the northerners that Abijah calls to account for even the counter-cultus (2 Chr 13:8–9), which was, in fact, initiated by Jeroboam according to the *Vorlage* (1 Kgs 12:26–31). Secondly, from the context "his master" should be construed as Solomon rather than Rehoboam. The verse reflects the situation described in its *Vorlage* (1 Kgs 11:26–27),[137] for Rehoboam has not been mentioned yet in Abijah's speech, while Solomon has been mentioned (13:6), to whom Jeroboam has been mentioned as "a servant" (13:6 עֶבֶד). Thirdly, "around him" in 13:7 should be construed as referring to Jeroboam rather than Rehoboam, for it is unlikely that the pronoun of third person singular (in the form of pronominal suffixes) which denotes Rehoboam, appears twice ("against his lord" (עַל־אֲדֹנָיו) in 13:6, "around him" (עָלָיו) in 13:7) before the proper noun Rehoboam is introduced (13:7). Rather it is more natural to read "around him" as referring to Jeroboam, for he has been introduced already. From a syntactical point of view, it is unlikely that a person would be mentioned in pronoun form twice even before the proper noun of the person was introduced, while it is more natural that a pronoun form of a person is used after the proper noun of the person has been introduced.[138]

While Williamson's attempt to harmonize 2 Chr 13:7 and the situation previously described (10:1ff) can be refuted as above, several points which indicate that Abijah is not presented as an approved flawless king, still remain unchallenged.

136. Williamson, *1 and 2 Chronicles*, 252.

137. Selman thinks that "the idea is taken from 1 Ki. 11:26–27" (Selman, *2 Chronicles*, 380).

138. Williamson also suggests, as a background of his argument, that, in Chronicles, for "each generation is responsible to God for its actions," now there is no excuse for keeping the secession of the northern tribes from the Davidic kingdom, in the reign of Abijah, who is presented as an authoritative Davidic king, while the northern kingdom has been never authorized by God in Chronicles (Williamson, *1 and 2 Chronicles*, 251), although the secession of the northern tribes in Rehoboam's reign happens by God's sovereignty for whatever reason. However, it is contradictory for Williamson to recognize, on the one hand, that "knowledge of 1 Kgs 11:29–39 is presupposed" (in 1 Kgs 11:29–39, God's promise of northern dynasty is apparent) in 2 Chr 10:15 (Williamson, *1 and 2 Chronicles*, 239), and to assert, on the other hand, that although the division of the kingdom is according to God's sovereignty in Rehoboam's reign, in the following generation i.e., Abijah's reign, the northerners have the right of secession no more.

3.3 Another Case of a Mixture of Truth and Lies in a Report in a Narrative of the Hebrew Bible

It is observed that a subtle mixture of a statement of objective facts and a lie appears in the Amalekite's lie to King David in 2 Sam 1:1–16. Although it is not precisely a speech or address, rather a report, it has similarities in that it is a content expressed through the mouth of a figure in a narrative.[139] It is evident that the young Amalekite's report of the death of Saul is a mixture of some true information and his own lie. That is, the previous passage which describes the death of Saul (1 Sam 31:1–6) shows that Saul was in a urgent situation, defeated and almost overtaken by Philistines in the battle of Mount Gilboa, and wished to be killed not by the hand of his enemy but by the hand of his own man, and he ordered it so. The passage also tells of the death of Jonathan, a son of Saul, with his two brothers. The Amalekite reports these facts to David as they were. However, he slightly fabricates the direct cause of Saul's death. While the previous passage shows that Saul killed himself by falling upon his own sword as his armor-bearer was unwilling to follow the order to kill him (1 Sam 31:4), the Amalekite reports that he himself killed King Saul, when Saul ordered him to do so (2 Sam 1:9–10).[140] It is a subtle mixture or combination of truth and lie. The mixture is, without doubt, for the expected profit of the Amalekite himself. It is strongly suspected that the Amalekite expected a reward from David, with the report that he himself killed King Saul, who was the enemy and persecutor of David.[141]

139. It can also be pointed out that the arguments between Job and his three friends are not black and white. That the statements of Job's three friends are not totally right is evident from the text (Job 42:7–8), though many parts of them appear to be correct statements. It is interesting that even Job himself has to repent of what he told his friends while he is vindicated by God of what he told of God (38:2; 40:2; 42:3). Although the case is a matter of correct statement and incorrect statement (not intended), rather than truth and lie, it shows that a statement of the mixture of two opposite ingredients is not alien in Hebrew literature.

140. The Amalekite's description of the situation of Saul's death, that "the chariots and the horsemen [of Philistine] drew close to him [King Saul]" (2 Sam 1:6) is at variance with the description of the narrator in 1 Sam 31 that "the archers [of Philistine] found him [King Saul]" (31:3). The disparity may imply that the Amalekite was not even present at the scene.

141. Cf. when Absalom was killed in the battle and the rebellion was subdued, Ahimaaz son of Zadok wants to carry the tidings to David, thinking it is good news to him, however, Joab does not allow it, saying, "Why will you run, my son, seeing that you have *no reward* for the tidings" (2 Sam 18:22). Although Hebrew text lacks the term "reward," the context makes the sense. Further, David's own understanding of the case is shown in 2 Sam 4:10, "when the one who told me, 'see, Saul is dead,' thought he

It is plain that the disparity between the account of Saul's death described in 1 Sam 31 and the content of the Amalekite's report of Saul's death in 2 Sam 1, tells the reader that the Amalekite is telling a lie mixed with reality, most probably for his own benefit.[142] What is interesting is that the narrator does not point out that the Amalekite is telling a lie, and leaves the judgment solely to his reader.[143] Neither does any character of the account in 2 Sam 1 realize that the young Amalekite told a lie,[144]

---

was bringing good news, I seized him and killed him at Ziklag—this was the reward I gave him for his news."

142. A similar view is proposed by majority scholars such as Keil, *I & II Chronicles*, 286; Fokkelman, *Narrative Art*, 640 ff; McCarter, *II Samuel*, 62–64; Gordon, *1 & 2 Samuel*, 208; Anderson, *2 Samuel*, 9–10; Payne, *Samuel*, 157. There are attempts to harmonize the two descriptions of King Saul's death. The third explanation for the disparity is that simply we have two traditions. For example, Brueggemann, following Smith (Smith, *The Books of Samuel*, 254), does not regard the disparity between 1 Sam 31 and 2 Sam 1 as evidence that shows that the Amalekite was lying. Being aware of many other scholars' view that the Amalekite fabricates his report of Saul's death, Brueggemann seems to think that the two accounts of the death of King Saul are distinguished traditions ("In fact there is no way to adjudicate the question of the historicity of either narrative"; Brueggeman, *First and Second Samuel*, 213). However, Brueggemann's view is not convincing, for it requires the presumption that the author (or the editor) of the present form of Samuel is a clumsy editor, which is most unlikely. Furthermore, Brueggemann fails to pay due attention to the fact that it is only through the report of the Amalekite (i.e., not a narrative narrated by the narrator himself) that the description of Saul's death is given in 2 Sam 1. A slight acknowledgement of the author's literary capability, and reader-sensitive consideration, will lead to our present interpretation. A convenient brief survey of the discussion of the issue of the disparity between 1 Sam 31:3–5 and 2 Sam 1:6–10 on Saul's death, is proposed by McCarter (McCarter, *II Samuel*, 62–64).

143. Leaving judgment to the reader is a characteristic of the Hebrew narrative. For example, in the famous case of Solomon's judgment which shows his God-given wisdom in 1 Kgs 3:16–28, the reader is so naturally invited to judge, the reader may not notice that it is himself or herself who judges the meaning of the text. That is, Solomon's order (NRSV, NIV versions add "first" to make it clear (i.e., "Give the first woman the living baby; Do not kill him. She is his mother" (v. 27)), however, the Hebrew text does not designate whom he refers to: the Hebrew text is simply תְּנוּ לָהּ אֶת הַיָּלוּד הַחַי (Give the woman the living baby). It is plain that which woman he refers to is confidently left to the reader's judgment. The reader's pre-understanding of the nature of motherhood is invited to interpret the passage, without notice, in this case. Walsh suspects that Solomon's order might be the wrong decision (Walsh, "Solomon in First King 1–5," 488–89), however, his suggestion is unnatural (this point will be discussed in chapter 3).

144. David's saying to the Amalekite when the young man was struck down and dying, "Your blood be on your head; for your own mouth has testified against you, saying, 'I have killed the Lord's anointed'" (2 Sam 1:16), can be construed that David suspected that it was possible that the Amalekite was telling a lie. However, it cannot be proved for sure.

and rebuke him for it, nor does the truth of King Saul's death happen to be revealed to the characters. Rather, David orders the Amalekite to be killed for his destroying the Lord's anointed, and the young Amalekite is executed by the hand of David's man.

The point of the account in 2 Sam 1 is not that David and his men were deceived foolishly by the Amalekite, but that David and his men have the virtue to be sorry to hear that King Saul the anointed was dead, although Saul was unjustly persecuting David. David and his men's tearing their clothes and mourning and weeping and fasting until evening for Saul, his son Jonathan, the army of the Lord, and the house of Israel (1 Sam 1:11–12), show how much David and his men honor and fear the God of Israel and love Israel their people.

Likewise, Abijah's lie about the situation of the division of the kingdom is plainly revealed through its disparity with the account of the division situation previously presented in 2 Chr 10. Abijah's speech is also an intentional mixture of some truth and lies (or distortion) made for his own benefit. As in the case of the lie of the Amalekite, neither the narrator nor any character in the account points out the lie; the judgment of Abijah's lie is left solely to the reader. As for how far Abijah's speech contains truth and lie, respectively, that judgment is also left to the reader, and it is not difficult to distinguish them. That is, the maintaining of the God-approved cultic practice in the Judahite kingdom and the wrong cultic practice in the northern kingdom is evident from the previous passages (2 Chr 11:14–15[145]). However, Abijah's description of the division situation of the united kingdom (13:7) is different from the previous passage (10:1—11:4).

The points of the account of Abijah are as follows. Firstly, the battle occurs in the situation where the pristine cult is distorted in the northern kingdom while the Judahite kingdom keeps it, as Abijah's speech describes. Secondly, the victory in battle does not come from superiority of human force, but from God's help (one of important messages of Chronicles[146]). The victory is due to God's responding to the cry of the Judahite army along with the priests' asking God's help by blowing their horns. Thirdly, God gives his blessing and help in spite of Abijah's faults, according to his covenantal promise to David, as a kind of confirmation,

---

145. "The Levites had left their common lands and their holdings and had come to Judah and Jerusalem, because Jeroboam and his sons had prevented them from serving as priests of the Lord, and had appointed his own priests for the high places, and for the goat-demons, and for the calves that he had made" (2 Chr 11:14–15).

146. This point will be discussed in chapter 7.

concrete example (or display), or exegetical material for the message[147] of the first history work.

As observed so far, the Amalekite's lie and Abijah's lie have many common elements, although the results of the two occasions seem to be quite different (i.e., the Amalekite's lie leads him to being killed, while after his speech Abijah defeats the northern army). The observation undermines the prevailing form-critical view of the speeches in Chronicles since von Rad's.[148]

3.4 Another Case of a Speech in Chronicles Containing a Mixture of Truth and Falsity

A distorted presentation of a situation in a speech appears within the scope of Chronicles, although it is not precisely a mixture of truth and lie as is the Amalekite's report (and Abijah's speech).[149] In the message of King Sennacherib of Assyria to the people in Jerusalem, an evidently distorted description appears as the speaker's interpretation of a situation. That is, "Is not Hezekiah misleading you, handing you over to die by famine and by thirst, when he tells you, 'The Lord our God will save us from the hand of the king of Assyria'? Was it not this same Hezekiah who took away his high places and his altars and commanded Judah and Jerusalem, saying,

147. That is, 1 Kgs 15:3–5, "He committed all the sins that his father did before him; his heart was not true to the Lord his God, like the heart of his father David. Nevertheless for David's sake the Lord his God gave him a lamp in Jerusalem setting up his son after him, and establishing Jerusalem; because David did what was right in the sight of the Lord, and did not turn aside from anything that he commanded him all the days of his life, except in the matter of Uriah the Hittite."

148. It is interesting to observe another case of a subtle mixture of truth and lie in a report in a New Testament narrative as well. It is observed in the Roman tribune Claudius Lysias' report of Paul's arrest to the governor Felix (Acts 23:26–30). In the report Claudius tries to conceal his mistake (i.e., to order Paul, a Roman citizen, to be examined by flogging, when it was illegal to flog a Roman citizen who was uncondemned) (22:24–29) and rather he fabricates that he tried to protect the Roman citizen, as if he had known of Paul's being a Roman citizen (23:27). The mixture of truth and lie in the report is understandable in the real life situation. Interestingly a fair judgment of the report is left solely to the reader, just as in the case of the Amalekite's report.

149. It is admitted that the mixture of this case is in a strict sense on a slightly different level of communication from the former case. That is, this case is of mixture of a real fact and a wrong interpretation of the fact, while the former is of a real fact and a false presentation of another fact. Nevertheless, the two cases are the same in that they are a mixture of true objectivity and false subjectivity.

'Before one altar you shall worship, and upon it you shall make your offerings'?" (2 Chr 32:11–12).[150] It appears, from early part of the chapter, that the Assyrian king misunderstood Hezekiah's taking away high places as an unfavorable action toward the God of Israel. He did not know that Hezekiah's taking away high places and altars was according to the law of Israel's God (Deut 12).[151] It is most probably according to his pagan understanding that building more worship places is a favorable act of a king toward his god, and destroying them is unfavorable act of the king to the god, which contrasts with the Chronicler's evaluation of the situation in 2 Chr 31:1b (cf. 31:21. also 13:17, 33:17). The judgment of the falsity of Sennacherib's interpretation of Hezekiah's religious reformation is left solely to the reader,[152] without any comment from the narrator.

150. In the parallel passage in 2 Kgs 18, the person who delivered King Sennacherib is the Rabshakeh (18:19). In the part of his speech, "But if you say to me, 'We rely on the Lord our God,' is it not he whose high places and altars Hezekiah has removed, saying to Judah and to Jerusalem, 'You shall worship before this altar in Jerusalem'" (v. 22); "Moreover, is it without the Lord that I have come up against this place to destroy it? The Lord said to me, Go up against this land, and destroy it?" (v. 25), it is implied that the Lord of Israel himself sent the Assyrian army to punish Hezekiah who had destroyed his high places and altars (although it is self-contradictory to the following insistence that Israel's God cannot save his people from the Assyrian king). The Chronicles conveys the same content to the reader in a shorter form with omission. For the general analysis of Rabshakeh's speech, see Fewell, "Sennacherib's Defeat," 79–90; Hyman, "The Rabshakeh's Speech," 213–20.

151. Another possibility is that the Assyrian king intentionally distorts the meaning of the Hezekiah's taking away high places in order to discourage the subjects of Hezekiah, knowing that it was Israelite law.

152. Williamson thinks that the falsity of the speech is very clear to the reader. Williamson directly quotes Childs' (*Isaiah and the Assyrian Crisis*, 110) understanding of the verse "Naturally for the reader the effect is just the opposite since he has been taught to value the reform as Hezekiah's greatest act of faithfulness" (Williamson, *1 and 2 Chronicles*, 383–84). Not a few scholars think that the speech is "a form of psychological warfare" (Dillard, *2 Chronicles*, 257). Tuell thinks that the speech was "aimed at dividing the community on a controversial point," for "presumably, there were many in Israel who did feel threatened and disenfranchised by Hezekiah's centralization policies." It is possible the speaker "plays on popular fears about the abolition of the by now ingrained Baal-religion" (McConville, *Chronicles*, 246). De Vries also states that "For the Hebrews this [i.e., Hezekiah's abolition of high places] would be a plus, yet it does touch a tender sore for any among them who might have been only halfhearted or eclectic in their Yahwism" [my insertion] (De Vries, *1 and 2 Chronicles*, 390). However, for some the mixed falsity of the speech comes from Assyrian's ignorance rather than a thoughtful tactic. Tuell thinks that "Sennacherib's words only demonstrate his total incomprehension of the ways of the Lord, and the faith of Israel" (Tuell, *First and Second Chronicles*, 227). In a similar view, Wilcock imagines interestingly that "There was surely at that point, to the puzzlement, derisive laughter from the walls of Jerusalem," for the misunderstanding of the speaker (Wilcock, *Chronicles*,

In this case, the falsity, mixed with reality, lies in the interpretation of the situation, while in the case of Abijah's speech, the falsity, mixed with the reality of the religious conditions, lies in the description of the division itself. Anyway, at least on this occasion, a subtle falsity mixed with reality is observed in Chronicles. When it is considered that the two speeches are the only substantial speeches that are delivered toward the enemy army in the situation of battle in Chronicles,[153] the common element of including a falsehood in order to undermine the enemy's morale is significant.[154]

Considering the above points together, if Abijah's speech is construed as a mixture of truth and falsehood, and the description of the division is a fabrication, then every detail of the division situation in 2 Chr 10 can be regarded as weighty and substantial information of the situation rather than an uncomfortable theological dilemma. The harmonization within Chronicles is sufficiently justifiable (i.e., 2 Chr 10 should be taken as it is and Abijah's speech is evaluated according to that information in 2 Chr 10, for it is natural to regard the narrator's description (2 Chr 10) as more trustworthy than the content of a character's speech). Rather, it seems that imposing a form-critical frame or form critically oriented rhetorical frame (or lens) (i.e., "royal speech" as reflecting precisely the author's view), upon the case has distorted or at least hindered a proper reading of the speech. The interpretative assumption that royal speeches precisely reflect the author's view needs to be reconsidered.

The near-consensus view produces its interpretation through a deductive approach, whose first proposition (i.e., royal speeches reflect the author's theology and view precisely, or major figures' speeches reflect the author's theology and view precisely) is not established through thorough exploration of the text (at least in the case of Abijah). Although the speeches in Chronicles seem to reflect the author's ideology to a significant extent, each one should be interpreted in the context and light of the whole interpretative assumption rather than be accepted as the exact

---

252). Whatever the nature of the speech is, and whatever the hearers' judgment of (or reaction to) the speech might be, it can be said that the reader is supposed to notice the falsity of the speech.

153. There are two more cases in which a word is proposed toward the opponents before battle. That is, in 2 Chr 25:18–19, King Joash of Israel to King Amaziah of Judah; in 2 Chr 35:21, King Neco of Egypt to Josiah. However, neither case really includes speech, but rather a private message (through envoys) to the opponent king alone.

154. Deboys shows his awareness of Rabshakeh's speech in his article on Abijah's speech (Deboys, "Portrayal of Abijah," 54), however, he does not pay attention to the common false elements of both speeches.

representation of the Chronicler's own perspective. The present approach is an inductive one based upon the text itself. When the deductive approach (which assumes the author's stance is precisely reflected in major royal speeches in Chronicles) cannot explain the distortion of the division situation in Abijah's speech and the nuance or complexity of the king's portrayal,[155] the first proposition (all major figures' speeches reflect the author's theology or view precisely) should be reconsidered. Furthermore, a combination of a correct statement of an orthodox ideology with pride, and a distorted statement of real facts, both for the speaker's sake, is not something alien to us, especially in a political situation, as Selman points out.[156] That the speech and the account should be construed as having greater complexity than it is usually regarded, will be supported in a later discussion of the literary characteristics of Chronicles.

4. CONCLUSION

In this chapter, the prevailing view which insists that Solomon is presented as blameless or impeccable in Chronicles was reconsidered. Firstly, it has been shown that there are many pieces of textual evidence which are against this view. Secondly, it was argued that no attempt to move the responsibility for the division of the kingdom from Solomon's shoulders to any other party, in interpretation of Chronicles, is successful or satisfactory. Thirdly, Abijah's speech and the related whole account of him in 2 Chr 13 was explored, for Abijah's description of the division situation is regarded as the Chronicler's stance, from which it has usually been accepted that in Chronicles the responsibility for the division is placed not on Solomon's shoulder but on Jeroboam's, in contrast to Kings' presentation. However, the near-consensus view was argued against, and it was proposed that Abijah's speech does not reflect precisely the Chronicler's view, in the description of the division of the kingdom.

---

155. E.g., the existence of idolatry in his day as revealed in 2 Chr 14:2, 4 [ET 14:3, 5], and the absence of any praising comment of the king.

156. Selman, *2 Chronicles*, 380. "Abijah's defence of his father Rehoboam (v 7) seems somewhat exaggerated in view of chapter 10, though the political device of presenting the facts in the best possible light is familiar enough!" However, Selman thinks that "Rehoboam was indeed inexperienced and weak-willed . . ." with which the present study does not agree.

3

The Problem of the
Interpretations of the
Solomon Narrative in Kings
and a New Interpretation[1]

1. INTRODUCTION

THE EXISTENCE OF A parallel story in Samuel-Kings provides the interpreters of Chronicles with a special vantage point. Through the comparison between the parallel accounts of the two works, interpreters have tried to detect the Chronicler's intentions. This is also applied to the Solomon account in Chronicles. That is, the interpreters of the Solomon account in Chronicles have sought to find out the author's intention in the account, in relation to, or in comparison with, the Solomon narrative in Kings. For example, and most significantly in terms of our concern, it has been proposed that the omission of the contents of chapters 2 and 11 of 1 Kings in the Chronicler's presentation of Solomon was intended by the Chronicler to present Solomon as flawless in Chronicles, on the basis that all the negative aspects of Solomon's reign in Kings appear only in those chapters.[2]

1. Early part of this chapter was published, in a slightly different form, in *Tyndale Bulletin* (62.1, 2011), 15–40, and is reused here with kind permission.
2. Japhet, "Chronicles, Book of," 525.

On the other hand, our understanding of the Solomon narrative in Kings, which is usually regarded as the *Vorlage* of the Solomon account in Chronicles, has been increased considerably in recent years. Since Parker's observation (1988) of the literary structure and its implication triggered the discussion on the narrative, many scholars have added their insights into the narrative. The increasing interest in the narrative eventually produced two monographs on the narrative, by J. J. Kang[3] and E. A. Seibert[4] in 2003 and 2006, respectively.

Unfortunately, recent study of the Solomon narrative in Kings, which has been quite considerably advanced in observing Solomon's faults or shortcomings, has not yet been applied to the interpretation of the Solomon account in Chronicles. In fact, interpretation of the Solomon narrative in Kings has not reached a consensus on a very important issue like the starting point of Solomon's corruption, while not a few scholars have recently contributed to, and considerably deepened, the understanding of the narrative through their valuable proposals.

This chapter will give a brief survey of recent studies of the Solomon narrative in Kings, including the most recent two monographs' views. After discussing the merits and weaknesses of those interpretations, and exploiting their insights, a new interpretation of the narrative concerning Solomon's corruption will be proposed, as an important preliminary or stepping stone to the interpretation of the Solomon account in Chronicles on the same issue. Approaching the narrative, special concern will be given to the narrative's presentation of the nature and process of Solomon's corruption, in order to secure the foundation of the interpretation of the Solomon account in Chronicles concerning Solomon's flaw(s). One would expect to detect a didactic lesson implanted in the narrative, concerning Solomon's turning from a pious king to an apostate, when one considers that the work is not a mere work of historiography but one with a didactic message or lesson for its reader, and that Solomon's turning from a pious king to an apostate is conspicuous and significant in the narrative and the book of Kings as a whole.

---

3. Kang, *The Persuasive Portrayal.*
4. Seibert, *Subversive Scribes.*

2. A SURVEY AND EVALUATION OF RECENT STUDIES

2.1. A Brief Survey of Recent Studies of the Solomon Narrative in Kings in Terms of Solomon's Corruption

Traditionally, the narrative was understood to have been composed in two parts, i.e., chapters 1–10 and 11, showing Solomon's achievement and prosperity under God's blessing, and Solomon's sin and God's punishment, respectively. This understanding is based on the plain fact that it is only in chapter 11 that the narrator's explicit criticism of Solomon's action appears.

This view was challenged by Noth (1957), who observed that the second part of the Solomon narrative begins from chapter 9, where God's warning at Gibeon against disobedience and apostasy appears, and Solomon's undue payback to Hiram (9:10–14) appears as the "first blot on Solomon's image."[5] Parker (1988) advanced Noth's view considerably, observing that the narrative has "a remarkable symmetry structure."[6] According to Parker, chapters 1–2 and 11:14–43 correspond as a frame story about Solomon's political enemies, and there are two sections, each being introduced by dream theophany (3:1–13 and 9:1–10a), and concluded by Solomon's attitude towards God (chapters 6–8; temple building, and 11:1–13; high place building and idol worshiping). The first section contains "domestic policy" and "labor relations," while the second contains "labor relations" and "foreign policy," in chiastic order. That means that the themes or materials in chapters 1–8 are "duplicated" in chapters 9–11 as a literary strategy to contrast the first section, "favorable" to Solomon, and the second, "hostile" to Solomon.[7] Parker's interesting observation of the narrative has triggered further scholarly discussions, which have considerably improved our understanding of the narrative.

Frisch (1991) challenged Parker's view, proposing that the narrative has not a bipartite, but a concentric structure, with the building of the temple as the center, and that the narrative ends not in chapter 11 but

5. Noth, *Deuteronomistic History*, 97.

6. Parker, "Repetition," 21.

7. Parker observes that the repetition structure implies "the two sides of Solomon's character." Chs 3–8 is favorable to Solomon because there Solomon's wisdom agrees with Torah, in contrast with 9:1—11:13 where his wisdom is at variance with Torah (ibid., 24–25). Sarvan's literary approach (1987) shows a similar understanding to Parker's view. However, he thinks that negative description of Solomon begins in the ominous mention of the future disasters, especially of the captivity in Solomon's dedicatory prayer in ch 8 (G. Sarvan, "1 and 2 Kings," 157).

12:24. In spite of the differing view of the range and structure of the narrative, Frisch's view is not different from Parker's in that negative description of Solomon begins from 9:10. A contribution of Frisch is his raising the question of why the negative aspect of Solomon's reign in 9:10—10:29 is presented implicitly while that in 11:1–10 is presented explicitly. According to Frisch, Solomon's material achievement in 9:10–10:29 is as God promised, and the author does not want to "conceal" it with an explicitly negative description of Solomon's reign in the passage.[8]

Brettler (1991), pointing out some problems of Parker's analysis,[9] provides a redaction approach to the narrative. According to him, 3:3—9:23 is "pro-Solomon," while 9:26—11:40 is "anti-Solomon," which is slightly different from Parker's and Frisch's divisions of the narrative.[10] Brettler's contribution is in his attempt to show how 9:26—11:10 is arranged to reveal Solomon's transgression against the king's stipulation in Deut 17:16–17. According to him, 9:26–10:25 is about "Solomon's wealth," 10:26–29 is about "Solomon's horses," and 11:1–10 is about "Solomon's foreign wives," corresponding to the three norms of the law of the king in Deut 17:16–17, which ban excessive wealth, many horses, especially Egyptian horse importation, and many wives for Israel's king. In this sense, he suggests that "1 Kgs 9:26–11:10 should be called 'Solomon's violation of Dt 17:14–17.'"[11] The tricky question of why "wealth" and "horses" are criticized implicitly while the "many foreign wives" matter is explicitly criticized, is answered by his redaction approach. That is, the "wealth" and "horses" passages were redacted from pre-existing material and simply pasted here, while the "many foreign wives" passage was "largely composed" by the redactor himself.[12]

---

8. Williams, who basically favors Parker's framework, tries to synthesize Parker's analysis with Frisch's and J. Walsh's (Walsh's view is very similar to Frisch's). Walsh, "Symmetry," 11–27; Frisch "Structure and its Significance," 3–14; Williams, "Once Again," 49–66. However, Williams does not provide improved understanding of Solomon's corruption, for his concern is confined only to structural analysis based on language data.

9. M. Brettler, "The Structure," 88. For example, the unbalanced word amount of the paralleled units, i.e., "the first section concerning 'Solomon's attitude towards God' is comprised of 155 verses (1 Kgs 6–8), while the second has only 13 (1 Kgs 11:1–13)."

10. According to Brettler, the frame accounts, i.e., 3:1–2 and 9:24–25, both mention (1) Pharaoh's daughter with the city of David, (2) building projects, and (3) Solomon's worship, encompassing the "pro-Solomon" section (Brettler, "The Structure," 89–90).

11. Ibid., 97.

12. Ibid., 96.

However, Knoppers (1996) argues against the application of the law of the king (Deut 17:16–17) to the Solomon narrative.[13] According to him, Solomon's wealth, many horses, and the importation of Egyptian horses, simply show the fulfillment of God's promise given to Solomon in 3:11–14, and the narrative should not be interpreted by the yardstick of the law of the king.[14] Rather Knoppers propounds that the Solomon narrative in Kings is a conspicuous example that reveals that the so-called Deuteronomist (i.e., the author of Kings) had a different stance from Deuteronomy. Knoppers, insisting that the law of the king should not be applied to Solomon's corruption, points out that 1 Kgs 11:2 has nothing to do with Deut 17:16–17, but with Deut 7:4 and Josh 23:12–13, which prohibit not excessive multi-marriage but intermarriage.[15] This observation is right, and requires more careful approach to the text of Solomon's corruption in 1 Kgs 11:1–10.

There is another important view, which sees Solomon's corruption from the early stage of the narrative. For example, McConville observes Solomon's intermarriage with Pharaoh's daughter in 3:1 as the first signal, and names it "the beginning of a 'return to Egypt' in the terms of Deut 17:16."[16] He also points out that the order of words in "king's house and God's house" in 3:1, and the comparative time scales in building God's house and the king's house in 6:38—7:1, are intended to betray Solomon's problematic priority. Furthermore, the introductory particle "רַק" (but) (3:2, 3) implies a negative evaluation of Solomon concerning high-place worship.[17] According to McConville, 1 Kgs 3 intends to show an already "flawed kingship" so that the reader should not have any expectation of permanent salvation in Solomon.[18] In fact, a greater number of scholars hold the view that Solomon's corruption is observed from the early stage

---

13. Knoppers, "The Deuteronomist and the Deuteronomic Law," 343; Knoppers, "Solomon's Fall," 399–401.

14. Ibid., 404. For Knoppers, 1 Kgs 1–10 is merely a description of nothing less than Israel's golden age.

15. There are other commentators who do not relate 1 Kgs 11:1–4 to the law of the king, but only to Deut 7:1–4 (or Exod 34:11–16), for example, Wiseman, *1 and 2 Kings*, 134; Gray, *1 & 2 Kings*, 252; Auld, *Kings*, 80. Jones relates 1 Kgs 11:2 with Deut 7:3–4, Exod 34:15–16, and Josh 23:12 (Jones, *1 and 2 Kings*, 233).

16. McConville, "Narrative and Meaning," 35.

17. Ibid. He refutes Noth's view that 3:2 is a Deuteronomic excuse for Solomon.

18. Ibid., 36. McConville's view of Solomon's early corruption is in accordance with his view of the Books of Kings as permeated with a "theology of grace" (46), which emphasizes "human fallibility" as its basic factor (36).

of his reign in the narrative, with certain variations.[19] For example, Eslinger (1989) interprets almost every action and speech of Solomon as Machiavellian, while Wiseman (1993) observes Solomon's faults only in his intermarriage with Pharaoh's daughter in 3:1 until chapter 11.[20] Between these two extremes, Bimson points out the unfairness of Solomon's administration between Israel and Judah in chapter 4,[21] and Walsh finds a discriminatory policy of corvée in 1 Kgs 5:27 [ET 5:13],[22] and so on.[23]

The authors of the recent monographs on the narrative, both Kang (2003) and Seibert (2006), also observe Solomon's faults or negative sides from early stage of his reign, although they have quite different concerns and approaches from each other. Kang begins to observe Solomon's fault in his bloodshed in chapter 2,[24] and Seibert observes Solomon's negative aspects even from chapter 1, raising the possibility that Nathan and Bathsheba persuaded David with a "concocted story."[25]

So far, through this brief survey, one fundamental problem has emerged. That is, there is no consensus even on the starting point of Solomon's corruption, though it is true that recent studies give more weight to the view that sees Solomon's faults from an early stage. To grasp the didactic message of the narrative on Solomon's corruption, it is very important to understand how the narrative describes the process of Solomon's turning from a wise king to an apostate. Therefore it is necessary to evaluate the scholarly views and to propose a new interpretation which accommodates various insights provided by the scholars.

---

19. For example, Provan, *1 and 2 Kings*; Walsh, "The Characterization"; Bimson, "1 and 2 Kings"; Eslinger, "Into the Hands," 123–82; Wiseman, *1 and 2 Kings*, 82. On 3:1, Wiseman comments, "This one was the beginning of Solomon's spiritual downfall"; Gray, *1 & 2 Kings*, 114; Nelson, *First and Second Kings*, 30; Brueggeman, *The Land*, 85–86; Gunn and Fewell, *Narrative in the Hebrew Bible*, 169; Olley, "Pharaoh's Daughter," 368; Hays, "Has the Narrator Come to Praise?," 149–74.

20. Most scholars who insist on Solomon's early corruption regard his intermarriage with Pharaoh's daughter as Solomon's significant fault. Naturally so, for the intermarriage is explicitly criticized by the narrator in ch 11.

21. Bimson, "1 and 2 Kings," 343.

22. Walsh, "The Characterization," 492.

23. For example, Provan and Bimson draw attention to ch 2 where Solomon executes several people in the process of the consolidation of his throne (Bimson, "1 and 2 Kings," 341; Provan, *1 and 2 Kings*, 31–42, especially 40).

24. Kang, *The Persuasive Portrayal*, 127–39, 299.

25. Seibert, *Subversive Scribes*, 115.

2.2. Evaluation of the Three Views on Solomon's Corruption

From the survey, it is possible to categorize the various views into three groups, according to their opinion on the starting point of Solomon's corruption. For convenience, the views which observe Solomon's corruption before the temple building are named "the early stage corruption view." The views which observe Solomon's corruption from just after the temple building, i.e., about chapter 9, are named "the middle stage corruption view," and the views which observe the corruption in the narrator's open criticism in chapter 11 are named "the late stage corruption view." Each view can be evaluated as follows.

A strong point of the "early stage corruption" view is that Solomon's intermarriage, which is criticized by the narrator in chapter 11, evidently appears at the early stage (3:1, cf. 7:8). However, those scholars who hold this view do not provide a reasonable explanation of why the narrator openly criticizes Solomon's fault only in the late stage (chapter 11).[26] Moreover, the view does not provide any explanation of why the narrative duplicates similar themes or materials, which Parker and Frisch (the middle stage corruption view) at least try to explain. It can also be pointed out that an excessive fault-finding is a feature of some interpreters who subscribe to this view. For example, Walsh suggests that the woman to whom Solomon orders the living child to be given (3:27) is the wrong woman, appealing to the Hebrew grammar of the pronoun.[27] Eslinger insists that Solomon is portrayed as irresponsible when he gives the verdict to cut the living child into two halves, questioning what would happen if the real mother had not conceded.[28] However, it is plain from the context of the text that Solomon gave the child to the real mother, and his first

26. Walsh tries to touch on this matter. He suggests that the author "antecedentally realizing the outcome" of the narrative, technically uses "gaps, ambiguities, and verbal subtleties that carry the negative characterization of Solomon' to 'shape and colour' the narrative negatively in the seemingly positive descriptions in chs 1–5 (Walsh, "The Characterization," 492–93). However, his suggestion cannot be a direct and sufficient answer to our fundamental question. Why does the author only implicitly criticize Solomon even when Solomon's faults can be read, and then later criticize Solomon openly? Brettler tried to explain this with his redaction theory as mentioned previously.

27. Ibid., 488–89.

28. Eslinger, "Solomon's Prayer," 138–39. In Eslinger's view, not only Solomon, but also God is interpreted as a selfish being who is struggling to get the upper hand, modifying the previous unconditional promise to conditional. In this sense, the concept of Solomon's corruption itself is probably meaningless in Eslinger's view.

verdict (3:25) is surely a well-calculated one based on an understanding of human nature.[29]

The "middle stage corruption" view is successful in providing an explanation of the duplication of similar materials or themes (Solomon's wisdom, wealth, administration, and corvée in chapters 3–8 and chapters 9–10) in the narrative by interpreting the first material as positive and the second as negative. However, these structural-analysis approaches over-simplify the narrative, consequently ignoring negative elements in the first section (chs 3–8), which are pointed out by "the early stage corruption" view. At least 3:1 (Solomon's marriage with Pharaoh's daughter) should be interpreted negatively in light of the open criticism of the marriage in 11:1–2.

The "late stage corruption" view observes Solomon's faults only where the narrator openly criticizes Solomon in chapter 11. The problem of this view is that it cannot explain the previous descriptions of Solomon's intermarriage (3:1; 7:8; 9:16, 24).[30] Knoppers' insistence that the mention of "Pharaoh's daughter" in 11:1 is a clumsy addition by a late scribe[31] is not a proper solution, and betrays a typical problem of redaction criticism, the error of circularity. This view also does not provide any explanation of the duplicated structure (chs 3–8 and chs 9–10).

Each view seems to have its grounds in the text to some extent. However, they seem to fall short of understanding the strategy of the narrative. Moreover, they do not pay sufficient attention to the process or development of Solomon's corruption. Hence, it will be worth seeking a device that shows the process of Solomon's corruption when we analyze the narrative. Another point that we need to consider is that, as has been shown in the cases of Eslinger and Walsh, a microscopic analysis of a limited passage cannot ensure objectivity in interpreting the reticent Hebrew narrative. To ensure objectivity, we need to pay attention to the literary technique or strategy of the narrative on a macroscopic level. Therefore, we will suggest and explain a certain literary technique or strategy which seems to be

---

29. For another example, Hays finds Solomon at fault in his not dancing humbly before the ark like David in the temple dedication ceremony (Hays, "Has the Narrator Come to Praise?," 170).

30. Knoppers insists that the whole of chs 1–10 should be interpreted as under God's blessing and that even in 11:1–2, the author "blames Solomon himself and not his wives for his malfeasance," overlooking the apparently problematic nature of his intermarriage (Knoppers, *Two Nations*, 145).

31. Ibid., 141.

employed to describe Solomon's turning process from positive to negative or the development of his corruption on a macroscopic scale.

2.3. A Brief Review of the Two Recent Monographs on the Narrative

The narrative was carefully approached by J. J. Kang in terms of rhetorical persuasion devices in his monograph (2003).[32] Kang tried to see, through the lens of a modern version[33] of Aristotle's theory, the narrative as a rhetorically well designed coherent unit. After that, E. A. Seibert proposed, in a monograph (2006),[34] a bold hypothesis that the narrative is a product of subversive scribe(s) who cheated his (or their) patron. Both Kang and Seibert pay their substantial attention to the presence of negative touches in the portrayal of Solomon in the narrative, although the two approaches are quite different from each other in terms of author's basic stance and interest.

J. J. Kang ultimately argues that Kings was produced in the exilic setting and the message (which he discovers by the rhetorical approach) contained in the Solomon narrative supports that view. He, in fact, tries to argue against the theory that the book of Kings is the product of the double redactions, i.e., Josianic and exilic ones. The theory that Kings is the product of the double redactions regards negative elements in the Solomon narrative as a trace of the Josianic redaction in which Solomon's faults should be presented in contrast to Josiah, the ideal king. Kang's stance is that the negative elements in the Solomon narrative do not require the Josianic redaction theory. Rather, he argues that the presence of Solomon's faults from the early part of the narrative onwards was intended to highlight the message that the hope of the exilic community is found only in God's mercy, not in human achievement. He supports this view by showing how the whole narrative is coherently well composed with rhetorical devices. In Kang's view, the Solomon narrative is a well-organized piece of literature even to the very details included for the purpose of rhetorical persuasion. In this sense, it can be said that Kang proposes an answer to the question of the presence of negative elements in Solomon's portrayal

32. Kang, *The Persuasive Portrayal*.

33. Kang employs the method drawn from Aristotle's classical rhetoric adapted by Kennedy and Perlman. (Kang, *The Persuasive Portrayal*, 80–99).

34. Seibert, *Subversive Scribes*.

in Kings according to his concern of compositional setting and purpose of the narrative.

Kang's study, however, does not explore a deeper question of the unusual subtlety with which the negative elements of Solomon are presented. Seibert's approach is a more square and direct answer to the question of why the positive and negative elements of Solomon's portrayal do coexist in the narrative in such a subtle way that "mutually contradictory readings" have been produced for the narrative. He explicitly articulates his awareness of this issue.[35] In fact his whole work is primarily intended to answer this issue.

It can be acknowledged that Seibert rightly raised the question about the subtle presence of negative elements in the overall positive portrayal of Solomon in the narrative, and his answer is simple. The subtle combination of positive and negative elements in Solomon's portrayal is the result of (a) subversive scribe(s)'s effort to cover their subversive intention in the portrayal of the king for whom they were working. In other words, the scribes pretended to write a propagandizing history for the royal house, on the one hand, but in fact tried to undermine their patron, on the other hand, revealing their faults or negative aspects in such a subtle way.

A few points concerning his view can be pointed out briefly here. The first is that it is doubtful that, given that Solomon's serious transgression explicitly and so plainly appears in the end (1 Kgs 11), the author(s) disguised Solomon's other faults in an implicit manner, in order to pretend that they were presenting the king in a positive light in the narrative. The present form of the narrative does not allow his view. Secondly, it can be pointed out that his overall presumption is unrealistic. That is, Seibert's thesis that the subversive scribes produced the narrative, implicitly criticizing Solomon's reign for those who could detect the subtle implication throughout the narrative, presupposes that the scribes expected that nobody on the king's side would notice the cunning subtlety and implicit criticism, while those of the opposite side would understand their intention. Considering the risk that the alleged scribes might have run when their intention might be detected, the presumption is unlikely. It is true that there is ancient Near East royal propaganda for royal establishment which is to some extent very similar to the Hebrew biblical narrative of certain kings' accounts, but to my knowledge, we do not have any ancient

---

35. Seibert, *Subversive Scribes*, 90–91, 181–82. He articulates this under the heading, "The Lack of More Compelling Explanations for Mutually Contradictory Readings."

Near East royal propaganda with covered subversive intention. This fact may indirectly indicate that such attempt was not realistic. Thirdly, our attention should be drawn to a general feature of the Hebrew biblical narrative. In general, reticence towards characters' behavior, leaving the judgment to the reader, is not something new. Seibert's allegation that the techniques of "covert critique" were employed by subversive scribes does not seem to consider the fact that not few faults of Abraham, Jacob, Isaac, for example, presented without apparent criticism, have nothing to do with propaganda, subversion, and subversive scribes.[36] Lastly, it should be pointed out that this kind of highly hypothetical approach is not necessary if the subtle presence of the critical elements throughout the text can be understood with identification of literary techniques employed to deliver its lessons and message effectively, even corresponding to the theological theme of the text.

3. A NEW APPROACH: MACROSCOPIC LITERARY STRATEGY, RETROACTIVE RE-EVALUATION TECHNIQUE AND ITS IMPLICATION OR MESSAGE

Even though it is true that a literary approach, as employed by Parker and Frisch, reveals meaningful structures and implications of a text and consequently contributes to a better understanding, it seems to overlook some important aspects of the text. Firstly, the reader's interpretation of a text is made progressively, in general, according to the reading process. The reader interprets the text on the basis of knowledge of the previous passages of the text and the present passage, without knowing the remainder of the text, at least in his or her first reading. So, it is natural that an author considers and exploits this quality of the reading process when he or she implants his or her literary devices in a text. Furthermore, it is natural to presume that the author of a biblical text assumed that the reader would read the text repeatedly, and tried to make use of the fact. When we consider the subtleties of the Bible text, it is hard to believe that the author would expect his reader to understand completely, at his or her first reading, every meaning implanted in the text.

---

36. Seibert introduced, to support his view, a few studies of other scholars who suggest some passages of Genesis meant to criticize King David (Gen 38) or Solomon's foreign policy (Gen 3) (Seibert, *Subversive Scribes*, 68–69). However, their views are not convincing, as their suggestions overly rely on their imagination.

Therefore, in order to identify the literary techniques of the text, it is important to reconstruct the reading process, imagining how the interpretation would be formed from the reader's perspective, and taking into consideration the effects that could occur through repeated reading of the text. Through this reconstruction of the reading process, the literary technique and its intended message may be detected. Even though it is true that the reconstruction requires a degree of imagination, it is also possible to secure objectivity to a certain extent, for there are supporting clues within the text. It is also important to consider what was expected by the author, in terms of his reader's prior knowledge, in the reader's reading and interpreting of the text. It seems that the expected pre-knowledge of the reader could also be detected from the clues in the text itself.

In this context, we suggest that the Solomon narrative contains three cases of the same literary technique, which requires the reader to do retroactive re-evaluation. The technique is very effective in revealing the insidious and furtive process of Solomon's corruption, plainly discernible and ensuring comparatively much more objectivity in interpretation; it reveals itself in a macroscopic view. It is observed firstly in the passages concerning Solomon's marriage with Pharaoh's daughter throughout the narrative (3:1; 7:8; 9:16, 24; 11:1), and secondly in the passage concerning Solomon's excessive wealth, maintaining many horses or importing horses from Egypt, and many wives to which the king's stipulation (Deut 17:16–17) is applied (9:26—11:10). Thirdly, it is observed in the passage concerning Solomon's oppression of the Israelites, which is indirectly revealed by the Israelites' complaint or protest after Solomon's death (12:1–14).

This literary strategy or technique is based on the premise of the reader's natural reading process. This technique works when the reader of the text reads it from the first sentence to the last without knowing the contents that will come next, at least at the first reading. The text is "intended to make sense as it is read cumulatively from beginning to end," as Provan states.[37] In fact, it is not a special premise but only a natural assumption that any author of literature would make concerning his or her reader, and exploit. Upon this basic understanding of the interpretative principle, the "retroactive re-evaluation technique" in the Solomon narrative can be identified. Tate explains this concept as follows:

> The author (storyteller) does not flatly state the case, but through the selective process, seeks to guide the reader into the construction of the message. The author invites the reader,

---

37. Provan, *1 and 2 Kings*, 4–5.

therefore, to become involved in and engaged by the story. The author seeks to move the reader from one event or scene to another, leaving sufficient gaps of information so that the reader can make necessary inferences. Story does not allow the reader to remain static.[38]

The author desired to construct a narrative in such a way that, given just enough hints, foreshadowing, and gaps, the reader might discover these facts on their own.[39]

The reader cannot stand outside the text, but becomes a participant, filling out the work, making connections between textual segments, evaluating new perspectives, and *reevaluating previous ones in light of new information*[40] *[my emphasis]*.

However, so far, this kind of insightful understanding of biblical narrative has not yet been applied comprehensively to interpreting the Solomon narrative.[41] The retroactive re-evaluation technique is an effective device to convey a significant lesson or message of the narrative, ensuring a more objective interpretation of the text by being observed in a macroscopic view rather than a microscopic view.

Exploring this technique in the narrative, we will also discuss the thematic background of the technique, i.e., the Exodus motif and, more importantly, the "return to Egypt" motif in the narrative. As a result of the main discussion, we will be able to reach a reasonable conclusion on Solomon's corruption, and accommodate some insights of the three main views on the starting point of that corruption, with critical evaluations.

38. Tate, *Biblical Interpretation*, 117. The quotation is from the section of "the Gospels and Acts." However, Tate's understanding of the New Testament narrative seems not to differ from the narrative of the Old Testament.

39. Ibid., 105–6. By "these facts," here, Tate means specific contents of a specific story of King David, i.e., David's self-verdict (2 Sam 12:5–6) and his four sons' following death for his sin. However, Tate's statement seems to contain a general principle that can be applied to other passages in the Old Testament narrative.

40. Ibid., 104.

41. Only R. Nelson seems to detect this device in the second case in his commentary (Nelson, *First and Second Kings*, 65–67).

4. THE FIRST CASE OF THE TECHNIQUE: SOLOMON'S INTERMARRIAGE WITH PHARAOH'S DAUGHTER (1 KGS 3:1; 7:8; 9:16, 24; 11:1-2)

Even though Solomon's intermarriage with Pharaoh's daughter is mentioned four times before chapter 11, it is never criticized openly on any of those occasions by the narrator. However, in 11:1–8, at last, the matter is clearly and crucially criticized, along with his idolatry, as part of Solomon's transgression against the law (Deut 7:3–4), which forbids intermarriage. The reader, who has probably overlooked the problematic aspect of Solomon's intermarriage with Pharaoh's daughter, is now required to re-evaluate the previous passages retroactively. Before we look into the mechanism of this device in the text, we need first to explore the thematic background of this case of the technique.

4.1. The Thematic Background of this Case of the Technique: The "Exodus Motif" and the "Return to Egypt" Motif

The "Exodus motif" which the Solomon narrative contains is extensively explored by Frisch.[42] Ironically, however, the "return to the Egypt motif"[43] is a substantial theme in the same narrative. In fact, Frisch does not distinguish the "return to the Egypt motif" from the "Exodus motif," dealing with both together under the title of the "Exodus motif." This is presumably because of their inextricable presentation in the narrative and also their intrinsic relationship. However, it is possible to distinguish the two motifs. It is interesting to observe how the two opposite themes *can be set in the same narrative that describes the period of one man's reign.* Before we think of the relationship of these motifs and its function in the narrative, it will be helpful to look into the way the two motifs appear in the text.

Regarding the Exodus motif, the manner in which the author describes the starting of the building of the temple by Solomon (6:1) implies that the ultimate purpose of the Exodus is now about to be accomplished, giving the impression of "at last."[44]

42. E.g., Frisch, "The Exodus Motif," 3–21. Frisch observes "the Exodus motif in 1 Kgs 1–14" in an extensive way. He insists that the Exodus motif has the unifying function of 1 Kgs 1–14. Oblath, "Pharaohs and Kings," 23–42. Oblath observes strong thematic and literary similarity between the Exodus narrative and the Jeroboam narrative.

43. E.g., Hays, "Has the Narrator Come to Praise?," 172: "reversal of the exodus."

44. Frisch, "The Exodus Motif," 6: "The association of the temple with the Exodus

> In the four hundred and eightieth year after the Israelites came
> out of the land of Egypt, in the fourth year of Solomon's reign
> over Israel, in the month of Ziv, which is the second month, he
> began to build the house of the Lord (1 Kgs 6:1).

Solomon's building of the temple can be also regarded as the fulfillment of Moses' prophecy concerning God's chosen worship place in the promised land (Deut 12:1–11). It is especially worth noting that peace and safety, a most important precondition of worshiping their God in his chosen dwelling place in the promised land (Deut 12:10), is described as having been secured before Solomon starts building the temple (1 Kgs 4:20—5:1 [ET 4:20–21], 5:4–5 [ET 4:24–25]). It is also worth remembering that the formal reason for the Exodus was to sacrifice to the Israelite God (Exod 3:1; 5:3; 8:21–24 [ET 8:25–28]; 10:24–26). The stated purpose of the three days' journey into the wilderness, for sacrificing to the Israelite God, or serving their God, should not be regarded as a mere pretense for escaping from Egypt. If the Israelites can stop their forced labor, which has been loaded upon them by the Egyptian ruler, in order to worship and serve their own God, they are not actually under Pharaoh's rule any more, but their God's, and consequently, their God can continue commanding what he wants, including, presumably, their coming out of Egypt, i.e., the Exodus. The implication of sacrificing and serving the Israelite God, stopping forced labor, is that they are their God's people, not Pharaoh's. Therefore, the building of the permanent temple for sacrificing to and serving the Israelite God by Solomon in the promised land has the significance that the Israelites have now accomplished their Exodus in its full sense,[45] as they have the peace and safety to serve their God without any hindrance. In a sense, Solomon can be labeled as a "new Moses" who takes over the first Moses' role and completes it.[46]

The reference to the "four hundred and eightieth year" (6:1) also reminds us of the Exodus, for it closely corresponds to the year counting in Exodus.

---

in 1 Kgs 6:1, therefore, seems to indicate that the erection of the Temple is the apex of the extended process that began with the Exodus from Egypt."

45. Ibid., "The erection of the Temple in Jerusalem represents the concretization and fullest embodiment of this 'you shall serve.'"

46. Parker, "Solomon as Philosopher King?," 81. "As Moses' successor, Solomon re-enacts key events in Moses' life. He judges Israel (cf. Exod. 18 and 1 Kgs 3), establishes a bureaucracy (cf. Num. 2–4 and 1 Kgs 4), disseminates the law (cf. Exod. 19–24 and 1 Kgs 8), builds Yahweh a throne (Exod. 25–31 and 1 Kgs 6), and promises reward for obedience to the law and punishment for disobedience (Deut. 12–26 and 1 Kgs 8)."

> The time that the Israelites had lived in Egypt was four hundred and thirty years. At the end of four hundred and thirty years, on that very day, all the companies of the Lord went out from the land of Egypt (Exod 12:40–41).

The year count in 1 Kgs 6:1 seems to correspond to the one in Exod 12:40–41, showing that a similarly significant historic event is occurring or a similarly significant historic epoch is dawning. When we consider the rarity of this kind of year count throughout the historical narrative in the Old Testament, it is all the more plausible that the intention of the year count in 1 Kgs 6:1, as part of the pair, is to present the temple building as an event of equal significance to the Exodus, and at the same time to imply that it is the completion of what was begun at the Exodus.[47] Additionally, the enshrinement of the ark of the covenant in the temple (8:9, 21), which is described as containing the two tablets given during the Exodus (in its broad sense),[48] also tightly links the Exodus event to the temple building.[49]

The importance of the "Exodus motif" is that it appears again after Solomon's death. It is not hard to notice that now Rehoboam, i.e., Solomon's successor, takes Pharaoh's role and Jeroboam takes Moses' role in chapter 12. That is, Jeroboam is the agent to deliver God's people from their "slavery."[50] As God hardened Pharaoh's heart in the original Exodus, now God hardens Rehoboam's heart to accomplish his divine will (12:15).[51] Naturally enough, a question is posed here: how can the "Exodus motif" appear immediately after the death of Solomon, during whose reign the completion of Exodus has been accomplished?[52] The answer to the question is simple. Israel has returned to Egypt again before Solomon's death. The "return to Egypt" motif links the two "Exodus motifs" and covers the period between them. Even though the first Exodus had been completed in Solomon's reign, Israel became an "Egypt" through Solomon's rule, and a new Exodus had to take place.

---

47. Nelson presents a similar view, when he states that, "the introductory chronology (6:1) makes the event of temple building the culmination of Israel's saga up to this point." Nelson, *First and Second Kings*, 46.

48. Frisch, "The Exodus Motif," 5. "the bounds of the exodus event can fairly be seen as encompassing everything from the bondage in Egypt up to the preparations to cross the Jordan after forty years of wilderness wandering."

49. Ibid., 7.

50. Provan, *1 and 2 Kings*, 104.

51. Ibid., 103.

52. In fact, the account of Hadad the Edomite (1 Kgs 11:14–22) also shows the "Exodus motif."

The "return to Egypt motif" has been noticed only fragmentarily by some scholars who observe Solomon's becoming a "Pharaoh," especially in chapter 9,[53] where Solomon is described as imitating an Egyptian tyrant in implementing his enormous building project and maintaining a standing army and forced labor system. In his building project, "store cities," "chariot cities," and "cavalry cities" especially remind the reader of Egypt.[54] Even though the Israelites do not go back to Egypt in a geographical sense, the Israelite kingdom itself is becoming an Egypt in a metaphorical sense. Additionally, the Israelites' complaint after Solomon's death (12:4), reveals that Solomon loaded on them a heavy yoke and disciplined them with whips, i.e., exploited and oppressed them (12:4, 10–11, 14) just as Pharaoh had done to their ancestors (cf. 8:51); that is, the Israelites experienced a similar thing to their ancestors. In other words, they have been living in an "Egypt" under Solomon's reign. However, in fact, the "return to Egypt" motif is already observed in Solomon's becoming Pharaoh's son-in-law (3:1) at an early stage. The frequent mentions of "Pharaoh's daughter" throughout the narrative (3:1; 7:8; 9:16, 24; 11:1), and, more directly, the mention of Solomon's making ships on the seashore of "the Red Sea" (9:26) and sending his men to Egypt to buy Egyptian horses and chariots (10:28–29), betray the progressive development of the "return to Egypt motif" as the narrative unfolds. Furthermore, the fact that the leader of the northern ten tribes, Jeroboam, is portrayed as a new Moses who has escaped being killed by a tyrant (11:40), and at last succeeds in delivering his people from the heavy yoke of the tyrant (12:3–20), also shows that the previous condition of the Israelites was like the one to which the original Moses was sent by God to save his people.

What, then, is the function of the "Exodus motif" and "return to Egypt motif," respectively, in the narrative? The "return to Egypt" motif characterizes the nature of Solomon's corruption while the "Exodus motif" acts as a foil to it ironically. In other words, the "Exodus motif" acts as a foil to the "return to Egypt motif" in the narrative in order to highlight the tragic process and result of Solomon's corruption, which is none other

---

53. "The Egyptian aura," "an Egyptian style of rule," Eslinger, "Solomon's Prayer," 148; "reversal of the Exodus," Hays, "Has the Narrator Come to Praise?," 172; "Solomon's first subtle look in the direction of Egypt," Parker, "Solomon as Philosopher King?," 84. Parker observes the first occasion which contains the "return to Egypt" motif, only in ch 9, with which this study does not agree; "an Israelite pharaoh," Hauer, "The Economics," 68. It is substantially discussed in Heaton, *Solomon's New Man*, 28–30, 162–78.

54. Eslinger, "Solomon's Prayer," 148.

than a "returning to Egypt" that would cause a new Exodus, i.e., the division of the kingdom. Solomon, the new Moses, became a Pharaoh, and a new Exodus had to take place![55]

4.2. A Brief Reconstruction of the Reading Process

Even if the reader has had some suspicion of the wrongfulness of Solomon's intermarriage with Pharaoh's daughter in 3:1, the following description of Solomon's love for God (3:3), which is very strong praise indeed, God's favorable theophany to Solomon (3:5–15a), which includes his satisfaction with Solomon's request (3:10), and Solomon's wisdom and prosperity, which is the very thing God has promised to him (3:12–13), have sufficient force to cause the reader to doubt that first suspicion. Therefore, it does not seem to be easy for the reader to maintain the suspicion that Solomon's intermarriage with Pharaoh's daughter in 3:1 is a serious problem that could lead to tragic consequences. Moreover, the fact that the subsequent mentions of "Pharaoh's daughter" as Solomon's wife (7:8; 9:16, 24) do not bear any plain criticism of the marriage, is likely to increase the reader's doubt about any previous suspicions he or she had, until the reader confronts the open criticism of the marriage in 11:1 and has to re-evaluate it retroactively.

4.3. The Mechanism and Effect of the Retroactive Re-evaluation Technique in this Case

McConville maintains that Solomon's misconduct is observed from ch 3 in his intermarriage with Pharaoh's daughter (3:1a), the problematic priority in building his house and God's house (3:1b), and the existence of high places (3:2, 3), showing a "flawed kingship" and conveying "the message that there could be no permanent salvation for Israel in a Solomon."[56] However, a question is raised. Did the author of the narrative expect such an observation from his reader on a first reading? The answer is negative. It will be sufficient enough to remember the fact that it has taken a

---

55. Frisch, "The Exodus Motif," 14; M. Oblath, "Pharaohs and Kings," 23–42. Oblath insists that Jeroboam was the model of Moses in the Exodus narrative, through the observation of the similarity of the two narratives with some other grounds. This study does not agree with his view, although, his analysis sufficiently shows the surprising thematic and literary similarity between the two texts.

56. McConville, "Narrative and Meaning," 35–36.

long time and the enormous efforts of many scholars to reach the present understanding of the presence of Solomon's faults in his early stage, and to recognize the subtlety and exquisiteness of the narrative. What, then, did the author expect his reader to discover of Solomon's faults from the text on a first reading? The most plausible answer to this question seems to be that the author expected the reader to realize the negativity of Solomon's intermarriage with Pharaoh's daughter when he reached 11:1–2, and to re-evaluate the previous passages regarding the marriage at that point. We can imagine that the author expected the reader to be able thereafter to begin to observe many other faults of Solomon in the account before chapter 11, standing upon this firm ground as an evident clue.

McConville is right in noticing Solomon's corruptive element in the early stage of his reign. However, McConville, like most others who see Solomon's corruption from this early stage, does not seem to consider the reading process[57] and the reader's epistemological experience throughout the narrative. The question is whether the reader could notice those things on a first reading with certainty. Hays, taking a similar stance to McConville, insists that "Solomon's intermarriage with Pharaoh's daughter" in 3:1 "should explode like a bombshell in the reader's mind" because Egypt always has very negative connotations in the Old Testament.[58] However, even for a sensitive reader who has a deep understanding of the meaning of the Egyptian motif in the Old Testament, and consequently had a strong suspicion of Solomon's fault in 3:1, it would not be easy to sustain it for the reasons presented above. As Hays himself admits, the author does not provide a negative description of Solomon openly until chapter 11, nor has the fragmentary implicit criticism of Solomon strong force "if analyzed one at a time in isolation."[59]

Hays insists that "the clear, but implicit references to Deuteronomy 17 at the end of 1 Kings 10 provide the strongest single supporting" evidence to confirm the previous subtle and implicit criticism of Solomon throughout the narrative.[60] However, it is doubtful whether the reader could decide that Solomon has been described negatively in a very subtle manner if the author had not criticized Solomon openly in chapter 11. Therefore, we should say that the decisive trigger which convinces the

57. Kang pays his attention to the "reading process" of the reader, to some extent, but he does not notice any substantial literary technique from that.

58. Hays, "Has the Narrator Come to Praise?," 161.

59. Ibid., 174.

60. Ibid.

reader of Solomon's missteps in the previous passages is the author's open criticism in chapter 11 rather than the end part of chapter 10, where the author seems to try to give the impression that Solomon has reached his peak, and even the Egyptian horse importing looks like a natural channel of increasing his or Israel's prosperity and security (10:26–29). The point where the reader can confidently decide that Solomon's corruption begins from the early stage of his reign, at least in the matter of his marriage, is evidently 11:1–2ff through the plain critical statement supplied by the narrator.

The first mention of Solomon's intermarriage with Pharaoh's daughter invites the reader, who is now required to re-evaluate the previous passages by the open criticism in chapter 11, to review critically the very early stage of Solomon's reign. It provides the reader with the possibility of an alternative overall understanding of the narrative before chapter 11. The occasional mentions of "Pharaoh's daughter" between chapter 3 and chapter 11 function as stepping-stones which keep the reader reminded of the existence of Pharaoh's daughter as Solomon's wife until the reader finally reaches the condemnation of the intermarriage in 11:1. In this sense, the intermediate mentions of "Pharaoh's daughter" (7:8; 9:16, 24) are like the pieces of bread scattered on the road for Hansel to trace back to his home later in the famous children's tale. But while Hansel failed because of thoughtless birds that came and ate up his pieces of bread, the author of the Solomon narrative seems to succeed in his device, because his markers cannot be deleted.

4.4. The Suitability of the Device in the Narrative

When we pay attention to (1) the relationship between "Solomon's intermarriage with Pharaoh's daughter" and the main theme of the narrative, i.e., the "return to Egypt" motif, (2) the significance and function of the mentions of "Pharaoh's daughter" in the various locations in the narrative, and (3) the term itself in anonymous form, we realize the suitability of the device, and this in turn supports our view that the material of "Solomon's intermarriage with Pharaoh's daughter" was used to constitute a substantial literary device in the narrative. Therefore, we will now explore the three points in order.

4.4.1. The Correspondence of the Term of the Device to the Main Theme of the Narrative

It is very clear that "Pharaoh's daughter," as an element of the literary device, corresponds well to the main theme or the "return to Egypt" motif that characterizes and reflects the nature of Solomon's corruption, which nullifies the effect of the Exodus. When we consider that the "return to Egypt" motif is a substantial or even a central theme, we can understand that it is not just a coincidence that "Pharaoh's daughter," who is a very pertinent symbol of Solomon's link to Egypt, is used as one of the building bricks of the literary device which is designed to convey the message of the dangerous and insidious process of corruption.

4.4.2. The Significance and Functions of the Device in the Various Locations

Once the reader realizes that Solomon's corruption started early, by noticing the link between 3:1 and 11:1, "Pharaoh's daughter" acquires a negative connotation throughout the narrative. Besides the basic function of "Pharaoh's daughter" which has been previously explained, each mention of "'Pharaoh's daughter" (3:1; 7:8; 9:16, 24; 11:1), clearly stating or implying Solomon's intermarriage, has a specific function in the narrative.

As for 3:1, 9:24, and 11:1, similar themes are clustered in each case. The contexts of both 3:1 and 11:1 contain the themes of "intermarriage" (3:1 and 11:1–3), "building project" (3:1 and 11:7–8), and "use of high places for worship" (3:2–3 and 11:7–8), constituting a "parallel" between 3:1–3 and 11:1–8, as rightly observed by Walsh.[61] The contexts of both 3:1 and 9:24 contain the themes of "Pharaoh's daughter" (3:1 and 9:24), "palace building project" (3:1 and 9:24), and "temple-sacrifice" (3:2 and 9:25), constituting a "parallel" between 3:1–2 and 9:24–25, as observed by Porten and Brettler.[62] In a sense, the three common themes are a

61. Walsh, "The Characterization," 477. Walsh observes that these three materials are described in ch. 3 positively, while in ch. 11 negatively. Hays, "Has the Narrator Come to Praise?," 161. Hays also pointed out the similarity between 3:1–3 and 11:1–8, following Fretheim's observation on the text (Fretheim, *First and Second Kings*, 62).

62. Brettler, "The Structure," 89–90. Brettler insists that the reason why the description of Pharaoh's daughter's entering her palace appears again in 9:24 anachronistically, in spite of the previous description of it in 7:8, is to constitute a frame which contains pro-Solomon material, by the "framing repetition." Brettler regards 3:1–2 and 9:24–25 as a frame containing pro-Solomon materials. Brettler observes that in the passage after 9:24–25, that is 9:26–11:10, Solomon is described as a transgressor of the

summary description of Solomon's life, reflecting his emotional desire, administration, and spiritual activity respectively. This means that whenever Solomon's life as an Israelite king is summarized in the narrative, his intermarriage with Pharaoh's daughter appears as an important part of it, which implies the crucial significance of the intermarriage in Solomon's life.

1 Kgs 9:16 also has an important role in reminding the reader of the intermarriage itself, by the mention of a dowry and by calling Pharaoh's daughter Solomon's "wife" for the first time. Solomon's inferior position to Pharaoh is implied by the mention of Pharaoh's conquest of a city within Palestine and his giving it to Solomon, his son-in-law, in the form of a present to his daughter.[63] Additionally, the surrounding passage of 9:16, i.e., 9:15–21, is replete with Egyptian imagery, for example, building of "cities of store," "cities of chariots," "cities of horsemen,"[64] and establishing "bond-service." The passage shows the image of Egyptian rule most intensively within the narrative, which concretizes the "return to Egypt" motif in the narrative, or Solomon's becoming a Pharaoh.[65]

The importance of the locus of 7:8 is recently revealed by Olley's literary structural analysis of the Solomon narrative. Olley observes that in the middle of the description of the temple building (6:1—8:66), there is the description of the palace for Pharaoh's daughter (7:1–12), and again, in the middle of the description of the palace building, there is Pharaoh's

---

king's stipulation of Dt 17:14–17. Porten also observes that the two passages match each other (Porten, "The Structure and Theme," 98–99).

63. McConville, "Narrative and Meaning," 36–37. McConville observes a "so-called frame-break" here, which betrays "the real measure of Solomon's achievement."

64. The "cities of store" is a conspicuous term for Egyptian imagery (Exod 1:11), while "cities of chariots" and "cities of horsemen" do not appear in the Exodus narrative. However, the fact that not only are "chariots" and "horsemen" closely associated with Egyptian military imagery (Exod 14:6, 7, 9, 17, 18, 23, 25, 26, 28; 15:1, 4), but also that the expressions "cities of chariots" and "cities of horsemen" seems to be applied forms of "cities of store," implies overall that the whole terms concerning "cities" contain Egyptian imagery.

65. Parker thinks that the slavery system in 9:21 is "Solomon's first subtle look in the direction of Egypt" (Parker, "Solomon as Philosopher King?," 84), which is contrast to McConville's view that Solomon's intermarriage with Pharaoh's daughter in 3:1 is "the beginning of a 'returning to Egypt,' in the terms of Deut 17,6." It is understandable that Parker, who insists that "in 1 Kings 3–8 Solomon is portrayed as the ideal king," making a dichotomous structural analysis on the Solomon narrative, cannot acknowledge the presence of negative Egyptian connotation in the earlier chapters. Nevertheless, Parker's observation of Egyptian connotation in 9:21 seems to betray the comparatively intense presence of Egyptian elements in the nearby passage of 9:16.

daughter herself (7:8).[66] Pharaoh's daughter therefore occupies the structural center of the whole Solomon narrative, implying that Solomon's corruption exists even in the heart of Solomon's seemingly most pious achievement.[67] When we think that the temple building is a consummation of the Exodus, in a sense the very presence of Pharaoh's daughter in the heart of the description of the temple building cannot but be significant, betraying the insidious presence of corruption. This observation was missed by Parker and Frisch, who have treated chapters 6–8 as a simple unit of temple building, ignoring the significant detailed structure within the comparatively large unit.

4.4.3. The Effect of the Anonymity of the Term

Pharaoh's daughter seems to be Solomon's chief wife, for a palace is built for her and she frequently appears in the narrative.[68] However, her name is not given and she remains simply as "Pharaoh's daughter" throughout the narrative.[69] This is conspicuous because we can observe many other names of characters who are less significant than Pharaoh's daughter in the nearby passages. Not only male officials' names (1 Kgs 4:2–19), but also many females' names are given. For example, Solomon's mother's name Bath-sheba, King David's last concubine Abishag, a Shunammite, Solomon's successor Rehoboam's mother, an Ammonitess, Naamah (1 Kgs 14:21), and Solomon's daughters, Taphath and Bas-math, who were given to local governors as their wives (1 Kgs 4:11, 15). In contrast to David's wives' names, which are given in 2 Sam 3:2–5, Solomon's chief wife remains strikingly anonymous.[70]

---

66. Olley, "Pharaoh's Daughter," 364.

67. Ibid., 368. In contrast, Bimson proposes the opposite view that, to emphasize the comparatively larger significance of the temple, the description of the palace is inserted or submerged in the description of the temple building, even though in its physical measure, the palace is bigger than the temple (Bimson, "1 and 2 Kings," 345–46). Younger also points out that the account of the construction of Solomonic palace is the "very pivot point" of "the account of the building and dedication of the Temple"; however he does not go further (Younger, "The Figurative Aspect," 166–67).

68. Ibid., 345.

69. It is interesting that the "daughter of Pharaoh" is only once described as Solomon's wife in 9:16.

70. Solomon himself has an extra name, i.e., Solomon's God-given name Jedidiah (2 Sam 12:25).

The anonymity of Pharaoh's daughter is well understood as a literary technique, which, as Reinhartz argues, "encourages readers to typify anonymous female character(s) rather than viewing them as individuals."[71] In this sense, "Pharaoh's daughter" is a well-chosen designation in order to be the representative of an enormous number of unnamed foreign wives. That is, in the narrative Pharaoh's daughter is simply the first of Solomon's enormous number of intermarriages or a representative of them, rather than a meaningful chief wife to Solomon. Furthermore, the term "Pharaoh's daughter" is more suitable than any Egyptian name of the princess for implying Solomon's resemblance to Pharaoh himself. In that sense, the term is appropriate for containing the "return to Egypt" motif, which characterizes the progress of Solomon's corruption as Solomon's transformation into an Egyptian ruler.[72]

Once it is recognized that the phrase "Pharaoh's daughter" is to be understood as a significant literary device of the narrative, Knoppers' insistence that "Pharaoh's daughter" in 11:1 is a clumsy insertion by a later scribe,[73] and that the whole account of 1 Kgs 1–10 is a positive description of Solomon's wisdom, fortune, and glory,[74] is not plausible. This is clear when we consider that the "return to Egypt" motif in the narrative is very plain, and that the previous mentions of "Pharaoh's daughter" are intended as conspicuous signs that reveal the process of the "return to Egypt," which has started from the early stage of his reign.

5. THE SECOND CASE OF THE TECHNIQUE: SOLOMON'S TRANSGRESSION AGAINST THE THREE NORMS OF THE KING'S STIPULATION (1 KGS 9:26– 11:8)

In the flow of the passage of 1 Kgs 9:26—11:8, the narrative stimulates and induces its reader to re-evaluate the first part of this passage (9:26—10:29) in light of the three norms of the king's stipulation (Deut 17:16–17).

71. Reinhartz, "Anonymous Women," 63.

72. Brueggemann, *1 and 2 Kings*, 43, pays attention to the anonymity of Pharaoh's name rather than Pharaoh's daughter's name. He insists that the anonymity of Pharaoh's name is intended to recall the Exodus situation, which has the same anonymity of name of the Egyptian ruler, quoted in Hays, "Has the Narrator Come to Praise?," 161.

73. Knoppers, *Two Nations*, 141. Cohen also thinks that the "Pharaoh's daughter" in 11:1 is a late addition (Cohen, "Solomon and the Daughter of Pharaoh," 26).

74. Knoppers, *Two Nations*, 57–134.

5.1. A Neglected Problem Concerning the Open Criticism in 11:1–10 and its Solution

When we observe the passage which includes "many foreign wives" in 1 Kgs 11:1–10, we find that the narrator is more sophisticated than Knoppers presumes,[75] because the theme of "many foreign wives" not only links with the norm of intermarriage, but also reminds the reader of the prohibition of "many wives" in the king's stipulation (Deut 17:17). Especially, in 11:3, 4, "wives" is twice related to "turning away his (the King's) heart" as in Deut 17:17. By providing the conspicuously enormous number of Solomon's concubines (11:3), the narrative makes it clear that the "wives" is really "many wives" as in Deut 17:17, as Brettler points out in his analysis of the Hebrew text.[76]

Possibly, one may still argue that the narrator's main criticism is clearly against intermarriage even though the problem of "many wives" might be implied in the same passage (11:1–10). However, the elaborately shaped arrangement of the description in 9:26—11:10, which is neatly matched with the king's stipulation, implies that the application of the king's stipulation has been intended.[77] That is, 1 Kgs 9:26—10:25 corresponds to the prohibition of excessive wealth (Deut 17:17b), 1 Kgs 10:26–29 to the prohibition of Egyptian horses (Deut 17:16), and 1 Kgs 11:1–10 to the ban of numerous wives (Deut 17:17a).

Therefore, we have two things which seem to be quite irreconcilable, that is, the structure or arrangement which supports the application of the royal law to Solomon, and the narrator's open criticism which seems to touch on the royal law only tangentially and implicitly. The question should then be raised, "Why does the narrator not apply the prohibitions to each matter in 9:26—11:10, but only to the 'many wives' matter, moreover why do so in an indirect manner, only hinting at the royal law prohibiting 'many wives'?" Two scholars who apply the royal law to the Solomon narrative have tried to explain the matter, even though they do not raise the question as precisely as we do now. They have tried only to explain

75. Knoppers thinks that the quoted law in 1 Kgs 11:1–2 is only related with Deut 7:4 and Josh 23:11–13 and, therefore, 1 Kgs 11:1–10 is not intended to be read in light of Deut 17:16–17 (Knoppers, "The Deuteronomist and the Deuteronomic Law," 343; Knoppers, "Solomon's Fall," 399–401).

76. Brettler, "The Structure," 91–92. He also points out the linguistic connection between the prohibition of "the extensive gold" (Deut 17:17) and Solomon's having extensive gold (1 Kgs 10:2, 10, 11).

77. Ibid., 90–92.

why the first two sins are criticized implicitly (1 Kgs 9:26—10:29) while the third one is criticized explicitly (1 Kgs 11:1–10). Brettler's approach is a historical-critical one. That is, 9:26—10:29 is pre-Deuteronomy material which was "probably originally positive illustrations of Solomon's wisdom" and has been taken as criticism now, while "11:1ff. is (largely) the composition or reworking of earlier traditions of Dtr."[78] Frisch's approach to this matter is, on the other hand, a literary-critical one. He thinks that in 9:10—10:29 Solomon is "merely implicitly criticized, for the author/editor does not conceal the material achievements of Solomon's reign" according to God's previous promises, within that passage.[79] However, neither of these scholars explains why, even in chapter 11, the narrator explicitly criticizes not the polygamy, according to Deut 17:17, but the exogamy. We can answer this question by supposing the literary technique employed there, that is, the retroactive re-evaluation technique.

5.2. The Reconstruction of the Reading Process

After God promised Solomon not only the wisdom for which Solomon had asked, but also riches and honor (1 Kgs 3:12–13), the evidence of God's implementation of his promise is sweeping throughout the narrative. The case of Solomon's wise judgment (3:16–28) is the first evidence of the implementation, coming directly after God's promise. The account of the administration of Solomon (4:1–19) also gives the reader the impression of a well-ordered ruling system probably reflecting Solomon's wisdom. In the following account, the description of the happy life of the Israelites (4:20; 5:5 [ET 4:25]) along with the reference to Solomon's wisdom as God-given (5:9 [ET 4:29]; 5:26 [ET: 5:12]) does not allow the reader to think otherwise than of the nation's happy situation under God's blessing. Then the narrative reaches the account of the temple building, and the way it starts (6:1) gives the reader the impression that Solomon is accomplishing a historic mission. The evidence of God's acceptance of the temple, which appears as the glorious cloud in the temple (8:11) along with the description of the gladness of people's hearts after the dedication ceremony (8:66), leads the reader to construe the whole process of the building of the temple in a positive light. However, in chapter 9, a

78. Ibid., 96.

79. Frisch, "Structure and its Significance," 13. Frisch has a similar view to Brettler about the original characteristics of the material which is now in ch 9 and 10, (Frisch, "Structure and its Significance," 14).

gloomy warning from God, which includes the destruction of the temple by God himself (9:6–9), Hiram's complaint about Solomon's reward for Hiram's cooperation in the building of the temple (and, probably, his palace as well) (9:10–14), and the existence of slavery in Israel (even though it is not of the Israelites) (9:17–21), could give the reader a more disturbing impression. On the other hand, the following overall atmosphere of chapter 10, which is full of the account of the overwhelming impression of Solomon's wisdom and glory upon a foreign queen (10:1–13) and the detailed description of Solomon's wealth, along with the mentions of his wisdom (10:4, 7, 23, 24), which appears again after an absence in chapter 9, will probably convince the reader that Solomon is now at the zenith of his receiving God's blessing.[80]

5.3. The Mechanism and Effect of the Retroactive Re-evaluation Technique and the Implied Message

We can say that the author of the Solomon narrative seems to be well aware of the king's law, in view of the exact correspondence between the description of Solomon's transgression and the three norms of the king's law. However, the author intentionally avoids the direct application of the king's law code to Solomon's act to better convey the intended messages to his reader; he openly criticizes only the intermarriage matter, but also hints at the problem of numerous wives. Here, the literary technique is employed to deliver its message in a more effective and impressive way, perhaps involving the reader in the experience of Solomon himself or of his contemporaries, who probably did not notice the transgression at the time, for it seems that the reader is liable to overlook Solomon's transgression against the king's law, especially in 9:26—10:29, because of the overall mood of immense prosperity which reflects God's blessing there. The narrative leads the reader to enjoy reading the description of Solomon's wealth and glory without noticing the transgression of the king's law. However, in 11:1–10, even though the open criticism is of Solomon's intermarriage, the narrative plainly provides a clue to remind the reader of the matter of the numerous wives in the king's law. Moreover, Egyptian horse importing in 10:26–29, which can be easily construed as a channel

80. Viviano, "Glory Lost," 344. About ch 9, "but it is not clear that either of these reports are intended to reflect negatively upon Solomon." Even though Viviano does not share our view (i.e., from the early stage) on the starting point of Solomon's corruption, his observation shows how the first time reader would read the passage.

of Solomon's wealth in that context, now turns out to be a conspicuous matter that helps remind the reader of the king's law, as R. Nelson rightly observes.[81] This reminder is reinforced by the consequent mention of the numerous wives matter, which is included in the negative evaluation of Solomon's act. Therefore, the reader has an increasing possibility of realizing that Solomon's acts are against the king's stipulation while reading the latter part of 9:26–11:10. On realizing that Solomon's acts have to be re-evaluated in the light of the king's stipulation, the reader is shocked by the fact that it was so easy not to notice the elements of transgression in the previous passage, because of its location in the midst of the on-going atmosphere of splendid blessing.[82]

This literary technique makes the reader realize the subtlety and insidiousness of sin or disobedience, especially in the situation where God's blessing is so abundant. In Solomon's case God's blessing upon him is so vivid that even a pagan queen acknowledges it and praises God for it. In such a situation it is very hard to notice that something is going wrong. In such a situation, even a transgression against God's law itself (i.e., Egyptian horse importing and trading) looks as if it is a channel of God's blessing.

The technique also makes the reader feel a strong need for the presence of God's law in his people's lives, to reveal transgression immediately and plainly. When the reader remembers the phrase, "It shall remain with him and he shall read in it all the days of his life, so that he may learn to fear the Lord his God, diligently observing all the words of this law and these statutes" (Deut 17:19), which is included in the king's stipulation,

---

81. Nelson, *First and Second Kings*, 67. "Yet no one with a Deuteronomistic theological background could ever have missed the broad hint of the last verses about horses from Egypt (10:28–29), which point directly to Deuteronomy 17:16." Richard Nelson is the commentator who notices the device of the retroactive re-evaluation technique to some extent in the present passage. See Nelson, *First and Second Kings*, 62–67.

82. A similar but not identical idea is proposed by a New Testament scholar, J. Staley, who maintains that the author of the fourth Gospel intentionally directs his reader to misunderstand particular passages, in order to maximize the effect of the message of the passages (Staley, *The Print's First Kiss*, 95–118). According to Staley, the implied reader of the John's Gospel can recognize his or her misunderstanding only after he or she has a false understanding concerning the passages, which is intended through literary strategy by the author. The reader is guided to regard himself or herself as being an "insider" in the early phase of the reading, but as the narrative unfolds, the reader is guided to realize that he or she is an ignorant "outsider." Through ongoing process, the reader can be a real "insider." Staley labels the literary technique as a "rhetorical strategy of "reader victimization"" (116) and proposes five examples of the technique, i.e., in John 4:1–2; 7:1–10; 10:40—11:18; 13:1–30; 20:30—21:25.

the reader really understands why such a command is included there. That is, the reader realizes the need for the presence of the law in order not to overlook an insidious progress of transgression.

It is surprising that no scholar who applies the king's law to the Solomon narrative has pointed out the problem of the indirect correspondence between the king's law and the narrator's open criticism in 11:1–10. However, their apparent failure to notice it, and their instinctive application of the king's law to the narrative, seems to show the basic fact that it is natural for us, as Bible readers, to interpret the narrative in the light of the Deut 17:14–20 law code. These scholars seem to have failed to go through the process of retroactive re-evaluation. It is perhaps because they, as experts, are too familiar with the Deuteronomic law code, and have related it to Solomon's acts, or have tried to deny the relation between them, from the first. In this way, the subtle literary technique of the narrative seems to have been left undetected till now.

This case of the technique is the subtlest of the three cases, and the reader could easily just pass over the clues that are intended to make him or her re-evaluate the previous passage. However, the reader can be expected to notice it in a later reading because the two other cases of the technique are much more evident. It is unquestionable that the later the reader realizes the subtlety of this case, the more strongly the message of the passage impresses the reader.

5.4. The Suitability of the Device for the Intended Message in its Location and Terms Used

When we consider the climactic quality of the passage of 1 Kgs 9:26—10:29 in the narrative, which includes the exclamation of the queen of Sheba about Solomon's glory and splendor,[83] we can understand the subtlety of the literary device in terms of its location. Even though the reader finds some awkwardness in Hiram's complaint against Solomon in 9:10–14, the subsequent descriptions of Solomon's achievement, wealth, and glory lead the reader to regard the passage as a description of Solomon's glory at its climax. The description of Solomon's glory through the eyes of the queen of Sheba (10:4–5) and the praise of Solomon's wisdom and blessing through her mouth (10:6–9) make a particularly vivid impression. The subsequent graphic account of Solomon's golden shields and throne

---

83. Bimson, "1 and 2 Kings," 350; Long, *1 Kings*, 120. Long regards the passage of the queen as "a climax" of the gathered encomium for Solomon before decline.

(10:16–20) also impresses the reader through its detailed description. The last part of chapter 10 (10:23–29) reiterates Solomon's wealth (10:23, 27), God-given wisdom (10:23, 24), and fame (10:24–25), and the reader is left with the impression that here is the climax of Solomon's glory. Therefore, when the reader realizes that the passage could or should be re-evaluated according to the norms of the king's law, the reader receives a strong jolt and learns keenly the insidiousness of the progress of sin, because it turns out that Solomon transgressed every norm of the king's law in the very climax of his glory.

As for the suitability of the terms employed by the device, the conspicuousness of the term "horses from Egypt" is crucial. The reader who knows the Deuteronomistic laws cannot miss this term, as Nelson points out.[84] "Many wives turning the king's heart away" (11:3 and 4) is also an evident mark that could be a trigger of the reader's remembrance of the king's law with the now stronger support of open criticism. However, in the context, it can be said that even though "horses from Egypt" is a very conspicuous term, the reader's recognition of its significance could be delayed by the climactic mood of the passage, as we have seen already. If the reader missed the hint of "horses from Egypt," "many wives turning his heart away" is another trigger with clearly negative force. If the reader has any suspicion about "horses from Egypt," his suspicion can soon be confirmed by the subsequent criticism in chapter 11. However, either way, he could realize the insidiousness of the progress of sin.

6. THE THIRD CASE OF THE TECHNIQUE: SOLOMON'S HEAVY YOKE UPON THE ISRAELITES (1 KGS 12:1–24):[85]

Basically, the account in 1 Kgs 12:1–20 describes how a political blunder is made by the new king Rehoboam, and how at the same time God's

---

84. Nelson, *First and Second Kings*, 67.

85. Although 1 Kgs 12:1–24 is located after the formal statement of the end of Solomon's reign (11:41–43), the passage should be considered as part of the Solomon narrative in the sense that it has a vital role in interpreting the account of Solomon's reign. That the formal statement of the end of a king is not necessarily the end of the account of the king, is insisted by Frisch, who proposes 1 Kgs 1—12:24 as the range of the Solomon narrative, pointing out that even though the formal statement of the end of David's reign appears in 1 Kgs 2:10–12, the account of Solomon is generally regarded as starting already in 1 Kgs ch 1 (Frisch, "Structure and its Significance," 7). It is noteworthy that Solomon is already designated as king in ch 1 (1:51, 53) along with the description of how he became king (1:43, 46, 48).

prophecy through Ahijah (1 Kgs 11:29–39) is fulfilled through the blunder. Surprisingly, the account also reveals that Solomon ruled the nation as a tyrant who put a heavy burden upon his people (12:4, 10, 11, 14) and disciplined them with whips (12:11, 14).[86] That Solomon's harsh rule upon Israelites is not denied by any party of Rehoboam's court in the account, makes the allegation of the Israelites unquestionable. Evidently, this is something unexpected by the reader, and it requires him or her to re-evaluate previous text, trying to detect Solomon's "hard service" and "heavy burden."

6.1. A Reconstruction of the Reader's Reading Process

When the reader reads the open criticism of Solomon's intermarriages and following apostasy in 11:1–8, it becomes clear that Solomon's fault or corruption started at least as early as chapter 3, where his intermarriage with the Pharaoh's daughter is first mentioned. After reading the content of God's judgment (11:9–13) and punishment (11:14–40) and the regnal ending formula (11:41–43), the reader is unexpectedly confronted with another problematic aspect of Solomon's reign in chapter 12. Interestingly, the issue is not mentioned in the narrator's open criticism in 11:1–8. The open criticism of Solomon in 11:1–8 mentions only his intermarriage and following apostasy.

6.2. The Mechanism of the Retroactive Re-evaluation Technique in this Case

The impressive description of the Israelites' peaceful and satisfactory life under Solomon's rule (4:20; 5:5 [ET 4:25]) would remain in the reader's mind. Although the description of the levy system of the temple building (5:27–32 [ET 5:13–18]) includes the Israelites' burden to some extent, the overall description of the levy does not give the reader the impression that the system was a heavy burden for the Israelites. First of all, the building

---

86. It is not alien to the author of Kings that through information given later a whole situation is more comprehensively presented. For example, the fact that King Ahab required an oath that they had not found Elijah when they would say, "He is not here," is revealed in 1 Kgs 18:10, without any previous mention of it. The information is given here in order to underline the danger that Obadiah faces now. Although it is not as dramatic as the case of the Solomon narrative, it shows that, for the author of Kings, supplying new information concerning a situation of which the previous passages do not mention is not unusual.

project has been described as a God-given task waited for long since the Exodus (6:1) and even as a privilege (e.g. 2 Sam 7:12–16, 1 Kgs 5:19 [ET 5:5]) given to Solomon, David's blessed successor, by God. Furthermore, continual praise of Solomon's wisdom (3:12, 28; 5:9 [ET 4:29], 5:14 [ET 4:34], 5:21 [ET 5:7], 5:26 [ET 5:12]) before the temple dedication, of which the last occasion occurs (5:26 [ET 5:12]) right before the description of the levy in chapter 5, apparently has a force that makes the reader regard the levy system which allows the workers to have two months' free time after one month levy work (5:28 [ET 5:14]) as a wise and humane one.[87]

When the reader reads the second account of the levy in chapter 9, he or she only finds an emphasis that Solomon does not make slaves of Israelites, but of "descendants who were still left in the land, whom the Israelites were unable to destroy completely" (9:21), while he makes soldiers and commanders, not slaves, of Israelites (9:22). The second description of Solomon's levy system leads the reader to think that after the temple is built, the Israelites become levy-free people.[88]

Apart from the two descriptions of Solomon's levy system, only once is "forced labor" mentioned in the context of God's punishment against Solomon's apostasy in chapter 11. That is, "The man Jeroboam was very able, and when Solomon saw that the young man was industrious he gave him charge over all the forced labour (סֵבֶל)[89] of the house of

---

87. Mettinger alternatively proposes that this passage means that "each man spent one month in Lebanon and two months at Solomon's 'house,' thus doing service for three months a year" (Mettinger, *Solomonic State Officials*, 135); however, his alternative interpretation does not affect the wise and humane quality of the corvee system executed by Solomon: "the duration of the duty, three months a year, is reasonable . . ."

88. By and large, there are two different views of the relationship between the accounts of the levy system in ch 5 and ch 9. Wiseman, *1 and 2 Kings*, 127; Provan, *1 and 2 Kings*, 86. Nelson, *First and Second Kings*, 64; Jones, *1 and 2 Kings*, 214; Parker, "Solomon as Philosopher King?," 80–81, 84–85; Walsh, "The Characterization," 481; 134; Mettinger, *Solomonic State Officials*, 134; Mendelsohn thinks that there is no contradiction between them (Mendelsohn, "Corvée Labor"). For example, Nelson thinks that 5:27–32 [ET 5:13–18] is about a temporary "civic duty," while 9:21–25 is about "forced levy of slaves." Provan thinks that 9:20–23 provides more details for the previous description of the levy system in 5:27–30 [ET 5:13–16]. Wiseman also insists that there is no ground to believe that the levy system in 9:20–23 is different from that of 5:27–30 [ET 5:13–16]. However, Gray and Cogan think that 9:20–22 is a late gloss, for the content of the description in 9:15–25 is contradictory to the previous description of the national levy system in 5:27–30 [ET 5:13–16], taking a historical-critical approach to the text (Gray, *1 & 2 Kings*, 222; Cogan, *Kings*, 309).

89. There are three major terms for the Solomonic levy system, that is, מַס (e.g., 1 Kgs 5:27 [ET 5:13]), מַס־עֹבֵד (e.g., 1 Kgs 9:21), and 1) סֵבֶל Kgs 11:28). Usually מַס is regarded as forced labor as civic duty, while מַס־עֹבֵד is understood as forced labor as

Joseph" (11:28). However, the point of the description is not to describe Solomon's levy system but to describe the process of God's punishment of Solomon's sin, and consequently, it is hard to expect the reader to catch the implication of the passage in terms of Solomon's levy system at first reading. In fact, the passage does not directly tell anything of the heaviness of the burden.

Therefore, the account of Solomon's heavy burden complained of by the northern tribes (12:4), admitted by Solomon's successor and his subjects, is surprising to the reader, as an unexpected issue. The surprise has the force of making the reader reconsider the previous passages of the Solomon narrative. The reader is stimulated to re-examine the previous passages to detect any clue that explains the "heavy burden" either immediately or in subsequent reading. The reader who has been overwhelmed by the impression of Solomon's wisdom, blessing, and glory throughout the narrative, would read the account from a different angle in order to detect any missing clues which can explain the "heavy burden" in the subsequent readings. It makes this another case of the retroactive re-evaluation technique in the Solomon narrative.

What would be the clue(s) which might explain the presence of the "heavy burden," when the reader reads the Solomon narrative in the light of 1 Kgs 12? As has been shown, from the description of his early reign, where the Israelites' satisfactory happy life is described (4:20; 5:5 [ET 4:25]), through Solomon's levy system for the temple building (5:27–30 [ET 5:13–16]), of which it is stated that all Israelites are "joyful and in good spirit" when the dedication feast is over (8:66), to the levy system of Solomon's later reign, which emphasizes that Solomon did not make slave-labor of Israelites, but of the Canaanites remnants in the land (9:15–23), the reader cannot detect the existence of a heavy burden upon the Israelites' shoulders.

However, it is not too difficult for the reader determined to detect a prime cause of the heavy burden to finally notice the clues in the narrative. The reader notices the presence of the "forced labor" of Israelites in 11:27–28, which is a different story from the description of the Solomon's levy system in 9:15–23. Therefore, the reader now notices that although no change of Solomon's levy system is described after 9:15–23, the levy system has been changed without explicit mention of it at some point after

---

slavery, according to the context of 1 Kgs 5 and 9. סֵבֶל occurs only three times in the Hebrew Bible (1 Kgs 11:28; Neh 4:11 [ET 4:17]; Ps 81:7 [ET 81:6]) with the meaning of "burden" or "labor of bearing burden" (Kellermann, "Sabal," *TDOT 10*, 141, 143).

9:15-23. Considering the different descriptions of Solomon's levy system in different stages of his reign in 5:27-32 [ET 5:13-18] and 9:15-23 (i.e., the presence of Israelites' levy in chapter 5 for the temple building, and the absence of it in chapter 9 after temple building), it is not unnatural for the reader to suppose that the system could change again in the latter part of Solomon's reign, for the good reason that appears in 11:27b ("Solomon built the Millo, and closed up the gap in the wall of the city of his father David").[90]

Moreover, when the reader notices that Jeroboam, who was the supervisor of the forced labor of the house of Joseph, becomes the leader of the ten tribes who complain of the heavy burden, and that not Judah and Benjamin but only the northern ten tribes secede from the Davidic dynasty, it raises the suspicion that Solomon's levy system had a discriminatory nature. The plausible discriminatory rule of Solomon is confirmed when the reader detects a discriminatory policy in the description of the food supply for Solomon and his household, where Judah is exempted in 4:7-19.[91] Although the whole people's satisfactory life is presented in 4:20; 5:5 [ET 4:25], in spite of their burden of the large amount of food supply for Solomon's court 5:2-3 [ET 4:22-23][92] (supplied only by the northern tribes), the presence of a discriminatory nature in Solomon's rule is confirmed anyway, and the reader may conclude that the discriminatory policy was applied to the levy system mentioned in 11:28 as well. Furthermore, the existence of "the land of good-for-nothing" in the northern part of the kingdom (9:14) is a contrast to the "the immense prosperity enjoyed in Jerusalem" (10:27).[93]

Additionally, a further consideration is possible here. Rehoboam's sending Adoram the taskmaster over the forced labor to the northern

90. Some think that the levy system for Israelites described in 5:27-28 [ET 5:13–14] has been maintained. For example, Cogan, *Kings*, 2000, 309. However, Cogan thinks that the statement that Solomon made no slavery of Israelites (9:22), is a later gloss, which is contradictory to the account of the levy system in ch 5.

91. There are two readings of 4:19b. "And there was one official in the land of Judah" (NRSV) and "He was the only governor over the district" (NIV). NRSV, in fact, includes the first word (Judah) of 4:20. John Bimson notices the discriminate nature, as does J. J. Kang.

92. Tribute from the neighboring nations is described in 5:1 [ET 4:21], which surely subdues to some extent any worry about the enormous amount of the food supply for Solomon.

93. Bimson, "1 And 2 Kings," 349. Bimson also points out that Solomon's paying Hiram with the northern cities implies that "Solomon's dues could no longer be raised by taxation" with negative tone.

tribes, and his being stoned to death, gives an impression that the issue is directly of the "forced labor." The fact that the first appearance of Jeroboam is in the context of a construction project (1 Kgs 11:27b "Solomon built the Millo, and closed up the gap in the wall of the city of his father David") supports this view. However, it is possible for the reader to understand "the heavy yoke" in a wider sense, i.e., not only forced labor, but also heavy taxation.[94] There are some clues that lead the reader to reach such a conclusion. That is, the reader can regard it as significant that the yoke is expressed in the two terms, "the hard service"[95] and "heavy yoke"[96] originally (12:4), although later on they are called "yoke" or "heavy yoke" alone (12:9, 10, 11(x2), 14). The northern Israelites' burden, like food supply (4:7–19, cf. 5:2–3 [ET 4:22–23]) not only for the palace but also military horses (5:8 [ET 4:28]), military service (9:22), and forced labor (11:28), can be detected as a possible cause of the "heavy burden" as a whole,[97] although it is admitted that in the early stage the people enjoy their life with some of them (4:20; 5:5 [ET 4:25]). With Solomon's maintaining excessive wives, a luxurious life, and army with horses (10:14–11:7) along with on-going construction projects after temple building[98] and immense taxation (10:14, 666 talents of gold for one year), (although it is admitted that some part of his wealth comes as gift from abroad (10:25)[99]) it is natural to find the presence of the "heavy yoke" upon the people's shoulders. Considering together these elements, the reader may conclude that "the hard service" and "heavy yoke" (although they are usually expressed as "heavy yoke" alone) actually means a complex duty of the northern tribes for Solomon's kingdom. Thus, the term "heavy yoke" can be understood as being used as a representative of the complex duties of the people. Probably in a later reading the reader will find out that the description of the Israelites'

---

94. In the introduction of the institution of kingship for Israel, it is well predicted that the Israelites will be suffering for their king's requirement of not only their various laborious services for him but also taxation (1 Sam 8:10–17).

95. עֲבֹדָה הַקָּשָׁה

96. עֻלּוֹ הַכָּבֵד (literally "his heavy yoke").

97. The charge of the food supply for the palace (4:7–19) and the charge of forced labor (4:6) are put side by side.

98. Solomon's palace (required the double time spent of the temple), and many cities including the Egyptian style cities (9:15, 17, 18, 19). Although these building projects are done by the forced labor of the remnant of Canaanites (9:20–23), it is evident that for some reason, northern Israelites are included in Solomon's work force later (11:27–28).

99. It should be pointed out that the gift from foreigners should be generously paid back as the case of the queen of Sheba shows (10:13).

peaceful and secure life in Solomon's early reign, as in chapter 4 and 5 (4:20; 5:5 [ET 4:25]), does not reappear in the latter part of the Solomon narrative, while most subjects which appear in the early part of the narrative reappear in the latter part. From this observation the reader may conclude that somewhere in the latter period of Solomon's reign, the people's life condition turned into the state of the "heavy yoke" being imposed upon their shoulders. In any case, overall, the content of 1 Kgs 12 has the power of making the reader read the description of Solomon's luxurious life and heavy expenditure again from a different point of view from the first reading. This re-evaluation of the previous passage is not strange for the reader, for the first case (i.e., of Solomon's intermarriage with Pharaoh's daughter, which is only later explicitly criticized) has opened his or her eye already to this trend of the narrative.

It is highly probable that through this process the reader may find out or realize that the process is done insidiously, for the exact time of the change does not appear clear in the text. Being placed even after Solomon's death, the evaluation of Solomon's reign through the people's mouth is regarded as the ultimate and final one. It is striking for the reader to observe that it is the evaluation of the king who had God-given wisdom and blessing so abundantly, and consequently, it makes the reader perceive the danger of insidious progress of sin or corruption even among the blessings of God.

Additionally, the heavy burden in chapter 12 as a negative connotation of Solomon's reign makes the reader conclude that the open criticism in 11:1–8 does not cover every fault of Solomon. This is because the open criticism provides the reader only with the information that Solomon's faults started as early as chapter 3 concerning his intermarriage and following idolatry against Deuteronomic law. Hence, the reader learns that some of Solomon's faults may be described without explicit criticism at that point in the narrative. The revealed heavy burden in chapter 12 persuades the reader that it is possible that there are even additional faults of Solomon that are not mentioned in the open criticism. In this sense, the reader is invited to investigate the whole narrative again from the start to find out Solomon's sin(s) or fault(s), which are implicit and insidious and consequently might have escaped his or her previous observation. This may help the reader detect Solomon's transgression in 9:26—10:29 which is against the king's stipulation in Deut 17:16–17, in an immediate re-reading or a subsequent reading.

7. ANOTHER CASE OF THE RETROACTIVE RE-EVALUATION TECHNIQUE IN THE BIBLICAL NARRATIVE

The retroactive re-evaluation technique is observed in at least one place elsewhere in the scope of the Hebrew biblical narrative. That is, the account of Mephibosheth (i.e., the son of Jonathan, the grandson of King Saul), and his servant Ziba. Although the story is scattered (2 Sam 4:4; 9:1–13; 16:1–4; 19:25–31 [ET 19:24–30]) across several chapters, the events between Mephibosheth, Ziba, and David make a coherent story. David shows his kindness to Mephibosheth for the sake of Jonathan, and orders Ziba (originally Saul's servant) to serve Mephibosheth. David also gives him the privilege of eating at the king's table, like one of the king's sons (9:1–13). However, when David has to leave Jerusalem for his life, and is suffering Absalom's rebellion, Ziba supports David and his men by supplying food. Replying to David's question of Mephibosheth, Ziba answers that "He remains in Jerusalem: for he said, 'Today the house of Israel will give me back my grandfather's kingdom,'" so David pledges to give Mephibosheth's properties to Ziba (16:1–4).

Absalom's rebellion is well prepared and very successful in its early stage (2 Sam 15:6, 13), and the fleeing David and his men's appearance is miserable (15:23, 30). In the very time of David's deepest trouble, Ziba's support seems to be true loyalty to the king. Mephibosheth's reaction to David's trouble, which is reported by Ziba, must disappoint David, and his pledge of Mephibosheth's properties is well understood. Mephibosheth, who did not come to show his faithfulness to David who was in trouble, seems to be a betrayer who repaid the king's mercy and grace with evil betrayal.

However, this was not the case. Ziba's report of Mephibosheth was a slander and false accusation, which was well calculated in order to get the upper hand of his master Mephibosheth, exploiting the time of King David's trouble. In the scene of David's returning to Jerusalem after defeating Absalom, the narrator plainly states that "Mephibosheth grandson of Saul came down to meet the king; he had not taken care of his feet, or trimmed his beard, or washed his clothes, from the day the king left until the day he came back in safety" (2 Sam 19:25 [ET 19:24]). The reason that he could not accompany to David when the king left Jerusalem, is also explained through the mouth of Mephibosheth (19:27–28 [ET 19:26–27]).[100]

---

100. The reaction of David to Mephibosheth seems to be odd. He does not punish

What matters is that when the reader reads the passage of David's being supported and reported to by Ziba, it is very easy to be deceived along with David by Ziba's slander. There are at least three reasons for this. Firstly, the scene of Ziba's meeting the king immediately follows the king's series of meetings with his faithful men, i.e., Ittai the Gittite (15:19–22), Abiathar and Zadok the priests (15:24–29), and Hushai the Archite (15:32–37) who faithfully accompany or try to accompany the king who is in trouble. Without any break, the flow of narrative has the power to make Ziba look like one of them. Secondly, it is easy for the reader to accept Ziba's report of Mephibosheth as truth, for anyway it is true that Mephibosheth does not appear in the scene to support David. Thirdly, in the stage of David's fleeing from Jerusalem, when it seems to be more likely that David will not be restored, it is unlikely that a servant would boldly slander his master to get the upper hand of him, it could be a dangerous gamble. It is very hard for the reader to suspect that the servant is so boldly gambling his fate, exploiting the king's trouble in this situation, until at last it turns out that the servant was in fact gambling his fate by supporting the fleeing king in rebellion, and by slandering his master so wickedly.[101]

Ziba for his false accusation of his master Mephibosheth. Rather David orders that Mephibosheth and Ziba should divide the land (2 Sam 19:30b [ET 19:29b]). Mary Evans proposes several possible reasons for David's action. Firstly, because Ziba provided "real help" anyway to David in his time in need, David's giving him the half of the land is a "wise and considered move." Secondly, "It could also be a petulant emotional reaction, showing an unwillingness to admit he has made a mistake and wanting to deal with the matter as quickly as possible." Thirdly, "The ambiguity in their presentation of David's reaction may be the writer's deliberate indication that the situation is not as clear cut as it might seem" (Evans, *1 and 2 Samuel*, 220–21). The first and second suggestions are unlikely, while the third is more likely when it is considered that Mephibosheth reaction which shows his loyalty to David described in 19:25 [ET 19:24], is just the description provided by the omniscient narrator not for David, but for the reader. Also, it should be considered that it is described that Mephibosheth "had not taken care of his feet, or trimmed his beard, or washed his clothes, from the day the king left" *only* "until the day he came back in safety." That is, it is most likely that Mephibosheth had to trim his beard and change his clothes before he came to the King David. The case of Joseph's preparation before his coming to an Egyptian king (Gen 41:14), might provide a similar case. Even when Joseph was "hurriedly brought out of the dungeon," he had to shave himself and change his clothes, before he came in and stood before Pharaoh, the king of Egypt. If the parallel case is taken into account, it is not difficult to explain why David had to react in an ambiguous manner. David could not know whether Mephibosheth had not taken care of himself or not, when Mephibosheth came to him, for Mephibosheth had cleaned himself up before he came to David.

101. Evans points out that "David accepted Ziba's story without question. This is understandable given David's natural distrust of Saul's family, shortly to be confirmed

It can be also said that not revealing the truth about Mephibosheth in the early stage (i.e., 2 Sam 16:1–4) but only in the late stage (i.e., 19:25 [ET 19:24]) is part of the literary device. That is, the truth is intentionally hidden from the reader, in order to mislead (i.e., intentionally lead) the reader to be deceived along with David, and then only later on, to re-evaluate Ziba's previous act and report in light of the new information.[102]

It is most likely that the reader is deceived by Ziba, like David, and later realizes the truth through the narrator-given information. Thus, the reader should retroactively re-evaluate Ziba's seemingly loyal support and his report of Mephibosheth, his master who did not appear to support the king. Whatever the larger picture of the narrative is intended to mean,[103] at the very least Ziba's case gives a good lesson that when one (especially as a leader) is in trouble and need, and well supported by someone who shows favor and even apparent loyalty, it is naïve to give him or her one's absolute trust, especially when the supporter talks evil of other(s). The lesson is delivered very effectively through the retroactive re-evaluation technique.[104]

8. CONCLUSION

In this chapter, it was shown that the near-consensus understanding of the Solomon narrative in Kings (that Solomon's faults appear only in 1 Kgs 2 and 11), which is regarded as the *Vorlage* of the Solomon account

by Shimei's actions. Mephibosheth's relationship with Saul is deliberately stressed, both by David and by Ziba. Also, since David's own son had betrayed him, it was easy to believe that one who had been treated like a son should behave likewise" (ibid., 205). It can be pointed out here that Evans is unconsciously mixing the force to move David to accept Ziba's report without question, with the textual force to persuade the reader. That is, for example, the following episode of Shimei could not have any influence upon David himself when he judges Ziba's report on the spot. But the episode can influence the reader's judgement of Ziba's report retroactively.

102. It is not clear why Satterthwaite thinks that this case provides the case which allows "two different readings" to be "equally plausible" (Satterthwaite and McConville, *Exploring*, 130).

103. Along with "animosity against David and loyalty to Saul . . . expressed by Shimei" in the following passage (2 Sam 16:5–13), the alleged Mephibosheth's betrayal, might have the effect to show "a brief glance at hopes still attaching to the family of Saul" (Ackroyd, *The Second Book of Samuel*, 150).

104. It is interesting to observe that the retrospective re-evaluation technique is noticed in the Solomon narrative in Septuagint, as well. When it is considered that the Solomon narrative (1 Kgs 1–12) in Masoretic text and that of Septuagint contain comparatively larger differences than other parts of the biblical narrative, it can be proposed that the technique is an essential device of the portrayal of Solomon in Kings.

in Chronicles, is not satisfactory, and this fact affects the interpretation of the Solomon account in Chronicles. Hence, this chapter proposed a new interpretation of the Solomon narrative in Kings concerning Solomon's faults. According to the present reader-sensitive approach (focusing on the reader's reading process and prior knowledge), it has been shown that Solomon's faults are characterized as his "returning to Egypt," and its concrete manifestations are his intermarriage with an Egyptian princess, his importation of Egyptian horses (and his violation against the king's law in Deut 17:16–17), and his Egyptian-style rule as a tyrant. It has also been shown that these materials are arranged to constitute a literary device that calls the reader to "retroactive re-evaluation" of previous passages, delivering the message of "insidious progress of sin" dramatically and effectively. Thus, the effectiveness of the reader-sensitive approach, in detecting the elaborate literary strategy that is planted in order to maximize the effect of conveying its message, was shown.

Moreover, from the new interpretation, it became plain that Chronicler did not intend to conceal the negative elements of Solomon in his writing. Rather, the re-appearance of these materials in the Solomon account in Chronicles requires a careful reading of the materials in terms of Solomon's faults. If Chronicles is also a reader-sensitive work, and it is generally acknowledged that the reader's prior knowledge of old tradition or its *Vorlage* is presupposed in many places in the work, it is worth scrutinizing whether the same materials are used, in Chronicler's Solomon account, in order to betray Solomon's faults.

4

The Nature and Purpose of Chronicles
A Working Hypothesis

1. INTRODUCTION

THE NATURE AND PURPOSE of a work should be identified through a detailed exploration of each part of the work. However, as Duke rightly points out, it is inevitable to presume the nature and purpose of the whole work, as a working hypothesis, in order to investigate or explore each part of the work, and this is to some extent a necessary circularity.[1] In order to approach the Solomon account in Chronicles, it is therefore necessary to presume the nature and purpose of Chronicles, as a whole, as a working hypotheses. In turn, our study of the Solomon account will examine some of the working hypotheses. It is not intended to prove or justify each assumption thoroughly, for that is an impossible task to achieve in the present dissertation. Nevertheless, it is necessary to make some assumptions or a working hypothesis, with some justification, as the starting point for the present study.

---

1. Duke, *The Persuasive Appeal*, 47.

2. THE NATURE AND LITERARY QUALITY OF CHRONICLES

2.1. The Nature of Chronicles

Asking about the nature of Chronicles raises the question of its genre. Several suggestions including Targum,[2] Midrash,[3] exegesis,[4] interpretation,[5] fiction,[6] preaching,[7] theological essay,[8] and so on, have been proposed regarding the genre of Chronicles. While it should be admitted that deciding precisely the nature of the work is an extremely tricky task to achieve, as Williamson states,[9] the present study presumes that Chronicles is first of all a work of historiography.[10] While the historical reliability of the work

2. Barnes, 316–19.

3. Johnstone, *1 Chronicles 1–2 Chronicles 9*, 23; Wellhausen, *Prolegomena*, 227; Zunz, *Die gottesdienstlichen Vorträge*, 34–38; Welten, *Geschichte und Geschichtsdarstellung*, 206. Welten sees the work as "historical Midrash." Johnstone follows J. Neusner (*Between Time and Eternity* (Encino: Dickenson, 52) in the definition of midrash as follows. "*Midrash* . . . represents . . . creative philosophy and creative historiography. As creative philology, the *Midrash* discovers meaning in apparently meaningless detail. It . . . uses the elements of language not as fixed, unchanging categories, but as relative, living, tentative nuances of thought. As creative historiography, the *Midrash* rewrites the past to make manifest the eternal rightness of Scriptural paradigms. What would it be like if all people lived at one moment? . . . *Midrash* thus exchanges the stability of language and the continuity of history for the stability of values and the eternity of truth."

4. Willi, *Auslegung*, 66–67; R. Coggins, "Theology and Hermeneutics in the Books of Chronicles," 278.

5. Ackroyd, "The Theology of the Chronicler," 276; Selman, *1 Chronicles*, 26: "the Chronicler's overall aim was to offer an interpretation of the Bible as he knew it. More precisely, his guiding principle was to demonstrate that God's promises revealed in the Davidic covenant were as trustworthy and effective as when they were first given, even though the first readers lived centuries after almost all the events he recorded."

6. Torrey, "Chronicler as Editor," 217.

7. Allen, *1, 2 Chronicles*, 20.

8. Ackroyd, "The Chronicler as exegete," 24.

9. Williamson, *1 and 2 Chronicles*, 21–23. Williamson concludes that "In conclusion, therefore, it emerges that we should beware of attempts simplistically to reduce to a single category the nature of the Chronicler's composition or his use of sources which was determined by it" (23).

10. Jones, *1 & 2 Chronicles*, 78–82; von Rad, *Old Testament Theology, I*, 347–48; Japhet, *I & II Chronicles*, 32; Fishbane, *Biblical Interpretation in Ancient Israel*, 380–81; Noth, *The Chronicler's History*; Braun, *1 Chronicles*, xxiv, "history in the pregnant sense of the term (facts plus interpretation) . . ."; I. Kalimi, "Was the Chronicler a Historian?," 73–89; McKenzie, *1–2 Chronicles*, 33–34. McKenzie defines the nature of Chronicles as "a theological rewriting of Bible history for instructional purpose" (34); Van Seters,

is being recognized more and more,[11] it is also still acknowledged that the Chronicler's way of writing history is different from the modern concept of history writing, in that it is more oriented by ideological or theological emphases.[12] However, it should still be granted that, as a historian, the Chronicler did not intend to fabricate or distort the historical facts, and could not deny already authoritatively established historical facts or traditions;[13] meanwhile it is naturally acknowledged that he was selective concerning his available materials in order to emphasize his own concerns and interests.[14]

It is also plausible that the Chronicler was conscious that he was writing "the second" work of historiography which covers the period from the beginning of the world to his time, i.e., the post-exilic period of Israel, in the sense that he was aware that his reader knew the first history already as authoritative, and that the reader's prior knowledge of it would affect the reading of his own work. Whether or not the Chronicler expected his work to attain the same status as the first one is another issue. But it can at least be said that the Chronicler expected his work to be read as a document that is basically in line with the established tradition or the authoritative ones.[15] There is evidence to show that he had a historical writing which is almost the same, at least, as the present form of the Pentateuch and

---

"The Chronicler's Account," 300; R. W. Klein, recently in an eclectic expression, "a work of historiography and of theology" (Klein, *1 Chronicles*, 19).

11. E.g., Jones, *1 & 2 Chronicles*, 12–13, 68–71, and 79–80; Williamson, *1 and 2 Chronicles*, 19–21 and *passim* ; Satterthwaite and McConville, *Exploring Histories*, 286–87.

12. Ibid., 81–82.

13. Payne, "The Purpose and Methods of the Chronicler," 68–60; Duke, *The Persuasive Appeal*, 109–116. "One can imagine that if the Chronicler flagrantly contradicted significant traditions, neither he nor his story would have been well received" (110), "it is important to note, in agreement with Willi, that the Chronicler did not offer a contradictory account to his audience. . . . The Chronicler did not seek to demonstrate that the earlier traditions were wrong" (112); "it appears probable that the Chronicler's methodology of interpreting tradition would not have stood out as abnormal or suspect to his audience" (115).

14. Dirksen's statement on the issue is noteworthy, "It is a cliché to say that Chronicles is not a history in the modern sense of the word. But if it is essential to historiography to give a coherent view of the period to be described and to lay bare underlying factors for developments, then Chronicles is most certainly historiography, also as regards its purpose. A coherent view depends on the historian's own position and attitude. . . . The aim set by the historian determines his selection from the sources and the way in which this material is revised and supplemented" (Dirksen, *1 Chronicles*, 10).

15. Willi even thinks that the Chronicler had the two first parts of the Hebrew Bible (Torah and Prophets) as canonical scripture in his day.

Joshua as authoritative historiography, and also as that of Samuel-Kings. For example, it is well known that the Chronicler evidently uses typology, when he describes the event of succession from David to Solomon, following the pattern of the succession from Moses to Joshua,[16] and shows that the Chronicler is not only aware of the previous tradition of the event, but also exploits his supposed reader's prior knowledge of the description of the event in the first history.[17]

Furthermore, that he uses a similar typology even within the scope of his own writing,[18] plausibly shows that he had an awareness that he was writing "the second history." This reveals that the relationship between parts of his writing is not different from that of his own writing and the first, authoritative, history.

If we accept, as a working hypothesis for the present study, that the nature of Chronicles is the second work of historiography, the following points can be proposed as a consequence. First, regarding the relationship with the first history, the Chronicler had to rely upon the established authority of the first one, in order to present his writing as acceptable to his readers.[19] As Duke suggests, the Chronicler could not have obtained any credence from his audience without giving them the impression that his work was firmly based upon the first history and did not deviate from it.[20] In this sense, the retained material from its *Vorlage* (about half

---

16. Williamson, "Accession of Solomon."

17. Among many, another interesting example is that the description of Manasses' idolatry (2 Chr 33:2–9) is according to the stipulation in Deut 18:9–14, as Selman points out (Selman, *2 Chronicles*, 520–21).

18. For example, the Chronicler describes King Hezekiah following the pattern of the Solomon description, as Williamson observes (Williamson, *Israel*, 119–25).

19. "Furthermore, it is true that on the whole he has handled his biblical sources more conservatively than others – perhaps because he accorded them a greater authority . . ." (Williamson, *1 and 2 Chronicles*, 23)

20. Duke, *The Persuasive Appeal, passim* in 105–38. Applying Aristotle's rhetorical theory, which maintains that three elements (or modes), i.e., logos, ethos, and pathos, are all needed to persuade an audience effectively and successfully. While ethos, which is about a rhetor's presentation of himself as "credible and worthy of trust," is usually presented by the rhetor's "good sense, good character, and good will," in a real rhetorical situation, the Chronicles needs applied features as a written material, for example, showing its respect of the established tradition, in order to gain its reader's or hearer's trust. "The Chronicler achieved a new portrayal of the past mainly by rearranging and omitting parallel material, rather than by contradicting important traditions. These modifications probably would not have appeared obtrusive or contradictory to his audience" (137). Payne also maintains the same stance (Payne, "The Purpose and Methods of the Chronicler.").

of Chronicles is similar to the first history[21]) deserves more careful and weighty attention than it sometimes receives. Japhet tries to prove that while the Chronicler uses many terms from the "pool" of established traditions, his theological stance is distinctive and unique.[22] However, the question still remains of whether the Chronicler intends to propose a new theology contradictory to the one of the established traditions. Secondly, exploiting the position of the second history, the Chronicler could omit a variety of materials, when it seems to be necessary simply for economy of writing, or to prevent his reader from being distracted by material that is not necessarily crucial or meaningful to his own point.[23] The Chronicler could use allusion in similar situations, but in that case, it is necessary that the reader is reminded of the omitted things through various forms of clues or hints. That is, the Chronicler tries to use his reader's prior knowledge of the omitted materials in a subtle way. Thirdly, writing a second history, itself, in the presence of the first one, means that the Chronicler has his own emphasis or message, which is distinct from that of the first one.[24] However, as has already been pointed out, his writing should not be contradictory to the first one, so that he can earn or preserve the reader's credit and deliver his own message effectively, of which the present study will provide an example. Finally, as a second history, it is not unnatural for the work to supplement the first one.[25] The supplementary aspect can appear in several ways, i.e., providing exegesis of the first one, providing a more nuanced presentation than the first one, and providing new information in certain cases. Being conscious of the first history, the Chronicler tried to do exegesis on the first one in some places, although not for the whole of the material. Further, in writing a second history, which overlaps

21. Rigsby, "The Historioraphy of Speeches and Prayers."

22. Japhet, *Ideology*, 19 and 505ff. Japhet observes that "At times, he [Chronicler] made use of a literary or stylistic tradition while either ignoring or altering its conceptual content" (ibid, 506).

23. Williamson seems to be on the same line when he maintains that "He (the Chronicler) frequently presupposes knowledge of passages in his *Vorlage* which he himself has not included, and indeed as a general rule the overall shape and order of work is dependent on the earlier composition" (Williamson, *1 and 2 Chronicles*, 22).

24. "But overall the Chronicler shows himself as the master, not the servant, of his sources, His is the last example of Israel's genius for retelling her sacred history in a way which applies its lessons creatively to the demands of a developing community" (ibid., 23).

25. This feature has been noticed by many scholars. For example, Braun, *1 Chronicles*, xxiii; Albright, "The Date and Personality of the Chronicler," 120; Childs, *Introduction*, 649–50.

in many periods or events with the first one, the Chronicler could present the same case in a more nuanced portrayal[26] than in the first one, providing his reader with a deepened or widened perspective. Furthermore, the Chronicler introduced new descriptions to certain cases, probably using different sources from those of the first history (for example, the death of Ahaziah, the Judean king (2 Chr 22:7–9; cf. 2 Kgs 9:27–28), and the genealogy of Benjamin (1 Chr 7:6 f; 8:1f.; cf. Gen 46:21, Num 26:38–41)).[27] Its purpose seems to provide a supplementary angle on the cases (the supplementary materials of the work exist in a way that serves his overall purpose of the work, rather than for their own purpose, i.e., as mere supplements).

2.2. The Literary Quality of the Secondary History

This study does not regard the book of Chronicles (or Kings) as a poorly written or edited piece of literature, which betrays editorial traces here and there and a lack of literary capability, as has been thought to be the case. Recent studies have begun to reveal the literary capability of the work.[28] For example, a close reading has discovered the exquisite analogy

26. Supplementary characteristics to the first historiography, a more nuanced picture, and omission and abbreviation on the basis of reader's prior knowledge are well summarized by Whybray's statement as follows. "They were probably regarded from the first as supplements to the earlier works giving a fuller picture of certain aspects of the reigns of the kings, while abbreviating, summarizing and omitting much of the earlier narratives as already familiar to the reader" (Whybray, *The Good Life*, 114–15).

27. Payne thinks that those cases show the credibility of the Chronicler as a historian who tried to be faithful to his sources, for they do not seem to serve any theological purpose, while undermining the acceptability of his new description for his reader, because it is impossible to reconcile to the *Vorlage* (Samuel-Kings) (Payne, "The Purpose and Methods of the Chronicler," 70). However, in our view, the Chronicler seems to intend to supply supplementary information about the case, which is reconcilable to the first one or the *Vorlage*.

28. For example, R. B. Dillard, "The Literary Structure of the Chronicler's Solomon Narrative," 85–93; L. C. Allen, "Kerygmatic Units in 1 & 2 Chronicles," 21–36; M. P. Graham, "Aspects of the Structure and Rhetoric of 2 Chronicles 25," 78–89; I. Kalimi, *Zur Geschichtsschreibung des Chronisten*, 1995. Ackroyd decribes it as "highly skilled arrangement and balance, pointing to a literary artist" (Akroyd, "The Theology of the Chronicler," 278); Braun describes the Chronicler as "a person of much greater literary skill than is usually attributed to him" (Braun, *1 Chronicles*, xxv); J. W. Kleinig also describes it in his concluding statement, "Chronicles seems to be a unified composition with its own literary integrity, purpose and message. And the Chronicler seems to have been a skilful author and well-versed theologian who reflected deeply on the authoritative tradition . . ." (Kleinig, "Recent Research in Chronicles," 76); "the criticism

between the presentation of Solomon-Huram-abi in Chronicles and that of Bezalel-Oholiab in Exodus,[29] and another analogy between the succession narrative of David-Solomon and that of Moses-Joshua[30] for their own theological emphases.

In the light of the point above, it will be presumed that the author's intention is reflected in the retained passages in the same way as in his own additional material. We will not give less weight to the retained material from the *Vorlage* than to the newly additional material in Chronicles.[31] In that sense, this study will not accept the stance of Japhet, following von Rad, which sees some retained passages as even contradictory to the author's (or editor's) own stance.[32] Rather the present study follows the stance of Williamson on this matter that the retained materials also precisely reflect the author's intention.[33]

Theological analysis of the text along with the literal analysis will be made, for, after all, literary techniques are the instruments to convey author's theology, and the two are essentially related to each other.

3. THE PURPOSE OF CHRONICLES AND RELATED ISSUES

The purpose of Chronicles, as in the case of the other biblical works, is connected with other issues, such as the date of composition,[34] the extent and

---

that sources have been incorporated rather crudely, or changed rather arbitrarily, has given way to growing admiration of the Chronicler's sophistication in employing and deploying sources" (48).

29. Dillard, "The Chronicler's Solomon," 296–99.

30. Williamson, "Accession of Solomon."

31. Contra Braun. Williamson also takes this position.

32. Von Rad, *Geschichtsbild*, 18; Japhet, *Ideology*, 8. "Although the Chronicler edited his source material quite comprehensively, he was not always systematic, and at times the text reveals not his opinion, but that of his source."

33. Williamson, *Israel*, 88. "We cannot accept that all parallel passages must be ignored, for if, as von Rad does, we find significance in the small changes that the Chronicler introduces, then it ought to be equally significant that he leaves other passages unchanged."

34. For example, Braun, *1 Chronicles*, xxv–xxix, Section of "Purpose and Date"; McKenzie, *The Chronicler's Use*, 25–26, "Purpose and Date." Later, McKenzie combines the issue of purpose with date of composition (McKenzie, *1–2 Chronicles*, 33–34, Section of "Genre and Purpose").

dates of late additions or recensions,[35] and so on.[36] Moreover, the extent of the work is an additional issue involved in the case of Chronicles. Concerning the extent of the Chronicler's work, the view that Chronicles and Ezra-Nehemiah had been produced by same author(s) had prevailed since Zunz (1832).[37] However, the consensus view has been challenged since Japhet (1968), who regards Chronicles and Ezra-Nehemiah as distinct literatures by separate authors,[38] and the latter view is prevailing in recent discussion. However, theoretically, even the same author could produce two distinctive writings with different ideological emphases or even linguistic styles,[39] reflecting the passage of time or by some deliberate intention. On the other hand, it is also possible that even two separate authors produce works that have common ideologies and similar linguistic styles. In light of this consideration, to discuss whether or not the two works were produced by a single author has an intrinsic limitation in reaching a decisive conclusion. The arrangement of the Hebrew canon, which always puts the two works separately, can be taken as the weightiest evidence.[40] Hence, the present study presumes that the two books are separate works, without the assumption or implication that the two writings are necessarily the products of two separate authors.

3.1. The Relationship between Chronicles and Ezra-Nehemiah

Many observations and points have been made by scholars on the view that the two books are separate works.[41] It will be sufficient to deal with only a

35. For example, Cross, "A Reconstruction of the Judean Restoration." For Williamson's refutation to Cross's theory see, Williamson, "Eschatology," 122ff.

36. For example, comparison of the theologies of Chronicles and Haggai, Zechariah 1–8 is used as a important criterion of deciding the date of Chronicles and consequently the purpose of the work by scholars like Throntveit (Throntveit, *When Kings Speak*, 97–107).

37. Zunz, *Die gottesdienstlichen Vorträge*; Ackroyd, "The Writings of the Chronicler," 510–12. Since Japhet, some scholars still maintains the old view. For example, Blenkinsopp, *Ezra-Nehemiah*.

38. Japhet, "Authorship of Chronicles and Ezra-Nehemiah." Japhet's view is supported by many following scholars. For example, Williamson, *Israel*; Kelly, *Retribution and Eschatology*.

39. Willi (Willi, *Auslegung*, 176–84), Welten, and Rudolph, think that the same author wrote the two distinctive works, while they do not consider the two works to have different ideologies or linguistic styles.

40. Williamson, *Israel*, 10–11; Willi, *Auslegung*, 176–84.

41. For example, Japhet, "Authorship of Chronicles and Ezra-Nehemiah.";

few of them here. The repetition of the first part of Ezra-Nehemiah at the end of Chronicles (or the other way round),[42] should be taken as having particular significance for the issue. In earlier days when the two works were generally regarded as one body by one author, this repetition was understood as major evidence for the unity of the two works.[43] However, as Welch pointed out and following scholars have agreed, the repetition itself in fact shows that the two works were not produced as one body, for "men do not take the trouble to stitch together two documents unless they have been originally separate."[44] However, it should not be overlooked that the repetition itself also betrays that there was a conscious effort to link the two works, unless it was a pure coincidence. If it was not a coincidence, it is plain that the author of the later work, whichever it was, willingly accepted the previous one, and intended to relate his own to the other one meaningfully.[45] Williamson, who argues for the separate authorship of the two works and also emphasizes the ideological difference between them, regards 2 Chr 36:22–23 as a later addition borrowed from Ezra 1:1–3 and modified.[46] However, the overall points he proposes to argue his view can be countered as follows. Firstly, Williamson thinks that the ending of Chronicles with וְיָ֫עַל is "quite unnatural" and maintains that 2 Chr 36:21 is a more plausible ending of the work. However, he overlooks the literary

Williamson, *Israel*, 7–11; Braun, "Chronicles, Ezra and Nehemiah."

42. Japhet (Japhet, "Chronicles, Book of," 532) and Williamson (Williamson, *1 and 2 Chronicles*, 419) agree that the Chronicler's work originally ended with 2 Chr 36:21 and 36:22–23 was added later on the basis of Ezra 1:1–3.

43. Zunz, *Die gottesdienstlichen Vorträge*, 22; Rudolph, *Esra und Nehemia*, XXII. Rudolph uses this case as the sole basis of his view that the two works are in unity.

44. Welch, *Post-Exilic*, 186; Williamson, *Israel*, 7; Kidner, *Ezra and Nehemiah*, 137. Williamson, in a similar stance, states that there is no other case like this in the Biblical texts, where repetition of a literary piece is used in order to indicate the succession of the two works (Williamson, *Israel*, 8). However, it is observed that the New Testament works, Luke and Acts shows a similar phenomenon, although the parallel passages are less precisely similar to each other than those of Chronicles and Ezra-Nehemiah. That is, Jesus' order for his disciples to stay in Jerusalem until they receive the promised one from above (the Holy Spirit), appears in the end part of Luke (24:49) and in the beginning part of Acts (1:4–5). Hamilton also suggests that Exod 1:1–6's resuming Gen 46:8–27 is a similar case, although he acknowledges that it is "not a perfect parallel" (Hamilton, *Historical Books*, 503).

45. Kidner shows the same view in remarking that "The fact that the final paragraph of Chronicles points the reader firmly to Ezra for the sequel can be argued either way; for while it makes a firm bond between the books it is also true that, as Welch remarked, "men do not take the trouble to stitch together two documents unless they have been originally separate'" (Kidner, *Ezra and Nehemiah*, 137).

46. Williamson, *Israel*, 9–10.

technique employed at this significant conclusion of the work. When the significance of the temple theme through the work is considered, its reappearance at the very end of the work is not only natural and meaningful, but also dramatic and skilful. Moreover, the seemingly abrupt ending provokes the reader into a dynamic expectation and a sense of being called to participate in this special and honorable task, as the final impression of the book.[47] When it is recalled that the genealogy which opens the work has the perspective of the whole of mankind and through the work the focal point of the whole world is nowhere else but the temple, the edict for the rebuilding of the temple is even the necessary conclusion. Secondly, Williamson admits that "on the assumption that Chr. was written after Ezr.-Neh.," one may propose that 36:22 ff. is designed to "indicate to the reader where the continuation of the story might be found." But he maintains that 36:21 is sufficient enough to do that role, for 36:20–21 already contains the idea of "the end of the exile" and "a clear indication of the liberation to be granted by the Persians (v. 20a). However, Williamson's approach to this issue may miss the real point. The repetition is not used merely to "indicate" to the readers where to look for a successive reading, but to make an impressive ending, and to remind the readers of the profound meaning and significance of the rebuilding of the temple among the returned exile community, and what its ongoing obligation or task should now be. Furthermore, in fact 36:21 is not sufficient to "indicate to the reader where the continuation of the story might be found." Thirdly and finally, Williamson also maintains that the different wording of Jeremiah's name (יִרְמְיָהוּ in 2 Chr 36:22 / יִרְמְיָה in Ezra 1:1) and "by mouth" (בְּפִי in 2 Chr 36:22 / מִפִּי in Ezra 1:1) between the two works is the result of later assimilation by a scribe who was conscious of the earlier verse i.e., 2 Chr 36:21(בְּפִי יִרְמְיָהוּ). This is possible, but no more than mere speculation. Instead, it is more likely that the very same phenomenon can be construed as pointing to the opposite conclusion. That is, the same form of language between 2

---

47. Selman also thinks that "to build him a house" in the last verse is "a deliberate echo of the central promise of the Davidic covenant (cf. 1 Ch. 17:11–12; 22:10; 28:6; 2 Ch. 6:9–10)" (Selman, *2 Chronicles*, 551). David Gunn also notices the significance of the last verse, and states that "The end of Kings is a gaping hole which, when we peer into it, loops us back to Deuteronomy, to where we stand "today" before Moses, "outside," pondering the invitation to enter and participate in a new gift. The end of Chronicles bridges that gulf surely, converts desolation into a Sabbath (2 Chr 36:21), and marches us resolutely toward an unambiguous goal—to build Yhwh a house. Cyrus' decree (36:23; Ezra 1:3) strikingly resumes David's charge to Solomon (1 Chr 22:6, 18–19)" (Gunn, "In Security," 147). A similar case is observed at the end of Jonah (4:10–11), with God's provoking question toward Jonah.

Chr 36:21 and 22 can be construed as evidence which shows that 2 Chr 36:22 ff. is an original part of the work, which reflects the author's inherent intention to link his work to Ezra-Nehemiah in a significant way.[48]

As for the composition order of the two works, the present study presumes that Ezra-Nehemiah was produced first, then Chronicles later. Again, while scholarly discussions are ongoing on this issue, only one more point will be noted here,[49] in order to support the assumption of this study. That is, the comparative observation of the list of the people and their population in Jerusalem in 1 Chr 9:2–34 and Neh 11:3–19, with the common-sense presumption that the population usually increases over time, leads to the tentative conclusion that Chronicles was produced after Ezra-Nehemiah.[50]

3.2. The Date of the Composition of Chronicles

Notoriously, different suggestions have been presented on the issue of the date of composition of Chronicles.[51] It should be acknowledged that a circular logic prevails regarding supposed evidence of later composition and supposed later additions; for example, by regarding a mark of later time as a later addition, one can maintain one's position of an earlier date. As Kelly suggests, following Selman, the dating of the original work and its later addition(s) are rather a matter of "starting points" of

48. Williamson thought that Japhet regarded 2 Chr 36:22f as original and fortuitously same to Ezra 1:1–3 (Williamson, *Israel*, 8). However, in fact Japhet also thinks that 2 Chr 36:22f is later addition on the basis on Ezra 1:1–3 (Japhet, *I & II Chronicles*, 1062, 1076).

49. For example, Williamson thinks that Chronicles (final form ca. 350 B.C.) predates Ezra-Nehemiah (final form ca. 300 B.C.) (Williamson, *Ezra, Nehemiah*, 47), while Japhet considers Ezra-Nehemiah (not "later than the first quarter of the fourth century BCE; Japhet, "Sheshbazzar and Zerubbabel," 89 n. 55) to predate Chronicles ("at the end of the Persian or, more probably, the beginning of the Hellenistic period, at the end of the fourth century BCE"; Japhet, *I & II Chronicles*, 27–28). Johnstone also predates Ezra-Nehemiah (Johnstone, "Guilt and Atonement," 114; Johnstone, "Reactivating the Chronicles Analogy").

50. Selman thinks that "the Chronicles version seems belong to a period approximately half a generation later than Nehemiah's list," on the observation (Selman, *1 Chronicles*); Kelly, "passage of a few years" on the same observation (Kelly, *Retribution and Eschatology*, 27). Kelly provides three more occasions that reveal, he believes, that "The Chronicler knew and made use of Ezra-Nehemiah" (Kelly, *Retribution and Eschatology*, 27–28); Riley has the same view (Riley, *King and Cultus in Chronicles*, 26).

51. For the various suggestions of the composition date, see the list provided by Throntveit, *When Kings Speak*, 97.

scholars.[52] For example, the early dating of ca. 515 B.C., suggested by Freedman, and followed by Newsome and Cross,[53] has its attraction in the fact that the cluster of the concerns—the Davidic dynasty, the temple, and prophecy—seem to point to its early composition, i.e., shortly after the return of exiles, when the expectation of restoration of the dynasty was lively. This view, however, requires that, for example, 1 Chr 1–9 be regarded as a later addition, because it includes conspicuous material that indicates a later-date composition. It is plain that this view almost unconsciously presumes that those concerns cannot be sustained in the post-exilic community for long.

On the contrary, other scholars like Selman and Williamson, thinking 1 Chr 1–9 is an integral part of the work, and consequently dating the composition at a later time, argue that there is no reason why an interest in the dynasty, temple, and prophecy should be extinguished after the early days,[54] or further point out that it is "most striking" to see that even after about two hundred years without a king, the Israelites maintained the hope for the restoration of their dynasty.[55]

Considering that the view that 1 Chr 1–9 is an integral part of the whole work has been more and more approved by recent studies,[56] and the simple fact that there is no clear evidence to show that 1 Chr 1–9 is a secondary addition, it is reasonable to take the genealogy in 1 Chr 3:17–24 as the most decisive clue to the date of composition. However, the ambiguity of this text, especially of verses 21–24, has produced diverse interpretations.[57] Although Williamson cautiously suggests that only two

52. Selman, *1 Chronicles*, 74; Kelly, *Retribution and Eschatology*, 26.

53. Braun also suggests the original shape of the book was formed about 515 B.C. and the final form was reached about 350–300 B.C. through the process proposed by Cross, while acknowledging that any time within the wide range of about 515–250 B.C. is possible. (Braun, *1 Chronicles*, xxix).

54. Williamson, "Eschatology," 129.

55. Selman, "The Kingdom of God," 170. Selman sees the composition date of Chronicles in ca. 400 B.C., leaving the possibility of any date in the fourth century (Selman, *1 Chronicles*, 71).

56. Johnstone, "Guilt and Atonement"; Johnson, *The Purpose of the Biblical Genealogies*, 44–55 (76), 69–71 (structure conforms to the narrative); Oeming, "'Vorhalle' 1 Chronik 1–9"; Selman, *1 Chronicles*, 75. Previously, Welch thought the genealogy chapters do not have unity and do not fit the narrative, regarding them as secondary addition (Welch, *Post-Exilic*, 185ff).

57. Kelly thinks "at least five generation after Zerubbabel" (Kelly, *Retribution and Eschatology*, 27), Japhet, "from seven to fourteen generations after Jehoiachin" (Japhet, *I & II Chronicles*, 26), Selman, "a minimum of five or a maximum of ten generations after Zerubbabel" (Selman, *1 Chronicles*, 70–71; LXX extends the genealogy to the

generations after Zerubbabel[58] are secured with certainty for the safest construction, it is not impossible to propose a reasonable construction of that part of genealogy. We can solve the problem of the alleged ambiguity. The crucial part is verse 21–22a; the names in verse 21 ("The descendants of Hananiah: Pelatiah and Jeshaiah, and the sons of Rephaiah, sons of Arnan, sons of Obadiah, and sons of Shecaniah") and 22a ("The descendants of Shecaniah: Shemaiah and his sons, Hattush, Igal, Bariah, Neariah and Shaphat, six") can be construed as each belonging to the same generation. The justification for this is as follows.

Firstly, there is no indication that the names in each verse come from different generations. If these names were intended to designate successive generations in each verse, 1 Chr 3:21–22a should be regarded as extremely odd or clumsy writing, which is unlikely, or a case of textual corruption, which does not need to be supposed, as will be explained in the following argument. Secondly, this construction is well harmonized with the appearance of Hattush, the descendants of David, the sons of Shecaniah in Ezra 8:3 (ca. 458) and Shemiah, son of Shecaniah in Neh 3:29 (ca. 445), in the three generations after Zerubbabel (ca. 538), in each case.[59] Thirdly, the elements that have been regarded as problematic to reasonable construction can be explained as follows. Regarding the uneven juxtaposition, i.e., Pelatiah and Jeshaiah, and the sons of Rephaiah, sons of Arnan, sons of Obadiah and sons of Shecaniah in verse 21, it is not strange to have this arrangement, if adoption is presumed here, as Jacob adopts Joseph's two sons as his own (Gen 48:5). Hananiah's adopting his four sons' children might have been the result of an epidemic or disaster of some kind, which may explain the unusual cluster of grandchildren through four sons. As for the seemingly problematic number six in verse 22, it is possible to explain in a wider perspective. It should be noted that the number of sons of a person is not usually given in the genealogy. While ordinal numbers appear for the sons of David (3:1–4a) and Josiah (3:15), the numbers of sons exceptionally appear from Zerubbabel's children to Elioenai's (19b–24). The introduction of numbers in this part can be regarded as an intentional device to clarify or demarcate a generation from others, where, otherwise, it would have been hard to discern each generation from others due to

---

eleventh generation after Zerubbabel)

58. Williamson, "Eschatology," 121; Williamson, *1 and 2 Chronicles*, 16. Williamson follows Harrison, *Introduction to OT*, 1155.

59. Selman, *1 Chronicles*, 101. However, Williamson regards 1 Chr 3:22 ff. as a secondary addition (Williamson, "Eschatology," 123).

its unusual complexity.[60] The seemingly incorrect number six at the end of verse 22 is explicable in this light. That is, the number is introduced ultimately to distinguish each generation from the others, and Shemaiah and his sons are possibly counted as one,[61] resulting in the total number of Shecaniah's sons being six. The absence of number at the end of verse 21 can be explained by its being unnecessary there, because the reappearance of the term "sons of Shecaniah" plainly indicates that the next generation is about to be introduced. Counting a generation as twenty-five years[62] (which is supported by the cases of Hattush (Ezra 8:3) and Shemaiah (Neh 3:29)), the last generation of the Davidic line, the sons of Ellioenai is ca. 413 (538 (Zerubbabel) – 125 (five generations) = 413). Thus, the composition date can be reasonably assumed to be between 413 and 388 B.C. (before the next generation appears). That means ca. 400 B.C. can be a reasonable date for the composition.[63]

Some scholars prefer later-composition dates, and argue that the part from verse 21b is a secondary addition,[64] or that the genealogy can be construed as having a maximum ten generations after Zerubbabel (or

---

60. Another intention of the introduction of the numbers this part of the geneal-ogy, seems to be to show the concern with the prosperity of the Davidic line in the re-cent generations, implying the restoration hope of the dynasty, which will be discussed later. Williamson sees "a witness to a continuing interest in the Davidic line" here (Wil-liamson, "Eschatology," 129), while not noticing the significance of the introduction of the numbers.

61. Cf. Gen 49:1–28 where it is clearly stated that the last blessing of Jacob is for twelve tribes of Israel (v. 28) and, Ephraim and Manasseh the sons of Joseph are count-ed as one, being absorbed in Joseph, although it has been already declared that the two became direct sons to Jacob just as Reuben and Simeon (Gen 48:5).

62. According to Albright, the average time span of a generation calculated from the ancient Near East royal lines is twenty to twenty-five years (Albright, "The Date and Personality of the Chronicler," 110).

63. While some scholars prefer this date, for example, Myers, *I Chronicles*, IXXX-VI–IXXIX; Selman, *1 Chronicles*, 71; Harrison, *Introduction to OT*, 1157, "closing decades of the fifth century B.C. or slightly later," many other scholars do not exclude ca. 400 B.C. for the composition. For example, Williamson who prefers "middle of the fourth century B.C." with the condition that the institution of "twenty four priestly courses" is the development "from two incidents from very late in the Persian period," thinks that a date "within the fourth century BC is most probable" (Williamson, *1 and 2 Chronicles*, 16). Braun who prefers the original writing about 515 B.C., and final edition about 350–300 B.C., leaves wide possibility as any date from about 515–250 B.C. (Braun, *1 Chronicles*, xxix). Kelly, "a date at some point in the fourth century BCE, perhaps the earlier half" (Kelly, *Retribution and Eschatology*, 27).

64. Williamson, "Eschatology," 123.

fourteen after Jehoiachin[65]). It is not hard to see that the phenomenon of the prolonged genealogy, through slight alterations,[66] in the Greek version (also, Syriac and Vulgate versions), is the result of failing to perceive the intention of the device of the numbers in the original genealogy. In those texts, the numbers neither fit in the altered genealogy neatly, nor are explainable. However, if the proposal of the construction of the genealogy suggested above is accepted, it excludes the possibility that 3:19–24 is later additional material after the original composition, and consequently, a more precise date is now given to reconstruct the *Sitz im Leben* of the work. Admittedly, dating the work on the basis of the analogy of the genealogy is somewhat narrowly based. However, it should also be noted that the work does not provide a more reliable and decisive hint than this.[67]

3.3. A Possible Sitz im Leben and the Purpose of Chronicles

As has been proposed already, if Ezra-Nehemiah precedes Chronicles, the composition date of Ezra-Nehemiah should fall between 425 B.C., when Nehemiah's return, cleansing the temple, and restoration of several backslidings occurred, and ca. 400 B.C., when Chronicles was produced.[68] The fact that the book of Nehemiah ends with Nehemiah's ongoing struggle in 425 B.C., and that Nehemiah the governor retired before 408 B.C. (or his successor took up the position in 410 B.C.) according to the Elephantine

65. In Japhet's calculation, taking twenty years for a generation and starting from Jehoiachin, the date falls between about 460 and 320 B.C. (Japhet, *I & II Chronicles*, 26). With other considerations, Japhet prefer "end of Persian or, more probably, the beginning of the Hellenistic period, at the end of the fourth century BCE" (Japhet, *I & II Chronicles*, 27–28).

66. From the "sons of Rephaiah" (v. 21), the Greek version changed plural "sons" into singular "son," and at the same time, the "son(s)" is construed as being linked to the previous name instead of to the next name.

67. Riley also relies upon the material as the crucial hint to decide the date. However, he avoids suggesting a more specific time than "the late Persian period" (Riley, *King and Cultus in Chronicles*, 26).

68. The present study presupposes that the date of Nehemiah's initial journey to Jerusalem is 445 BC according to the near consensus view (which sees the Artaxerxes in Nehemiah as Artaxerxes I), and that the date of Ezra's journey to Jerusalem is 458 B.C. according to the traditional view (which sees the Artaxerxes in Ezra as Artaxerxes I). A major alternative view of the date of Ezra's journey comes from seeing the Artaxerxes as Artaxerxes II. Another alternative view comes from reading "seventh year of Artaxerxes (I)" as "thirty-seventh year of Artaxerxes (I)." For a convenient summary of the scholarly discussion of the chronological order of Ezra and Nehemiah, see Williamson, *Ezra and Nehemiah*, 55–68 Hamilton, *Historical Books*, 504–6.

papyri (discovered in 1903), may support this view of Ezra-Nehemiah's composition date. From these presumptions, it is possible, with a certain degree of speculation, to reconstruct the *Sitz im Leben* and the basic motif or purpose of Chronicles as follows. Chronicles was produced to encourage the people of the post-exilic community to keep maintaining the temple cult, and hope for the future in the face of ongoing challenges that were undermining the accomplishment of the restoration until and through the Ezra-Nehemiah program. In such a situation, the people needed to be reminded of the positive meaning of the temple and its services, as a token of hope, which is closely related to the Davidic covenant, as Kelly suggests,[69] together with practical lessons for their present life. Reminding the people of the true meaning of the temple, which had been rebuilt among them by and as a token of the sovereign grace of God, must have been a stimulus for the people. They were experiencing ongoing challenges or setbacks which were against or undermining the restoration program.

This view is well matched with the fact that (1) Chronicles is located at the end of the Hebrew canon, and (2) the beginning part of Ezra-Nehemiah reappears at the end of Chronicles so that it becomes clear that the initial restoration described at the end of the Chronicles (although challenges and setbacks keep impeding it, as is shown in Ezra-Nehemiah), has the implication that the Davidic covenant would be fulfilled some day in the future by the sovereign God who had enabled the temple to be built again.

While the *Sitz im Leben* of Ezra-Nehemiah, and Chronicles, is uncertain, because of the paucity of knowledge of the Persian period, if the composition date above is accepted, a plausible situation of Chronicles and Ezra-Nehemiah can be suggested. When it was decided that Nehemiah should leave his post as Jerusalem governor ca 410, he might have wished, good leader that he was as shown through the work, to prepare or to establish some devices for his absence. The device, on one hand, would enable the community to keep the restoration program started since Zerubbabel's return, and on the other hand, prevent the backsliding of the program. The possibility of the backsliding had been fully revealed by what had happened during his short absence (Neh 13:4 ff.).

---

69. Kelly's conclusion is agreeable in this regard. Kelly concludes that "although Ezra-Nehemiah showed that the initial Return appeared to have failed to obtain its bright objectives of a renewed and faithful community (this seems the likeliest way of reading the rather dismaying conclusion in Nehemiah 13, in which the sin of intermarriage persists), the Chronicler nevertheless affirms that earlier work of restoration as a decisive and positive stage in 'building Yahweh's house,' and he puts it in the context of God's irrefrangible promise to David" (Kelly, *Retribution and Eschatology*, 233).

It is plausible that Nehemiah ordered a narrative document to be produced which would show the history of the restoration program from the beginning, with rich lessons that he had learned from earlier events of history and his own experience, and that, he hoped, would live long in the hearts of the people and his successors, in order to continue or maintain the program. An able and creditable man was appointed for this serious task, and sufficient materials with the necessary information, including Nehemiah's diary or memoir, were provided for this purpose.[70] Having the necessary material in his hand, the author might not necessarily have needed a long period of time in order to produce a work of such size.[71] To make the reader realize that the restoration program had not finished yet and how easily backsliding could happen, the work should end the way it does now (Neh 13). It implies that continuous alert and effort should be sustained. The intended arrangement of the material 13:4bff., after the mark of "before this" (וְלִפְנֵי מִזֶּה) (13:4a), in order to put the following meaningful episodes at the end of the work, can also be explained in the same light. In this sense, the possibility that Ezra wrote "Ezra-Nehemiah" at Nehemiah's request cannot be excluded, as Talmudic tradition suggests.[72] Furthermore, the fact that the style of editorial material of Ezra-Nehemiah is similar to that of Ezra's memoirs, but unlike Nehemiah's, may support this view.[73]

---

70. According to 2 Maccabees, which was "a letter purporting to be addressed by the Jews of Jerusalem and Jud[a]ea to the Jews of Egypt it is recalled that Nehemiah in his day 'founded a library and collected the books about the kings and prophets, and the writings of David, and letters of kings about votive offerings'" (2 Macc 2:13, quoted in Bruce, *The Canon of Scripture*, 38), it is probable that Nehemiah was concerned with producing a document like Chronicles, except his own memoirs.

71. Contrary to Williamson's conjecture of the long period process of the composition of Ezra-Nehemiah (Williamson, *Ezra, Nehemiah*, xxxiii–xxxvi). Kidner's view agrees with the present proposal of the composition date. He states that "we shall not need to postulate any appreciable interval between the events and their recording." Kidner suggests "at any time from the last years of Darius II (423–404) onward" (Kidner, *Ezra and Nehemiah*, 138).

72. Baba Bathra 15a states that "Ezra wrote his book and the genealogies of the Book of Chronicles up to his own time . . . who then finished? Nehemiah the son of Hacaliah" (quoted from Japhet, *I & II Chronicles*, 23). If "his book" is "Ezra-Nehemiah," then this Talmudic tradition is well matched with the present proposal of the composition date and *Sitz im Leben* of Ezra-Nehemiah and Chronicles. That is, both Ezra-Nehemiah and Chronicles were separately produced at the request of Nehemiah in his day, with a short interval between.

73. Kidner, *Ezra and Nehemiah*, 138.

Presupposing the *Sitz im Leben* of the composition of Ezra-Nehemiah as above, it is possible to reconstruct that of Chronicles with some degree of speculation. After Nehemiah left his office (most likely to return to Susa, the capital of the Persian empire), Nehemiah's hope proved to be vulnerable (Neh 13:4ff.). Sooner or later, without the presence of an excellent leader like Nehemiah, cultic order and its maintenance became easily neglected. Hence, the overall faith of the community needed, on the one hand, to be stimulated by a theology of immediate retribution, and on the other hand, to be encouraged by the ultimate hope of dynastic restoration through the grace of a sovereign God, which is guaranteed by the rebuilt temple.

Furthermore, to emphasize the significance of the restoration community as God's chosen community around the temple, and consequently to infuse them with a solemn sense of duty, a history on a vast scale, which starts with the beginning of the human race and ends with the starting point of the restoration program, should be produced.[74]

As for the author of Chronicles, presuming ca. 400 B.C. for the composition date,[75] the possibility that the author is Ezra (the co-worker of Nehemiah) is not necessarily excluded.[76] However, it is still impossible to

---

74. Having proposed the above as a possible *Sitz im Leben* of the composition of Chronicles, it will be too much to suggest here whether Chronicles was produced by following an order from Nehemiah now being remote from Jerusalem or somebody else, or by the author's own will, and also whether the task of producing Chronicles was given to the one who had produced Ezra-Nehemiah not long time before, or to somebody else.

75. The evidence for this date, together with the relevant bibliography, is provided in Bright, *A History of Israel*, 398–99.

76. Albright thinks that the identity of the Chronicler is Ezra on the grounds that "the Chronicler's literary peculiarities" appear most conspicuously in Ezra 7–10, Neh 8–10 and that there are many common expressions and words between the Chronicler's and the Ezra memoirs, following Torrey (*Composition*, 11–20; *Ezra Studies*, 238–48), while both scholars presume single authorship of Chronicles and Ezra-Nehemiah (Albright, "The Date and Personality of the Chronicler," 119). As for Ezra's time, Albright proposes that Ezra came to Judea in the reign of Artaxerxes II (404–359) rather than Artaxerxes I (465–425), and takes the early fourth century as the composition date (104–24). On the other side, Harrison similarly takes the "closing decades of the fifth century B.C." or slightly later time for composition date (Harrison, *Introduction to OT*, 1157), and admits that it is compatible with the authorship of Ezra in regards composition date (1153). But he does not think that Ezra is the Chronicler for the reason that there are "significant differences in style, historical and theological perspective, the treatment of source material, and the basic metaphysic of history . . . in the two compositions" (1157). However, deciding whether the Chronicler is Ezra or not is not the concern of the present study.

identify him with any certainty, except to say that the author was able to get the basic documents from the temple archives, the authoritative institution or from Ezra or Nehemiah themselves (in case he is the same person who produced Ezra-Nehemiah). The conspicuous concern of the work for the Levites and the temple singers has been regarded as suggesting the possibility that he was one of them. However, it should be admitted not only that the view cannot be maintained with any substantial certainty,[77] but also that it can be construed as simply reflecting the author's concern for cultic duty and praise.[78]

3.4. The Themes and the Purpose of Chronicles

The diverse suggestions of the composition date are related not only to specific indicative passages in the work,[79] but also to a supposed specific purpose of the work. Proposing a specific purpose, for example, anti-Samaritan propaganda,[80] is closely related to identifying the composition date of the work. The current scholarly trend is that one single purpose cannot explain the complexity of the work.[81] Rather, theological themes,

77. Selman, 1 Chronicles, 71.

78. Rudolph, "Problems," 407–8.

79. For example, Hellenistic armies and catapults (2 Chr 26:15), which were proposed by Welten as a mark of late date (Welten, Geschichte und Geschichtsdarstellung, 199–200) though this is squarely refuted by Williamson (Williamson, Israel, 83–86); "darics" (1 Chr 29:7) named after Darius I (522–486 B.C, cf. Williamson, "Eschatology," 123–26) and not known to have been minted before 515 B.C. (Selman, 1 Chronicles, 71); "birah" (Persian loan-word, 1 Chr 29:1, 19); the genealogical list of five to ten generations (because of ambiguity of the passage) after Zerubbabel in 1 Chr 3:19–24 (while Greek, Syriac and Vulgate versions contain eleven generations after Zerubbabel, pointed out by Throntveit in Throntveit, When Kings Speak, 98); plausible quotation of Zech 4:10 in 2 Chr 16:9, which is, however, refuted as evidence of the contemporary composition (Williamson, 1 and 2 Chronicles, 15–16), 2 Chr 36:20–23. The absence of Greek trace in the work is usually taken as evidence that Chronicles was produced before the influx of Greek influence upon the post-exilic Israel community on the basis that Greek terms are absent in the work. It means that the date seems to be earlier than the third century B.C. (Newsome, "Chronicler and His Purposes," 202–3; Albright, "The Date and Personality of the Chronicler," 104–24; Williamson, 1 and 2 Chronicles, 16.)

80. Noth, Chronicler's History, 97–106; Galling, Chronik, Esra, Nehemia; Plöger, Theocracy and Eschatology, 40, 404.

81. Japhet, I & II Chronicles, 43–44. "It is doubtful, however, whether one single and unilateral purpose would account for such an enormous enterprise, with all its complexities of content and form. Chronicles is not a manifesto devoted to a specific political movement but a more general and comprehensive theological stock-taking,

which are conspicuous in the work, are the main concerns of recent scholarly discussion, as reflecting the author's interests and concerns. Reflecting this tendency, some major scholars do not treat the issue of the purpose of the work in the sense of specific political propaganda, which had been the usual area of scholars' concern regarding the purpose of Chronicles.[82] Rather, the genre[83] or its main theological themes are treated under the title of the Chronicler's purpose in their work.[84]

In the discussion of the themes of Chronicles, fortunately, there is agreement on many issues among scholars, with of course some disagreements on details or on other subjects. Areas of agreement include God's active intervention in history,[85] immediate retribution,[86] emphasis on the heart's devotion to God,[87] emphasis on cult and cultic ceremony,[88] emphasis on the temple,[89] emphasis on the Davidic monarchy,[90] the prominence of the Davidic monarchy and the Jerusalem temple as the twin institutions installed by God, the unity of the reigns of David and Solomon,[91] and the

---

striving to achieve a new religious balance in the face of a changing world. . . . It is from this 'total' perspective that the grand historical and theological enterprise should be judged" (43–44).

82. For example, "Apology for Judaism" (Pfeiffer), "Justification of the Levitical Priesthood" (von Rad), "Legitimacy of the Dynasty" (Freedman). Scholars cannot and do not insist on only one single purpose of the work in a strict sense, because of the complexity of the work. For example, Noth acknowledges that the legitimacy of the Davidic dynasty and Jerusalem temple as an important concern of the Chronicler, while maintaining that the emphasis serves ultimately as anti-Samaritan propaganda (Jones, *1 & 2 Chronicles*, 107). As for W. Rudolph, both anti-Samaritan and anti-eschatological (in other word, realized theocracy perspective) propaganda is the purpose of Chronicler's work (Williamson, "Eschatology," 118).

83. Jones, *1&2 Chronicles*, 109–10, "An Interpretation of History"; McKenzie, *1–2 Chronicles*, 33–34, "Genre and Purpose."

84. For example, Japhet, *I & II Chronicles*, 43–49.

85. For example, Jones, *1&2 Chronicles*, 113–17; Hooker, *First and Second Chronicles*, 6–7, 10.

86. For example, Braun, *1 Chronicles*, xxxvii–xxxix; Williamson, *1 and 2 Chronicles*, 31–33; McKenzie, *1–2 Chronicles*, 51–52.

87. For example, Braun, *1 Chronicles*, xl–xli; Klein, *1 Chronicles*, 47; Williamson, *1 and 2 Chronicles*, 30–31; John C. Endres, "The Spiritual Vision of Chronicles," 1–21.

88. For example, Jones, *1&2 Chronicles*, 126–30; Thompson, *1, 2 Chronicles*, 35–36.

89. For example, Braun, *1 Chronicles*, xxix–xxxi; Williamson, *1 and 2 Chronicles*, 28ff; Selman, *1 Chronicles*, 56–59; McKenzie, *1–2 Chronicles*, 49–50; Dirksen, *1 Chronicles*, 12–13, 19–20.

90. For example, Jones, *1&2 Chronicles*, 122–26; Selman, *1 Chronicles*, 45–51.

91. For example, Braun, *1 Chronicles*, xxxv; Williamson, *1 and 2 Chronicles*, 27; McKenzie, *1–2 Chronicles*, 48. In the earlier discussion, Im proposes the excellence

inclusive "all Israel" concept.[92] It is also acknowledged that some of these themes overlap each other to a certain extent. Among those observations, not a few themes are closely related to the interpretation of the Solomon account in Chronicles. In this sense, the Solomon account is crucial for the understanding of the theological stance and the purpose of the whole of Chronicles. Most of those (near-consensus) views are accepted by the present study with small modifications or comments on the "divine activity" view and the "immediate retribution" view.

Regarding the "divine activity in history" theme, it should be acknowledged that an active God not only appears in the retribution situations,[93] but also in his initiative on the matters of the establishment of the monarchy and the project of the temple building. That is, concerning the monarchy, God himself changes monarchies (1 Chr 10:14), and makes his promise with eternal effect (1 Chr 17:12, 14), which is "unilateral"[94] and different from the previous case (1 Chr 17:13) according to his arbitrary will, appointing the first Davidic successor (1 Chr 22:9–10). As for the temple building, God himself chooses the place for the temple (1 Chr 21:18–19 cf. 1 Chr 22:1), the temple builder (1 Chr 22:9–10), and even the plan of the temple (1 Chr 28:11–19, especially 28:12, 19). On the immediate retribution theme, the present study acknowledges that it is true that the "immediate retribution" perspective is a strong point of the work, however, it also notices that other retribution perspectives, i.e., accumulative retribution and "grace given to the undeserving" perspectives (e.g., 2 Chr 21:7) appear in the same work.[95] (That the Solomon account itself is

---

of David in Chronicles (Im, *Davidbild in den Chronikbüchern*), while Mosis sees the most ideal king in Solomon (Mosis, *Untersuchungen*). In Mosis's view, Saul, David and Solomon provide a distinctive framework for the following period. For him, Solomon is more ideal than David. However, his view is seriously refuted by Williamson on several grounds (Williamson, "Eschatology," 132–33).

92. For example, Braun, *1 Chronicles*, xxxv–xxxvii; Williamson, *1 and 2 Chronicles*, 24–26; Jones, *1&2 Chronicles*, 117–22; McKenzie, *1–2 Chronicles*, 50–51; Selman, *1 Chronicles*, 51–53.

93. For Japhet's view that God's action in history is mainly shown in his retributive action (Japhet, *I & II Chronicles*, 44–45).

94. McKenzie, *1–2 Chronicles*, 48.

95. Contra Japhet (Japhet, *I & II Chronicles*) "Reward is mandatory, immediate and individual. Every generation is requited for its own deeds, both good and evil, with no postponement of recompense; there is no accumulated sin and no accumulated merit" (44). In this regards, Selman's statement is noteworthy, "A number of David's descendants are treated more positively than in Kings, not because the Chronicler is any more lenient but because he sees in their lives explicit evidence of God's kindness to the undeserving. In fact, it is precisely because the Chronicler does not believe in

an example of this will be shown later.[96]) Having said this, we do not need to deny that the newly introduced emphasis on the scheme of "immediate retribution" in Chronicles has its own purpose: the work, with "immediate retribution" examples, makes "an urgent call to repentance" to the reader.[97]

3.5. The Restoration Hope and the Purpose of Chronicles

Another issue, which is closely related to the interpretation of the Solomon account of Chronicles, is whether the hope of restoration of the Davidic monarchy is reflected in the work.[98] In fact, this issue is also closely related to the purpose of the work. Unfortunately, scholarly opinions are divided into three positions on this issue. One can be called an "eschatological

---

automatic retribution that his account of rulers such as Solomon, Rehoboam (2 Ch. 11–12), Abijah (2 Ch. 13), and especially Manasseh (2 Ch. 33) differs so substantially from that of Kings." Selman also points out that "cumulative" attribution is present in Chronicles. (Selman, *1 Chronicles*, 62–63). In a similar stance to Selman, Rudolph also sees grace of God as the prevailing theology in the work (Rudolph, "Problems," 404–6). For the most systematic argument of this position, see Kelly, *Retribution and Eschatology*, 29–134; Kelly, "'Retribution' Revisited," 206–27; Klein, "The God of the Chronicler," 120–27. P. Dirksen describes it, "so the 'retribution' does not involve any kind of automatism. On the contrary, God's goodness and forgiving nature are paramount," pointing out the added material in 2 Chr 7:13–16 to the text of 1 Kgs 8.

It is plain that Jehoram, in spite of his evil deed, is preserved by the virtue of David or God's covenant with David (2 Chr 21:7). The case cannot be explained in the "immediate retribution theology," of which Japhet who advocates the dominance of the theology does not provide any explanation in her commentary (Japhet, *I & II Chronicles*, 809–10). Recently, Murray observes that not only "retribution" motif, but also "revival" motif in Chronicles, and he thinks that "revival" motif is "within the whole foundational Davidic-Solomonic narrative (1 Chron 11—2 Chron. 9) . . . actually bulks far larger than the retributional motif . . ." (81) (D. Murray, "Retribution and Revival," 77–99).

96. Contra McKenzie.

97. For McConville, "repentance" is one of the two aims of Chronicler's message to his contemporaries. The other is the message of salvation (McConville, *Chronicles*, 4–5).

98. Kelly categorizes scholars' positions under four distinctive titles, "messianic expectation that focuses upon an ideal Davidic king," "hopes of a dynastic restoration, either at the time of Zerubbabel or later (royalist hope)," "eschatology which nevertheless dos not involve monarchic restoration or a messianic expectation," and "non-eschatological and non-messianic," and provides the lists of scholars and their works according to these categories in his article which deals precisely with this issue (Kelly, "Messianic Elements"). For his third category, which is exceptional and will not be treated in this study, he puts R. Mosis (Mosis, *Untersuchungen*, 164–69, 211–14) and S. Japhet, (Japhet, *I & II Chronicles*, cf. 1077), however, it is doubtful that Japhet's view can be called in relation to "eschatology."

messianic hope," in the sense that the restoration of the Davidic monarchy is associated with a totally new order of the world which is different from the past and present,[99] while another can be called a "royalist hope," in the sense that the restoration of the Davidic monarchy is expected to happen within the same order of the world as the past and present one.[100] Far from those two positions, some scholars think that Chronicles justifies the *status quo* as the realization of Israel's ideal that previously appeared in the David-Solomon golden age, in the form of, now, cultic restoration in the comparatively peaceful post-exilic period under the authority of the Persian empire.[101] The basic stance of the present study is that, while it should be acknowledged that it is hard to prove that there is an explicit eschatological messianic hope in Chronicles, compared to prophetic writings in the post-exilic period,[102] the hope of restoration of the Davidic monarchy still underlies the whole work.

The reasons for this stance are as follows. First, the hope of monarchical restoration is most obviously detected in the frequent mention of the "eternity" of God's promise of the Davidic monarchy (e.g., 1 Chr 17:14). Second, it is evident that there is a clear, close, and mysterious association of the monarchy with the kingdom of God (e.g., 1 Chr 28:5), which by its own nature cannot fail.[103] Third, the restoration of one part of

99. For example, Keil, *1 & 2 Chronicles*; von Rad, *Geschichtsbild*; Stinespring, "Eschatology in Chronicles."

100. For example, Noth, *Chronicler's History*, 105–6; Wilda, "Das Königsbild"; Williamson, "Eschatology."

101. Rudolph, *Chronikbücher*, xiv-xxiii; Caquot, "Messianisme," 119–20; Bickerman, *Ezra to Maccabees*, 30; Rudolph, "Problems," 408–9; Riley, *King and Cultus in Chronicles*; Braun, *1 Chronicles*, xxvii. Rudolph, presupposing that the same author produced Chronicles and Ezra-Nehemiah, sees full realization of the idea of theocracy in Neh 12:44—13:3 (Rudolph, "Problems," 409). Plöger, *Theocracy and Eschatology*.

102. However, scholars such as Stinespring think that there is clear eschatological messianic hope in the work on the basis that the presentation of King David and the feature of supposed eschatological Messiah of the days is very similar. Stinespring, "Eschatology in Chronicles," 214–15. "The Messiah must be both *king* and *redeemer*. He must overthrow the enemies of Israel, establish the kingdom of Israel, and rebuild the temple; and at the same time he must reform the world through the kingdom of God, root out idolatry from the world, proclaim the one and only God to all, put an end to sin, and be wise, pious, and just as no man had been before him or ever would be after him. In short, he is the great political and spiritual hero at one and the same time" (J. Klausner, *The Messianic Idea in Israel*, tr. by W. F. Stinespring, 392). Also, it should be reminded that other biblical literatures like Zechariah 12–14, Daniel, (Joel without messianism but with eschatological faith) produced in the post-exilic period, contain so-called "eschatological messianism."

103. "Chronicler is quite clear that kingship and the kingdom in Israel ultimately

the twin institutions, the temple, strongly implies that the other institution is expected to be restored somehow.[104] Fourth, if, as is described in the case of the temple, God's sovereign grace is the source of the restoration, there is no reason that the monarchy, which has more abundant promise than the temple itself, will not be restored by God or his sovereign grace. Furthermore, when it is considered together with the fact that a significant theme of the work is that a change of fate always happens through repentance, even in an extremely gloomy situation, there is no reason why the Davidic monarchy cannot be restored in future in the perspective of Chronicles. Fifth, the continuing interest of Davidic line is shown in the

---

belong to God (1 Chr 10:14; 17:14; 29:23; 2 Chr 9:8; 13:8). . . . Since kingship is grounded in God, however, there is no question that it will continue beyond the exile" (McKenzie, *1–2 Chronicles*, 47–48). "'Kingdom of Yahweh' occurs in various forms only fifteen times, while 'kingdom of God' does not appear at all. 'Kingdom of Yahweh' in Pss 22:9 [*sic*]; 103:19; 145:11–13; Obad. 21; Dan. 2:44; 3:33 (EVV 4:3); 4:31 [EVV v. 34: my reference]; 6:27 (EVV v. 26); 7:14, 18, 27; 1 Chr. 17:14; 28:5; 29:11; 2 Chr. 13:8" (Selman, "The Kingdom of God," 162, and n. 7 on the same page). Selman argues that "God's kingdom is permanently linked with the Davidic dynasty" (Selman, "The Kingdom of God," 167). Selman maintains in his understating of 1 Chr 17:14, that "the juxtaposition of "my kingdom" and "his throne" confirms by divine decree that both kingdoms are to be permanent" (Selman, "The Kingdom of God," 164).

104. Selman seems to be on the same line when he states that "Despite Israel's current reduced circumstances and loss of the Davidic monarchy, the rebuilt temple is a visible sign that God is still at work. . . . They must take seriously the occupation of the land, and worship the God who promises eternal kingship to David line. God's purposes remain incomplete, and the future lies open to all who believe that God will not abandon what he has started. . . . He will yet keep his promise to set one of David's descents "over his house and his kingdom for ever (1 Ch. 17:14)" (Selman, *1 Chronicles*, 65). Selman's pointing out that "the kingdom of God is reflected in both 'houses' of the Davidic covenant, the Davidic dynasty and the Solomonic temple," is also significant here (Selman, "The Kingdom of God," 164); "this association between the temple and the kingdom of God was founded in the Davidic covenant. According to that covenant, the temple would be built by David's heir and successor. . . . Only when God's own house was established by Solomon's accession could David's successor build the house of God. . . . The latter house or temple was therefore a symbol of the former house or dynasty (1 Chr. 17:10–14). . . . Although the Davidic monarchy had long since disappeared, the rebuilt temple was very much a present reality. His [i.e., the Chronicler's] concern for the temple, its personnel and its practices was doubtless meant to encourage his contemporaries to take its worship seriously as a sign of their faith in the promises of God. By maintaining its sacrifices and not neglecting its Levites and priests, Israel might not only find continuing atonement for their sins but hope ultimately in the kingdom of God. The temple, therefore, whether Solomon's or Zerubbabel's, was not an end in itself, but a sign of something even greater than Solomon" [my insertion]. (Selman, "The Kingdom of God," 170). Kelly also notices the strong link between the temple and the Davidic covenant (Kelly, *Retribution and Eschatology*, 231).

genealogy,[105] even counting the numbers of the Davidic descendants in the comparatively recent period of the composition (1 Chr 3:20, 22, 23, 24), significantly leaving number seven at the end (1 Chr 3:24).[106] Sixth, reference to the seventy-years land Sabbaths (2 Chr 36:21) and the ensuing restoration of the temple (36:22–23) may hint at the possibility of the restoration of the Davidic dynasty, for the law of land Sabbaths as the result of God's punishment on Israel (Lev 26:34–35, 43) is closely related to the restoration promise of God who remembers his covenant with his people in its original context (i.e., his covenant with Jacob, that with Isaac, and that with Abraham in Lev 26:42; his covenant (through Moses) with those whom God brought out of Egypt in Lev 26:45–46). When the close relationship between the temple building and the Davidic dynasty is also considered, the reference to the land Sabbaths (2 Chr 36:21) and ensuing temple building (2 Chr 36:22–23) may also hint at the restoration of the Davidic dynasty, which was established through God's special covenant, unlike the Saulide dynasty. While it is obvious that Chronicles contains a variety of messages,[107] it should also be acknowledged that Chronicles sheds light on a future hope of the restoration of the Davidic monarchy.[108]

On the other hand, the post-exilic community did not regard its days as an ideal theocracy, as shown plainly in Neh 9:36–37 which confesses its state as that of servitude to foreign power. Rudolph's attempt to reduce this gloomy atmosphere by pointing out that "Ezra in Ezra ix 8f. has no word to say against heathen domination, but expresses rather the friendliness of the Persian authorities in their restoration of the Jerusalem temple,

---

105. Williamson, "Eschatology," 129.

106. Riley, maintaining that there is no Davidic restoration hope in Chronicles, points out that "The presence of the Sauline genealogy, therefore, makes it impossible to point to the David genealogy in 1 Chronicles 3 as a proof of the Chronicler's interest in a Davidic restoration . . ." (Riley, *King and Cultus in Chronicles*, 50–51). It is fair to admit that the Davidic genealogy itself cannot alone be a proof for the restoration hope of the dynasty, in the presence of the Sauline genealogy, which continues contemporarily. Nevertheless, it should be admitted that the Davidic genealogy (which shows significantly seven contemporary descendants) can be an element which alludes to the restoration hope of the dynasty, along with other stronger hints at the hope.

107. Begg, "'Seeking Yahweh' and the purpose of Chronicles"; Schaefer, "The significance of seeking God." Schaefer's proposal of the purpose of Chronicles is fully accepted by Duke and is employed as the basic presupposition of Duke's rhetorical analysis of Chronicles (Duke, *The Persuasive Appeal*).

108. Knoppers also believes that "the Chronicler is a monarchist," pointing out that in the Chronicler's description of Jehoshaphat's reformation, although it was written in the post-exilic period when the community did not have a king, the king's role was presented as vital (Knoppers, "Jehoshaphat's Judiciary").

and the peace and security which they guarantee,"[109] is not convincing. Firstly, Ezra 9:8 ff. itself has nothing to do with Neh 9:36–37, so cannot be used to dismiss it. Secondly, even in Ezra 9:8 the post-exiles condition is described not as "full relief," but "little (מְעַט) relief in our bondage." Furthermore, assuming 2 Chr 36:22–23 as an original and intentional link to Ezra-Nehemiah, designed by the Chronicler, it is hard to see that the Chronicler regarded his post-exilic community as an idealized theocracy and tried to reflect it in Chronicles.

Now, a question may arise: if Chronicles contains the hope of monarchical restoration, should not a subversive intention against the Persian empire, at least, have been hinted at in the work? It is plain that no subversive intention appears explicitly through the work. Rather, it is clear that, by virtue of or in the support of the Persian empire or the emperor who was used by God's will, the restoration of the temple was possible. Should not this observation be understood as evidence that supports the "already realized restoration" view? The question can be answered as follows. The failure of Israel as a God-established kingdom after all means that there is no hope on Israel's side. Only God can do something for the future of Israel, more specifically the restoration of the Davidic monarchy and the kingdom, as is the case with the temple. In this sense, the Chronicler dared not to agitate his people to rise against the foreign empire in any way, which, moreover, is acknowledged as God's means of grace for Israel, at the moment. All the Israelites can do is to wait for the sovereign God's gracious initiative on this matter. The way and time do not depend upon the Israelites, and consequently even the Chronicler himself cannot direct his people in a specific way on that matter. Therefore, lessons like "seek the Lord with whole heart" are a guideline for the people concerning how to live waiting for the restoration of the monarchy which will be achieved through the sovereign will of God.[110]

109. Rudolph, "Problems," 408.

110. Johnstone shows a similar view in stating that "It [Chronicles] offers a theology of hope in the dawning age that only God can bring about through the transformation of the present conditions of human life. And it endorses a pattern of life to be followed meantime as Israel awaits the fulfillment of these hopes" [my insertion] (Johnstone, *1 Chronicles 1–2 Chronicles 9*, 9). Mason's words "They are neither to plot rebellion nor to despair" (Mason, *Preaching the tradition*, 42) also express this stance well, although he does not see any hope of restoration of the Davidic dynasty (rather, he thinks that the Davidic dynasty is assimilated into the priestly theocracy), with which this study does not agree.

3.6. The Implication of the Nature and Purpose of Chronicles as the Working Hypothesis of the Present Study

The stance introduced above, which has resulted from the consideration of the nature and purpose of Chronicles, implies important points for the interpretation of the Solomon account. (1) As the co-establisher of both the temple and the monarchy, in the sense that David prepared the building project and Solomon accomplished it, and David initially received the promise of the dynasty and Solomon established the dynasty by his succession,[111] Solomon's portrayal is expected to be similar to David's.[112] In this sense, it is more probable that Solomon is presented as having flaws like David rather than flawless in contrast. (2) With the hope of monarchical restoration, Chronicles needed to describe the David-Solomon reign as an ideal to some extent, for that period was the most glorious in the history of Israel. In this sense, it is not unnatural that the glorious aspect of the reign became the main focus of the accounts of the two kings, for the period to be a model of the restoration of the monarchy and the kingdom in future. (3) If Chronicles is the second history, which relies heavily upon the authority of the first one, it is plausible that the Chronicler could not intend to hide Solomon's flaws which appear in the first one, but rather, possibly, should even hint at Solomon's flaws in order to obtain his reader's acceptance as far as the hints do not distract him or her from the presentation of the glorious aspects of Solomon. Moreover, if it is plain that a certain hint is inevitable to unfold the story-line of the history, specifically, the cause and result of the matter of division of the kingdom, it is more plausible that the Chronicler had no reason to hide Solomon's flaws which are involved in the division. (4) If God's graceful initiative is the fundamental source of the monarchy or the kingdom, it is not problematic for Solomon as well as David to have some flaws in his presentation. In fact, their flaws can highlight by contrast the sovereign grace of God, so that the case may give strong hope to the reader.

111. "Solomon's accession therefore a crucial moment . . . for God thereby established David's dynasty" (Selman, "The Kingdom of God," 168).

112. It can be reminded that Solomon's conquering of Hamath-zobah (2 Chr 8:3) is added in Chronicles, in order to present him as being similar to David as warrior, according to Japhet (Japhet, *Ideology*, 488), even taking the risk of undermining the image of temple builder as one who enjoys total peace.

4. CONCLUSION

In this chapter, several working hypotheses on the nature and the purpose of Chronicles are proposed, which includes related issues such as the date and setting of the composition. If it is accepted that the nature of Chronicles is a second history which relies heavily upon the first one as authoritative, then the interpretation of the Solomon narrative in Kings should be cautiously considered as prior knowledge of the supposed reader. (Hence comes the need to propose a satisfactory interpretation of the Solomon narrative in Kings, concerning his faults.) If one of the major purposes of Chronicles is to give hope of future restoration, by emphasizing God's grace given in spite of human faults (although immediate retribution theology is truly acknowledged to be emphasized in short term perspective in the work), then it is more likely that Solomon is not presented as an impeccable king (while it is acknowledged that as a model of the golden age of Israel, David and Solomon's united kingdom is presented more or less in an ideal color).[113]

113. The present chapter has proposed hypothetical stances of the present study on a variety of issues concerning the nature and purpose of Chronicles. However, the prime proposal of the dissertation, i.e., a new interpretation of Solomon's faults in Chronicles, using a reader-sensitive approach, is not heavily dependent on the detailed discussions of the present chapter. The nature of Chronicles as a second history that relies upon and exploits the reader's pre-knowledge of the first authoritative history is the most crucial working hypothesis. Other proposals on the related issues were proposed in order to reconstruct a plausible or possible *Sitz im Leben* of the composition of the work, and those proposals are not necessarily indispensable. In other words, the new interpretation is possible with other assumptions of the purpose, composition date, or *Sitz im Leben* of the work than the one proposed here.

5

Two Literary Features
of Chronicles

1. INTRODUCTION

THE LINGUISTIC CHARACTERISTICS OF Chronicles have been explored
by many scholars, especially in relation to those of Ezra-Nehemiah.[1] The
theological characteristics of Chronicles have also been debated on issues
such as "idealized David and Solomon," "Davidic dynasty," "eschatology,"
"immediate retribution," whether in relation to those of Ezra-Nehemiah
or not.[2] It could be said, however, that comparatively less attention has
been given to the literary characteristics of Chronicles as a whole, although
several analyses of limited passages have been attempted.[3] R. Duke's work

1. For example, Curtis and Madsen, *Chronicles*, 27–36; Driver, *Introduction*, 535–
40; Japhet, "Authorship of Chronicles and Ezra-Nehemiah"; Polzin, *Typology of Biblical
Prose*; Williamson, *Israel*, 37–59; Throntveit, "Linguistic Analysis and the Question of
Authorship"; Talshir, "A reinvestigation of the linguistic relationship"; Blenkinsopp,
Ezra-Nehemiah, 49–51.

2. For example, Kelly, *Retribution and Eschatology*; Williamson, "Eschatology";
Williamson, *Israel*, 60–70; Dillard, "Reward and Punishment"; Wellhausen, *Prolegomena to the History of Ancient Israel*, 203–10; von Rad, "Levitical Sermon." For a list of
the study of retribution, see Dillard, "Reward and Punishment," 164.

3 "In contrast to language and theology, much less attention has been given in research to the literary aspect of these works" (Japhet, "Chronicles and Ezra-Nehemiah,"

(1990) opened a rhetorical approach to Chronicles, applying Aristotle's framework to Chronicles as whole.[4] Recently I. Kalimi (1995) proposed firstly a comprehensive and systematic approach to the Chronicler's literary techniques.[5] While his study focuses on the techniques themselves, the literary techniques have not been used to interpret a substantial piece of Chronicles. Our present concern is not to provide a comprehensive exploration of the literary characteristics of Chronicles, but to identify two main literary characteristics of the work, which are both significant and relevant to our present discussion. That is, firstly, the greater complexity of Chronicles concerning presentation of kings, and secondly, the allusion technique in the work.

2. THE MORE COMPLEX PRESENTATION OF KINGS IN CHRONICLES THAN THAT IN KINGS

Some biblical scholars have seen the Chronicler's presentation as rather simplistic. For example, the observation that the Chronicler did not treat the history of the northern Israel, but only the Judahite kingdom (with a few exceptions), has tended to lead to the conclusion that the Chronicler's concern was limited to the Judean kingdom. Secondly, many scholars

---

306). According to Japhet, the reasons for the lack of literary study of Chronicles and Ezra-Nehemiah, are two. Firstly, "literary analysis" is a comparatively new field. Secondly, the two works have been regarded as a "compilation," of "inferior artistic merit" (307). Japhet only suggests two examples of Chronicles' literary characteristics. However, her attempt to identify Chronicles' literary characteristics is preoccupied with a concern to prove separate authorship of Chronicles and Ezra-Nehemiah, and her illustration is not meaningful to our discussion. For an example of a literary approach to Chronicles, Dillard, "Literary Structure, Solomon Narrative." Comparatively more literary approaches have been attempted to Ezra-Nehemiah; see the list in Japhet, "Chronicles and Ezra-Nehemiah," 307.

4. Duke, *The Persuasive Appeal.*

5. Kalimi, *Zur Geschichtsschreibung*; "The Contribution," 190–212; "Paronomasia," 27–41. Kalimi observes, for example, textual harmonizations, antitheses, omission, allusion, chiasmus, inclusion, narrative resumption and paronomasia as the Chronicler's literary techniques. He insists that many passages which are regarded by modern scholars as "late additions," "errors," "erasures," and "textual emendations" can be understood in light of the literary techniques instead. His collection of a variety of literary techniques employed in Chronicles is highly valuable. However, his approach does not consider a dynamic reader-factor in literary technique, for example, the reader's reading process. On the other hand, there are scholars who apply a literary approach to a text of Chronicles. For example, Eskenazi, "A Literary Approach to Chronicles' Ark Narrative in 1 Chronicles 13–16," 258–74. On the other hand, for an example of an overly reader-centered approach, see G. Snyman, "Tis a Vice," 91–113.

have thought that conspicuous omission of materials from the account of David's and Solomon's reigns was intended to idealize the two kings, "fashioning an image without blemish."[6] Consequently, the commentators have seen the account of the two kings as a rather simplistic piece of literature, i.e., accounts of totally idealized kings.[7] Thirdly, the observation that many additional materials and comments contribute to the immediate retribution principle, has even given the impression that one of the major aims of the Chronicler is simply to emphasize that principle.[8] Fourthly, the many additional comments and evaluation added to the deeds of kings in the Chronicler's work have given the impression that Chronicles is simplistic literature with clear evaluations.[9]

However, the alleged "simplicity" of Chronicles has been challenged in various ways recently. Firstly, despite the Chronicler's omitting most material about the northern kingdom, the concept of Israel in Chronicles never excludes the northern tribes, as Williamson successfully shows.[10] Secondly, the omissions in the accounts of David's and Solomon's reigns may be construed as being intended to keep the focus upon the temple issue, rather than to idealize the two kings, as we have argued already in chapter 2. Thirdly, the immediate-retribution principle cannot cover Chronicles, as is successfully proved by B. Kelly.[11] On the one hand, the principle of immediate retribution is highlighted on a number of occasions, but on the other hand, the principle of accumulative retribution and the principle of grace given to the undeserving, is maintained as in its *Vorlage*. Fourthly, although Williamson observes that the Chronicler's presentation reveals a "black and white" clarity in judgment of right or wrong,[12] this does not mean that the Chronicler's presentation of a king is simplistic. Rather, some additional comments to its *Vorlage* contribute to evaluating only an individual deed of a king on a certain occasion, rather than the king himself or his reign as a whole. This tendency is observed

6. Japhet, "Chronicles, Book of," 527.

7. For example, Japhet's and Dillard's commentaries.

8. For example, Dillard, "Reward and Punishment"; Dillard, "The Reign of Asa."

9. Williamson, *Israel*, 68.

10. Ibid., 87–140.

11. Kelly, *Retribution and Eschatology*, 29–134.

12. Williamson, *Israel*, 68. "a history in which . . . circumstances are idealized into black and white situations where right and wrong are immediately recognizable." This had been pointed out by J. Liver on page 225 of "History and Historiography in the Book of Chronicles" (Hebrew) in *Studies in Bible and Judean Desert Scrolls* (Jerusalem: 1971), 221–33, as Williamson observes.

in the work, as below, to reveal that the Chronicles provides a more nuanced or complex (than its *Vorlage*, if there is any), two-sided, and subtle presentation than it seemingly appears to, exploiting the reader's prior knowledge, as is shown in Deboys' exemplary study.[13]

2.1. The Greater Complexity in the Cases of Good Kings

The presentation in Kings and Chronicles of the so-called good kings, i.e., Asa, Jehoshaphat, Hezekiah, and Josiah, shows that, along with the tendency to add their positive elements to the *Vorlage*, the Chronicler also had the tendency to add or emphasize negative elements.

2.1.1. *The Greater Complexity in the Presentation of Asa*

The account of Asa's reign in Kings, i.e., its *Vorlage* (1 Kgs 15:9–24), presents him positively overall, as expressed in "Asa did what was right in the sight of the Lord, as his father David had done" (15:11) and "the heart of Asa was true to the Lord all his days" (15:14b), although his shortcoming is not concealed by the mention of his not moving "high places" (15:14a). The account of Asa in Chronicles not only retains most of the content of its *Vorlage* including the evaluation above, with slight variations in some cases (1 Kgs 15:11 // 2 Chr 14:1 [ET 14:2] "Asa did what was good and right in the sight of the Lord his God;" 1 Kgs 15:14b // 2 Chr 15:17b), but also conspicuously adds more material which contributes to the positive presentation. That is, Asa is presented more positively in Chronicles than in Kings, especially in the accounts of his "commanding Judah to seek the Lord, the God of their ancestors, and to keep the law and the commandment" (2 Chr 14:3 [ET 14:4]), of his victory over the Ethiopian army and consequent plunder in Gerar, through his trusting in and praying to God (2 Chr 14:8–14 [ET 14:9–15]), and of his encouraging the people to "enter into a covenant to seek the Lord, the God of their ancestors, with all their heart and with all their soul," or to "take an oath to the Lord" (2 Chr 15:9–15).

However, it is plain that materials which contribute to a negative presentation of Asa were also added in Chronicles. That is, firstly, a negative evaluation, through the seer Hanani's rebuke, of Asa's relying on King Ben-Hadad of Aram for relief from King Baasha of Israel, taking silver and

---

13. Deboys, "Portrayal of Abijah."

gold from the treasures of the house of the Lord and the king's house and sending them to the king of Aram for an alliance (2 Chr 16:7–9), while in its *Vorlage* only a factual description of the event (1 Kgs 15:16–22) appears. Secondly, Asa's rejection of the seer's rebuke and putting him in prison (2 Chr 16:10a). Thirdly, Asa's inflicting cruelties on some of the people (2 Chr 16:10b). Fourthly, Asa's seeking help from physicians rather than seeking the Lord on the occasion of his foot disease (2 Chr 16:12), while there is only a mention of his foot disease in its *Vorlage* (1 Kgs 15:23b). In spite of these additional negative presentations, Asa's status as a standard for his son Jehoshaphat (2 Chr 20:32a) is maintained, as is the case in its *Vorlage* (1 Kgs 22:43 [ET 22:43a]). Thus, it can be said that Asa's portrayal in Chronicles is more complex than that in its *Vorlage*.

2.1.2. *The Greater Complexity in the Presentation of Jehoshaphat*

The case of Jehoshaphat shows a similar tendency to that of Asa. The account of his reign in its *Vorlage*, 1 Kgs 22:41–51 [ET 22:41–50], presents him positively, as expressed in "He walked in all the way of his father Asa" (who is described as having done "what was right in the sight of the Lord, as his father David had done" (1 Kgs 15:11), "whose heart was true to the Lord all his days" (15:14b), and did "not turn aside from it, doing what was right in the sight of the Lord" (1 Kgs 22:43 [ET 22:43a]), although his shortcomings are not concealed by the mention of his not moving "high places" (1 Kgs 22:44 [ET 22:43b]), just as in the case of Asa (1 Kgs 15:14a).[14] Conspicuously many materials both positive and negative are added in Chronicles, like the case of Asa.

14. The matter of high places in the descriptions of Asa's and Jehoshaphat's reigns requires some textual speculation. While both kings' failures in removing high places are mentioned respectively in Kings (1 Kgs 15:14a; 22:44 [ET 22:43b]), in Chronicles each king's removing high places and failure in removing them are mentioned, respectively (Asa's removing them; 2 Chr 14:2, 4 [ET 14:3, 5]. His failure; 2 Chr 15:17. Jehoshaphat's removing them; 2 Chr 17:6. His failure; 2 Chr 20:33). The mentions of each king's removing and not removing do not need to be understood as a textual contradiction or an editorial trace, but rather can be understood as a realistic statement which reflects the king's attempt to remove them and probably a temporary success, with a failure in the end. A similar pattern is observed in Kings, too. As for male temple prostitutes, it is reported that Asa removed them from the land (1 Kgs 15:12a), while it is also reported that Jehoshaphat removed them in his own days. How can Jehoshaphat remove the male temple prostitutes who had been removed already? In this case, a clue to the answer is revealed in the text. That is, it is "the remnant of the male temple prostitutes who were still in the land" that Jehoshaphat removed in his days. The phrase "in the days of his father Asa" attached to " the remnant" also support

Among the positive materials are the statement that Jehoshaphat "sought the God of his father and walked in his commandments" (2 Chr 17:4a), "in the earlier ways of his father (his father David)" (2 Chr 17:3), the description that he sent his officials and Levites to teach the people in Judah the contents of "the book of the law of the Lord" (2 Chr 17:7–9), brought the people from Beer-Sheba to the hill country of Ephraim back to the Lord (2 Chr 19:4), appointed judges over people, instructing the judges to do their job righteously (2 Chr 19:5–11), and responded piously to the invasion of the united army of Moabites, Ammonites, and some of the Meunites, setting himself to seek the Lord, proclaiming a fast throughout all Judah (2 Chr 20:1–3), praying before the assembly of Judah and Jerusalem in the house of the Lord (2 Chr 20:5), and encouraging the people to trust their God and his prophet (2 Chr 20:20), which resulted in a great victory and consequent peace (2 Chr 20:22–30).

However, it is clear that in spite of these additional positive materials the Chronicler did not intend simply to idealize Jehoshaphat in every aspect, for he highlighted the king's faults more evidently by adding negative materials, as in the case of Asa. The Chronicler added the account of the seer Jehu's rebuke of the king's alliance with the king of the northern Israelite kingdom after Jehoshaphat's joint campaign with the northern Israelite king over Ramoth-gilead (2 Chr 19:1–2), while in Kings, the relational fact of the two kingdoms is tersely described, "Jehoshaphat also made peace with the king of Israel" without any evaluation statement (1 Kgs 22:45 [ET 22:44]). Furthermore, Eliezer's prophecy, which criticizes Jehoshaphat's alliance with Ahaziah, the king of Israel, and foretells the wreckage of Jehoshaphat's ships, a product of the alliance, as God's punishment (2 Chr 20:36–37), highlights Jehoshaphat's wrong relationship with the wicked king of Israel in the sight of God, while in Kings, only the factual account of the ships' wreckage is mentioned, which is followed by an episode that possibly implies an alliance of the two nations on the sailing (1 Kgs 22:49–50 [ET 22:48–49]).

To sum up, the presentation of Jehoshaphat in Chronicles is like a picture where both a lighter tone and a darker tone are added to several parts of the basic painting, resulting in a picture with a starker contrast of colour. In other words, a more nuanced or complex picture. In light of this

---

the conclusion that Asa's attempt to remove the male temple prostitutes had been done and succeeded to some extent, however, it had not been such a thorough success that Jehoshaphat did not have to try it again. In the same way, in the description of Josiah, the occasion of removing of idols from the land appears repeatedly (2 Chr 34:3b–7 and 2 Chr 34:33).

observation, it is noteworthy that the Chronicler adds the episode where Jehu son of Hanani the seer rebukes and praises the king at the same time (2 Chr 19:1–3), which is a peculiar combination. Thus, it can be said again that the portrayal of Jehoshaphat is more complex than that in its *Vorlage*.

2.1.3. The Greater Complexity in the Presentation of Hezekiah

Both Kings and Chronicles describe Hezekiah as doing "what was right in the sight of the Lord, just as his ancestor David had done" (2 Kgs 18:3; 2 Chr 29:2), which is a label of an exemplary king.[15] It is significant that while Kings' account of Hezekiah's reign contains comparatively few passages about his cultic activity, which is positively described (2 Kgs 18:4–6), and a comparatively large number of passages of the Assyrian invasion (2 Kgs 18:9—19:37), Chronicles' account of the king's reign contains a comparatively large amount about his cultic activity, which is also positively described (2 Chr 29:3—31:21), and comparatively shorter account about the Assyrian invasion (2 Chr 32:1–23). In spite of the large difference in the proportion, those passages present similar evaluations of the king, as a pious and God-trusting exemplary king.

However, concerning Hezekiah's sickness and God's miraculous sign as a guarantee of his recovery from the sickness (2 Kgs 20:1–19; 2 Chr 32:24–26, 31[16]), the Chronicler's description increases the complexity of the account in terms of the evaluation of the king, by adding evidently negative elements and evaluation to the overall very positive portrayal of the king, such as mentioning Hezekiah's heart's pride (2 Chr 32:25) and God's wrath executed and postponed as a result (2 Chr 32:25b, 26b). Furthermore, the additional material which reinforces the overall positive portrayal of Hezekiah in the end part of his account, i.e., "his good deeds" concerning source material (2 Chr 32:32a), "all Judah and the inhabitants of Jerusalem did him honor at his death" (2 Chr 32:33) also add complexity

15. The positive Davidic standard is only attached to Asa (1 Kgs 15:11), Hezekiah (2 Kgs 18:3), and Josiah (2 Kgs 22:2) in Kings, while it is attached to Jehoshaphat (2 Chr 17:37b, There is another reading), Hezekiah (2 Chr 29:2), and Josiah (2 Chr 34:2) in Chronicles. Hezekiah's being the first class king is shown also in 2 Kgs 18:5, i.e., "He trusted in the Lord the God of Israel; so that there was no one like him among all the kings of Judah after him, or among those who were before him."

16. Although the contexts of Babylonian envoy appear different from each other, i.e., in Kings visiting for Hezekiah's sickness (2 Kgs 20:12), while in Chronicles inquiring about the miraculous sign (2 Chr 32:31), the miraculous sign seems to be the same one which appears as a sign of God's promise of Hezekiah's recovery, and the verse 2 Chr 32:31 seems to be actually in the same context.

to the Hezekiah account along with the added explicitly negative elements in 2 Chr 32:25.

2.1.4. The Introduced Complexity in the Presentation of Josiah

As for Josiah, the king is in sum evaluated in terms of the positive Davidic standard, i.e., "walking in all the way of his father David," like Hezekiah in both works (2 Kgs 22:2a; 2 Chr 34:2a), with additional comment, "he did not turn aside to the right or to the left" (2 Kgs 22:2b; 2 Chr 34:2b), showing that he is an exemplary king.[17] It is significant that while Kings' account of Josiah's observance of the Passover (2 Kgs 23:21–23) is comparatively short, and the account of his destroying idols (2 Kgs 23:4–20, 24) is comparatively long, Chronicles' account of his observance of the Passover (2 Chr 35:1–19) is comparatively long and the account of his destroying idols (2 Chr 34:3b–7, 33) is comparatively short. As is the case with Hezekiah, the large difference in the proportion of the two themes has nothing to do with the evaluations of the king, i.e., a pious and God-trusting first-class king. However, it is plain that the Chronicler introduced into his portrayal of Josiah a nuance or complexity which does not appear in his *Vorlage*, for while in Kings the account of the king's death is only described in a brief factual report without any evaluation (2 Kgs 23:29), the Chronicler clarifies the king's fault, i.e., his not listening to God's voice through Neco's words (2 Chr 35:21–22b). When we consider that the materials in the end part of his account (i.e., all Judah and Jerusalem's mourning for Josiah (2 Chr 35:24b), the prophet Jeremiah's lamentation for Josiah (2 Chr 35:25), and the mention of "his faithful deeds" (2 Chr 35:26) in terms of source material, which underline Josiah's being a good king) are added in Chronicles, the negative element of his death becomes more conspicuous, producing a nuanced or complex portrayal of the king. In fact, Kings does not appear to contain any negative elements in the account of Josiah.

2.2. The Greater Complexity in the Cases of Bad Kings

As the converse of the point above, the Chronicler's presentations of the kings who are so-called bad kings in Kings, i.e., Rehoboam, Abijah, and Manasseh show that the Chronicler has the tendency to add or emphasize

---

17. 2 Kgs 23:25 "Before him there was no king like him, who turned to the Lord with all his heart, with all his soul, and with all his might, according to all the law of Moses; nor did any like him arise after him."

positive elements to the *Vorlage*, while maintaining and highlighting their negative elements, ultimately resulting in more complex presentations of the kings.

2.2.1. *The Greater Complexity in the Presentation of Rehoboam*

Rehoboam's portrayal in Kings does not contain any explicit evaluation of the king in the scope of his reign, while his people Judah's doing "what was evil in the sight of the Lord" is described with a clearly negative evaluation (1 Kgs 14:22–24). An explicit evaluation of the king only appears as a negative model for his son's reign later (1 Kgs 15:3a). In contrast, the Chronicler provides a clear evaluation of the king in the end part of the account of his reign, "He did evil, for he did not set his heart to seek the Lord" (2 Chr 12:14). Rehoboam's case is a conspicuous example of the "black and white" feature of the Chronicler's presentation, in the sense that the Chronicler provides a clear "right or wrong" evaluation of each deed of kings. However, it does not mean that the Chronicler's portrayal of a king is simplistic. In fact, with clear evaluation of an individual period or deed of a king, the Chronicler's portrayal of a king, as a whole, is more complex than its *Vorlage*. In other words, on the one hand, the Chronicler provides a clear evaluation of a certain deed or period of a king, and on the other hand, the Chronicler's portrayal of the king shows or emphasizes two contrasting elements, his merits and faults. Rehoboam's case provides a good example of this. In Chronicles, Rehoboam is described as following David and Solomon's good model for the first three years of his reign (2 Chr 11:17).[18] After the three years, the king is described as abandoning the law of the Lord, with his people (2 Chr 12:1). That is, Rehoboam's short-lived loyalty to God and the following betrayal are distinctively described in Chronicles, producing a nuance or complexity that is absent in its *Vorlage*. The subsequent invasion by Shishak, the Egyptian king, is clearly described in Chronicles as God's judgment or discipline on Rehoboam and his people for their betrayal (2 Chr 12:2, 5–8), while only a factual report of the invasion and its result is described in Kings (1 Kgs 14:25–28). Furthermore, Chronicles contains the repentance of the king and Israelite leaders and a consequent recovery of the nation (2 Chr 12:6–7, 12b),

---

18. For a detailed study of the materials which has been added or devised by the Chronicler to account of the first three years of Rehoboam's reign, see Knoppers, "Rehoboam in Chronicles," 432–37.

which is completely absent in Kings, making the Chronicler's presentation of the king's reign still more nuanced or complex than its *Vorlage*'s.

2.2.2. *The Greater Complexity in the Presentation of Abijah*

As for Abijah, he has a negative evaluation in Kings (1 Kgs 15:3) with only one factual report of his reign, the war with Jeroboam (1 Kgs 15:7), in a comparatively short account (1 Kgs 15:1–8), which even includes a comment about King David's piety and God's faithfulness to David (1 Kgs 15:4–5), and consequently has even less space for Abijah himself. By contrast the account in Chronicles does not contain any explicit evaluation of the king, and is a comparatively long account (2 Chr 13:1–22); the Chronicler's portrayal of the king has been construed by most scholars as presenting the king as positive, on several bases.[19] First of all, Abijah's speech has usually been regarded as a typical case of the so-called "royal speech," which means that the Chronicler's ideology or stance is expressed through the mouth of the main figure. This view strongly implies that Abijah is a righteous speaker and king commended by the Chronicler.[20] Secondly, the following victory over the northern army was regarded as proof of Abijah's righteousness. Thirdly, the mention of Abijah's enemy Jeroboam's being struck by the Lord (2 Chr 13:20), Abijah's "growing strong" (13:21a), and having a big family (13:21b), are construed as God's blessing on Abijah, proving his righteousness.

However, this view needs reconsideration. This was proposed already in chapter 2, but needs to be reintroduced here briefly. Firstly, it is plain that Abijah's speech cannot be regarded as precisely reflecting the truth,[21] although it is acknowledged that some parts of it (i.e., 2 Chr 13:5,[22]

19. For example, Curtis sees the reign of Abijah in Chronicles as "one of great glory," and thinks that "The Chronicler gives no inkling of" the negative evaluation of the king in his *Vorlage* (Curtis and Madsen, *Chronicles*, 373).

20. The view is well captured in Mason's statement that "If he is to be the bearer of exemplary theological truths to the apostate North he can hardly merit such a judgment [i.e., the negative evaluation of Abijah in Kings] by the Chronicler" [my insertion] (Mason, *Preaching the Tradition*, 39).

21. Even Curtis who believes that the Chronicler described Abijah as free from his negative evaluation described in its *Vorlage*, thinks that 2 Chr 13:7 is "very different from" the situation described in 2 Chr 10:1ff, "where Rehoboam appears hard and defiant and brings about the rupture by his domineering manner" (Curtis and Madsen, *Chronicles*, 375).

22. Caquot, who sees the realized theocracy in the post-exile temple community, does not think that 13:5 which states the eternal nature of Davidic dynasty, reflects

8–11) really do reflect the ideology of the Chronicler. That is, while the criticism of Jeroboam's false religion is in line with the Chronicler's general ideology, the situation of the division of the kingdom stated in 2 Chr 13:7 is contradictory to the text which describes the case previously (2 Chr 10:1–15; 11:1–4a). The division was not caused by Rehoboam's being young and irresolute as Abijah describes it (2 Chr 13:7b), but by God's will, as is evidently stated (2 Chr 10:15; 11:4). Furthermore, far from Abijah's statement, Rehoboam was neither young, nor irresolute, in fact it is described that he was forty-one years old (2 Chr 12:13)[23], chose the hard line (2 Chr 10:13–14), and was resolute enough to start a war to regain the northern tribes (2 Chr 11:1).[24] The fact that Abijah's speech cannot be regarded as flawless undermines the view that he is a good or righteous king.[25] Secondly, the victory over the northern army has nothing to do with Abijah himself, it is gained by Judah's trust as the text explicitly states (2 Chr 13:18). Rather, it is suspected that Abijah's name is intentionally omitted there, for in similar situations a king and his people are usually mentioned together (e.g., Jehoshaphat, 2 Chr 20:3–13, Hezekiah, 2 Chr 32:20–21), if not the king alone (Asa, 2 Chr 14:9–11 [ET 14:10–12], Jehoshaphat 2 Chr 18:31b).[26] Thirdly, neither Jeroboam's being struck by

---

the Chronicler's stance, but only Abijah's own legitimacy against Jeroboam (Caquot, "Messianisme," 119). However, the present study presumes that the Chronicler shows the hope of restoration of the dynasty.

23. It is admitted that in spite of a not young age of forty-one, "young" could be used to mean the new king's inexperience in his job (cf. the case of Solomon in 1 Chr 22:5; 29:1. Williamson points out that the almost identical terms "young and irresolute" (נַעַר וְרַךְ־לֵבָב) were used of Solomon at 1 Chr 22:5 and 29:1 (Williamson, 1 and 2 Chronicles, 253).).

24. Selman thinks that Abijah's statement that Rehoboam was "young and irresolute," is the right expression to mean being "inexperienced and weak-willed"; however, he thinks that Rehoboam, being forty-one years old, was "fully responsible for his folly," and consequently, "Abijah's defence of his father Rehoboam (v 7) seems somewhat exaggerated in view of chapter 10," although it is understandable as an embellished political statement (Selman, 2 Chronicles, 380).

25. Kissling, Reliable Characters, 20.

26. Deboys notes this omission of Abijah's name regarding the prayer. However, he does not take it seriously in terms of negative evaluation of Abijah (Deboys, "Portrayal of Abijah," 51). He dismisses the significance of the omission of Abijah's name in the prayer, on the ground that the involvement of people in events is emphasized in Chronicles, taking the example of 2 Chr 31 where all Israel is emphasized as the subject of demolishing idols (being compared to 2 Kgs 18 (Hezekiah emphasized)). However, Deboys' argument on this matter is not convincing, for the case is of prayer and it should be better compared to Asa and Jehoshaphat's cases of prayer with their people.

the Lord for his own sin (2 Chr 11:14–15) against the Lord, nor Abijah's growing strong and having a big family necessarily demonstrate Abijah's righteousness. Rather, it is questionable why there is no mention of God's or the narrator's explicit approval of Abijah in the whole account, if these are really intended to confirm Abijah's righteousness, in accordance with the Chronicler's usual black and white presentation.[27] In fact, it is more natural to construe the description of Abijah's growing strong and his family's prosperity without any praise of him, as being simply intended to provide concrete cases of its *Vorlage*'s mention of God's undeserved favor upon him as a descendant of David (1 Kgs 15:4). Fourthly, as Deboys rightly observes, the following king's clearing of the idols from Judah (2 Chr 14:2, 4 [ET 14:3, 5]) suggests that the Chronicler did not intend to present Abijah in only a positive light.[28]

Hence, it is reasonable to see the presentation of Abijah in Chronicles as consistent with its *Vorlage*. In total, no merits of Abijah appear in the account, except his proud speech, and even that is suspected of distorting the truth. Therefore, although it is true that the Chronicler's presentation of Abijah seems to have a more positive atmosphere than that of its *Vorlage*, its hints at Abijah's negative aspects still produce a nuanced or complex presentation of the king when compared to its *Vorlage*.

2.2.3. *The Greater Complexity in the Presentation of Manasseh*

The portrayal of king Manasseh in Kings is a one-sidedly negative presentation (2 Kgs 21:2–16) as the first evaluation states, "He did what was evil in the sight of the Lord, following the abominable practices of the nations that the Lord drove out before the people of Israel" (21:2). No single statement is provided to present him in a positive light. His practices of

27. Deboys points out that "It was noted that the Chronicler has not one word to say against Abijah. But it is surely no less striking that he has not one word to say in his favor" (ibid., 50). Deboys rightly raises questions about the view of Abijah's flawlessness in Chronicles' presentation, on textual bases, however he does not find false element of Abijah's speech on the matter of division situation.

28. Deboys points out that Maacah, i.e., Asa's mother's idolatry (2 Chr 15:16) was probably possible under Abijah's connivance (ibid., 51–52).

It is significant that the Chronicler carefully states that in spite of Asa's religious purification, "the high places were not totally taken out of Israel" (2 Chr 15:17) (cf. 14:2 [ET 14:3]) before he states Jehoshaphat's removing the high places (2 Chr 17:6). If the Chronicler is this aware of the sequence of removing high places, it is highly likely that the description of Asa, Abijah's son's moving away various idols, has a not little allusion to Abijah's day.

idolatry and abominations are described in detail (21:3–8), followed by the content of the prophets' words against him (21:11–15).

In contrast, the portrayal of the same king in Chronicles introduces positive materials for his evaluation, Manasseh's repentance after God's discipline, and consequent recovery (2 Chr 33:11–17). However, it retains the overall negative evaluation of him at the beginning of the account, which is verbally identical to the Kings' evaluation of him in 2 Kgs 21:2 (2 Chr 33:2). In addition, the content of the prophets' words against the king and his people (2 Kgs 21:11–15) is replaced with the simple mentioning of the source material of the contents of the words (2 Chr 33:18b). In this context, it seems natural that Manasseh is described as a model of idolatry and repentance at the same time, in his son Amon's evaluation (2 Chr 33:22–23). All of these cases, as a whole, show that the presentation of Manasseh in Chronicles has a complexity which is absent from its *Vorlage*.

2.3. The Greater Complexity in the Cases of Average-Quality Kings

Joash, Amaziah, and Uzziah (Azariah), who are evaluated as average quality kings in Kings (2 Kgs 14:3; 15:3), are also described in Chronicles with a similar touch to that we have seen so far.

2.3.1. The Greater Complexity in the Presentation of Joash

Regarding Joash, the evaluation of the king is good in general, but with conditional statements in both Kings and Chronicles (2 Kgs 12:3 [ET 12:2]; 2 Chr 24:2), such as "because the priest Jehoiada instructed him," or "all the days of the priest Jehoiada." The absence of reference to David as the standard, which is employed positively to evaluate only Hezekiah and Josiah (2 Chr 29:2; 34:2)[29] also implies that the king is not a wholly exemplary king. The account of King Joash's restoration project in the temple, even urging the chief priest Jehoiada, seems to show his zeal for God in both works (2 Kgs 12:5–17 [ET 12:4–16]; 2 Chr 24:4–14). Joash's shortcomings are probably implied in the account of his giving away "all the votive gifts that Jehoshaphat, Jehoram, and Ahaziah, his ancestors, the kings of Judah, had dedicated, as well as his own votive gifts, all the gold found in the treasuries of the house of the Lord and of the king's house"

---

29. There is a case where David is referred to in order to criticize a king, the evaluation of king Ahaz (2 Chr 28:1b), while in Kings there are three cases (1 Kgs 15:3; 2 Kgs 14:3a; 16:2b (//2 Chr 28:1b)).

to the invader king Hazael of Aram (2 Kgs 12:18–19 [ET 12:17–18]), although the action of Joash is not criticized explicitly in Kings. While this account is omitted in Chronicles, the Chronicler added much more serious faults of Joash. That is, the account of Joash's turning his back on God to serve idols after Jehoiada's death (2 Chr 24:17–18a), with explicitly negative comment (24:18b, 19, 24) including the interpretation of the defeat by the army of Aram as God's punishment (24:24), and his order to stone the inspired prophet Zechariah, the very son of his benefactor Jehoiada, with explicitly negative comment (24:22). Therefore, it is plain that the Chronicler highlighted a dark side of the generally well-evaluated king, making his portrayal more complex.

2.3.2. *The Greater Complexity in the Presentation of Amaziah*

As for Amaziah, it is clear in Kings that, while the overall evaluation is positive—"He did what was right in the sight of the Lord" (2 Kgs 14:3a)—he is evaluated as an average-quality king when he is explicitly described as being short of the Davidic standard and only paired with his father Joash (2 Kgs 14:3b), along with the mention of his failure to remove high-places (2 Kgs 14:4). In Chronicles, the overall evaluation of the king takes a more condensed form, "He did what was right in the sight of the Lord, yet not with a true heart" (2 Chr 25:2), omitting the comparison with David, and that with Joash as well, but still reflecting a similar average-quality marking of kings. His being overall a good king is exemplified in both works in his not putting to death the children of his father's murderers according to the law of Moses (2 Kgs 14:5–6; 2 Chr 25:3–4). In contrast to this similar stance in his positive portrayals, the dark side of the king shows different degrees of negative description in the two works. That is, while in Kings, accounts of two wars, one ending in victory, the other defeat, are simply factual descriptions, in Chronicles, additional materials contribute to increase the negative evaluation of the king in both cases. Firstly, regarding Amaziah's war against the Edomites, while Kings' description is an extremely brief factual report without any evaluation (2 Kgs 14:7), the Chronicler added the account of God's disapproval of the king's hiring the northern Israelite army, followed by the king discharging them according to a man of God's words. The subsequent damage done by the discharged northern Israelite army (2 Chr 25:10, 13) is probably construed as a cost of the primary misdeed of hiring the army, which God disapproves of (2 Chr 25:7). Other additional materials, of Amaziah's serving the gods of the people of Seir after his victory over the Edomites, and of his rejecting the rebuke of a prophet sent by God, also increase the negative tone of the king's portrayal. Secondly, Kings' description of Amaziah's war against the northern Israelites is only a factual account without any evaluation (despite its being a comparatively long account), i.e., only the king's challenge against Jehoash, king of the northern kingdom, and its tragic results, his being defeated and exploited (2 Kgs 14:8–14), whereas the Chronicler added a crucial statement that interprets the war as God's punishment for Amaziah's idolatry (2 Chr 25:20), which makes the neutral account of Kings into a negative account as a whole. To sum up, the Chronicler's presentation of king Amaziah increases the complexity of his *Vorlage* by adding negative tone to the overall positive account of the king.

2.3.3. The Greater Complexity in the Presentation of Uzziah

As for Uzziah (Azariah in Kings), the king is positively evaluated in general in Kings, "He did what was right in the sight of the Lord" (2 Kgs 15:3a), while his not being a "wholly exemplary" king is shown both in his being compared to his father Amaziah as a standard, not to David (2 Kgs 15:3b), and his not removing high-places (2 Kgs 15:4). Chronicles' description of the king in general is not very different from the one of Kings, while retaining the Amaziah standard (2 Chr 26:4b), omitting the high-places matter, but adding a conditional statement on his good deeds—"in the days of Zechariah, who instructed him in the fear of God" (2 Chr 26:5a). As for Uzziah's dark side, in Kings there is only the factual description of his being struck by the Lord and becoming a leper (2 Kgs 15:5a), whereas in Chronicles there is a plain account of his becoming proud when he became strong by God's favor (2 Chr 26:16a) along with a detailed description of his prosperity (2 Chr 26:5b–15) by God's help (2 Chr 26:5b, 7a, 15b), also with explicitly negative evaluation of his deed (26:16b) and a much more vivid description of this tragic event (26:16b–21a). It is plain that the Chronicler made the portrayal of the generally good king more complex and double-edged than that of Kings, by adding more negative explicit evaluation and more vivid descriptions of the king's misdeeds in spite of God's abundant blessing upon him, which is also absent in his main *Vorlage*.

2.4. A Case of the Greater Complexity in the Presentation of David

The significance of David's fault in the case of the census (1 Chr 21) is described in a stronger tone in Chronicles than its *Vorlage*, while his fault is less clearly presented in the case of Bathsheba and Uriah in Chronicles than in Kings (the allusion of the adultery and killing will be discussed later), as Selman points out.[30] The combination of these two presentations in opposite directions seems to constitute a greater complexity in the Chronicler's overall presentation of David.

2.5. A Case of the Greater Complexity in the Presentation of Solomon

A section of Solomon's portrayal in Chronicles also shows that the Chronicler has the tendency to increase the nuance or complexity of its portrayal of kings, when compared to its *Vorlage*. On the one hand, Solomon's being a king of peace who does not shed blood is strongly emphasized (1 Chr 22:7–9; 28:2, 5–6),[31] which do not appear in its *Vorlage*. On the other hand, the Chronicler added the unique report of Solomon's military action (2 Chr 8:3). In Kings, Solomon does not initiate any war or battle, but enjoys peace with his people (1 Kgs 5:4–5 [ET 4:24–25]), although his suffering from his enemies as a punishment from God for his idolatry is described in the end part of the Solomon narrative (1 Kgs 11:14, 23, 25–26). In Kings, Solomon is never described as a conqueror, maintaining his image of a king of peace, while in Chronicles his being a king of peace, who does not shed blood, is more emphasized. At the same time his being a conqueror is also added in Chronicles, producing a more nuanced or complex presentation of him than in Kings.

2.6 Conclusion: The Implication of the Observation of Greater Complexity in the Presentation of Kings in Chronicles

The above cases show the increased nuance or complexity of portrayal of kings in Chronicles, compared to that in Kings. The increased or newly

---

30. Selman, *1 Chronicles*, 201–2.

31. It is noteworthy that "peace" is mentioned four times, including the meaning of his name Solomon, in the single verse (22:9), giving a strong impression of Solomon's being a king of peace in contrast with the adjacent negative mention of "blood shedding" of David (22:8).

introduced two-sidedness of the kings' portrayal encourages us to read out the same quality from the Solomon account. Although the portrayal of David and Solomon is in several ways distinct from the following kings, the cases of David and Solomon mentioned above indicate that the portrayal of David and Solomon is no different from the following kings regarding the tendency for increased nuance or complexity. Those examples above concerning the nuanced or complex presentation of David and Solomon may be just a few instances of many. Therefore, it is justifiable to scrutinize the Solomon account with the expectation that his overall positive presentation in fact has some nuance or complexity in it.

3. THE TECHNIQUE OF ALLUSION IN CHRONICLES

Not a few scholars[32] believe that the Chronicler exerted his freedom to the extent that the original context of the material which he used is ignored, or even that the Chronicler simply used the materials from the first history, in order to create his own history which is to replace the first history. However, the view contradicts the widely accepted observation that the Chronicler presumed the reader's prior knowledge of the existing texts or the first history, as Childs points out. Childs points out the problems of the view that "the Chronicler's purpose lies in suppression or replacing the earlier tradition with his own account." Two reasons among the three that he proposes have special relevance to the present study. "First, the Chronicler often assumes a knowledge of the whole tradition on the part of his readers to such an extent that his account is virtually incomprehensible without the implied relationship with the other accounts (cf. I Chron. 12.19ff.; II Chron. 32.24–33). Secondly, even when he omits a story in his selection he often makes explicit reference to it by his use of sources." As an example of the second case, Childs mentions the Chronicler's "explicit reference to the prophecy of Ahijah" (2 Chr 9:29).[33] Although Childs does not mention the more explicit and significant passage in 2 Chr 10:15, the present study agrees with his view. On the assumption that Chronicles is the second history, dependent on the authority of the first one, it is more likely that the Chronicler tried to respect the stance of its *Vorlage* and also

32. For example, Willi, Mosis, Ackroyd, Knoppers, Sugimoto, De Vries. For the list of various strata of the view, see Sugimoto, "Chronicles as Independent Literature," 62 nn. 3, 4; 63 nn. 5, 6, 7, 8. The view can be divided into several subcategories, possibly, as Sugimoto suggests (ibid, 62–63). For a recent example of the view that the Chronicler tried to replace the previous tradition, see Mitchell, "The Ironic Death of Josiah."

33. Childs, *Introduction*, 646–47.

exploit it; Childs insists that the Chronicler did not attempt to replace or suppress the previous tradition, but instead used it.[34] Allusion technique is plainly in tune with this presumption.[35]

3.1. The Need for the Technique of Omission and Allusion in Chronicles

It is widely acknowledged, as mentioned above, that the Chronicler presumed the reader's prior knowledge of the content of the *Vorlage*. It means that he exploited the reader's prior knowledge when he omitted some materials.[36] It is not difficult to deduce or explain why the Chronicler

---

34. Ibid., 646–47. Childs observes that "it is a basic error of interpretation to infer from this method of selection that the Chronicler's purpose lies in suppressing or replacing the earlier tradition with his own account" (646). Johnstone also thinks that "the Chronicler (or, at least, the final compilers and canonisers of Scripture) has no intention of abrogating or suppressing these earlier forms" (Johnstone, "Reactivating the Chronicles Analogy," 17). Williamson states that "it is true that on the whole he has handled his biblical sources more conservatively than others – perhaps because he accorded them a greater authority . . . " (Williamson, *1 and 2 Chronicles*, 23).
   Some other scholars too think that Chronicles is not a "rewriting," for example, Selman thinks that even the account of Abijah is not a rewriting of the account of Kings (Selman, *2 Chronicles*, 377), while Braun thinks that the account of Solomon alone is an exceptional case of rewriting in Chronicles (Braun, *1 Chronicles*, xxxiv, 'significance," 131–36): "In contrast to his usual method of dealing with his *Vorlage*, his account of Solomon's reign amounts to a virtual rewriting of that history." As for the evaluation of kings, for example, the evaluation of king Amaziah shows how the Chronicler followed the stance of its *Vorlage*, while presenting it in his own way for his own reasons. That is, the evaluation of Amaziah is described in Kings as "He did what was right in the sight of the Lord, yet not like his ancestor David; in all things he did as his father Joash had done" (2 Kgs 14:3), while the evaluation becomes simpler in Chronicles as "He did what was right in the sight of the Lord, yet not with a true heart" (2 Chr 25:2). Although the Chronicler omitted the name David as the standard, the Chronicler's new description still maintains his *Vorlage*'s view of the grade or evaluation of the king, i.e., an average-quality king.

35. Kalimi observes allusions as a literary technique employed by the Chronicler (Kalimi, *Zur Geschichtsschreibung*, 172–90). S. Weitzman also treats allusion as an important literary technique in his article which suggests that "Tobit 12–13 contains an allusion to Dt 31–32 that was intended by its author and was recognized by Tobit's original audience" (Weitzman, "Allusion, Artifice, and Exile," 49–61). A close relationship between reader's prior knowledge and allusion technique in a literature is investigated by J. Pucci, in the realm of western literature tradition, in his monograph *The Full-Knowing Reader*.

36. For example, Williamson thinks that "He [the Chronicler] frequently presupposes knowledge of passages in his *Vorlage* which he himself has not included . . ." [my insertion] (Williamson, *1 and 2 Chronicles*, 22). Ackroyd states that "Often we

had to employ omission, when we consider his situation. Firstly, the time scale of Chronicles, from the first man in Genesis to King Cyrus's order for the reconstruction of the temple, is wider than Samuel-Kings' time span. Secondly, many additional materials were necessary to emphasize his own points. These two points, at least, must have required the Chronicler to be selective in employing his source materials. For example, the Chronicler added extra materials in terms of the temple-building preparation along with the David-Solomon succession (1 Chr 22–29 cf. David's administration in 26:29–27:34), religious reformations of pious kings (e.g., 2 Chr 15:8–15; 17:7–9; 29:3–31:21), repentance (e.g., 2 Chr 33:10–17), wars (sometimes much more detailed accounts) (e.g., 2 Chr 13:2b–19; 14:7–14 [ET 14:8–15]; 20:1–30; 25:5–14; 28:5–8), prophets' activities (e.g., 2 Chr 15:1–8; 16:7–10; 19:1–3; 20:37; 21:12–15; 24:19–22; 25:14–16; 28:9–15), additional descriptions of kings' reigns (e.g., 2 Chr 17:10–19; 19:4–11; 26:5–15), not to mention some fragmentary historical information (e.g., 2 Chr 8:3), lists of names or genealogies (e.g., 1 Chr 1:51–9:34; 1 Chr 12) and so on,[37] for his own purposes. Hence, it must have been essential for the Chronicler to present his account in an economical way, or condensed form, as much as possible. To achieve this, it was necessary for him to omit some material that is not necessary or may distract his reader from his point, exploiting the supposed reader's prior knowledge of the first history, sometimes to its extreme.

The Chronicler also exploited the reader's prior knowledge when he employed the technique of allusion. Many commentators identify the presence of allusions in Chronicles to the first history or the old tradition. The reason for the Chronicler's employing the technique of allusion is more complicated than the cases of omission. It is not only related to an economical way of writing, but also to the subtlety required to solve this dilemma. Firstly, due to the need to cover a wider range of history than Samuel-Kings, and even add additional materials, he had to omit as much as possible. Secondly, at the same time, he had to sustain the flow

may observe that he assumes that his readers know the story being told, or that they know the form in which the story existed in the older presentations; *by an allusion*, by a brief summary, by a comment, *he invites a particular kind of understanding*, pointing in the direction of a particular moral or theological insight" [my emphasis] (Ackroyd, "The Theology of the Chronicler," 276). Selman also states that "One of the reasons for omitting this material is that the reader is expected to have a working knowledge of much of Samuel and Kings, and also of many other parts of Scripture" (Selman, *1 Chronicles*, 35).

37. For example, the Chronicler added the content of the psalm (1 Chr 16:8–36), which had been sung in the ceremony of the ark moving into Jerusalem.

of the history that was already known to his reader through reminding the reader of the omitted material. Thirdly, on top of the previous two points, he had to avoid distracting his reader from his own emphases. To meet such needs, the allusion technique seems to have been employed, for those needs cannot be satisfied through any other literary device than the technique of allusion.

3.2. The Definition of the "Technique of Allusion" in the Present Study

While there may be various definitions of allusion,[38] the present study defines the concept of technique of allusion as follows. It is a literary skill, which exploits the supposed reader's prior knowledge and is designed to remind the reader indirectly of certain contents, which are omitted or partially presented, in order not to distract the reader's mind from the main point of the present text. In other words, the reader is reminded of the omitted contents through the linkage of the alluded and the allusion without direct comment or evaluation.[39]

38. M. Silva, a NT scholar, describes well the "broad range of scriptural uses" that is covered by "allusion," in his discussion of Paul's allusion to OT. According to Silva, allusion in its broad sense covers "loose quotations, references to events, intentional appeals to specific passages, verbal similarities used (perhaps unconsciously) to express a different idea, broad undercurrents of themes, even totally unintentional correspondences" (Silva, "Old Testament in Paul," 634).

Gunn and Fewell, and Sommer discuss the concept of allusion in the context of the Hebrew Bible, suggesting their own respective definitions. For Gunn and Farewell, allusion is something that objectively exists as a similarity between an earlier text and a later text, while intertextuality as a counter concept exists only in the reader's mind, i.e., as a subjective entity (Gunn and Fewell, *Narrative in the Hebrew Bible*, 165). For Tate, allusion happens when "one author (perhaps sometimes unconsciously) frames a story or an episode like one written much earlier" (Tate, *Biblical Interpretation*, 102). In discussing allusion, other important issues are raised. For example, Sommer points out that when we explore allusion we firstly question whether a text follows the other or the two texts follow a common source (Sommer, "Exegesis, Allusion and Intertextuality," 488).

39. Kalimi provides a definition of allusion (*Anspielung*) in a wider sense, i.e., "Die Anspielung ist ein Signal, das für den aufmerksamen Leser eine Beziehung vom jeweils vorliegenden Text zu einem anderen schafft, und zwar durch markante Wiederholung einer sprachlichen Einheit (Vokabel oder Ausdruck)" [The allusion is a signal, which for the careful (sensitive) reader, creates a link between one given text to another, through the conspicuous repetition of a linguistic unit (word or phrase): my translation] (Kalimi, *Zur Geschichtsschreibung*, 172). Kalimi regards "allusion" as a distinctive literary technique in Chronicles, and provides a list of various kinds of allusion in Chronicles, using a chapter in his work (chapter 10, 172–90), for example,

3.3. The Various Types of the Technique of Allusion in Chronicles

In spite of most commentators' frequent use of the terms "allude" and "allusion" or their equivalent in describing Chronicles' literary features,[40] the contents that are alluded to are not considered as interpretative elements to constitute the meaning of the text. It is also noticeable that allusion has not been treated as a technique in the classic works that have tried to explore the literary technique of the narrative of the Hebrew Bible.[41] It is suspected that the reason for the lack of study of the allusion technique lies in the nature itself of the technique. That is, the technique functions in an implicit way by its nature, covering or hiding itself to some extent.

There are various types of allusion technique in Chronicles, outlined below. The titles do not necessarily reflect a precise meaning or feature of each category, but are used simply for our convenience in distinguishing one from another.

3.3.1. Abbreviation Allusion

Abbreviation allusion means that the Chronicler presented only the core material or simply mentioned the existence of a certain thing or matter, expecting that the reader, with his or her prior knowledge, should perceive his presentation as an understandable abbreviated form of the original account or tradition.

1. It is evident that the first two verses of the book, the simple enumeration of names from Adam to Noah, presume the reader's prior knowledge of a preliminary history or the first history, which contains the relationships between the protagonists. If not, the enumeration of names cannot have any sense of genealogy without the basic expression of "who begot whom" or "son of" (e.g., 1 Chr 3:10–16; 5:4–6a). This technique reappears in 1 Chr 1:24–27, covering Shem to Abraham. These are among the cases that show the extent to

regnal ending form (*Schlußformeln*). He also treats omission (*Auslassungen*) in a separate chapter (chapter 4, 80–91). His collection of a variety of literary techniques employed in Chronicles is highly valuable.

40. For example, Selman acknowledges that from the beginning to the ending, in Chronicles, "quotations from and allusions to other parts of the Old Testament are frequent" (Selman, *1 Chronicles*, 26).

41. Alter, *Art*; Berlin, *Poetics*; Bar-Efrat, *Narrative Art*; Sternberg, *The Poetics of Biblical Narrative*. None of them treats the allusion technique. Gunn and Fewell treat it only in relation to intertextuality, without substantial depth.

which Chronicles was written in an economical manner, exploiting the reader's prior knowledge.[42]

2. In the opening verse of the Solomon account in Chronicles, the expression "Solomon . . . established himself" (2 Chr 1:1a) is generally construed by commentators as alluding to "the disorder" which was present just before Solomon's first enthronement (1 Kgs 1–2), for the expression is always used in a context which presumes "a time of difficulty" or "some considerable effort" (2 Chr 12:13; 13:21; 17:1; 21:4), as Williamson points out.[43]

3. When the Chronicler describes the fact that Saul "did not keep the command of the Lord" in 1 Chr 10:13 as the reason for his death, he must refer to the series of occasions in which Israel's first king failed to obey God's word given by Samuel the prophet,[44] which appears in its *Vorlage*, for it is plain that Chronicles' text so far has not mentioned any disobedience of Saul to God. This means that the Chronicler expects, by this abbreviated presentation, his readers to recall the cases of Saul's disobedience.

4. While Kings describes the content of prophets' words against Manasseh in 2 Kgs 21:10–16, the Chronicler simply mentions the fact that the words had been written in a certain book (2 Chr 33:18b), probably expecting that his simple mention would remind the reader of the content of the prophets' words which appear in its *Vorlage*.

3.3.2. Presupposing Allusion

While every case of allusion basically presupposes the reader's prior knowledge of a certain matter or account, presupposing allusion refers especially to cases where without the prior knowledge of the reader which functions as supplementary to the text, the account does not make sense by itself. If

42. "In this way, the whole of Genesis has been spectacularly reduced to a single chapter" (Selman, *1 Chronicles*, 39). "C's audience must also have been well-versed in the traditions of Genesis: his use of its genealogical framework must have functioned for his readers (and for such a highly sophisticated work of learning with its detailed modification of a written text one must assume an audience primarily of readers) as a kind of cryptic code, allusively bringing to mind in the most condensed form possible the stories of the primeval and of the patriarchal periods" (Johnstone, *1 Chronicles 1–2 Chronicles 9*, 25).

43. Williamson, *1 and 2 Chronicles*, 193.

44. Selman, *1 Chronicles*, 35.

we do not acknowledge the presence of the allusion technique in this case, then the description should be construed as clumsy or irrelevant.

1. The retrospective mention that David had an alliance with the Philistines in the battle against Saul, as the background to some of the Manassites' coming to David (1 Chr 12:20–22 [ET 12:19–21]), might be abrupt and odd, if the reader's knowledge of the account or story of David's early exiled life was not presumed.[45]

2. If the first enthronement ceremony of Solomon, as it appears in Kings, is not supposed to be part of the reader's prior knowledge, the phrase "the second time" in the context of the enthronement ceremony of Solomon in 1 Chr 29:22 must be, by itself, a puzzling phrase.[46]

The seemingly contradictory presentations of Solomon's enthronement between the two works (1 Kgs 1:5–53; 1 Chr 28:1—29:23) have been well recognized. In Kings, Solomon's succession is a hurried one in the face of Adonijah's revealed ambition for the throne, whereas in Chronicles, it appears to be a well-prepared succession without any hurry. However, the Chronicles statement "They made David's son Solomon king a second time" in 1 Chr 29:22b should be considered seriously. That is, Kings' description of Solomon's succession is presupposed as his first enthronement, and the Chronicler's description is of Solomon's second enthronement ceremony.[47] Although it is acknowledged that the Chronicler, for his own reasons, chose the second occasion of Solomon's enthronement rather than the first occasion which appears in Kings, it is plain that he did not try to rewrite the event of Solomon's succession described in Kings. Rather he did not neglect to inform his reader of his account's describing a different, second occasion of Solomon's enthronement,

---

45. Childs, *Introduction*, 646–47. Childs thinks that the passage is "virtually incomprehensible without the implied relationship with the other accounts." He also thinks that 2 Chr 32:24–33 is the same case, which is not very convincing.

46. It is noteworthy that in the *Vorlage* the previous kings to Solomon (i.e., Saul, David), have a ceremony of becoming king twice, respectively (Saul in 1 Sam 10:19–24 and 11:14–15 ("renew the kingship" (הַמְּלוּכָה...וַנְחַדֵּשׁ)); David in 2 Sam 2:4 and 5:3. cf. for Joshua in Num 27:18–23 (cf. Deut 34:9) and Deut 31:3–8). Williamson proposes that the first enthronement and ensuing power struggle are presupposed by the author and hinted at as well.

47. Williamson too thinks that Solomon's first enthronement in 1 Kgs 1 is presupposed here by the Chronicler (Williamson, *1 and 2 Chronicles*, 187).

strongly presuming or alluding to the first one in Kings.[48] Therefore, Braun's understanding that the Chronicler wrote a new history on this occasion, i.e., the succession of Solomon, which he regards as a contrast to the usual case of Chronicler in terms of his usage of Samuel-Kings as his main source, is misleading.[49]

3. Jeroboam's flight from King Solomon and his return from Egypt in 2 Chr 10:2 would be an abrupt and incomprehensible statement, if the reader did not have prior knowledge of 1 Kgs 11:26–40, where the reason why he had to flee from Solomon is accounted for.[50]

4. The account of Shemaiah the man of God's prophecy which declares that the division of kingdom is the work of God, and therefore the southern kingdom should not try to regain the northern territory and tribes through war, and the southerner's obedience to the prophecy in 2 Chr 11:1–4, would be an incomprehensible episode, if the reader did not have the prior knowledge of the content of 1 Kgs 11:1–40, where Solomon's sin and God's declaration of the secession of the northern tribes as punishment for Solomon's sin are explicitly stated.

5. It is also noteworthy that in Chronicles, Jeroboam's becoming king of the northern kingdom has not at this point been mentioned, but it is stated that the war is against Jeroboam (2 Chr 11:4b). That means that the Chronicler presupposed the reader's prior knowledge of it in 1 Kgs 12:20, where Jeroboam's becoming the king of the northern Israel is mentioned.[51]

6. King Rehoboam's rejection of the people's claim for a lightened yoke upon them, which will result in the division of the kingdom, is described as a fulfillment of the prophecy of Ahijah the Shilonite to Jeroboam son of Nebat (2 Chr 10:15), without any previous account in Chronicles of its contents, not to mention its context or background, except the simple mention of "the prophecy of Ahijah the Shilonite" among source materials or further information sources (2 Chr 9:29). It might appear to be an abrupt comment, if the reader does not know the account of 1 Kgs 11:29–39. Hence, it is evident that the

---

48. Contra Knoppers.

49. Braun, *1 Chronicles*, xxxiv.

50. Williamson, *1 and 2 Chronicles*, 239.

51. Although it has been revealed that Jeroboam is an important figure among the northern tribes, it has not been shown from the text so far that he is the leader of the northern tribes, the object of the war.

Chronicler assumes his reader's prior knowledge of the Kings' account or an equivalent of it.[52] Furthermore, it can be suggested not only that this verse is in line with the Chronicler's well-acknowledged perspective, which regards God's prophecy and its fulfillment as an important driving force of Israel's history (e.g., 1 Chr 11:2; 17:3–15; 2 Chr 36:22–23),[53] but also that the alluded account of 1 Kgs 11:29–39 inevitably reminds the reader of the cause or background of the prophecy, i.e., the apostasy of Solomon in 1 Kgs 11:1–8. Ahijah's prophecy in 1 Kgs 11:29–39 contains the fact of Solomon's apostasy (11:33, 39a). That means that the Chronicler presumes the reader's prior knowledge of Solomon's corruption.

Knoppers does not admit that the Chronicler presupposed the reader's prior knowledge of the content that appears in Kings on the matter of the division of the kingdom, including the cause or background of it. He tries to read the text only in its own light, and insists that the presentation of Rehoboam in Chronicles is totally different from that in Kings.[54] According to him, the blame for the division of the kingdom falls solely upon Jeroboam in Chronicles, for, in his view, Rehoboam is presented positively in his first three years, within which the schism happens, which means that the blame for the division of the kingdom does not fall upon Rehoboam in Chronicles.[55] Solomon also cannot be an object of blame on the matter of the division, for he takes it for granted that Solomon's reign is described as an "unblemished tenure"[56] in Chronicles and the ideal state of the united kingdom. However, Knoppers fails to recognize that the present issue is not whether Rehoboam is depicted as a "victim"[57] and

---

52. Selman, 2 Chronicles, 363; Williamson, 1 and 2 Chronicles, 239.

53. Selman, 2 Chronicles, 363.

54. Knoppers, "Rehoboam in Chronicles."

55. The grounds on which he insists that Rehohoam is positively presented in his early reign is, for example, conspicuously additional material for the period seems to be positive. That is, his fortification of many cities (2 Chr 11:5–12), refugees from Israel (2 Chr 11:13–17), prospering family of Rehoboam (2 Chr 11:18–21), his wise administration (2 Chr 11:22–23). Also the frequent appearance of the word of root, חזק (strengthening) is construed by Knoppers as a mark of positive presentation of Rehoboam (2 Chr 11:11, 12, 17; 12:1, 13; 13:7, 8). On this point, Knoppers diverges from other scholars who put some amount of the responsibility for the division upon Rehoboam (e.g., Williamson, 1 and 2 Chronicles, 238).

56. Knoppers, "Rehoboam in Chronicles," 434. For Knoppers' understanding of Solomon's reign, 429–30.

57. Ibid., 437–39.

also positively in his early reign, but whether Solomon's misdeeds as the ultimate cause of the division described in the *Vorlage*, are hinted at or denied in Chronicles.

According to Knoppers, the mentions of Ahijah's prophecy and its fulfillment in 2 Chr 10:15, and the prophecy of Shemaiah in 2 Chr 11:2–4 only show "divine sovereignty," and do not allude to Solomon's misdeeds in the *Vorlage* at all; the division of the kingdom is accounted for solely by "Jeroboam's usurpation and Rehoboam's faint-heartedness" with the excuse of his inexperience,[58] as Abijah's speech emphasizes.[59] The omission of the account of God's punishment against Solomon (1 Kgs 11:26–40), including God's promise of the northern kingdom to Jeroboam (1 Kgs 11:31, 35, 37–38), and the addition of the refugees from Israel, as the result of the problematic counter-cultus of Jeroboam (2 Chr 11:13–17), are also construed by Knoppers as proof of the Chronicler's intention to present Jeroboam more negatively[60] in order to lay the whole weight of blame for the division upon him.[61]

However, Knoppers' argument can be refuted as follows. Firstly, it is not likely that the prophecies of Shemaiah and Ahijah only show "divine sovereignty" vaguely as he insists. If the division is merely the result of Jeroboam's unauthorized usurpation and the weakness of the inexperienced Rehoboam, why does God prevent Rehoboam's rightful action to regain the lost territory? God's stopping the rightful action, saying that "for this thing is from me" (2 Chr 11:4) is not reasonable or understandable, if it is the case that Jeroboam is not authorized to become the king of northern territory and Rehoboam, at least at this stage, is a positively described king as Knoppers suggests. Secondly, Knoppers' view seems to be unable to explain the evident passage of Solomon's oppressive rule which is recognized not only by the rebel party (2 Chr 10:4) but also by Rehoboam's party (2 Chr 10:11, 14). Thirdly, if the Chronicler wanted to deny any responsibility of Solomon on the matter of the division of the kingdom, he could have omitted even the mentions of the prophecies of Ahijah and Shemaiah, which, however, he did not do. Fourthly, as we have

---

58. Ibid., 439.

59. Ibid., 437–39. Knoppers believes that Abijiah's speech reflects the exact perspective of the Chronicler, which we have contested already.

60. Ibid., 434–36.

61. Ibid., 439–40.

seen already, the view that Abijah's speech reflects the exact perspective of the Chronicler is not tenable, for Rehoboam's response to the rebel party was never weak in the crucial two cases, i.e., his harsh response (2 Chr 10:14) and his determination to regain the lost territory, not hesitating to initiate a civil war (2 Chr 11:1). Fifthly, it should be pointed out that Jeroboam's problematic counter-cultus is more directly and negatively described in Kings (1 Kgs 12:25–31), which is omitted in Chronicles. Therefore, it is hard to say that the Chronicler tried to depict Jeroboam more negatively in his writing on this matter, in order to present him as an unauthorized "villain." Moreover, the omission of God's promise to him, and his becoming the king of the northern kingdom officially, might be explainable without any assumption of the Chronicler's intention of presenting Jeroboam more negatively than in its *Vorlage*. That is, it is more likely that the Chronicler presupposed his reader's awareness of the omitted content, as we have been seeing.

3.3.3. Allusive Hints

Allusive hints refers to cases where certain of the Chronicler's descriptions seem to strongly imply some omitted tradition, a description that does not seem very necessary in the context, but functions as a crucial clue to remind the reader of a particular omitted tradition.

1. The account of the bringing of the ark to the city of David ends abruptly in Chronicles, with the mention of Michal's despising the dancing David in her heart (1 Chr 15:29). The ending by itself is not a very relevant piece of the account in the context, in contrast with its original form in its *Vorlage*, where the consequent result, i.e., Michal's barrenness (2 Sam 6:20–23), in the larger context of the decline of Saul's house in contrast to David's house, makes the whole episode meaningful. Without the mention of Michal's despising David dancing, the whole ark-moving episode might have been more neatly concluded in Chronicles. Hence, it is reasonable to think that the Chronicler curtailed the original episode, expecting his reader to be reminded of the ensuing events. The ensuing episode of the argument between David and Michal, and Michal's barrenness, is omitted because it might distract the reader from the main point of the ark-moving episode in Chronicles. Nevertheless, the ensuing events should be recalled or hinted at through the introductory mention

of Michal's despising David, for the reminded account of Michal's barrenness is consonant with the clear statement of Saul's being punished by God for a proper reason in Chronicles (1 Chr 10:13–14).

2. David's remaining at Jerusalem while Joab was attacking Rabba in 1 Chr 20:1b, seems to strongly imply his adultery with Bathsheba, which occurred as a consequence of his remaining in Jerusalem. The phrase retained from the *Vorlage*, "In the spring of the year, the time when kings go out to battle . . ." (1 Chr 20:1a / 2 Sam 11:1a) also maintains the implication that David does not behave properly as a king, which becomes evident in the *Vorlage* as the story unfolds. Those phrases seem to be used as a significant foreshadowing of David's disgraceful deed to follow in its *Vorlage,* and do not seem very necessary in the present context of the account, if the Chronicler did not intend to hint at the ensuing misdeed of David. This observation leads us to conclude that this verse is intended to remind the reader of the whole account of the affair and possibly even the murder of Uriah.[62] This means that the Chronicler did not intend to conceal David's faults, but to recall them without any serious distraction from his present emphasis in the account.

3.3.4. *Typological Allusion*[63]

Typological allusion means the case where the Chronicler's presentation of a certain account has a similar pattern to an account of previous tradition, strongly implying that the event or figure described now has continuity with the previous one, together with the significance of it. It is plain that the Chronicler's intention to link the present description to an earlier one, i.e., its prototype, is unthinkable without the presupposition of the supposed reader's prior knowledge of the earlier tradition. It is noteworthy that the Chronicler uses typological allusion not only between an earlier tradition and his own writing, but also within his own writing.[64]

---

62. Selman, *1 Chronicles*, 196: "evocative allusion"; Williamson, *1 and 2 Chronicles*, 140: "probably . . . he assumes knowledge of the fuller account" (Willi, *Die Chronik*, 57ff.).

63. For a list of cases, see Dillard, "The Chronicler's Jehoshahat," 17.

64. It includes the resemblance between the portrayal of Solomon and that of David, between the portrayal of Hezekiah and that of David and Solomon, between the portrayal of the reign of Ahaz and that of Jerohoam (shown by Williamson), and between Asa and Jehoshaphat (shown by Dillard).

1. The presentation of the temple building follows the pattern of the tabernacle construction in several ways. Firstly, God is described as the original designer of every details of the sacred temple and its furniture in Chronicles (1 Chr 28:11–19) as in the case of the tabernacle building (Exod 25:9–40). Secondly, the call for the materials for the building of the temple by David the leader and the people's willing response to it in Chronicles (1 Chr 29:6–9) resembles Moses' call for the material and the people's willing response to it in the case of the building of the tabernacle (Exod 35:4–9; 36:3–7). Thirdly, detailed description of the temple being built (2 Chr 3–4) resembles the similarly detailed description of the tabernacle being built (Exod 36:1—39:32). Fourthly, the skilled artisan Huram-abi's being employed for the temple construction (2 Chr 2:12–13 [ET 2:13–14]; 4:11–16) resembles the case of Bezalel and Oholiab for the tabernacle construction (Exod 35:30—36:2; 37:1; 38:22–23). Fifthly, the presence of the Lord's glory accompanied by a cloud, overwhelming the priests there, in the dedication ceremony (2 Chr 5:13–14) resembles the almost identical phenomenon in the case of the tabernacle when the construction is finished (Exod 40:34–35).[65]

2. As the temple building resembles the tabernacle building, the chief builders of the temple, Solomon and Huram-abi in Chronicles, resemble Bezalel and Oholiab in Exodus in many aspects, as Dillard rightly points out.[66] Solomon resembles Bezalel in his being chosen by God as the main builder for the building task (1 Chr 22:9–10; 28:6—29:2 // Exod 31:1–11; 35:30—36:2; 38:22–23), in his being of the tribe of Judah (Exod 31:2; 35:30; 38:22), and in his receiving wisdom from God (2 Chr 1:7–12; 2:11 [ET 2:12] // Exod 31:1–3; 35:30–35). Furthermore, the description of Solomon's going to the bronze altar plainly described as having been built by Bezalel in Chronicles (2 Chr 1:5), which is absent in its *Vorlage*, can be construed as a conscious effort of the Chronicler to link Solomon to Bezalel. That the Chronicler consciously tried to link the two figures becomes more probable when we consider that, apart from Exodus, the name of Bezalel appears only in Chronicles (1 Chr 2:20; 2 Chr 1:5) in the

---

65. Selman provides a similar observation, but some of his points are not convincing. (Selman, *1 Chronicles*, 41).

66. Dillard, "The Chronicler's Solomon," 296–99. Dillard notes that his student Mr. Terry Eves has provided the basic idea.

context of the tabernacle building.[67] The description of Huram-abi in Chronicles also seems intended to hint that the figure is following the model of Oholiab who worked in the tabernacle building. Dillard points out Huram-abi's early involvement in the building task (2 Chr 2:11–13 [ET 2:12–14]), his skill not only in bronze work but also others, such as textiles (2 Chr 2:13b [ET 2:14b]), and his mother's belonging to Dan (2 Chr 2:13a [ET 2:14a]), which resembles the description of Oholoiab (his early involvement in the tabernacle building in Exod 31:1–6, his variety of skills in Exod 35:30—36:2; 38:23, and his father's being from Dan in Exod 31:6a; 35:34; 38:23). This betrays the Chronicler's intention to link the two figures, as they are described differently in the *Vorlage* (Huram's late appearance in 1 Kgs 7:13–47, his work only in bronze in 1 Kgs 7:14, his mother's being Naphtali in 1 Kgs 7:14[68]).[69]

3. The description of the succession of David and Solomon resembles that of Moses and Joshua.[70] Williamson rightly observes similarity at five points, and convincingly argues that the account of the succession from Moses to Joshua in the Pentateuch and book of Joshua was used as a model of the Chronicler's description of the succession from David to Solomon, enumerating the similarities as follows. Firstly, as Moses is disqualified from leading the people into the promised land, David is disqualified from building the temple. Both figures want to do it, but God rejects them and lets it be done by their respective successors.[71] Secondly, several elements or phrases used in the installation of Joshua reappear in Solomon's installation. That is, "Be strong and bold" in Deut 31:7, 23; Josh 1:6, 7, 9 and 1 Chr 22:13; 28:20, "Do not fear or be dismayed" or equivalents in Deut 31:6, 8; Josh 1:9 and 1 Chr 22:13; 28:20, "The Lord your God is with you" or equivalents in Deut 31:6, 8, 23; Josh 1:5, 9 and 1 Chr 22:11, 16; 28:20;

---

67. Ibid., 296.

68. Dillard suggests a possible harmonization of the contradictory descriptions between Kings and Chronicles concerning Huram-abi's mother. For example, Dan in 2 Chr 2:13 [ET 2:14] could be used as a regional name rather than a tribal name. See ibid., 298.

69. Ibid., 297–98.

70. Williamson, "Accession of Solomon," 351–56; Braun, "Solomon the Chosen Temple Builder," 586–88 ; Dillard, "The Chronicler's Solomon," 293–95.

71. Williamson also observes that "peace" and "rest" commonly appears in Joshua and Solomon in terms of their tasks (Josh 11:23; 21:44, etc. / 1 Chr 22:9, 18) (Williamson, "Accession of Solomon," 351–52).

2 Chr 1:1, and "He will not fail you or forsake you" or equivalents in Deut 31:6, 8; Josh 1:5 and 1 Chr 28:20. Furthermore, the promise of success or prosperity commonly appears as the supposed result of the observation of the law in Josh 1:7–8 and 1 Chr 22:12–13; 28:7–9.[72] Thirdly, Solomon is commanded to succeed David twice, once more or less privately (1 Chr 22:6–16) and the other more publicly (1 Chr 28:1–10) "in the sight of all Israel," by David, while Joshua is commanded to succeed Moses twice, once privately by God (Deut 31:23), and the other publicly (Deut 31:7) "in the sight of all Israel" by Moses. Fourthly, in both cases, the people's full-hearted acceptance of the new leader and obedience to him is described (Deut 34:9 and 1 Chr 29:23–24). Fifthly, in both cases, the Lord's exalting or magnifying the new leader after the installation, usually in the sight of Israel, is described (Josh 3:7; 4:14 and 1 Chr 29:25; 2 Chr 1:1).[73]

The purpose of this typology is not hard to recognize. By reminding his reader of the model case of the present one, exploiting the reader's prior knowledge, the Chronicler intended to bring into relief the significance or meaning of the present case impressively or effectively without any direct explanation. For example, it is probable that the Chronicler tried to show the complementary nature of the relationship of David and Solomon, by patterning the description after that of Moses and Joshua, whose relationship is preparation and fulfillment, i.e., a complementary one, as Williamson argues.[74]

---

72. Three elements of installation, encouragement, description of the task, and assurance of divine aid, are spotted first by Lohfink. Since his discovery, the discussion of the typology between the two cases has developed (Lohfink, "von Moses auf Josue").

73. Williamson, "Accession of Solomon," 351–56. Dillard adds one more point to these. That is, both new leaders lead the people into "rest," Joshua in Josh 11:23; 21:44 and Solomon in 1 Chr 22:8–9. Besides, Dillard points out two more similarities, which are not necessarily exclusive similarities of the two accounts. Firstly, both leaders use aliens in the service of the tabernacle or the temple. That is, Joshua employs the Gibeonites for the service of worship place (Josh 9:26–27), and Solomon conscripts foreign labor for the construction of the temple (2 Chr 2:16–17 [ET 2:17–18]; 8:7–10). Secondly, both leaders receive divine wisdom as a gift (Deut 34:9; 2 Chr 1) (Dillard, "The Chronicler's Solomon," 294).

74. Williamson, "Accession of Solomon," 356–69. Another of Williamson's points of similarity is that by following the pattern of the succession of Moses and Joshua, the Chronicler intended to present the reign of David and Solomon as a unitary period (356–57).

3.3.5. Allusion by Conflation

"Allusion by conflation" refers to the cases where the Chronicler's presentation of a certain account not only re-presents the apparently identical one from the *Vorlage*, but also reminds the reader, through subtly additional materials, of another account which has common elements or a similarity to the main one in its *Vorlage*.

1. It is observed that the account of David's adultery and murder in Second Samuel 11–12, and the account of David's sin of the census in Second Samuel 24, have several common elements. That is, firstly, in both cases David makes the confession "I have sinned" (חָטָאתִי), marking a turning point in both narratives (2 Sam 12:13 and 24:10). Secondly, David's sin brings about death (2 Sam 11:17–26; 12:15–19 and 24:15). Thirdly, a prophet is sent to rebuke David (2 Sam 12:1–4 and 24:11–14).[75] What matters is that God's punishing sword, which appears only in the account of Bathsheba and Uriah in the *Vorlage* (2 Sam 12:10), appears in the account of the census in Chronicles (1 Chr 21:12, 16, 27), while it is unclear how the angel's sword works in regard to the plague upon the people. This "sword" element added to the account of the census means that the David's sin concerning Bathsheba and Uriah can be more easily recalled here.

   Furthermore, Ornan's four sons hiding themselves from the angel or his sword (1 Chr 21:20) can be construed as a significant link between the census account in 1 Chr 21 and the adultery and murder account in 2 Sam 11–12. Williamson proposes the possibility that the phrase, "his four sons" came from textual corruption, regarding it as "not contributing further to the development of the narrative."[76]

---

75. Selman observes several similarities between the account of David's adultery and murder in 2 Sam 11–12 and the account of David's census in 1 Chr 21, acknowledging the basic fact that there are some similarities already between 2 Sam 11–12 (adultery and murder) and 2 Sam 24 (census). He points out that there are two more similar points between 2 Sam 11–12 and 1 Chr 21 than between 2 Sam 11–12 and 2 Sam 24. That is, the sword of the Lord as the instrument of punishment (2 Sam 12:10 // 1 Chr 21:12, 16, 27, 30) and God's "forgiveness through his covenant promises" (2 Sam 12:24–25 cf. 2 Sam 12:10 // 1 Chr 21:28—22:1 cf. 1 Chr 21:29–30). However, Selman's putting 2 Sam 12:13 and 2 Sam 24:16 together as a similar point under the title, "David is forgiven by God's word of promise" is not convincing, for 2 Sam 24:16 can in no way be construed as a promise. Selman also introduces Johnstone's significant view that David's adultery in 1 Sam and David's census in 1 Chr are both a "hinge" or "pivot" of each story line, which implies an underlying similarity between 2 Sam 11–12 and 1 Chr 21. (Selman, *1 Chronicles*, 201).

76. Williamson, *1 and 2 Chronicles*, 149.

However, it is unlikely that "his four sons' (אַרְבַּעַת בָּנָיו) was confused with "his servants coming on" (עֲבָדָיו עֹבְרִים) (2 Sam 24:20) as he suggests. In fact, it is possible that "his four sons" can be construed as having a significant meaning and function here in relation to the account of David's adultery and murder in 2 Sam 11–12. After the sin of adultery and murder, David's four sons died one by one,[77] in keeping with his own pronouncement that the robber of a lamb should pay four fold (2 Sam 12:6), based on the property law in Exod 21:37 [ET 22:1], as Tate sharply observes.[78] The tragic death of David's four sons is nothing but a fulfillment of the Lord's word of punishment or discipline of David, i.e., "Now therefore the sword shall never depart from your house" (2 Sam 12:10). Therefore, for the reader who is acquainted with the whole story of David's discipline or punishment for his sin of adultery and murder, in the form of losing his four sons, Ornan's four sons hiding themselves with their father from the Lord's sword in 1 Chr 21 might be a reminder of the account of David's adultery and murder in its *Vorlage*.

Finally, it can be added that David's sin concerning Bathsheba and Uriah is strongly hinted at, as we have seen already as a case of "Allusive Hints." Therefore, it seems that through several devices of allusion technique here in 1 Chr 21, the Chronicler alluded to the omitted tradition in this combined or coalesced form, although the main account of David's sin of adultery and murder is omitted in his work.

---

77. The firstborn infant baby between David and Bathsheba (2 Sam 12:14–18), Amnon (2 Sam 13:28–33), Absalom (2 Sam 18:14–15), and Adonijah (1 Kgs 2:23–25).

78. Tate, *Biblical Interpretation*, 104–5. Tate observes that, interestingly, as David himself declared, not realizing that he was passing the sentence upon himself, "he shall restore the lamb fourfold" (2 Sam 12:6), he pays for his sin with his four sons' lives as four lambs. Tate points out lamb-elements of each son's death. The first son dies on the seventh day like a firstborn male lamb in the sacrificial system (Num 29). The second son Amnon dies where sheepshearers are gathered. The third son Absalom is described with lamb image in his long hair and annual hair shearing and his hair's weight. Absalom is also described as having "no blemish" like the sacrificial lamb. Absalom is caught in "thick branches" with his hair like "a ram caught in a thicket by its horns" which was slain in the place of Abraham's son Isaac. The fourth son Adonijah "went to grasp the horns of the altar" (1 Kgs 1:50), which has "sacrificial imagery," but he was soon killed.

3.4. Conclusion: The Implication of the Presence of the Allusion Cases in Chronicles

Presenting the reigns of kings, the Chronicler seems to exploit the reader's prior knowledge of the contents of the *Vorlage* by omitting some parts of its *Vorlage* for particular reasons, while at the same time reminding the reader of the omitted contents through the technique of allusion. If it is valid that there are various types of technique of allusion employed in Chronicles, as we have explored so far, it plainly indicates that the Chronicler presumed his reader's prior knowledge, trying to exploit it for his own reason or purpose. It will be shown later how various types of allusion technique are employed in the account of Solomon in 2 Chr 1–9 (or 10), which will produce a new interpretation of the account concerning Solomon's faults.

4. CONCLUSION

In this chapter, two literary characteristics of Chronicles, which are closely related to its nature as the second work of historiography, were proposed. Firstly, kings are generally presented with increased or newly introduced nuance or complexity in Chronicles, compared to its *Vorlage*. It is true that in many ways David and Solomon's reign is described in a distinctive manner from other kings. Nevertheless, it is detected that David and Solomon's portrayal has an increased nuance or complexity like other kings' general cases. If that is accepted as a possibility, it is expected that Solomon's faults can be detected in his account.

Secondly, through case studies, various kinds of allusion technique are shown as literary characteristics of Chronicles. If the increased nuance or greater complexity and technique of allusion are accepted as literary characteristics of Chronicles, much more attention should be paid to small hints, which may have a negative sense, in the Solomon account in Chronicles, in order to find the intended meaning of the account. This chapter suggests that it is justifiable to pay very close attention to the subtle presentation that is involved with Egyptian elements in the Solomon account in Chronicles, which have negative implications in the reader's prior knowledge.

6

The Deuteronomic Law
and Chronicles

1. INTRODUCTION

DILLARD STATES THAT NEITHER the Deuteronomist nor the Chronicler applied the law of the king (Deut 17:14–20), which bans Israelite kings from importing Egyptian horses and accumulating gold and silver for themselves, to the Solomon narrative or account, and he is surprised at his own observation that even the Deuteronomist did not apply the stipulation to the Solomon narrative in Kings (which is part of the so-called Deuteronomistic History).[1] According to Dillard, the importation of Egyptian horses and wealth accumulation are presented as God's blessing in both works. However, contrary to Dillard's view, the present study has proposed in chapter 3 that the so-called Deuteronomist or the author of Kings applied the stipulation in a subtle way to maximize the effect of his message, i.e., the insidious progress of sin and the pressing need of the presence of the law in the life of Israel to check hard-to-detect sin. Then what should be said of Chronicles, of which it has been presupposed, in this study, that it relies heavily upon the previous history work as its basic stance?

1. Dillard, "The Chronicler's Solomon," 290 n. 3.

The law (Torah) of Moses or its equivalents with a variety of titles, is mentioned as an established authority for an action or plan over six times more frequently in Chronicles than in Kings, where it is mentioned only three times (2 Kgs 14:6; 23:21; 23:24).[2] Not only has the frequent appearance of the Mosaic law as a source of authority in Chronicles long been noticed, but also the influence of Pentateuchal law on the book's historical narrative has been recognized.[3] However, while some scholars have suggested that the laws of the Chronicler were different from what we have now,[4] the Pentateuchal law has not been taken into consideration seriously as a factor that helps interpretation of the account of Solomon. For example, while Curtis maintains that the importation of horses from Egypt in Solomon's time is probable, even resorting to the reference of Deut 17:16, he does not seem to have any concern to apply the law to decide the meaning of the text of 2 Chr 1:14–17.[5] The early commentators who saw a close link between the Pentateuch and Chronicles, seem to be so preoccupied with the historical aspect of the text that their commentaries are filled with comments on whether the horses were imported from Egypt (מִצְרַיִם) or *Muzri* and so on, without any mention of the possibility of the application of the Deuteronimic law in order to decide the intended meaning of the text.

2. Japhet notices only two cases (2 Kgs 14:6; 23:21), overlooking 23:24 (Japhet, *Ideology*, 235). Myers also provides a similar comparison, although his calculation is based upon his assumption that Ezra-Nehemiah is also the Chronicler's work (Myers, *I Chronicles*, LXXVIII).

3. Willi, *Auslegung*, 48ff; von Rad, *Geschichtsbild*, 1; Japhet, *Ideology*, 239.

4. Von Rad, *Geschichtsbild*, 63 and n. 106; Rudolph, *Chronikbücher*, xv; Milgrom, *Levitical Terminology*, 80 n. 46, 307; Eissfeldt, *Introduction*, 539.

5. Curtis and Madsen, *Chronicles*, 318–19. Curtis mentions Deut 17:16 here against a historical critical view which sees that "Egypt is an agricultural not a pastoral country; it lacks the broad plains suitable for the rearing of large number of horses. Egypt was therefore probably only the market; the raising ground was elsewhere" (Barnes, *The Books of Chronicles*, 145 n. 16; almost the same views in Elmslie, *The Books of Chronicles*, 172 n. 16; Slotki, *Chronicles*, 162 n. 16). However, Curtis proposes that "Horses were introduced into Egypt by the Hyksos (during the period of the thirteenth to the seventeenth dynasties, 1788–1580 B.C.," Breasted, *History of the Ancient Egyptians*, p. 425), and in later dynasties the "stables of Pharaoh contained thousands of the best horses to be had in Asia" (Ib. p. 195), hence the importation of horses and chariots, which were widely used in Egypt, into Palestine would have been most natural (v. 17)." Curtis adds that "The securing of horses from Egypt is also strongly favoured by Deut. 1716, Is. 311."

Noth's distinction between the Deuteronomistic history (Deuter-onomy–Kings) and the Chronicler's history (Chronicles–Nehemiah),[6] formed a framework in which scholars see the Old Testament histories. And it has affected, by its nature, the understanding of the relationship between the Deuteronomic law and Chronicles. Noth's view seems to help form an attitude which sees Chronicles as fundamentally different from Deuteronomy. On the other side, although von Rad emphasizes a close link between the Deuteronomic law and Chronicles,[7] he does not think that the law mentioned in Chronicles is the same law that we have in canonical form.[8] Hence, it is not surprising to notice that even after the close relationship between the Pentateuch and Chronicles had been recognized by scholars like von Rad, commentators neglected to apply the Deuteronomic law to the text of Chronicles in order to decide its meaning, especially that of the account of Solomon. For example, Myers observes that "there is a much stronger emphasis upon Moses and the Torah than in the corresponding books of the Deuteronomist,"[9] and "The Torah was thus the official standard according to which the life and activity of nation and individuals were judged,"[10] but he does not show any attempt to apply the law of the king in Deut 17:16, which bans importation of Egyptian horses, to the account of Solomon in Chronicles.[11] Furthermore, McConville, who even proposes that Deuteronomy should be construed as an ancient Israelite constitution, and consequently insists on its ancient origin,[12] does

6. Noth divides the Old Testament histories into two distinct parts in his influ-ential work, *Überlieferungsgeschichtliche Studien*. Reflecting the distinction of the histories in his view, the work was translated into two separate volumes in English (Noth, *Überlieferungsgeschichtliche Studien*. Noth, *Deuteronomistic History*; Noth, *The Chronicler's History*, 29–106).

7. Von Rad even refers to Chronicles as a "nomistic view of history" (*nomistische Geschichtsbetracht*) (von Rad, *Geschichtsbild*, 1), and demonstrates that more Deutero-nomic than Priestly elements are found in Chronicles (134). See also Willi, *Auslegung*, 48ff.

8. Von Rad, *Geschichtsbild*, 40ff.

9. Myers, *I Chronicles*, LXXVIII.

10. Ibid., LXXIX. Myers also observes that the Chronicler "was steeped in every aspect of the Torah" and that "The importance of the Torah may be judged by the fact that kings and kingdom, cult and ministrants were under its judgment. . . . Moreover, the Chronicler scrutinized every phase of politics and religion for possible viola-tions of its demands, which he applied rigorously to all life and conduct..." (Myers, *I Chronicles*, LXXIX–LXXX).

11. Myers, *II Chronicles*, 4–7, 54–59.

12. McConville, "Deuteronomy," 198–99; McConville, *Deuteronomy*, 38–40.

not apply the king's law in Deut 17:16 in interpreting the Solomon account in Chronicles.

While the relationship between Deuteronomy (or its law) and Chronicles has not yet attracted close scholarly attention,[13] recent studies of the Solomon account in Chronicles have also precluded the application of the law to the text because the commentators with only a few exceptions have agreed that Solomon is presented as idealized or flawless.[14] Rather the account has been generally regarded as a conspicuous proof text which reveals the different stance between the Deuteronomic theology and the Chronicler's theology.[15] The result of this trend is that many commentators still fill the analysis in their commentaries of 2 Chr 1:14–17 and 9:25–28, where Solomon's importation of Egyptian horses and his wealth is depicted, with comments about historical or textual issues (or comparison) (e.g., the comparison between 1 Kgs 5:6 [ET 4:26], 10:26, 2 Chr 1:14, and 2 Chr 9:25 where the numbers of chariot horses and stalls appear).[16]

However, there are several points that encourage interpreters to consider the possibility of applying the law to the text. Firstly, it is observed that while it is true that the Davidic covenant is a major theme of Chronicles, the Sinai covenant and Mosaic law also have their place as a foundation of the Davidic one in Chronicles.[17] Secondly, it should be pointed out that the emphasis on the law is even stronger in Chronicles than in its parallel text of the so-called Deuteronomistic history. The fact that "the law" (the Torah or its equivalent) is mentioned nineteen times in Chronicles, as the

13. For example, when R. E. Clements discusses the relationship between Deuteronomy and other parts of the Old Testament, he does not include Chronicles in the discussion, while he includes the Pentateuch, the Former Prophets, and the Latter Prophets (Clements, *Deuteronomy*, 95–100).

14. For example, Kelly and Selman.

15. For example, the issue of "mixed marriages" is the first case of Williamson's enumeration of the cases which shows the different ideological stances between Chronicles and Ezra-Nehemiah. Williamson proposes that Chronicles shows different stance from Ezra-Nehemiah's, while Ezra-Nehemiah follows the Deuteronomic laws (Williamson, *Israel*, 60–61).

16. For example, Dillard, *2 Chronicles*, 74; Williamson, *1 and 2 Chronicles*, 196, 235–36.

17. Selman, *1 Chronicles*, 48–49. In a similar stance, Japhet thinks that "David and Moses have their own well-defined, separate spheres of authority in the book of Chronicles. David's authority does not conflict with or supersede that of Moses. Each has his own authority, and David's actions complement and supplement Moses" commandments" (Japhet, *Ideology*, 237–38). On the other side, there are scholars like von Rad and Wilda, who see more emphasis upon David or Davidic law than Moses or Mosaic law (e.g., von Rad, *Geschichtsbild*, 63, 136; Wilda, "Das Königsbild," 47–52).

legitimate authority of a certain action or plan, while it appears only three times in the parallel text, simply demonstrates this, as already mentioned. The emphasis upon the law in Chronicles is most conspicuously shown in the fact that even God himself, in its parallel text (1 Kgs 8:25), is replaced with "the law" in Chronicles (2 Chr 6:16).[18] Additionally, the point that religious reformations by some good kings are done on the basis of the Sinai covenant tradition, or by the standard of the law, is emphasized more in Chronicles than in Kings (2 Chr 15:9–15; 17:7–9; 19:4–11; 29:15–35; cf., 2 Chr 34–35 // 2 Kgs 22–23), as Selman rightly observes.[19]

In this chapter, several aspects of the Chronicler's work will be considered in order to support the stance that it is valid to apply the law, especially the law of the king in Deut 17, to the Solomon account in order to capture the intended meaning of the text. Before moving to consider theological, literary, and historical aspects concerning this issue, each case that mentions the law (Torah) or its equivalent in Chronicles needs to be explored briefly as a starting point.

2. OBSERVATION AND ANALYSIS OF THE REFERENCES TO THE LAW IN CHRONICLES

For a basic understanding of the concept of the law in Chronicles, it is necessary to observe and analyze the nineteen cases where the "law" (or its equivalents) is referred to. It is especially worth scrutinizing the passages to consider whether or not "the law" is used mostly in a cultic sense by the Chronicler (i.e., the law that bans idolatry, and promotes the proper worship of God, as distinct from the law that deals with social justice, for example). The prevailing view that when the Chronicler used "the law," he only had cultic affairs[20] in mind seems to be another factor which prevents

18. Throntveit, *When Kings Speak*, 58. Throntveit also accepts "the usual explanation" for the alteration, i.e., the "the post-exilic emphasis on the law as a way of life" (Ackroyd, *I & II Chronicles, Ezra, Nehemiah*, 112.

19. Selman observes that "The Chronicler also sees the positive value of covenant law as something which was continually relevant and effective rather than a relic left over from the past" and that "though this has led to David being viewed as a second Moses, it only serves to underline the supremacy of the Mosaic law itself. It is the Mosaic law which is the basis of a succession of reform movements, which are given greater prominence as a succession of related events than in Kings" (Selman, *1 Chronicles*, 49).

20. Japhet, *Ideology*, 235. Japhet states that "In Chronicles, it appears some twenty times, and almost all the examples pertain to the cult." In this line, Japhet discusses the issues of (the book of) "the law" in the section titled "Worshipping YHWH in the

interpreters from applying the law of the king's in Deut 17:14–20 (that is not about worship) to the Solomon account in Chronicles in order to reach the intended meaning of the text.

1. First Chr 16:40. David arranged cultic personnel "to offer burnt offerings to the Lord on the altar of burnt offering regularly, morning and evening, *according to all that is written in the law of the Lord that he commanded Israel.*"

   It is quite clear, from the context, that David's effort here was in order to fulfill the cultic regulations in the law (daily (morning and evening) burnt offering: Exod 29:38–42; Num 28:3–8). However, it should not be overlooked that the words "written in" implies the very existence of the book of the law, which might cover not only cultic regulations but others as well (therefore, the "all" means every regulation concerning the specific cultic performance, but not every regulation of the whole book). It is also noteworthy that the stipulation involved is not found in Deuteronomy but in other books in the Pentateuch.

2. First Chr 22:12. In his charge to Solomon, David said, "Only, may the Lord grant you discretion and understanding, so that when he gives you charge over Israel you may keep *the law of the Lord your God.*"

   It is not clear whether or not the content of the law mentioned here only concerns cultic affairs. However, from the context, which is related to the kingship over Israel, it is more likely that the meaning of the law here has a wider or more comprehensive sense rather than cultic stipulations only.[21]

3. Second Chr 6:16. In his prayer for the temple dedication ceremony, Solomon prays "Therefore, O Lord, God of Israel, keep for your servant, my father David, that which you promised him, saying, 'There shall never fail you a successor before me to sit on the throne of Israel, if only your children keep to their way, to walk in *my law* as you have walked before me.'"

Temple" in her work (i.e., 234–44 in Japhet, *Ideology*, 222–47).

21. Myers states that "The Torah was thus the official standard according to which the life and activity of nation and individuals were judged. Solomon was urged by his father to observe the Torah of the Lord so that his rule might prosper (I Chron xxii 12)—here the Torah is thought of as a body of statutes and ordinances set for the guidance of the nation" (Myers, *I Chronicles*, LXXIX).

While it is noteworthy that "to walk in *my law*" has replaced the "to walk before me" in the parallel passage in its *Vorlage* (1 Kgs 8:25),[22] it is not clear again here what the law means exactly. Nevertheless, for a similar reason to case (2), it is more likely that the law here has a wider sense rather than only cultic stipulations, for the context is about the kingship over all of Israel for which cultic regulations are only part of its comprehensive system, although they are a crucial factor of the kingdom.

4. Second Chr 12:1. In the description of the early years of King Rehoboam, "When the rule of Rehoboam was established and he grew strong, he abandoned *the law of the Lord*, he and all Israel with him."

    Again it is not clear what exactly "the law" means here. However, it is likely that King Rehoboam's sin is of idolatry, i.e., plainly a cultic matter in reference to the expression in 12:5, "You abandoned me," in 12:8 "serving me," and the case of Manasseh, where it is described that the king's idolatry (2 Chr 33:2–7a) affects the nation or the people of Israel (2 Chr 33:9a cf. 2 Kgs 21:9), which seems to be similar to Rehoboam's case.

5. Second Chr 14:3 [ET 14:4]. In the description of King Asa's early reign, it is stated that Asa "commanded Judah to seek the Lord, the God of their ancestors, and to keep *the law and the commandment*."

    Again what "the law" refers to here is not clear. However, the context 14:2 [ET 14:3] and 14:4 [ET 14:5][23] which encompasses 14:3 [ET 14:4] describes the cultic reformation of Asa, i.e., the destroying of idolatry, to make it more or less clear that the law and the commandment here is primarily cultic.

6. Second Chr 15:3. The prophet Oded encourages King Asa, who has shown his trust in God in the battle against Cushite army of one million, saying of the past situation of Israel, "For a long time Israel was without the true God, and without a teaching priest, and without *law*."

---

22. It is interesting to observe that God commands Abraham to "walk before me, and be blameless" (Gen 17:1b), and later tells Isaac that "Abraham obeyed my voice and kept my charges, my commandments, my statutes, and my laws" (Gen 26:5), commanding him not to go down to Egypt.

23. "He took away the foreign altars and the high places, broke down the pillars, hewed down the sacred poles" (14:2 [ET 14:3]); "He also removed from all the cities of Judah the high places and the incense altars. And the kingdom had rest under him" (14:4 [ET 14:5]).

This again is not clear. It can be suggested that the law mentioned here mainly concerns cultic stipulations, because the ensuing event, after the exhortation and encouragement of Oded (15:2–7), is a more thorough eradication of idolatry (15:8). However, the expression "teaching priest" in 15:3, which appears just before the "law," should not be overlooked. The "teaching priest" presupposes the people who learn "the law" from him. If the law is just about cultic matters, the term is not very relevant here, for cultic matters are supposed to be performed mainly by priests or cultic personnel, and do not have much to do with ordinary people. Furthermore, the following description of the covenant renewal ceremony (15:9–15), which resembles the Sinai or Moabite covenant ceremony (Exod 24:8; Deut 28:69 [ET 29:1] cf. Deut 31:9–13) that is evidently of the whole comprehensive law of the God, should be considered carefully. Therefore the idea that the "law" in this context could mean a more comprehensive law of the Lord cannot be dismissed.[24]

7. Second Chr 17:9. In the description of King Jehoshaphat's reformation, the king's officials (שָׂרָיו) (17:7a) with Levites (17:8a) and priests (17:8b), being sent by the king, "They taught in Judah, having *the book of the law of the Lord* with them; they went around through all the cities of Judah and taught among the people."

Here, the presence of the law in the form of a book first appears in Chronicles, although it has been already implied in the case of (1), i.e., "written in the law" 1 Chr 16:40. Probably, the meaning of "teaching priest" in the case of (6) (2 Chr 15:3) is illustrated here, although in this case not only priests but also the king's officials and Levites fulfill the role of the teachers of law. For the same reason proposed already in (6), the content of the law here can be construed as more than mere cultic stipulations. In fact, it is clearer here that the content of the law is beyond the confines of cultic regulations,

24. It is noteworthy that teaching Israel is one of the three roles of Levites in Moses" final blessing. Among the blessings on each of Israel's tribes (Deut 33), the roles of Levites are mentioned as (1) delivering oracle with Urim and Thummim, (2) teaching Israel God's ordinances and law, and (3) performing cultic ceremonies such as placing incense before God and burnt offerings on the altar (Deut 33:8–10). In the book of Malachi as well, whose composition date is definitely near to Chronicles, the role of the tribe of Levi is described as speaking "true instruction" to the people of Israel (Mal 2:6–7). It is interesting to observe that the following passage is not of cultic, but of social iniquity of the people (i.e., intermarriage and divorce) (2:10–16), which seems most likely to be the result of the Levites' failure to teach true instruction of the Lord to Israel.

due to the implication of "king's officials and Levites" sent by King Jehoshaphat. That is, firstly, it should be considered that for the cultic performance, only priests and Levites who themselves know the cultic regulations would have been sufficient, and consequently they do not need to be teachers on cultic affairs for ordinary people, who do not need to have much knowledge for their cultic duty. Secondly, that the main subject or force of this campaign is the king's officials, while the priests and Levites accompany them, shows that the main subjects of the law lecture are most likely ordinary affairs associated with social or judicial regulations. Therefore, it is natural to regard the law in this case as having a wider sense than mere cultic regulations.

8. Second Chr 19:10. In the program of his reformation, King Jehoshaphat exhorts the judges whom he himself has appointed in each city (19:8), saying "whenever a case comes to you from your kindred who live in their cities, concerning bloodshed, *law or commandment, statutes or ordinances*, then you shall instruct them, so that they may not incur guilt before the Lord and wrath may not come on you and your kindred. Do so, and you will not incur guilt."

It is quite clear that the "law" here with the "commandment, statutes, or ordinances," means judicial stipulations. Firstly, this is simply shown in that King Jehoshaphat's exhortation is given to no one else but the judges who have been appointed by the king in each city in order to treat or judge civil cases. Secondly, that the "law" and its altered titles or titles for different kinds of stipulations[25] appears side by side with "bloodshed," which apparently means cases of murder or manslaughter, also makes it clear that the law here (and its equivalents or different kinds of stipulations) is about social and judicial stipulations. It should be pointed out that law appears here without the slightest implication of cultic matters, without even a mention of priests. This case is one of the most powerful pieces of evidence that the concept of law in Chronicles surely extends beyond cultic affairs.[26]

---

25. Japhet introduces several opinions on the different titles, see Japhet, *Ideology*, 246 n. 156. However, it can be said that the numeration of the titles is Deuteronomic anyhow (e.g., the last two titles in Chronicles (מִשְׁפָּטִים, חֻקִּים) are exactly same to the last two in Deut 4:45).

26. It is noteworthy to see that the term "guilt" (אָשָׁם), which has the same root to guilt-offering (e.g., Lev 5:25 [ET 6:6]), is used for the case which is apparently not of idolatry or cultic affairs. And it is also noteworthy that in the context of this case, a distinction appears between God's matters (2 Chr 19:11a) and the king's (2 Chr 19:11b), which probably mean cultic affairs and social affairs respectively, and also that Levites

9. Second Chr 23:18. In the cultic restoration which followed the political restoration of the Davidic kingship, the priest "Jehoiada assigned the care of the house of the Lord to the Levitical priests whom David had organized to be in charge of the house of the Lord, to offer burnt offerings to the Lord, *as it is written in the law of Moses*, with rejoicing and with singing, according to the order of David."

Apparently, the law mentioned here is involved with cultic performance. Nevertheless, as the phrase "written in" implies a book and there is no decisive evidence that there has been a book that contains only cultic stipulations, the concept of the law here as it is, may go beyond the cultic boundary. It seems to be worth noting that a book or scroll appears in a previous passage, 2 Chr 23:11 which is closely related to this, although it does not have a title which includes the term "Torah."

In the event of restoration of the Davidic kingship (2 Chr 23:11), in order to finish the reign of Athaliah, who usurped the Judean kingship after her son Ahaziah's accidental death (22:10–12), the priest Jehoiada arranges to crown Joash the legitimate Judean king, "Then he (Jehoiada) brought out the king's son, put the crown on him, and gave him *the covenantal regulations* (הָעֵדוּת); they proclaimed him king, and Jehoiada and his sons anointed him; and they shouted, 'Long live the king!'"

A covenant book or scroll appears here. For the same reason already proposed in (2) and (3), that the occasion concerns kingship over the nation, the content of the covenant seems to extend beyond cultic affairs. Moreover, it is hardly deniable that this occasion or event has strong linkage to the king's law itself (Deut 17:14–20), where it is described that having a copy of the law book and reading it on a daily basis (Deut 17:18–19) is one of the most important duties of an Israelite king.[27]

10. Second Chr 25:4. When Amaziah killed his servants who had murdered his father the king, after the royal power was firmly in his hand (25:3), "he did not put their children to death, *according to what is written in the law, in the book of Moses*, where the Lord commanded,

are given the role of שֹׁטְרִים, which is usually interpreted as officials (2 Chr 19:11).

27. It is noteworthy that in Ps 132:12 ("If your sons keep my covenant and my decrees (בְּרִיתִי וְעֵדֹתִי) that I shall teach them, their sons also, forevermore, shall sit on your throne"), which can be regarded as reflecting Nathan's oracle of God's promise of the Davidic dynasty, עֵדֹת is mentioned side by side with בְּרִית as something to keep or obey.

'The parents shall not be put to death for the children, or the children be put to death for the parents; but all shall be put to death for their own sins.'"

Having the parallel passage in its *Vorlage*, 2 Kgs 14:6, the Chronicler does not show any dissent to the fact that the law, in the book of Moses, contains more than mere cultic matters (it should be remembered, here, that the presumption of the present study is that the retained material from its *Vorlage* should have the same weight as the additional material from the Chronicler). Hence, it is probable that the cases of (1) and (9), which involve the phrase "written in" the law or the book of law (or its equivalents), also presuppose a law book which contains law about non-cultic affairs.

11. Second Chr 30:16. After the restoration of the temple in first month of the first year of King Hezekiah's reign, in the following second month, the priest and the Levites "took their accustomed posts *according to the law of Moses the man of God*; the priest dashed the blood *that they received* from the hands of the Levites" (Hebrew text lacks *that they received*).

It is apparent that here the law is clearly associated with cultic affairs,[28] while the meaning of "the law of Moses," is not clear in this narrow context.

12. Second Chr 31:3. In King Hezekiah's cultic restoration program, "The contribution of the king from his own possessions was for the burnt offerings: the burnt offerings of morning and evening, and the burnt offerings for the Sabbaths, the new moons, and the appointed festivals, *as it is written in the law of the Lord*."

It is apparent that the law here is associated with the cultic performance. However, the implication of the "written in" as mentioned before (cases of (1), (9), and (10), especially in the light of case (10), where the phrase is used for non-cultic affairs) should not be overlooked. Furthermore, it is most probable that Num 28–29 is presupposed here, in the sequence of the offerings, i.e., daily offerings, Sabbath offerings, new moon offerings, as Williamson rightly observes.[29]

13. Second Chr 31:4. In Hezekiah's restoration program, "He commanded the people who lived in Jerusalem to give the portion due to the

28. The alleged discordance between the law in the Pentateuch and the description in Chronicles will be discussed in the following section.

29. Williamson, *1 and 2 Chronicles*, 198 (cf. 374). Dillard also sees Num 28–29 behind the text (Dillard, *2 Chronicles*, 250).

priests and the Levites, so that they might devote themselves to *the law of the Lord.*"

It is quite clear that "the law" here is of cultic affairs, for the field that the priests and the Levites devote themselves to is mainly the cultic area (although the cases of (6) and (7) show that Israelite priests and Levites have the role of teachers for the ordinary people on non-cultic affairs). It is noteworthy that the practice of giving the portion due to the priests and the Levites, may presume a wide range of texts in the Pentateuch, i.e., Lev 6:7–7:36 [ET 6:14–7:36]; Num 18:8–32; Deut 14:27–29; 18:1–8; 26:1–15.

14. Second Chr 31:21. In the resumptive description of King Hezekiah's cultic reformation, it is stated that "And every work that he undertook in the service of the house of God, and in accordance with *the law and the commandment* (וּבַתּוֹרָה וּבַמִּצְוָה), to seek his God, he did with all his heart; and he prospered."[30]

The exact meaning of "the law and the commandments" is not clear by itself. The context of the passage, 2 Chr 31:2–20, which is about Hezekiah's reformation of the religious system or affairs for the temple service, seems to suggest that "the law and the commandments" mentioned here are the cultic stipulations involved. However, it cannot be easily dismissed that the syntax of the passage suggests, through the paralleled prepositions "in" (בְּ), that "the service of the house of God" and "the law and the commandments" are separated items in his faithfulness to God. If the latter evidence is accepted as more significant than the former, "the law and the commandments" here could mean non-cultic stipulations.[31]

15. Second Chr 33:8. In his own comment on King Manasseh, the Chronicler reminds his reader of God's promise to David and Solomon, "I will never again remove the feet of Israel from the land that I

---

30. While NRSV construes "*in* accordance with the law and the commandments" as the same status with "*in* the service of the house of God" and regards "every work that he undertook" as the title, NIV leaves the Hebrew text as it is, concerning the preposition "*in*" (בְּ), "In every work that he undertook *in* the service of God's temple and *in* obedience to the law and the commandments, he sought his God, and worked wholeheartedly. And so he prospered" (NIV). Whichever interpretation is chosen, the result is the same in that Hezekiah's reformation concerning temple affairs and his obedience in the law and commandments are distinct from each other.

31. A similar pair of titles, "his statutes and his commandments" (אֶת־חֻקָּיו וְאֶת־מִצְוֹתָיו) appears in Deut 4:40, ending with מִצְוָה. It is interesting to see that the text following Deut 4:40 is of non-cultic matters (i.e., the law of refuge cities).

appointed for your ancestors, if only they will be careful to do all that I have commanded them, *all the law* (כָּל־הַתּוֹרָה), *the statutes* (הַחֻקִּים), *and the ordinances* (הַמִּשְׁפָּטִים) *given through Moses."*[32]

It should be acknowledged that the portrayal of the reign of Manasseh, as a background to this passage, is almost all of cultic affairs, i.e., Manasseh's abominable idolatry and apostasy (2 Chr 33:2–7a). That seems to suggest that the law, the statutes, and the ordinances mentioned here are cultic only. However, the repetition of "all," and the phrase "given through Moses," may suggest the opposite, implying a more comprehensive law system. This is more probable when it is considered that in case (8), in 2 Chr 19:10, where the variety of the titles of stipulations, i.e., law (תּוֹרָה), commandment (מִצְוָה), statutes (חֻקִּים), ordinances (מִשְׁפָּטִים) appear, the context evidently indicates that the terms are of non-cultic affairs as analyzed there. Likewise, the variety of the stipulation titles here seems to imply a wider range of stipulations than cultic stipulations only.

16. Second Chr 34:14. In the eighteenth year of Josiah's reign, when the temple was being repaired (34:8), the discovery of the law book is described as follows, "While they were bringing out the money that had been brought into the house of the Lord, the priest Hilkiah found *the book of the law of the Lord given through Moses.*"

There are roughly three different views on the identity of the book of the law which was discovered in the reign of Josiah. Firstly, since de Wette's epoch-making work, *Dissertatio Critica* (1805), the book of the law has been construed by many as Deuteronomy, either in its canonical form or a variation of it.[33] Secondly, some suggest that the book cannot be Deuteronomy or a similar-sized document, but only part of Deuteronomy. One of the grounds for this view is that the book could not have been read twice within a day (2 Kgs 22:8, 10), if it had been the whole of Deuteronomy as it is now.[34] Thirdly, some

32. Cf. similar to the numeration of the titles in Deut 4:45. "the decrees and the statutes and ordinances" (הָעֵדֹת וְהַחֻקִּים וְהַמִּשְׁפָּטִים).

33. Some of the Church Fathers suggested that the book found in the reign of Josiah was Deuteronomy; however, while they thought that the book was compiled by Moses, de Wette suggested that Deuteronomy was composed much later. On the discussion of this issue, see Eissfeldt, *Introduction*, 171–76.

34. For example, Selman, *2 Chronicles*, 531–32; Eissfeldt, *Introduction*, 173. Eissfeldt and Selman's reasoning is not based upon the text of Chronicles, but upon Kings, for Chronicles does not retain the first reading by the scribe Shaphan before he read it again to the king. Eissfeldt suggests another reason for his view, that the designation,

argue that the book can be identified as the whole of the Pentateuch. For example, Williamson and Japhet both point out the alteration from "read it" (וַיִּקְרָאֵהוּ) (2 Kgs 22:8, 10) to "read in it" (וַיִּקְרָא־בוֹ) (2 Chr 34:18), as evidence that the Chronicler construed the book as the Pentateuch.[35] This observation can solve the problem of the book being read twice in a single day.

The other title of the same book, i.e., "book of the Covenant" (סֵפֶר הַבְּרִית) which appears in 2 Chr 34:30 provides a clue to settle the matter. The identical term "book of the Covenant" appears in Exod 24:7, and the context of the appearance seems to suggest that the content of the "book of the Covenant" is Exod 20:22—23:33, which is a mixture of cultic, ethical and social stipulations. A wider observation allows it to include also the Decalogue (Exod 20:1–17. cf. also see the mention of "covenant" in Exod 19:5), which is given before the interruption caused by the frightened people of Israel in the face of God's awesome presence (Exod 20:18–21).[36] However, the concept of the "book of the Covenant" cannot be decided by this observation only, for Deut 28:69 [ET 29:1] shows that there is additional content of the covenant. That is, "these are the *words of the covenant* that the Lord commanded Moses to make with the Israelites in the land of Moab, in addition to *the covenant* that he had made with them at Horeb." The actual content of the stipulation in "the words" given in the land of Moab seems to appear in Deut 12:1—28:68, and it is also the mixture of cultic and ethical stipulations, and a special commandment, "blotting out Amalek" (Deut 25:17–19). The fact that Moses records the laws in a book or scroll (Deut 31:9, 24. cf. 29:13-14, 19 [ET 29:14–15, 20] "as all curses of *the covenant* written in *the*

book of the law (סֵפֶר הַתּוֹרָה) excludes the narrative part of Deuteronomy (chs. 1–11, 27–34). However, as Selman's suggestion that "the Torah" can be better interpreted as "instruction" or "teaching" (Selman, *2 Chronicles*, 532), is more probable, Eissfeldt's second point is not very convincing.

35. For example, Williamson, *1 and 2 Chronicles*, 402; Japhet, *I & II Chronicles*, 1030. Japhet also points out that the change from "all the words of the book" (2 Kgs 22:16) to "all the curses that are written in the book" "seem to lead in the same direction." She also regards the title "the book of the law of the Lord given through Moses," which appears only in Chronicles in the context, as pointing to a similar conclusion.

36. Eissfeldt insists that the content of the book of the covenant is originally only the Decalogue (Exod 20:2–7), regarding Exod 20:22—23:33 as a secondary addition on the grounds that that part is out of place (Eissfeldt, *Introduction*, 213–17). However, his observation is not decisive, as R. E. Clements shows that some laws that seem to be out of place (e.g., Deut 16:21–17:7) can be construed as an essential part of the text in a closer reading (Clements, *Deuteronomy*, 77).

book of this law" in 29:20 [ET 29:21]; cf. "the words of the covenant that were written in his book" in 2 Chr 34:31) and orders that the law book be kept beside "the ark of *the covenant*" (Deut 31:25–26) strongly suggests that the book of the law in Deut 31:26 is also called "book of the Covenant" and that the "book of the Covenant" has increased in its contents, as the laws given in Moab are added to the laws given in Horeb. Hence, it becomes clear that intrinsically the concept of the book of the Covenant cannot be restricted to Deuteronomy, but includes at least some part of Exodus, i.e., other parts of the Pentateuch, whether of cultic or non-cultic stipulations, because Deuteronomy itself links its covenant stipulations to the earlier covenant which appears in Exodus. This view can be strengthened by the observation that more similarity is found between the covenant ceremonial situations in Exod 24:3–8 and in 2 Chr 34:29–32 than in Deut 28:69–31:30 [ET Deut 29–31] and in 2 Chr 34:29–32 (see especially the phrases [my own literal translation for comparison] "he took the book of the covenant and *he read into the ears of the people*" (וַיִּקְרָא בְּאָזְנֵי הָעָם) (Exod 24:7a), and "and *he read into the ears of them* all of the words of the book of the covenant" (וַיִּקְרָא בְּאָזְנֵיהֶם) (2 Chr 34:30b), while "*so I will speak into the ears of them*" (וַאֲדַבְּרָה בְּאָזְנֵיהֶם) (Deut 31:28) or "*and Moses recited into the ears of* all the assembly of Israel" (וַיְדַבֵּר מֹשֶׁה בְּאָזְנֵי כָּל־קְהַל יִשְׂרָאֵל) (Deut 31:30)).

The same concept of the book can be applied to the following cases (17), (18), and (19), which show the same context.

17. Second Chr 34:15. It follows that "Hilkiah said to the secretary Shaphan, 'I have found *the book of the law* in the house of the Lord;' and Hilkiah gave *the book* to Shaphan."

18. Second Chr 34:19. At last, Shaphan informed King Josiah of the discovery of the law book, and read it aloud to the king. "When the king heard the words of *the law* he tore his clothes."

19. Second Chr 35:26–27. At the epilogue of Josiah's reign it is stated that "Now the rest of the acts of Josiah and his faithful deeds in accordance with *what is written in the law of the Lord*, and his acts, first and last, are written in the Book of the Kings of Israel and Judah."

Following cases (1), (9), (10), and (12), "written in" appears again in this last case. It can be pointed out that case (10) is of non-cultic affairs and (12) is based not upon Deuteronomy but Num 28–29.

So far, the concept of Torah in Chronicles has been scrutinized through the observation of each case that refers to it. Through this observation, several points can be proposed. Firstly, the concept of "the law" in Chronicles cannot be confined to Deuteronomy, but includes other parts of the Pentateuch. Several cases show that the stipulations from Exodus, Numbers are presupposed in the concept of the law. Additionally, it will be helpful to observe that although "the book of the law" is not directly referred to, Lev 26:34–35 is quite plainly presupposed in 2 Chr 36:21 which explains or interprets the seventy years" desolation of the land of Israel as the land's Sabbaths which had not been kept because of the Israelites' disobedience to the law of God. As shown already in chapter 5, if it is accepted that the succinct name list in 1 Chr 1 is intended to indicate the genealogy in Genesis, it can be said that each part out of the Pentateuchal five books is presupposed at least partially in Chronicles.[37] Hence the general view that the law in Chronicles means "more than simply the contents of Deuteronomy"[38] is well supported. Secondly, as shown in several cases, non-cultic laws are plainly presupposed in Chronicles in either an explicit or implicit way. Hence, it has become clear now that, contrary to Japhet's view[39] that "the law" in Chronicles in most cases means cultic matters, the concept of the law in Chronicles encompasses both cultic and non-cultic stipulations even more clearly than it does in Samuel-Kings.

It is true that in some cases the law mentioned is plainly of cultic matters. However, it is necessary for the case of the so-called Deuteronomistic history (i.e., Samuel–Kings) to be considered here. In the Deuteronomistic history, the assessment of a king is without exception related to cultic affairs (i.e., whether he got rid of idols or the high places). However, this does not mean that the Deuteronomist was only concerned with cultic affairs; it has already been shown in chapter 3 that the author of the Solomon narrative in Kings had an awareness of the non-cultic law (cf. 2 Kgs 14:6). Likewise, although it is admitted that the cultic ceremony is the most conspicuous concern which appears in the presentation of a king's religious reformation in Chronicles and that cultic affairs seem to be the

---

37. The trend of the post-exilic period that parts of the Pentateuch other than Deuteronomy are construed as the "law" is also exemplified in Ezra-Neh. For example, a stipulation from Lev 6:5–6 [ET 6:12–13], which is of wood supply for the altar, seems to be presupposed in Neh 10:35 [ET 10:34]. For a brief introduction to the discussion of the identification of Ezra's law book (Neh 8:1), see Kidner, *Ezra and Nehemiah*, 158–64.

38. Enns, "Law of God," 895.

39. Japhet, *Ideology*, 235.

main concern in Chronicles as shown in pious kings' reformation (e.g., Hezekiah, Josiah), it should be also admitted that they do not necessarily mean that cultic affairs are the sole concern of the Chronicler. The emphasis upon cultic matters both in Kings and Chronicles may simply reflect the plain fact that cultic issues, i.e., worship of God or idols, whether in a proper way following its ceremonial stipulation, are the most fundamental element of religion, and consequently can be presented as a yardstick for the whole picture of the religious condition of the nation. For example, if a king and people are failing to worship God properly, it is not necessary to inspect other areas of their life to see the condition or state of their religious life. Secondly, it should be pointed out that, overall, the link between non-cultic law and narrative is more prominent in Chronicles than Kings, as King Jehoshaphat's case conspicuously shows. Considering this together with the fact that Chronicles emphasized the law more than Kings, it is natural to conclude that the concept of the law in Chronicles most likely includes the Deuteromic law of non-cultic affairs. Therefore, there is no reason to think that the Chronicler did not intend to apply the king's stipulation in Deut 17:14–20 to the Solomon account because his concept of the law was only or mostly of cultic affairs.

3. CORRESPONDENCE BETWEEN CHRONICLES AND THE PENTATEUCHAL LAW

The discussion of the contents or identity of the law in Chronicles had been founded for a long time on the hypothesis that the Chronicler wrote or produced both Ezra-Nehemiah and Chronicles. Hence, in the discussion, several passages in Ezra-Nehemiah were frequently referred to, to decide the identity of the law. For example, Neh 10:35 [ET 10:34] (cf. 13:31), is cited as a proof that the law referred to by the author (i.e., the Chronicler) is not the same as what we have now, for "the wood offering" matter mentioned in the passage does not have any counterpart in the Pentateuchal law,[40] while the passage states that that matter was done according to the law (i.e., "as it is written in the law").[41] Moreover, naturally

40. Von Rad, *Geschichtsbild*, 1930, 41.

41. For another example, the silence over the Day of Atonement (the tenth day) in Neh 8, while the chapter mentions the affairs of the first, second day and the fifteenth day of the month (the seventh month), is cited as a proof that the day of the atonement was not yet known (cf. Lev 23). Also it is alleged that the poll-tax of one-third of a shekel (Neh 10:33 [ET 10:32]) is contradictory to Exod 30:11–16. Kidner proposes an explanation of how these problems are "more apparent than real" (Kidner, *Ezra and*

and reasonably enough on the one-author hypothesis, the identity of the law book which Ezra used (Neh 8:1ff., cf. Ezra 7:12, 25–26) has attracted scholarly attention in the discussion (this issue will be treated briefly later in one of following sections). Without doubt, on the one-author hypothesis, the content or identity of Ezra's law book reflects the author's concept of the law.[42] That von Rad begins his discussion with "the Ezra book" when he explores the Chronicler's view of the law simply reflects the trend.[43] However, our following discussion of the issue will be confined within the scope of Chronicles alone, because the assumption of the present study is that Chronicles and Ezra-Nehemiah are not necessarily one work.

3.1. Correspondence between the Law in Chronicles and the Pentateuchal Law

Challenging the well-established view of the common authorship of Ezra-Nehemiah and Chronicles, and proposing a view of separate authorship of the works, Japhet tries to figure out the concept of the law for the Chronicler, solely within the scope of Chronicles. Taking a milder stance than von Rad, supposing the possibility of the difference of the concept of the law between the Pentateuch and Chronicles,[44] but not clearly denying that the Chronicler had the Pentateuch as it is now, she insists that the Chronicler's resort to the law is mainly due to his need of its authority rather than his concern for the old law itself. In other words, Japhet thinks that the Chronicler was not necessarily strictly bound to the traditional theology or norms, as she tries to show the uniqueness and independence of the ideology of Chronicles in general in her work.[45] However, re-examination of the two cases that have been proposed by Japhet as examples of her point,

---

Nehemiah, 162–63).

42. There are a few scholars who see the whole or most part of Ezra as fictional, such as O. Kaiser, C. C. Torrey. For them the content of the law book that Ezra brought has no substantial significance.

43. Von Rad, *Geschichtsbild*, 38–41. Von Rad, like Kittel and Noth, maintains that there is evidence that the Chronicler's law was not exactly the same as what we have in the Pentateuch.

44. "It is indeed probable that the Chronicler's text differed somewhat from the one we know; the question is: how extensive was the difference – was it great enough to clarify all the phenomena discussed above? It seems more likely to me that these deviations stem from the Chronicler's free, interpretative way of approaching all his sources, including the Torah. Bickerman terms this approach "emancipation from the authority of tradition"; *Ezra to Maccabees*, p. 21" (Japhet, *Ideology*, 244 n. 149).

45. Ibid.

shows that the alleged discrepancy between the law in the Pentateuch and the law in Chronicles can be questioned. The two exemplary cases proposed by Japhet, and the refutation against each one, are as follows.

1. Second Chr 30:15–16: "They slaughtered the Passover lamb on the fourteenth day of the second month. The priests and the Levites were ashamed, and they sanctified themselves and brought burnt offerings into the house of the Lord. They took their accustomed posts according to the law of Moses the man of God; the priests dashed the blood that they received from the hands of the Levites" (Heb lacks *that they received*).

    Japhet points out that the priests' sprinkling of blood (i.e., dashing of blood) of the Passover lamb, and the Levites' role, i.e., giving the blood to the priests, in the passage is not articulated in the Pentateuch. It is true that sprinkling of the sacrificed animal's blood by priests does not appear in the case of Passover, while it appears in other sacrifices performed in the Pentateuch. It is also true that "the law does not tell us who gives them the blood to sprinkle," as she points out. Does this therefore mean that the Chronicler had some laws which are not included in the present Pentateuch, or that the Chronicler arbitrarily referred the performance to his own imaginary Mosaic law?

    However, without presuming the Chronicler's arbitrariness or a now-unknown stipulation of the Passover performance, it is possible to understand the passage. The two sentences, "They took their accustomed posts according to the law of Moses the man of God" and "the priests dashed the blood that they received from the hands of the Levites" can be interpreted as not so tightly bound. Regarding the dashing (or sprinkling) of the blood, it is possible that not the specific action of the priests' dashing (or sprinkling) blood, but simply the priests' role as the main performers in cultic ceremony in general, is referred to by "their accustomed posts according to the law of Moses the man of God." As for the Levites' role, the priests and the Levites' taking their post may simply mean their general relationship in cultic performance, i.e., the relationship of the main executors (or conductors) and their helpers rather than the specific performance in which the priests dashed (or sprinkled) the blood and the Levites gave the blood to the priests.[46] When the plain fact

---

46. It is noteworthy that the last words of David define the Levites' duty as "to assist the descendants of Aaron for the service of the house of the Lord" or to "attend

that "according to the law of Moses the man of God" is referred to "their accustomed posts" (literally "their position as prescribed of them," עָמְדָם כְּמִשְׁפָּטָם) is considered, it is more likely that the thing which was in the Chronicler's mind was the comparative roles of the priests and the Levites (i.e., the priest as leading conductor, the Levite as assistant) rather than a specific action of the priests or the Levites in the cultic affairs.[47] Having said this, even if "according to the law of Moses" does not mean the present Pentateuchal law, but reflects a later tradition as the interpretation of the law for the practical use in the cultic performance, it can still be said that the Chronicler did not deviate from the law.

2. First Chr 15:15: "And the Levites carried the ark of God on their shoulders with the poles, as Moses had commanded according to the word of the Lord."

   Japhet points out that the phrase "as Moses had commanded according to the word of the Lord" does not mean to refer to a specific stipulation, but "a conclusion based on" three other passages (Exod 25:12–15, Num 4:4–15, and Num 7:9) in the Pentateuch. Exod 25:12–15 mentions only how the poles should be made and placed for the ark. Num 4:4–15 mentions only that poles should be put in places for the holy objects of the tabernacle to be carried. Num 7:9 refers only to the responsibility of the sons of Kohath to carry holy things in general on their shoulders, without even mentioning poles. She also points out that the term used for "poles" (מוֹט) in 1 Chr 15:15 is not used to denote the poles in the relevant passages in the Pentateuch, but the term used in the relevant passages (Exod 25:13, 14,15; Num 4:6 (for the ark) cf. Num 4:8, 11, 14 (for other sacred

---

the descendants of Aaron, their kindred, for the service of the house of the Lord" (1 Chr 23:28a, 32b). Although David's order is given to adapt the role of Levies to new circumstances (i.e., the permanent settlement of God's tabernacle in a fixed place), it basically reflects the original concept of the relationship between the Levites and the priests (Num 3:1–9, especially 3:6, "Bring the tribe of Levi near, and set them before Aaron the priest, so that they may *assist* him,"; Num 18:1–2, especially 18:2, "So bring with you also your brothers of the tribe of Levi, your ancestral tribe, in order that they may be joined to you, and *serve* you while you and your sons with you are in front of the tent of the covenant." cf. 8:19).

47. Curtis' understanding is the same as the present work. He states that "no specific law is here meant, but the general law constituting the orders of the priests and Levites with their respective functions" (Curtis and Madsen, *Chronicles*, 475). Japhet perceives Curtis's view, but does not provide any refutation of it (Japhet, *Ideology*, 240 n. 136).

materials)) is בַּדִּים.[48] Japhet proposes two possibilities to explain the change of terms. Firstly, the Chronicler may have indicated another method of transport. Secondly, in the Chronicler's day the usage may no longer have distinguished between the two terms.[49] Japhet adds that even if the difference is only of the matter of the vocabulary usage, the Chronicler's reference to the Pentateuch "remains general and imprecise." [50] However, it is most likely that the Chronicler chose the "precise" term for his contemporaries' better understanding, of which even Japhet herself admits the possibility.[51]

What, then, is the implication of the Chronicler's referring in this way to the Pentateuchal law? It should be acknowledged that the Chronicler's reference to the Pentateuchal law is not word-for-word quotation. However, in terms of the correspondence between the law in Chronicles and that of the Pentateuch, it can be said with certainty that the Chronicler's understanding and application of the stipulations of the Pentateuch is based on or is within the scope of the present Pentateuchal law. In other words, it cannot be said that the Chronicler's concept of the law departs or deviates from the Pentateuchal law, although the Chronicler's re-use or application of it may be described as "general and imprecise."

If the discrepant cases proposed by Japhet, who emphasizes the theological independence and uniqueness of the Chronicler from the earlier biblical traditions, are as above, it could be said that the extent of the alleged discrepancy between the Chronicler's law and the Pentateuchal law is not serious, or in other words, not decisive.

Additionally, apart from Japhet's examples, one other example also shows that the alleged discrepancy between the law in Chronicles and the Pentateuch is not decisive. 2 Chr 29:34 has been noted as an instance which reveals the discrepancy between the Pentateuchal law and the Chronicler's law.[52] It is plain that in 2 Chr 29:34 the task of slaughtering and flaying the burnt offerings is done by the priests with help from Levites, while the

---

48. Japhet, *Ideology*, 242–43. The term (מֹטֹת) appears in Lev 26:13 as meaning "bars" of yoke in a different context.

49. BDB shows that the two terms have the same meaning "poles" (BDB, 94, 557). It is noteworthy that בַדִּים is used in 2 Chr 5:8, 9 (twice) as it appears in its parallel passage in 1 Kgs 8:7, 8 (twice).

50. Japhet, *Ideology*, 243.

51. Ibid., 516.

52. For example, Snaith, "The Historical Books," 110–11; Williamson, *1 and 2 Chronicles*, 359–60; Selman, *2 Chronicles*, 491.

same task is defined as the work of the offerer himself in Lev 1:5–6. The seeming discrepancy between the two works can be explained as follows. Firstly, it should be noticed that the phrase "as it is written in the law" does not appear in the context. This means that at the very least we cannot be sure that the author does intend to link the performance to any stipulation. Secondly, it should be acknowledged that while the stipulation in Lev 1:5–6 is intended for the ordinary burnt offering performed by an individual offerer, the case presented in 2 Chr 29:34 is a collective burnt offering initiated by the king for the special event of the temple rededication (2 Chr 29:3, 10, 19, 21, 24, 28, 29, 31, 32, 35), as Dillard points out.[53] It is not an unreasonable idea that the task of slaughtering and flaying the burnt offering can be transferred to the priests in order to maintain the order and show more respect for the special national cultic performance.[54]

Recently, Talshir proposes three cases which suggest that the Chronicler tried to harmonize seemingly different stipulations, which belong to different traditions in the Pentateuch (i.e., P and D), on the same subject. Talshir's three cases are, firstly, Solomon's observance of the date of the Feast of Tabernacles in 2 Chr 7:8–10 (in relation to Deut 16:3, 1 Kgs 8:65–66 / Lev 23:36, Num 29:35), secondly, the way of cooking Josiah's Passover lamb in 2 Chr 35:13 (in relation to Deut 16:7 / Exod 12:9), and thirdly, the nature of Josiah's Passover offering in 2 Chr 35:7f (in relation to Deut 16:2 / Exod 12:5). He thinks that the Chronicler's attempt to harmonize different strata of the Torah itself reflects that "the Chronicler regarded the laws of the Torah as one entity" (389).[55] If his view is accepted, it can be deduced that the Chronicler must have been sensitive to the detailed stipulations in the Pentateuch and approved of all of them, regardless of the tradition to which each stipulation belongs. The harmonization by the Chronicler means that he did not try to discard any stipulation of any tradition.

When the points discussed so far in this section are considered together, it can be concluded that the nature of the Chronicler's reference to the law (Torah) contains flexibility and fidelity at the same time. The flexibility means that the Chronicler was not confined to word-for-word

---

53. Dillard, 2 *Chronicles*, 237, 235–36.

54. Japhet does not see any proof of the discrepancy between the Pentateuchal law and the Chronicler's law in the case of 2 Chr 29:34. Rather, she understands that the case in 2 Chr 29:34 is an "*ad hoc* measure," or "*ad hoc* solutions" is in accordance with the "*ad hoc* adjustments" in the case of the Passover in 2 Chr 30 (Japhet, *I & II Chronicles*, 930–31). In other words, Japhet notices and acknowledges the flexibility of the Chronicler's attitude towards the law.

55. Talshir, "Canon-Related Concepts," 389–90.

quotation, but was free to synthesize the stipulations and also felt free to change the vocabulary used, for his own purpose or convenience. The fidelity means that the Chronicler basically did not try to deviate from the Pentateuchal law, but remained in the confines of the law, while he felt free to modify it to re-use in his own context or his quotations. The flexible attitude of the Chronicler concerning the law is also glimpsed in his description of King Hezekiah's observance of the Passover feast, which is held in the second month instead of in the first month, according to the inevitable condition of the situation (2 Chr 30:2–3). The Chronicler does not show any hesitation or negative attitude towards this, which is evidently a flexible practice of the law. Rather, the flexible practice of this case is described in a tone of full acceptance and a positive atmosphere (2 Chr 30:12, 20, 26–27).[56] Although the flexibility of this last case exists on a different level of meaning from that of the previous ones, it can be said that all the cases in common betray or reflect the Chronicler's flexible attitude towards the law.

Another example of the flexible attitude of the Chronicler appears in a quotation of the Pentateuch law in terms of King Amaziah's revenge in 2 Chr 25:4 ("Fathers shall not *die* (יָמוּתוּ) for their children, nor children shall *die* (יָמוּתוּ) for their fathers; each shall *die* (יָמוּתוּ) for his own sins").[57] This is the only case where a stipulation of the Pentateuchal law is cited again in Chronicles after it has been quoted in Samuel-Kings. The quoted stipulation is changed from that of its *Vorlage* (2 Kgs 14:6) ("Fathers shall not *be killed* (יוּמְתוּ) for their children, nor children shall *be killed* (יוּמְתוּ) for their fathers; each shall *be killed* (יָמֵת) for his own sin"), while the original stipulation is "Fathers shall not *be killed* (יוּמְתוּ) for their children, nor children shall *be killed* (יוּמְתוּ) for their fathers; each shall *be killed* (יוּמְתוּ) for his own sin" (Deut 24:16). It is observed through comparison

---

56. It is interesting to observe that flexibility already appears in the law itself. The Passover feast should be held in the first month (Lev 23:5–8; Num 28:16–25; Deut 16:1–8; cf. Exod 12:1–28). But on the first occasion of the Passover feast in wilderness, a case occurs which requires exception to the day of holding the feast (Num 9:1–8). That is, some who became ceremonially unclean on account of a dead body could not join the feast at the appointed time. God's reply to the inquiry about this, is that those who are unclean or away on a journey at the appointed time in the first month, should keep their Passover in the second month (Num 9:10). Considering the severe punishment, whatever it exactly means, which is supposed to be given to those who fail to keep properly the Passover (Exod 12:19 "shall be cut off from the congregation of Israel"; Num 9:13 "shall be cut off from his people"), the flexibility is astonishing. Anyway, it is plain that in the Pentateuchal law, flexibility in observance of the Passover already appears.

57. The NRSV does not reflect this change.

of the three versions of the same stipulation, that there is a measure of difference in Chronicles' quotation from both the Deuteronomy stipulation and the Kings quotation, while there is a slight difference in the Kings' quotation from that of Deuteronomy.[58] When it is considered that the Kings quotation is almost the same as Deut 24:16, and that the Chronicler relied heavily upon old tradition (which is our assumption or working hypothesis), it is more likely that the Chronicler too had the same or a very similar law to that which the author of Kings had. Therefore, we can conclude that the Chronicler felt free to change small details of it in his re-quotation. In other words, this case indicates that even when the Chronicler had and knew a certain Pentateuchal stipulation, he felt free to change the stipulation in its details. This means that when the Chronicler's quotation of a certain law is not precise, it does not necessarily mean that the Chronicler's law was different from the present Pentateuchal law.

It can be added here that a case of the flexible application of the law to a narrative context also appears in the New Testament, as Williamson observes.[59] For example, it appears in Luke's description and quotation of the law concerning the case of Jesus' purification ceremony in Luke 2:22–24, 27. Joel B. Green points out that in at least five ways, Luke's statements about the law's requirements are not strictly in accordance with what the law actually says.[60] While there are some who view the discrepancy as a result of Luke's ignorance of the law,[61] there are others who think that the seeming discrepancy is the result of Luke's attempt to combine the separate rites of purification of the mother and redemption of the firstborn child.[62] In other words, the discrepancy can be dismissed when it is ascribed to Luke's flexible attitude towards the law.[63] When it is considered that there

---

58. It is admitted that Lemke's suggestion that differences in Chronicles from Kings might have been caused not by his own theological intention, but by the fact that he had a different version of the old tradition from the present form of Samuel-Kings, could be a possible explanation of the case (Lemke, "The Synoptic Problem").

59. Williamson, *Ezra, Nehemiah*, xxxviii. Williamson maintains that "we should not expect such exactitude from an author in antiquity: the citations of the OT in the NT show similar variation . . ." (Williamson, *Ezra, Nehemiah*, xxxviii).

60. Green, *The Gospel of Luke*, 140.

61. Fitzmeyer, *The Gospel according to Luke I–LX*, 421.

62. Nolland, *Luke 1–9:20*, 117–18, 124.

63. Again, another possibility is that Luke's description simply describes or reflects the cultic practice of Jesus' days which is based upon the interpretation at the time of the related laws of childbirth. In this case, too, the view that the present form of the Pentateuchal law was a legitimate authority at that time, remains undamaged.

is no doubt that Luke's Old Testament was no different from ours,[64] it is most likely that the flexible quotation and application of the Pentateuchal law was a trend in the post-exilic community.

3.2. Correspondence between Two Narratives in Chronicles and the Deuteronomic Law

It cannot be denied that certain stipulations in Deuteronomy are echoed in the narrative of Chronicles, and the echoes reveal the close relationship between the two works. For example, Jehoshaphat's reformation of the judicial system of Israel in 2 Chr 19:5–11 reflects the stipulations in Deut 16:18—17:13, as most commentators agree.[65] There is ample evidence which shows that the Chronicler was well aware of the stipulations of Israelite judges in Deut 16–17, including the following:

1. Both texts refer to the same situation in that the case is brought to the court from the provinces (2 Chr 19:10 / Deut 17:8).[66]

---

64. Williamson, *Ezra, Nehemiah*, xxxviii.

65. Williamson, *1 and 2 Chronicles*, 289–91; Selman, *2 Chronicles*, 416, 420; Dillard, *2 Chronicles*, 147; McKenzie, *1–2 Chronicles*, 293. Selman points out that common concern for "right attitudes in relation to human law, and for the purposes and presence of God" appears both in Deut (16:20; 17:12) and the text of Chronicles. Williamson describes the link of the two works as "based . . . on" (2 Chr 19:6 / Deut 1:17), "similar to" (2 Chr 19:7 / Deut 16:17; 10:17), and "draws in particular on . . . for its legal presupposition" (2 Chr 19:9–10 / Deut 17:8ff). However, concerning the order of composition date, scholars" views diverge. While Selman thinks that Deuteronomic law is "applied to a new situation" (Selman, *2 Chronicles*, 418, 420), Williamson thinks that "the essential elements of the judicial reform as described in Chronicles are earlier than the present form of Deuteronomy" (Williamson, *1 and 2 Chronicles*, 288–89) (It is not clear how Williamson, who maintains that the Chronicler must have had the present form of Pentateuch (Williamson, "Accession of Solomon," 361), can harmonize his view with this occasion). Dillard too observes that "the present form of Deuteronomy is later than the source which the Chronicler used for the account of Jehoshaphat's reform" while he admits "the dependence of 19:5–11 on Deut 16:18—17:13." Japhet emphasizes the differences in details between the two works (i.e., for example, judges and officers" (Deut 16:18) / "judges" (2 Chr 19:5, 8), "in all your towns" (Deut 16:18) / "in the fortified towns" (2 Chr 19:5), etc), in order to argue against Wellhausen's view that the text in Chronicles is a pure fabrication by the author on the basis of Deuteronomy. Japhet thinks that the differences suggest that the text is not intentional fabrication but authentic information (Japhet, *I & II Chronicles*, 770–74, 775–78).

66. Japhet, *I & II Chronicles*, 777.

2. The establishment of a high court in Jerusalem as shown in 2 Chr 19:8[67] corresponds to Deut 17:8ff where it is commanded that there should be a high court in the God-chosen city.[68]

3. The threefold undesirable things that the judges should avoid in Deut 16:19, i.e., "to distort justice," "to show partiality," and "to accept bribes," reappear in 2 Chr 19:7, as something with which God, the model or master of the judges, is not associated.[69]

4. It is suggested by Japhet that the appearance of "judges" (שֹׁפְטִים 2 Chr 19:5, 6) alongside "officers" (שֹׁטְרִים 2 Chr 19:11) reflects the judicial system in Deut 1:15–16 and Deut 16:18–19 (cf. Josh 8:33).[70]

5. It is suggested by Selman that "the priests' role alongside the judges' " in Deut 17:9, 12 (cf. 1 Sam 2:25; Jer 18:18) is reflected in 2 Chr 19:8.[71]

6. While it is fair to say that the appearance of tribal leaders (i.e., "the heads of fathers' houses") in the legal system as shown in 2 Chr 19:8 differentiates the text from the law in Deut 17:8–9,[72] it should still be noted that the appearance of the tribal leaders in the system cannot be an alien idea in Israel's juridical system, for it is plain that they have been "the backbone" of the system for a long time as shown in Deut 19:12, as Selman points out.[73]

67. Although there are various views on the matter of Jerusalem court, which entails a textual difficulty at the end of verse 8, the basic fact that there is a high court in Jerusalem is generally agreed. That is, while Williamson (also Curtis) thinks, supporting the translation of NEB, LXX, Vulgate versions, that the Jerusalem court also treats "the disputed cases of the inhabitants of Jerusalem" (v. 8b), others (Dillard, Selman) think, supporting the versions of RSV (i.e., the end of the verse 8 is read "they had their seat at Jerusalem" (literally "they lived in Jerusalem"), while MT and RV reads "they returned to Jerusalem," which seems not to make sense due to verse 4 and the first part of verse 8), that the passage only describes the Jerusalem court as a high court. (Curtis and Madsen, *Chronicles*, 1910, 404; Williamson, *1 and 2 Chronicles*, 290–91; Dillard, *2 Chronicles*, 149; Japhet, *I & II Chronicles*, 776–77; Selman, *2 Chronicles*, 418–20).

68. Japhet, *I & II Chronicles*, 777; Selman, *2 Chronicles*, 420. Selman sees that the Deuteronomic law of Deut 17:8–13 is "applied to a new situation." It is plain that while Deut 17:8–13 simply mentions "the place that the Lord your God will choose" and a court in the place, the Chronicles text mentions "Jerusalem" and the court.

69. Japhet, *I & II Chronicles*, 775. Williamson points out that the text of Chronicles combines Deut 10:17 (Williamson, *1 and 2 Chronicles*, 289).

70. Japhet, *I & II Chronicles*, 775, 779.

71. Selman, *2 Chronicles*, 418.

72. For example, Japhet, *I & II Chronicles*, 773, 777. Japhet states that " 'the heads of fathers' houses' cannot be regarded as developed from Deut. 17" (777).

73. Selman, *2 Chronicles*, 420. Selman enumerates more proof texts, i.e., Ezra

7. It is noteworthy that it is "(between) one kind of homicide and another" that begins both the lists of various kinds of cases which should be brought to a high court in 2 Chr 19:10 and Deut 17:8, as Japhet observes[74] (NRSV"s translation "bloodshed" in 2 Chr 19:10, and "one kind of bloodshed and another" in Deut 17:8 obscures the identity of the texts). It is plain that "the bloodshed" (or homicide) matter appears in exactly the same wording (i.e., בֵּין־דָּם לְדָם: literally, "between blood to blood") in both the cases from the same contexts of a high court (Deut 17:8b / 2 Chr 19:8a). That is, when Jehoshaphat, establishing the judicial system of Israel, gives instruction to certain Levites and priests whom he appoints as judges of the high court in Jerusalem, the case of "bloodshed" or "homicide" is the first one which is enumerated as a case to be treated in the court, and then followed by general provisions, thus it reads "concerning bloodshed, law or commandment, statutes or ordinances" (2 Chr 19:10). In the corresponding Deuteronomic law, the case of "bloodshed" (or homicide) comes first and is followed by less serious cases. Thus it reads "one kind of bloodshed and another, one kind of legal right and another, or one kind of assault and another—any such matters of dispute."

From the observation of the correspondence seen above, it can be said that on the one hand, the Chronicler was aware of the previous tradition quite precisely and reflected it to some extent in his writing, but on the other hand he felt free to put old traditions in new forms, which were required in order to emphasize his own concerns (in this case, the Chronicler emphasizes the law, which is conventionally presented in the wording of "law, command, decrees, and ordinances" as here, as the ultimate object the high court should aim to guard). This might be a case which reveals the flexibility of the Chronicler's style in re-use of or reflecting old traditions in his own context or concern.

A similar phenomenon is observed in the account of King Manasseh, who is at the opposite end of the spectrum of Israel's kings in terms of their virtue or loyalty to God. Manasseh's sin is enumerated as "He made his sons[75] pass through fire in the valley of the son of Hinnom, practiced soothsaying and augury and sorcery, and *dealt with mediums and with*

10:14; Matt 26:57.

74. Japhet, *I & II Chronicles*, 778. Japhet describes the identity as "exactly the same form and the same first doublet."

75. NRSV ignores the plural and translates it as singular "son."

wizards (וְעָשָׂה אוֹב וְיִדְּעֹנִי)" in 2 Chr 33:6. This undeniably echoes the stipulation in Deut 18:10–12, "No one shall be found among you who makes a son or daughter pass through fire, or who practices divination, or is a soothsayer, or an augur, or a sorcerer, or one who casts spells, or who *consults ghosts or spirits* (וְשֹׁאֵל אוֹב וְיִדְּעֹנִי), or who seeks oracles from the dead."[76] What a comparison of the two texts plainly shows is that, to some extent, the Deuteronomic law is reflected quite precisely and, on the other hand, a flexible and free modification and addition of new materials is apparent. The plural "sons" appears in 2 Chr 33 while the singular "son" and "daughter" is denoted in Deut 18. The name of the specific place where the abominable cult is performed, "the valley of the son of Hinnom," is added in 2 Chr, and only four of the seven practices of sorcery are enumerated, in different grammatical forms but in the same order.[77]

From the observation of these two passages above (those of King Jehoshaphat and Manasseh), two points can be made. (1) Both cases show the flexibility and fidelity in the Chronicler's attitude toward the law and his quotation and application of it, as has been suggested previously. It is observed that the Chronicles' narratives reflect a combination of a quite precise quotation or reflection of the Deuteronomic law alongside a loose or flexible correspondence to it. (2) Interestingly, both cases are involved with the stipulations of the Israelite institutional offices which are addressed in Deut 16:18—18:22, covering the stipulations of judges, king, priests and Levites, and prophet. It means that the king's stipulation in Deut 17:14–20, which is located between the two stipulations involved with the cases above, is also most likely included in the Chronicler's consideration, if Deut 16:18—18:22 is accepted as a set or unit. When it is considered that it is quite unlikely that the direction of the influence between the two works is from Chronicles to Deuteronomy, it can be said that the existence in the author's mind of the rules about the offices, including the king's law, is guaranteed. At the very least, the two cases show the extent to which the Chronicler was conscious of the stipulations in Deuteronomy.[78]

76. This is observed by most commentators. For example, Selman, *2 Chronicles*, 520; Japhet, *I & II Chronicles*, 1006. According to Japhet, "This verse is a clear reflection of Deut. 18.10."

77. Japhet provides a similar but shorter comparison of the two texts (Japhet, *I & II Chronicles*, 1006).

78. Additionally, Kleinig's interesting article is noteworthy. He proposes that "the institution of the choral rite" established by David, which seemingly is an unauthorized cultic institution against Mosaic law, in fact has its ground in the Pentateuchal law including Deuteronomy (Kleinig, "The Divine Institution," 1992). For example, he proposes that in the Chronicler's view David's "instruction to perform liturgical song"

4. A LITERARY CONSIDERATION OF THE RELATIONSHIP BETWEEN CHRONICLES AND DEUTERONOMY (OR THE PENTATEUCH)

The literary creativity of the Chronicler has been recognized by a number of scholars with various stances since C. C. Torrey.[79] However, literary features of Chronicles have not attracted much scholarly interest, for several reasons. According to Japhet, "literary analysis is a relatively new field of biblical scholarship," and the general view of the work as "compilations" with "inferior artistic merit," and "the difficulty . . . of peculiar idiom have not encouraged research" on this aspect of the work.[80] Even when literary features of Chronicles have been discussed recently, it has usually been in relation to Ezra-Nehemiah, in order to consider the issue of common or separate authorship of the two works. For example, the presence of the Levitical sermon in Chronicles, and its absence in Ezra-Nehemiah, has been pointed out as an indication of the separate authorship of the two works.[81]

While literary connection between Chronicles and Deuteronomy (or the Pentateuch) is not a subject which has received much scholarly attention,[82] the reappearance of fragmentary pieces from the Pentateuchal tradition in Chronicles has attracted the attention of some scholars such as G. von Rad.[83] However, in spite of the apparent reappearing of

---

(1 Chr 6:16–17 [ET 6:31–32]; 16:41; 23:4–5, 30–31; 25:1; 2 Chr 8:14; 23:18; 29:25; 35:15) is about obeying "the command to rejoice in Deuteronomy"(Deut 12:6–7, 11–12, 18; 16:10–11; 26:11; 27:6–7) in relation to "the regular sacrificial ritual at the temple."

79. Torrey, "Chronicler as Editor," 157–173 and 188–217 (= *Ezra Studies*, 208–51); Noth, *Chronicler's History*, 89–95; Welten, *Geschichte und Geschichtsdarstellung*, 5, 205; Ackroyd, "The Theology of the Chronicler," 273–89. The present study does not agree with these stances. For example, Torrey's basic view of Chronicles is that the Chronicler wrote both Chronicles and Ezra-Nehemiah, and the nature of the work is imagination or fabrication of the Chronicler himself, with which the present study does not agree.

80. Japhet, "Chronicles and Ezra-Nehemiah," 307.

81. Japhet also points out that the formula description of king's death and burial appear in Chronicles, and do not in Ezra-Nehemiah (ibid., 307–8), which, however, is a point without consideration of the different contexts of the two works. See also Williamson, *1 and 2 Chronicles*, 11; Newsome, "Chronicler and His Purposes," 214–15.

82. As an exceptional example, Anne M. Solomon proposes that the structure of Chronicles and Ezra-Nehemiah follows that of the Pentateuch. (Solomon, "The Structure of the Chronicler's History").

83. Von Rad provides the most comprehensive list of the Chronicler's re-use of the Pentateuchal materials (von Rad, *Geschichtsbild*).

Deuteronomic or Pentateuchal elements in Chronicles, the significance of the phenomenon has been underestimated in those scholars' views which pay attention mainly to the uniqueness and independence of the Chronicler's theology over against the previous tradition,[84] while Willi construes Chronicles as exegesis.[85] For example, Japhet dismisses the significance of the Deuteronomic or Deuteronomistic terms reappearing in Chronicles, regarding them as just borrowed terms or expressions from the traditional language pool.[86] However, Williamson makes an excellent case for the literary connection between the two works. In his discussion, how the pattern of the succession from David to Solomon follows that of Moses and Joshua is analyzed in detail from a typological perspective,[87] and consequently the extent of the literary relationship between Deuteronomy

84. For another example, Weinfeld's list of "Deuteronomic Phraseology" includes the appearance of the deuteronomic terms in Chronicles without showing any specific concern for it (Weinfeld, *Deuteronomic School*, 320–65). Weinfeld does not distinguish "deuteronomic" and "deuteronomistic" as the present study does. He uses "deuteronomic" as the term which covers Deuteronomy, the Deuteronomistic History, and Jeremiah (Weinfeld, *Deuteronomic School*, 8).

85. Willi, *Auslegung*. Willi fails to notice the pattern in Chronicles that follows the accession model from Moses to Joshua in the wide scale, although he includes "typology" as a kind of exegetic device.

86. Japhet, *Ideology*, 19, 506.

87. Williamson, "Accession of Solomon." There is convincing observation by several scholars that the pattern of the transition of the leadership from Moses to Joshua was used by the Chronicler as a model for his presentation of that from David to Solomon. Since Lohfink (1962) had identified three elements of installation formula in Deuteronomy and Joshua, Porter (1970) and McCarthy (1971) suggested a developed and enlarged observation of the same issue. Later, R. Braun (1976) and Williamson (1976) pick up the issue, almost at the same time, and suggest fuller grown observations. Lohfink proposes that (1) the encouragement (Josh 1:6a), (2) the description of the task to achieve (Josh 1:6b), and (3) the promise of God's accompaniment (Josh 1:9b), are the three elements of commission formula. Although Braun points out that "promise of God's accompaniment" is so general in the OT, and cannot be a specific element, he, basically adapting the observation of Lohfink (Lohfink, "von Moses auf Josue") and D. J. McCarthy (McCarthy, "An Installation Genre?") of the commission of Joshua, points out that the literary pattern of the commission of Solomon follows that of Joshua. Braun's observation of the common elements of the two accessions are, (1) the command to keep the law, (2) the promise of prosperity, (3) the fourfold encouragement (be strong, be bold, do not fear, do not surprised), (4) the commission occurs first privately, and then later public. For Braun, the dependence of Solomon's case on the pattern of Joshua, emphasizes the fact that Solomon is divinely commissioned for his mission (i.e., the temple building) (Braun, "Solomon the Chosen Temple Builder," 588). There seems to be an error in printing. Braun suggests 4 points but he uses numbers 1, 2, 3, then 5, omitting 4. (Braun, "Solomon the Chosen Temple Builder," 586–88).

(or the Pentateuch) and Chronicles is shown convincingly. This analysis shows not only how closely the two works are related in literary aspects, but also that the literary connection between the two works is not simply one of language but of meaning and implication.

Williamson observes five points which are common to the description of the succession from Moses to Joshua (in Deuteronomy and Joshua), and that from David to Solomon (in Chronicles), as shown in chapter 5 already.[88] The typology or modeling by the Chronicler has the following purposes, according to Williamson. Firstly, as the transition of the leadership from Moses to Joshua welds Deuteronomy and Joshua as a continuous story, the similar description of the kingship transition from David to Solomon contributes to presenting the two kings' reign as unity. Secondly, as the case of Moses and Joshua shows the "complementary nature" of the two persons' works, the similar description of the case of David and Solomon by the Chronicler is intended to show that David and Solomon are complementary in their function.[89]

Additionally, Williamson points out a crucial implication from the tight typology which exists between Deut 34:9 and 1 Chr 29:24 (his fourth point).[90] Deut 34:9 has usually been regarded as "either a direct continuation or a recapitulation" of the account of Joshua's commission in Num 27:12–23 (which is regarded as P, i.e., non-Deuteronomic[91]), the tight typology suggests that Deut 34:9 was already in the present place. Hence, Williamson concludes that "the Chronicler had the Pentateuch before him in its final and completed form."[92]

Williamson's analysis clearly shows that the Chronicler's dependence upon the previous tradition is not merely on the level of vocabulary or term borrowing.[93] Rather, it shows that the Chronicler was borrowing and exploiting the meaning of the tradition, in order to express his own

88. See the third point of *3.3.A. Typological Allusion* in chapter 5.

89. Williamson, "Accession of Solomon," 356–59.

90. In Hebrew the similarity is more vividly shown.

91. Although the terms "P" and "D" are employed in the discussion it does not necessarily mean that the hypothesis of the documents is presupposed in the discussion. The terms are simply used here to indicate certain parts of the OT.

92. Williamson, "Accession of Solomon," 361. Williamson states that "our findings provide fresh evidence against any attempt to divide up the work of the Chronicler on the basis of his adherence to one or another of the Pentateuchal sources, and even suggest that the effort so frequently made to establish which of the sources had greatest influence upon him is misguided" (Williamson, "Accession of Solomon," 360–61). The assertion is proposed by Williamson as one of three implications of the study.

93. Contra Japhet.

theology of history. However, Williamson does not articulate what is implied very naturally in his observation. That is, the typology itself shows that the reader's supposed prior knowledge of the succession from Moses to Joshua must have been considered by the Chronicler, as a hermeneutical element to constitute the meaning of his presentation of the succession from David to Solomon. That is, the reader is able to perceive the meaning and implication of the repeated succession pattern in Chronicles, only when he or she also knows the pattern of the Pentateuchal succession account and its implication. In other words, the effect of following the previous pattern that appears in Deuteronomy and Joshua is operative only when the reader knows the previous one and its meaning and implication. The conclusion suggests, for the interpretation of the Solomon account in Chronicles, that it is probable that the Chronicler expected that his reader would know the Deuteronomic law, which includes the law of the king, and would apply it to capture the intended meaning of the Solomon account.[94]

5. THEOLOGICAL CORRESPONDENCE BETWEEN CHRONICLES AND DEUTERONOMY

The Chronicler's conspicuous concern for Levites, temple singers, the performance of Passover ceremony, and so on, suggests that the author has a special interest in cultic affairs. In tune with this observation, it is suggested by some that the Chronicles is closer to the so-called Priestly work than the Deuteronomic history.[95] Nevertheless, a close and strong connection between Chronicles and Deuteronomy has been the subject of scholarly discussion. For example, so-called immediate retribution theology, which is regarded as a characteristic of the Chronicler's view of history, whether it is construed as an exclusive theology or part of a wider theology for cause-and-effect perspective in Chronicles, seems to be closely related to the Deuteronomic stance.

94. Also, Eskenazi proposes that "Chronicles is patterned after Deuteronomy" in many ways, for example, concerning David and Moses" role, through his literary approach to the ark narrative in 1 Chr 13–16 (Eskenazi, "A Literary Approach to Chronicles' Ark," 273–74).

95. Ackroyd suggests that the Chronistic History is closer to the Priestly work than to the Deuteronomistic History, (Ackroyd, *Chronicler in His Age*, 252–72, 273–89). Jones also observes that "dehistorization" for "theologizing" is a common element to the Priestly work and the Chronicler"s work, while it is "less obvious in the Deuteronomistic History" (Jones, *1&2 Chronicles*, 112–13).

There is a variety of views concerning the way the cultic or priestly material and the Deuteronomic material combine in Chronicles. For example, while Rothstein and Hänel regard the P document as the basic material and the D document as additional, Welch believes that the D document constitutes the basis of the narrative, and the P document was applied later, contrary to Rothstein and Hänel's view.[96] Ackroyd takes a middle position, suggesting that the Chronicler's intention was to combine the two materials from the start.[97] However their suggestions may be evaluated, they show the undeniable connection between Deuteronomy and Chronicles. That is, although scholars disagree about how the cultic or priestly material and Deuteronomic material combine in Chronicles, it is undeniable that they all think that there is an evident connection between Chronicles and Deuteronomy.[98]

It can also be pointed out that apart from the concrete discussion of the way the distinctive materials combine in Chronicles, in a wider sense, the influence of the Pentateuch as a whole upon Chronicles has been noticed since Wellhausen, who sees Chronicles as a work of historiography written in the perspective of the Pentateuch,[99] followed by von Rad.[100] Childs' and Talshir's observation of the Chronicler's effort to harmonize concerning seemingly discrepant traditions in the Pentateuch,[101] also implies that at least the Chronicler did not intend to suppress the

96. Rothstein and Hänel, *Das erste Buch der Chronik*; Welch, *The Work of the Chronicler*. The terms P and D document do not presuppose that the present study accepts the JEDP hypothesis (as Wenham shows, the hypothesis has been strongly challenged in recent decades, see Wenham, *Exploring the OT: the Pentateuch*, 172–83). However, for the convenience of denotation, those conventional terms are used here.

97. Ackroyd's suggestion is noteworthy in this regard. Observing on the one hand, the Chronicler's emphasis upon the cultic affairs, which has been pointed as the characteristic of Chronicler's works (i.e., Chronicles-Ezra-Nehemiah) since Wellhausen, and on the other hand, acknowledging the strong connection between the theology of Deuteronomy and of Chronicler's works, Ackroyd concludes that the Chronicler tried to combine the Priestly theology and the Deuteronomistic theology in his work, exemplifying the Jerusalem temple as a combination of the two theologies (Ackroyd, "The Theology of the Chronicler," 282–84).

98. The complicated relation between the traditions is well summarized by Snaith's observation that "The relation of the Chronicler's writings to the JEDP scheme is confused" and "It is evident that the relations between the Chronicler and D and P are still obscure" (Snaith, "The Historical Books," 110–11). Snaith introduces a variety of views suggested by scholars in regards to the relationship between previous traditions in Chronicler's works (Snaith, "The Historical Books," 110ff).

99. Japhet, *Ideology*, 239 n. 134.

100. Von Rad, *Geschichtsbild*, 1. "nomistische Geschichtsbetracht."

101. Childs, *Introduction*, 648–49; Talshir, "Canon-Related Concepts," 388–90.

Deuteronomic tradition in his work. As shown in the previous section, the argument which insists on the difference between the law in the present Pentateuch and the law which the Chronicler worked with, does not have any firm grounds; their stances point in the same direction, supported by the fact that there is undeniable linkage between the two works. Moreover, it should be remembered here that the previous section of the literary consideration of the two works raised the strong possibility that Chronicles was influenced by or based upon the completed Pentateuch, rather than a possible partial stratum of it (although it is impossible to prove this with absolute certainty).

The following cases are presented as only some examples to show the theological connection or correspondence between the two works; a thorough survey would be too big a task to achieve here and will not be necessary for the present discussion. Although it is not intended to present an exhaustive list of the cases of theological connection between Chronicles and Deuteronomy (or the Pentateuch), it will be sufficient to point out the extent of the connection between the two works in theological aspects which might have significant implications concerning the interpretation of the Solomon account in Chronicles. That is, cases referring to Solomon and the temple in 1–4, to the law in 5–7, and a related issue in 8.

1. The concept of "rest" as the precondition of temple building, which is conspicuous in the context of God-chosen worship place in the future, in Deuteronomy (Deut 12:8–11 (הַמְּנוּחָה (9), וְהֵנִיחַ (10)), reappears with emphasis in Chronicles in terms of Solomon's temple building. It is well known that the connection between "rest" and "temple building" is plainly observed in the Deuteronomistic history in line with the Deuteronomic stipulation. That is, in the Deuteronomistic history the issue of temple building appears for the first time in the context of "rest" (2 Sam 7:1; in the verb form, i.e., הֵנִיחַ) in the reign of David, then of Solomon (1 Kgs 5:17–19 [ET 5:3–5] (הֵנִיחַ) (5:18 [ET 5:4]), 8:56 (מְנוּחָה)). What should be noticed is that in a sense the connection between "rest" and "temple building" is reinforced in Chronicles. R. Braun makes an important point in this regard. That is, in Kings, the reason that David could not build the temple is described as his being engaged in many wars with his enemies (1 Kgs 5:17–19 [ET 5:3–5]), giving the impression that David's being busy in his wars is the main reason.[102] In contrast, in Chronicles, the

---

102. The obtaining of the "rest," through war, as David achieves, also appears in Josh 22:4.

reason that David was not allowed to build God's temple is described as his having shed much blood, and Solomon's qualification as the temple builder is described as his being a "man of rest" (אִישׁ מְנוּחָה) (1 Chr 22:9, while David is described as "man of war" (1 Chr 28:3)). In other words, "rest" is emphasized in Chronicles, as a qualification of the temple builder, while it is not apparent in Kings. Furthermore, it can be pointed out that God's giving the name "Solomon," which has apparently the same meaning as "rest," appears in Chronicles in the context of temple building (1 Chr 22:9–10), while it does not appear in Kings. Additionally, it can be pointed out that the order (or pattern) of the original wording וְהֵנִיחַ לָכֶם מִכָּל־אֹיְבֵיכֶם מִסָּבִיב "give you rest from your enemies all around" (Deut 12:10b) reappears more precisely in 1 Chr 22:9 (וַהֲנִחוֹתִי לוֹ מִכָּל אוֹיְבָיו מִסָּבִיב "give him rest from all his enemies on every side") than that in 2 Sam 7:1 הֵנִיחַ לוֹ מִסָּבִיב מִכָּל אֹיְבָיו "he had given him rest from all his enemies around him."[103] Considering the several observations above, it can be said that overall the connection between "rest" and "temple building," which originally appears in Deuteronomy, is reinforced in Chronicles, even more strongly emphasized than in Kings.[104]

2. The law of cult centralization (Deut 12) is even better corresponded to in Chronicles than Kings, on the following grounds. Firstly, the explicit description of the occasion of choosing the temple site appears in Chronicles (i.e., 1 Chr 22:1) but not in Kings. Secondly, concern for the high places, as a resultant concern for the centralization of the cult place, is observed in Chronicles at least as strongly. It is admitted that the frequent mention of whether a king abolished or maintained the high places in Kings as a Deuteronomistic concern does not appear with the same frequency in Chronicles.[105] However, this does not necessarily mean that Chronicles lacks the interest in

103. 2 Sam 7:1 and 1 Chr 22:9 are the verses where the most similar phrase to Deut 12:10b appear from the Deuteronomistic history and Chronicles respectively. English translation (NRSV) does not reflect the precise order of the wordings.

104. Braun, "Solomon the Chosen Temple Builder," 583–84.

105. In Kings it is mentioned thirty times, in 1 Kgs 3:2, 3, 4; 11:7 (twice); 12:31, 32; 13:32, 33; 14:23; 22:44 [ET 22:43b]; 2 Kgs 12:4 [ET 12:3]; 14:4; 15:4; 15:35; 16:4; 17:9, 11, 29, 32 (twice); 18:4; 18:22; 21:3; 23:5, 8, 9, 13, 19, 20 (including four times of the Northern Kingdom, in 1 Kgs 12:31, 32; 13:32, 33 and twice in Josiah's cleansing in the Northern territory, in 2 Kgs 23:19, 20). In Chronicles, nineteen times, in 1 Chr 16:39; 21:29; 2 Chr 1:3, 13; 11:15; 14:2 [ET 14:3], 14:4 [ET 14:5]; 15:17; 17:6; 20:33; 21:11; 28:4, 25; 31:1; 32:12; 33:3, 17, 19; 34:3 (including two times of "the high place in Gibeon" in 1 Chr 16:39; 21:29).

the same issue of the centralization of the cultic place. Rather, the Chronicler shows his maintaining the same position to that of its *Vorlage* through some exemplary cases throughout the work (i.e., the abolishing of the high places in 2 Chr 1:3 (cf. 1 Kgs 3:2–3); 14:2, 4 [ET 14:3, 5]; 15:17; 20:33; 28:25; 31:1; 32:12;[106] 33:3, 33:17, 19; 34:3), and his sensitivity to the issue is even more vividly presented by some cases that do not appear in its *Vorlage*. In 2 Chr 33:17, it is cautiously and significantly noted that the high places that Manasseh allows after his repentance of his previous idolatry, are only for the sacrifices to God. That is, "The people, however, still sacrificed at the high places, but only to the Lord their God." It must have been that the Chronicler felt that some excuse should be provided for the fact that even after Manasseh's repentance high places were maintained in the land. On the other hand, the popular use of the high place for idolatry is plain through the case of King Ahaz (which does not appear its *Vorlage* either), that is, "In every city of Judah he made high places to make offerings to other gods, provoking to anger the Lord, the God of his ancestors" (2 Chr 28:25). From the observations above, it can be concluded that the Chronicler maintained the same interest in the issue of high places as his *Vorlage*, while the omissions of comments on high places are supplemented through exemplary cases. Moreover, the work provides new information on the same issue, as the second work of historiography.

The case of Solomon's offerings in high places does not depart from the stance observed above, which appears in 2 Chr 1:3–5 (compared to 1 Kgs 3:2–3). While the Kings' presentation excuses Solomon's offering his sacrifices in the high places by mentioning that the temple has not yet been built (1 Kgs 3:2), the Chronicles' presentation simply emphasizes the authorized status of the place where Solomon offers his sacrifices, by noting that God's tent of meeting and the original bronze altar of the tabernacle are there at the high place at Gibeon (2 Chr 1:3, 5). It has been suggested that the Chronicler presented Solomon's using the Gibeon high place more positively than the author of Kings did, although it is recognized that even in the Kings' presentation an excuse for Solomon's using high places is provided. While the Kings' presentation might be interpreted as

---

106. The phrase "his high places and his altars" plainly shows that at least in the foreigner's (i.e., Sennacherib king of Assyria's or his officers) view some high places are for the God of Israel.

having a negative implication, as the sentence "Solomon loved the Lord, walking in the statutes of his father David; only, he sacrificed and offered incense at the high places" (1 Kgs 3:3) probably has,[107] the Chronicler changed the passage with more positive material in order not to give any negative nuance on the matter of Solomon's using the high place. In conclusion, the Chronicler's stance is not different from that of Kings on the matter of Solomon's using high places. Whether the Kings' presentation was intended to paint Solomon negatively or provide only the excuse on the matter of his using high places, the author's sensitivity about the matter of high places is evident in either case, and it is in tune with the continuing concern for the high places throughout the work. The Chronicler also shows his concern for the high places, not with a similar approach, however, but with new information on the matter.

3. It is plain that the idea that God chooses a king (Deut 17:15) for Israel to establish a dynasty (Deut 17:20) corresponds well with Samuel-Kings, which is demonstrated in God's choosing Saul (1 Sam 10:24), David (2 Sam 6:21; 1 Kgs 8:16; 11:34), and even Jeroboam (1 Kgs 11:29 ff., especially 11:38), and so on. Although the correspondence is not described in exactly the same manner, the idea of God choosing a king for Israel is not absent from Chronicles. That is, regarding Saul, his having been chosen by God is implied in 1 Chr 10:13–14, and as for David, it is clearly described in an indirect manner (in the sense that the narrator's comment does not state it) in, for example, 1 Chr 11:2b, 3, 9; 12:19 [ET 12:18]; 14:2; 17:7, 12–14, 25, and it can be said that even Jeroboam's being chosen or appointed by God is implicitly described in Chronicles (2 Chr 10:15b; 11:4). Additionally, God's choosing Solomon in Chronicles is not for the general purpose of establishing a king or dynasty for Israel as shown in Deut 17, but

107. For example, McConville even denies the presence of the excuse for Solomon, maintaining that "No sooner is Solomon's kingdom 'established' (1 Kgs 2, 46) than he marries Pharaoh's daughter (3,1), a move which is clearly political, and which we cannot but see as the beginning of a 'return to Egypt,' in the terms of Deut 17,6. The marriage in itself breaches Deut 7,3, and aims a blow at the purity of Israel. Still in 3,1, the writer raises a further question about Solomon's priorities when, in a twist of the play on *bayith* in 2 Sam 7, he records the building of the king's own house before that of YHWH. (The hint is reinforced by the time-scales mentioned in 6, 38; 7, 1.) In view of these features of 3,1, it is likely that the note in 3,2 that the people were still sacrificing on the high places because the house of the LORD had not yet been built, far from being a deuteronomic excuse for Solomon, is a rebuke for him" (McConville, "Narrative and Meaning," 35).

for the special purpose of the temple building. Nevertheless, the idea of God's choosing a king is still the common element both in Deuteronomy 17 and the cases of Solomon in Chronicles (1 Chr 28:6, 10; 29:1). That is, the idea of God's choosing Solomon can be regarded as an advance from God's choosing a king in general, i.e., for Israel, as shown in Deut 17. The more so, when we consider the crucial importance of the temple building in the context of Israel as the God-chosen nation, and Solomon's being chosen by God for the crucial and special project is as significant a thing as being the first successor who establishes the dynasty.[108] Deuteronomy mentions neither the building of the temple, nor God's choice of a king for that purpose. However, it is not strange that the Deuteronomic stance that emphasizes so strongly God's choice of the future worship place (Deut 12:5–14, 17–26; 14:23, 25; 15:20; 16:5–6, 11, 15, 16; 17:8b, 10; 18:6) (which is even better corresponded to in Chronicles than in Kings as mentioned already) may be transferred or extended to God's choice of a king for the immensely significant project. In fact, God's choosing Solomon in Chronicles is a unique and special occasion, without parallel, after God's choosing David, as Braun rightly observed.[109]

4. Solomon's temple dedication prayer (2 Chr 6) includes and reflects the Deuteronomic concept and theology (or ideology) of retribution, together with the terms of Deuteronomy, i.e., drought (Deut 28:24 / 2 Chr 6:28), locusts (Deut 28:38, 42 / 2 Chr 6:28), pests (Deut 28:21–22 / 2 Chr 6:28) and so on, which appear in Deut 28.

Summing up the observations (1) to (4), when it is considered that the temple building is the focal subject in the reign of David and Solomon, the theological correspondence between Chronicles and Deuteronomy is significant. That is, the Chronicler inherits and reflects the Deuteronomic theology in these cases, and even shows a

---

108. According to Williamson, Solomon's success of building the temple is "the major condition for the eternal establishment of the Davidic dynasty" (Williamson, *1 and 2 Chronicles*, 192).

109. Braun, "Solomon the Chosen Temple Builder," 589. Deuteronomy shows the idea of the God-chosen king and the perpetuation of his dynasty on the condition that he and his descendants observe the law (Deut 17:15, 20). In the Deuteronomistic History, this rule is confirmed in God's choice of David (1 Kgs 11:34) and God's promise of the perpetuation of David's dynasty on the same condition (1 Kgs 2:4; 8:25; 9:4–5) (Weinfeld, *Deuteronomic School*, 4–5).

conscious effort to advance the Deuteronomic theology in terms of the temple building.[110]

5. It has been shown already that the concept of the law is not confined in scope to cultic stipulations. For example, the case of King Amaziah's revenge of his father (2 Chr 25:4), where the Deuteronomic law that commands that children shall not be put to death for the parents and vice versa is resorted to, shows that the Chronicler's concept of the law (or Torah) goes beyond cultic matters. Japhet points out the variation in the quoted stipulation as showing the independence of the Chronicler's theology. She maintains that "for the Chronicler this is a key to a different theological principle: vicarious punishment is to be avoided not only in the sphere of human judicial procedure, but also in the divine management of the world; the strictly individual character of retribution is a universal and absolute rule."[111] However, it is more likely that the Chronicler's change of the stipulation from "being killed" to "die" did not mean such a subtle difference, when his flexible attitude toward the old traditions in dealing with and quoting them for his own generation is considered.[112] Rather, it should be more significantly construed that most probably the slightly varied quotation itself reveals that the Chronicler's re-use of the passage is not just his mere compilation of previous materials, but his conscious choice and incorporation of the material, regarding it as relevant in his presentation. Most of all, it should be pointed out that whether the variation can be construed as accidental or intentional, the basic fact that the Chronicler tried to quote the Deuteronomic stipulation as the standard to judge an instance, within the same stance on Deuteronomy as a whole (if the variation can be construed as not serious or crucial), cannot be denied.

110. Although it is not a correspondence between Deuteronomy and Chronicles, it should be pointed out that in a wider range, concerning the completion of the holy building, Chronicles echoes the Pentateuchal tradition. That is, the presence of God's glory in the temple after the completion of the temple (2 Chr 7:1–2) echoes Exod 40:34–35, where a similar phenomenon is described after the completion of the tabernacle.

111. Japhet, I & II Chronicles, 861. Japhet refers to Greenberg, "Some Postulates," 20–27. McConville harmonizes the two seemingly contrasting theological stances. He proposes that Exod 20:5f (2 Kgs 23:25f) "speaks of God's own application of his justice and love in history, according to his mysterious ways," while Deut 24:16 (2 Kgs 14:6) "legislates for human judicial processes" (McConville, Chronicles, 214).

112. It is evident that the context shows it is about the king's execution rather than divine punishment.

6. The case of Jehoshaphat's reformation (2 Chr 17:7–9; 19:4–11) shows that the concept of the law in Chronicles is not merely of cultic affairs but encompasses civil and social affairs, as discussed in the previous section. What is significant here is that what Jehoshaphat tried to realize in the nation is exactly what the Deuteronomic law commands (Deut 16:18–20; 17:8–13[113]). When it is considered that the content of Jehoshaphat's reformation does not appear in its *Vorlage*, it should be acknowledged that the Chronicler had an intention to connect the Deuteronomic law and his portrayal of King Jehoshaphat, as some scholars admit.[114]

7. The description of the high priest Jehoiada's giving the covenant (הָעֵדוּת) to young Joash in his kingship inauguration ceremony (2 Chr 23:11), which does not appear in its *Vorlage*, also strongly reflects the Deuteronomic law in Deut 17:18–19 where it is commanded that the Israelite king should have a copy of the law and read it all his days to keep the stipulations in it. In this light, it is most likely that, at minimum, the content of the covenant includes the king's law in Deut 17:14–20, not to mention other fundamental commandments.[115] It is true that there are diverse views on the identity (or nature) of the covenant (הָעֵדוּת). When it is taken seriously that the king's important duty is clearly described as reading and keeping the law or even more,[116] it is quite plausible that the king received the law book in his coronation ceremony, as a symbolic act. This case can be one that shows that the Chronicler did intend to link his own writing to Deuteronomy.

---

113. On the connection of the two passages, Talshir agrees that 2 Chr 19:10 "early echoes" Deut 17:8 (Talshir, "Canon-Related Concepts," 388).

114. For example, Selman, *2 Chronicles*, 420; Dillard, *2 Chronicles*, 147; Williamson, *1 and 2 Chronicles*, 288–89; Japhet, *I & II Chronicles*, 777; Talshir, "Canon-Related Concepts," 388. Talshir thinks, considering together Neh 8:7f where the Levites" ministry to have the people understand the law appears, that the account of not simply reading the law but teaching it to the people reflects the custom of the Chronicler's day, not admitting that 2 Chr 17:9 describes a real occasion. But his suggestion is without evidence, and he only points out the fact that there is no parallel passage in its *Vorlage* (Talshir, "Canon-Related Concepts," 387).

115. Hence, the ban on Egyptian horse importation in the stipulation cannot be ignored in the interpretation of the Solomon account in Chronicles.

116. Williamson, *1 and 2 Chronicles*, 282. Williamson states that "It is true that the king was probably thought of as responsible for instruction in the law; cf. G. Widengren, *JSS* 2 (1957)."

Summing up (5)–(7), concerning the law or the equivalent in Chronicles, the correspondence between the concept of the law in Chronicles and that of Deuteronomy, at least in the first case, cannot be denied. Rather, it can be suggested that the correspondence is supplemented in the Chronicler's presentation, and consequently the correspondence between Deuteronomy and Chronicles looks even closer than that between its *Vorlage* and Deuteronomy. The phenomenon viewed in the cases of (6) and (7) can be construed as the Chronicler's supplementary intention in writing the second history.

8. The prophecy of Huldah (2 Chr 34:23–28) plainly maintains a Deuteronomistic stance:[117] a Deuteronomistic view of the postponement of God's punishment (2 Chr 34:28), reappears in Huldah's prophecy in Chronicles. Although many scholars such as Williamson and McKenzie emphasize "retribution in each generation" as a characteristic of Chronicles' presentation of history,[118] this case, together with the end part of Chronicles" non-immediate retribution stance (2 Chr 36:15–16), shows that the Chronicler's view of history goes beyond a simple retribution theology, although it is admitted that emphasis upon it, as compatible with other perspectives, is clearly one of his concerns. If we accept that Chronicles maintains a non-immediate retributionist view of history (as a characteristic of the second work of history, which is expected to show more the complex (or nuanced) reality of history), we do not need to conclude that the division of the kingdom after Solomon's death should be attributed to someone else. Likewise, Solomon's prosperity should not be necessarily attributed solely to Solomon's obedience to God (contra McKenzie[119]).

117. Japhet, *I & II Chronicles*, 1033. Japhet admits that "The prophecy of Huldah is a characteristic Deuteronomistic speech, full of Deuteronomistic expression," while she believes that "Huldah's prophecy is a secondary element in its Deuteronomistic context." The present study does not agree with Japhet's view that the prophecy is secondary, for it seems to come from her preconception of the Chronicler's theological stance. It is also noteworthy that the divine promise of prophets in Deut 18:15, 18 is more frequently fulfilled in Chronicles than the Deuteronomistic History as Zimmerli points out. He states that "Even more clearly than in the Deuteronomistic History, the prophets are depicted functionally as proclaimers of God's law after the manner of Moses, whose authority they bear" (Zimmerli, *Old Testament Theology*, 181).

118. Williamson, *1 and 2 Chronicles*, 1982, 251 ("the Chronicler regards each generation as being directly responsible to God for its actions without reference back to previous circumstances") and *passim*; McKenzie, *1–2 Chronicles*, 51–52 ("Each person and each generation is responsible for his or her own behavior").

119. McKenzie, *1–2 Chronicles*, 231, 255, 256, 259.

So far, through the exploration of three subjects, the temple building which is the central subject of the Solomon account, the law, and the
retribution, it has become clear that the Chronicler's presentation shows
strong links to the Deuteronomic stance or theology. When it is considered that the first subject is just about the main focus of the account, and
the next two are quite closely related to Solomon's sin (or disobedience)
and its punishment, it suggests that it is quite possible that the Chronicler's
understanding of Solomon's reign is firmly based upon the Deuteronomic
stance or theology, especially the king's stipulation in Deut 17:14–20.

It should also be taken into consideration that not a few scholars
admit that the Davidic covenant, although it is emphasized in Chronicles,
does not replace the Mosaic covenant in the work,[120] or that the Sinai
covenant is presented as a foundation of the Davidic covenant in Chronicles.[121] It is true that the Chronicler shows unique emphases in his work in
comparison with other books of the Old Testament (if not, there would be
no reason to write another work of historiography at all), but it does not
necessarily mean that his stance is intended to replace or deny the previous tradition.[122] Rather, as has been shown above, many consistent ideas
between Chronicles and others are observed.

6. CONCLUSION

In this chapter, the close relationship between Chronicles and the Deuteronomic law was explored.[123] Firstly, it was shown, through examining

120. Jones, *1 & 2 Chronicles*, 128. (Japhet introduces the opposite viewers (Von
Rad and Wilda), although herself agree with Jones, Williamson. Japhet, *Ideology*, 238
n. 131).

121. Selman, *1 Chronicles*, 48–49. Selman states that "in the Chronicler's thought
the Sinai covenant is the foundation of God's promises to David."

122. Jones states that "although he was addressing the situation of the post-exilic
Jerusalem community, he was not basically at variance with the great tradition reflected in the works of other biblical historians" (Jones, *1 & 2 Chronicles*, 129). Johnstone
states that "One may guess that the author belongs to the levitical school, whose office
it is to expound scripture with a hermeneutical flair which combines faithfulness to
tradition with the independence and freedom of theological creativity" (Johnstone,
"Reactivating the Chronicles Analogy," 19). However, until recently the view that the
Chronicler tried to replace the previous tradition has been proposed. For example, see
Mitchell, "The Ironic Death of Josiah."

123. After all, de Wette and Wellhausen's old view that many parts of Chronicles
are not authentic material, which is not accepted by many commentators these days,
is due to nothing but the high-level correspondence between the Pentateuch and
Chronicles.

each case where "the law" (Torah) appears, that "the law" referred to in Chronicles means more than merely cultic instructions, contrary to the arguments of some. Secondly, the alleged discrepancy between the Pentateuchal law and the Chronicler's law was also examined, and it was shown that there is no substantial discrepancy between the two. Thirdly, this chapter highlights, through some exemplary cases, the close relationship between Chronicles and Deuteronomy (or the Pentateuch) from theological and literary points of view, to support the argument that the Chronicler presupposed the Deuteronomic law. Considering the theological connection between Chronicles and Deuteronomy, together with the literary one, it should be acknowledged that Chronicles, which includes the Solomon account, is very closely related to Deuteronomy on the level of theology and its stance. Japhet, emphasizing the theological independence of the Chronicler, maintains that the Chronicler only used Deuteronomic or Deuteronomistic terms from the language pool.[124] However, we have shown that not only the Deuteronomic or Deuteronomistic terms but also Deuteronomic ideas and theology plainly reappear in a number of places in Chronicles.[125]

By proving that the law referred to in Chronicles includes non-cultic matters, and by highlighting the close relationship between Chronicles and Deuteronomy (or the Pentateuch) in regard to literary and theological aspects, this chapter suggests that there is no reason why the king's stipulation (Deut 17:14–20) and the non-cultic stipulations, should not be applied to the interpretation of the Solomon account in Chronicles. Torah, i.e., the law of the Lord, which is frequently referred to in the literature, should be included as a hermeneutical element in the interpretation of the text,[126] unless it is proved that the law (Torah) mentioned in Chronicles is anything other than Torah which includes Deuteronomy or part of it (i.e., Deut 17:14–20).

---

124. Japhet, *Ideology*, 19, 506.

125. Therefore, the alleged theological uniqueness, difference, and contrast in terms of Chronicles' theology observed by Japhet, requires a re-examination. Unfortunately, the re-examination cannot be carried out thoroughly in the present study due to the lack of space. However, the observations proposed in the present study can be a partial contribution by showing, although limited in several cases, that the Chronicler's view cannot be described as being contradictory to the previous tradition, especially the Pentateuchal or Deuteronomic theology.

126. For example, Talshir states that "At the time Chr was written, the Torah was the very core of the people's religious life," and shows the ground (Talshir, "Canon-Related Concepts," 386ff).

7

A New Interpretation of the Solomon Account in Chronicles

1. INTRODUCTION

THE PREVIOUS CHAPTERS HAVE been supporting cumulatively the position that it is possible or justifiable to hold that the Chronicler's presentation of Solomon has a negative tone, in the following respects:

1. The nature of Solomon's corruption in Kings is the "return to Egypt," as has been shown in chapter 3. It should be noted that all of the three elements of the "return to Egypt" theme in Kings reappear in Chronicles, even in significant ways (conspicuous repetition, Solomon's own reservation (i.e., "My wife shall not live . . ." as shown in 2 Chr 8:11), and the political background of the kingdom division), which will be discussed later. This might suggest that the reader of Chronicles is supposed to understand the nature of Solomon's corruption in Kings' presentation from his or her prior knowledge, and is to interpret the account of Solomon in Chronicles accordingly. Further, the new interpretation of the nature of Solomon's corruption in Kings indicates that the omission of the contents of 1 Kgs 1–2, 11 can no longer be sufficient evidence of idealizing Solomon, for Solomon's

corruption is not confined to those chapters, but exists elsewhere. Moreover, it has already been well recognized that the Chronicler's omissions or additions in the Solomon narrative are mainly in order to focus the reader's attention on the temple building, rather than to idealize Solomon.[1]

2. Given that a feature of Chronicles is its greater complexity compared to its *Vorlage* in each king's portrayal, and that allusion is an important technique of Chronicles, as has been seen in chapter 5, it is possible to reason that the faults or negative aspects of Solomon are presented in Chronicles in an implicit way, through the technique of allusion. It is not difficult to explain why the Chronicler had to treat Solomon's faults through allusion in Chronicles. Firstly, the Chronicler had to present Solomon the temple builder as positively as possible, in order to emphasize the hope through the temple. Secondly, the Chronicler had no intention to rewrite the history, nor was it possible to rewrite the history, for neither the description of the flow of the history nor the prior knowledge of the reader allows it. Therefore Solomon's faults had to be described at least in an indirect or implicit way. To meet these two requirements, which seemingly present a dilemma, the Chronicler had both to overlook and to acknowledge Solomon's faults, which was possible through the technique of allusion.

3. Additionally, when it is considered that the presence of the law or the book of law, which certainly includes the king's law (Deut 17), is apparent in Chronicles, as seen in chapter 6, it is also likely that Solomon's importation of Egyptian horses, his intermarriage with Pharaoh's daughter, and his exploitation or oppression of the Israelites, are presented in a negative sense, although not criticized explicitly, in order to avoid unnecessary distraction from the main theme of the text.

All the points mentioned above suggest that the Solomon account in Chronicles can be interpreted as having negative elements in presenting the king, not by accident[2] but by the author's intention. Therefore, it

---

1. Dillard, 2 *Chronicles*, 2: "not just Solomon's sins are missing but also some accounts which would have enhanced a favorable portrayal of the king. Since the Chronicler's account of Solomon's reign is given almost exclusively to his concern with the temple (2 Chr 2–7), narratives not showing any involvement with the cult are omitted."

2. Ibid., 88–89; Japhet thinks that in Chronicles, the reality of Solomon's heavy yoke, which appears in Kings, is "systematically suppressed" and the Northerner's

is worth exploring some conspicuous materials which might have been intended to show negative aspects of Solomon, i.e., the three "Egyptian" elements in the account of Solomon in Chronicles, for the author might have expected the reader's prior knowledge of the "Egyptian" elements to help constitute the meaning of the text. Before dealing with each case, it is necessary to consider the reader's prior knowledge with which he or she interprets the Solomon account.

2. RECONSTRUCTION OF THE PRIOR KNOWLEDGE OF THE READER OF THE SOLOMON ACCOUNT IN CHRONICLES

The assumption of the present study is that the author of Chronicles wrote the work with the perspective or expectation that the reader would understand or interpret the work with his or her prior knowledge of Deuteronomy or Kings material.[3] While it is impossible to suppose every single part of the reader's prior knowledge, nevertheless an attempt to reconstruct the contents of the reader's prior knowledge is essential to a reader-sensitive interpretation of the account. The contents fall, by and large, into two categories. The first is the prior knowledge which the reader would have before his or her reading Chronicles (e.g., the Pentateuch). The second is the one that the reader would obtain in the process of his or her reading of the preceding parts in Chronicles, before he or she reached the Solomon account (i.e., 1 Chr 1–29).

2.1. The Reader's Prior Knowledge Before Reading Chronicles

In the first category, the Chronicler, as the author of the second history, not only presupposes but also exploits the reader's understanding of the first history. This is evident in the frequent cases of allusion and

---

demand is just a pretext for rebellion that is well described 2 Chr 13:6–7 in Abijah's speech. Therefore, according to Japhet, Rehoboam's acknowledgement of the reality of Solomon's heavy burden is just a result of Chronicler's failure to adapt and modify his materials into a new and consistent account. "These literary and historical tension and inconsistencies cannot be reconciled to our full satisfaction, as they are the inevitable results of the logic and dynamic of adapting existing material to the framework of a new historical philosophy" (Japhet, *I & II Chronicles*, 653).

3. In this study, for the interpretation of the Solomon narrative in Kings, a similar presumption has been used. That is, the reader's prior knowledge of Deut 17:14–20 is presupposed in the interpretation as shown in chapter 3.

bold omission. As for the precision and depth of the ideal reader's prior knowledge, it can be measured and illustrated by the typological comparison between the Moses-Joshua succession in Deuteronomy-Joshua and the David-Solomon succession in Chronicles, as Williamson suggests.[4] In order that the intention of the close typology may be achieved, the reader must have a deep and precise prior knowledge of the details of the Moses-Joshua succession case, and the implication of it, as well, which has already been shown.[5]

Hence, the present study presupposes that the reader is supposed to know about the nature of Solomon's corruption in the Kings' presentation. This position is strengthened by another aspect of the reader's prior knowledge. That is, it is most likely that the Deuteronomic law, especially the law of the king (Deut 17:14–20), is presupposed by the reader, for it is probable that the post-exilic community, which might have been the first readers of the work, regarded the Deuteronomic law or Deuteronomy, or even the Pentateuch, as an authoritative standard divinely given.[6] Hence, it is again most likely that it is natural for the supposed reader of Chronicles, unlike most recent commentators, to apply the king's stipulation to the account.

Therefore we can conclude that the reader is supposed to understand that the responsibility for division of the kingdom is put upon Solomon's shoulders, and that Solomon's intermarriage which leads him to apostasy, his importation of the Egyptian horses (along with his maintaining many horses), and his selfish accumulation of extreme wealth which placed a heavy burden upon his people, all have negative connotations as Solomon's faults or shortcomings.

2.2. The Reader's Prior Knowledge Obtained through the Reading of the Parts of Chronicles Preceding the Solomon Account

As for the second category, what can we suppose that the reader already knew through reading the preceding parts to the Solomon account in Chronicles (1 Chr 1–29)? To try to reconstruct the whole of this prior knowledge is beyond the task of the present study. Here, only selected contents will be briefly pointed out, which could have had an influence on

4. Williamson, "Accession of Solomon."

5. See the section, "A Literary Consideration Between Chronicles and Deuteronomy."

6. The point was discussed in chapter 6.

the reader's understanding of the Solomon account (2 Chr 1–10[7]). We will observe the contents in two ways, looking first at the prior knowledge of the characteristics or style of the work, and then at the prior knowledge of the subject or theme of the work.

First of all, from the very start, in 1 Chr 1:1–4, the reader finds it a characteristic of the literature that the author condenses a large amount of tradition into an extremely short expression; this will prove to be a common style through the whole work.[8] Consciously or unconsciously the reader starts to become accustomed to the presentational method of the work. In other words, the reader begins to learn and is prepared to accept the tendency to *omission*, and learn to be reminded of omitted traditions through simple, small hints or *allusions*, from the very start of the work.

Twice, the genealogies and name lists in 1 Chr 1–9 reach the time of the author and his first reader (in the end part of 1 Chr 3, and 1 Chr 9:1–34). This gives the reader not only the impression of a grand setting of the work, a magnificent flow of history, but also brings into relief the significance of the present time.[9] It is, also, not hard for the reader to realize, through several conspicuous comments or additional short episodes (e.g., the comment of the birthright of the first-born given unto the sons of Joseph (1 Chr 5:1–2), and the description of Jabez's birth, prayer, and his life (1 Chr 4:9–10)), that this part of the work is not a mere abridgement of the first history, but a distinctive work with its own information and flavor. It gives the reader the expectation that the work will display its own fresh perspective and emphases, while it does not suggest that the work will go beyond the overall frame of the inherited tradition.[10] That is, the reader begins to be prepared to accept fresh perspectives, emphases, and *new information* in a familiar framework of history, in the rest of the work.[11]

---

7. The ordinary account of Solomon's reign appears from 2 Chr 1 to 9 with the usual regnal statement of the king's starting his reign first, and the king's death and burial last. However, 2 Chr 10 should be included, for it contains significant information about Solomon's reign.

8. The point has been already discussed in an earlier chapter. Observing even the omission of the verbs which should designate the relationship (i.e., father-son) between the enumerated names, the reader begins to realize one characteristic of the literature. That is, the literature presupposes the reader's prior knowledge of the old tradition and exploits it.

9. It may highlight the fact that the present community is the continuing forefront of God's grand purpose.

10. The different names (from that of Genesis) in the Levites tribe in 1 Chr 3 can be construed as an attempt to provide supplementary information.

11. For more comprehensive messages and implications of 1 Chr 1–9, see Oeming,

The radical turn from the genealogical part of the work to the detailed account of Saul's death (1 Chr 10:1–14; the first proper account of the entire work), which is introduced by the genealogy of Saul's ancestors and descendants (1 Chr 9:35–44), also gives the reader a taste of the author's radical way of writing. First of all, the narrative, which begins with the situation of the Israelite king's being killed in a battle, itself strongly implies that the author presupposed the reader's prior knowledge of the overall story of the king, for without this, starting the narrative with the very last part of the king's reign would not be a natural or expected way of writing a history. Further, in the explanatory comment of the death, the proposed reason is the king's transgression against the word of Yahweh, without any details at first (10:13–14). Whether the "king's transgression against the word of Yahweh" means specific events[12] or is a general evaluation of his life and reign,[13] it would be poor way of accounting for an Israelite king's tragic death, if the reader's prior knowledge were not presupposed here. It is plain that the following mention of King Saul's consulting a medium (אוֹב) (10:13b) does not constitute the whole of the king's transgression, for that part is introduced with the "and also" or "and even" (וְגַם) which clearly distinguishes the general transgression of the king against Yahweh's word from the king's specific transgression, the consulting of the medium. Therefore, it is plain that *omission* is employed here with small hints or *allusions*. The bold *omission* of the implied information, however, does not dismay the reader now, for the reader acknowledges, consciously or unconsciously, that the author's way of writing presupposes the reader's knowledge of the first history and is in a sense exploiting it.[14]

When the reader begins to read the text from 1 Chr 11 where the account of David begins, it is very obvious to him or her from the start that the preceding story of David is omitted here, as with King Saul. The reader's prior knowledge of the preceding story of David is presupposed by the author. The sudden introduction of all Israel's coming to David at Hebron and their requesting David to become their king (11:1–3) surely

---

"*Vorhalle*" 1 Chronik 1–9.

12. Most commentators suggest that it means the occasions of 1 Sam 13 and 15, while Talgum includes 1 Sam 22.

13. Williamson following Mosis, suggests (*1 and 2 Chronicles*, 95).

14. One may raise a question about "the king's not inquiring of Yahweh" in 1 Chr 10:14a, which seems to contrast with 1Sam 28:6 where Saul's endeavor to inquire of God is emphasized. However, 1 Chr 10:14a can be better translated as "not seek Yahweh," as a general evaluation of the king's attitude towards God, rather than "not seek the guidance from Yahweh," as Williamson suggests (ibid., 95).

presupposes the reader's familiarity of the whole situation. The first episode of David has several *allusions* to the preceding omitted story. The Israelites' saying, "For some time now, even while Saul was king, it was you who commanded the army of Israel. The Lord your God said to you: It is you who shall be shepherd of my people Israel, you who shall be ruler over my people Israel" (1 Chr 11:2), effectively and economically alludes to the most significant facts of David's military activities and merits under King Saul, and God's promise or preordination of David as king of Israel. Further, "according to the word of the Lord by Samuel" in the context of Israel's anointing David king over Israel (1 Chr 11:3) reminds the reader of the omitted story of God's choosing David among Jesse's sons (1 Sam 16).[15] Presupposing the reader's prior knowledge, bold *omission* based upon the reader's prior knowledge, and effective *allusion* to omitted stories, all appear in the first account of David and make the reader accustomed to such trends or features of the work.

The following account of David's conquering Jerusalem (1 Chr 11:4–9) accustoms the reader to another characteristic of the work, adding *new information* in retelling a familiar old account. In fact, providing *new information* in a familiar frame of history has already appeared in the genealogies in 1 Chr 1–9. In the retelling of the famous event of conquering Jerusalem, the subject who achieves the conquest is named as Joab, while the first history does not articulate his name, his role, or his merits in the conquest (2 Sam 5:6–10). Thus, the reader acquires *new information* that does not appear in the famous story of the first history.

Having Joab as an introduction or link, the Chronicler provides a mixture of David's warriors' names, anecdotes about their bravery, and David's increasing military strength blessed by God (1 Chr 11:10—12:41 [ET 11:10—12:40]). This part of the work also shows the same features described above, *allusions* and *new information*. Reading this part, the reader confronts, in several places, meaningful names of places or situations that remind him or her of omitted accounts, including "to David at the cave of Adullam" (11:15),[16] "to David at Ziklag, while he could not move about freely because of Saul son of Kish" (12:1), "As he [David] went to Ziklag . . . " (12:21 [ET 12:20]),[17] "when he [David] came with the Philistines for the

15. Furthermore, "These are the numbers of the divisions of the armed troops who came to David in Hebron to turn the kingdom of Saul over to him, *according to the word of the Lord* . . ." (1 Chr 12:24 [ET 12:23]).

16. The cave of Adullam appears as David's shelter in 1 Sam 22:1; 2 Sam 23:13.

17. Ziklak appears as David's refuge town in 1 Sam 27:6; 30:1, 14, 26; 2 Sam 1:1; 4:10.

battle against Saul" (12:20 [ET 12:19]).[18] *New information* includes several lists of names (11:41b–47, 12:3–8 [ET 12:3–7], 12:10–14 [ET 12:9–13], 12:21 [ET 12:20], 12:24–38 [ET 12:23–37]),[19] additional short descriptions or stories in regards to the lists (12:1–2, 12:9 [ET 12:8], 12:15–16 [ET 12:14–15], 12:39–41 [ET 12:38–40]), and an episode (12:17–19 [ET 12:16–18]).

The following account of the next (and still early) stage of David's reign, is composed of (1) David moving the ark into Jerusalem (the first attempt: 1 Chr 13, the second attempt: 1 Chr 15–16), (2) David building his palace and his children born in Jerusalem (1 Chr 14:1–7), and (3) David defeating the Philistines twice (1 Chr 14:8–17). If the reader has perceived the flexible attitude of the author, with the time order oriented to theme or subject as shown above, while of course maintaining the general time order, the rearrangement[20] of the events would not disturb him or her. It becomes clear to the reader that the ark has greater weight in the work than in the first work of history, when he or she sees that the bringing of the ark is presented as the first event after David's being made king over all Israel (1 Chr 12:39 [ET 12:38]), and that a significant amount of *new*

18. In Samuel, the episode appears in 1 Sam 28:1–2; 29:1ff.

19. In the parallel list to the first history (e.g., 11:26–41a), alteration of names is observed. Exploring the alteration is not the present concern of our discussion.

20. In the first history, the order of the events is as follows. (1) building the palace and fathering children (2 Sam 5:11–12, 13–16), (2) defeating the Philistines twice (5:17–25), (3) the first attempt to bring the ark to Jerusalem (6:1–11), (4) the second attempt to bring the ark to Jerusalem (6:12–19). The rearrangement of the order of the events is explained in various ways. For example, Mosis explains that the account of the first attempt to move the ark is rearranged before that of the battle with the Philistines in order to show that the victory over the Philistines is due to David's faithfulness to God which is shown in his attempt to bring the ark to his place (Mosis, *Untersuchungen*, 55–61). On the other hand, Braun does not deny that Mosis' view is probable, but suggests that the Chronicler simply put the battle account between the accounts of the two attempts to bring the ark, for there is a three-month time gap in which the ark was at the house of Obed-edom (1 Chr 13:14 / 2 Sam 6:11) between the two attempts, although he does not insist that it means that the battle happened in the gap time necessarily, because the work is not precisely chronological (Braun, *1 Chronicles*, 178). However, Mosis' explanation of the Chronicler's motive for the rearrangement is not convincing. When it is considered that the transgression of the law in the first attempt is emphasized, it is hard to think that the first attempt is presented as the cause of the victory over the Philistines. Therefore it is more reasonable to think that the rearrangement simply highlights David's cultic priority rather than any other affairs, and also possibly that the three months time gap is considered. We can safely say that by placing the first attempt to bring the ark as the first event after David's enthronement, the Chronicler underlines the significance of cultic performance or even temple building for the kingdom.

materials or information of cultic matters is added in regard to the event (1 Chr 13:1–4; 15:1–24; 16:4–6; 16:7–36; 16:37–42). With this observation, the reader also sees the emphasis on keeping the law through the explicit explanation of the failure of the first attempt, from the mouth of David (15:13), and explicit description of the observance of the law in the second attempt (15:11–12, 14–15, 26).[21]

When the reader sees that several episodes and lists across a wide time span are collected here not in a precisely chronological order, but in the single theme of David's military strength blessed by God, he or she perceives the flexible attitude of the author in writing history. It is plain that some materials are arranged according to subject, while the work unfolds the history in a chronological order by and large. For example, the name list of David's thirteen children who are born in Jerusalem (14:3–7) is added to the account of the building of his palace in Jerusalem (14:1–2), while it is most likely that the births of the children take several years at least, and the Philistines' attacks against David (14:8–17) soon after his becoming king of Israel occur before some of the thirteen children are born.

Additionally, when the reader reads the conspicuous description of how Michal despises King David leaping and dancing, at the second attempt to bring the ark to the city of David (1 Chr 15:29), and realizes that the expected outcome of this (i.e., the conversation between Michal and David, and consequent childlessness of Michal (2 Sam 6:20–23)) does not follow, it can remind him or her of the feature of bold *omission* in the work.

The theme of the ark is taken over by (or linked to) the theme of temple building (preparation) in the remaining part of the account of David's reign (1 Chr 17–29). The account of God's promise of a dynasty to David and David's response to it (1 Chr 17) is followed by the account of David's military campaigns and episodes (1 Chr 18–20). Most of these accounts are the same as in the first history with little alteration.[22] Then the account of David's problematic census resumes the topic of temple building by ending the episode with the account of deciding the location of the temple (1 Chr 21:1—22:1).[23] The rest of the account of David's reign

---

21. In the account of the second attempt to move the ark in 2 Sam 6:12–19, it is not explicitly explained why the first attempt did not succeed, while, in the second account, carrying the ark upon the Levites' shoulders, according to the law of moving the ark, is observed (1 Chr 15:13–15).

22. A few alterations of names (e.g., Joram (2 Sam 8:10) to Hadoram (1 Chr 18:10)), numbers of military units (1 Chr 19:7, 18—already discussed in "Solomon's Egyptian horses and chariots"), etc., are observed.

23. Of the overlapping of David's adultery and census in his confession in

(22:2—29:30) is largely about the preparation for the temple building, with cultic affairs which are mostly related to the temple, and is *new information* to the reader.[24] The large proportion of the account, which is closely related to the temple building, forces the reader to recognize the greatly strengthened emphasis on the temple and cultic matters in the work, when compared to the first history.[25]

It should be pointed out that, on the other hand, the long narrative of David committing adultery and murder and the following tragic punishment from God in the first history (2 Sam 11:1—20:22; 1 Kgs 1; 2:13–25[26]), is totally omitted in the present work. However, in the account of the capture of Rabbah (1 Chr 20:1–3), the retained description of David's staying in Jerusalem (20:1), which is the introductory part of the account of David's adultery in the first history, is conspicuous to the reader, and reminds him or her of the result that follows. The conspicuousness of the mention of David's remaining in Jerusalem is strengthened by the fact that the inclusion of the statement of David's staying in Jerusalem even comes at a cost to interpretation of the smooth flow of the account. While in the first history Joab's calling David to Rabbah which has been almost conquered, in order to attribute the merits of conquering to the king (2 Sam 12:26–28), and David's coming to and conquering the city, are described (2 Sam 12:29), in Chronicles Joab is described as the one who captures the city (1 Chr 20:1), and somewhat absurdly David appears in the latter part of the account as being present in Rabbah, without any mention of his coming there. In other words, if the mention of David's staying in Jerusalem were omitted, the flow of the account would be smoother. Hence, it can be suggested that the description of David's staying in Jerusalem

---

Chronicles discussed by Selman, see chapter 4.

24. The exception is, the materials in 1 Chr 27 which are of David's army divisions (27:1–15), officers of tribes (27:16–22), and the king's civil officials and counselors (27:25–34 partially parallel to 2 Sam 20:23–26) with a short comment on David's census (27:23–24).

25. In this sense, Wellhausen's statement that "his clearly cut figure [David] has become a feeble holy picture, seen through a cloud of incense" is understandable (Wellhausen, *Prolegomena*, 182). Nonetheless, David's military campaigns, episodes, and lists are not presented in the level to be overlooked in Chronicles. Furthermore, it should be pointed out that new materials on the military subjects are added in the Chronicler's presentation of David.

26. Adonija is the forth son of David who is killed to pay the sin of David as discussed already in chapter 4 (in the section, "The Technique of Allusion in Chronicles").

is most probably intended to remind the reader of the omitted story of David's adultery.[27]

In contrast to the radical *omissions*, the reader can see interesting *new information* in the account of David's preparation for the temple building (1 Chr 21–29, cf. 1 Chr 17). Apart from various cultic orders and lists of cultic personnel established by David, the description of the blueprint of the temple that has been given to David by God's spirit (1 Chr 28:11, 12–19) is conspicuous, along with an emphasis on Solomon's being pre-ordained as the God-chosen temple builder with full qualifications (1 Chr 22:6–11 cf. 28:6, 10; 29:19); both highlight Solomon's divine obligation to build the temple in his reign. Further, the reader observes Solomon's enthronement (1 Chr 29:22–23) in the context of temple-building prepa-ration (i.e., 1 Chr 28 is of David's disqualification from temple building (28:2–3), God's choice of Solomon as temple builder (28:5–6), God's blue-print of the temple building (28:11–19), David's admonition to Solomon as the temple builder (28:9–10, 20–21), the devotion of temple-building materials by David and leaders (29:1–9), and David's praise to God over the materials gladly devoted for the temple building (29:10–20)). These points prepare the reader to expect a temple-centered presentation of Solomon's reign in the following Solomon account.

Additionally, a careful reader cannot overlook the mention of Solo-mon's enthronement as "a second time" (שֵׁנִית) in 1 Chr 29:22. Without any previous account of the first enthronement, the reader cannot but under-stand that Solomon's enthronement with a struggle for succession in the first history (1 Kgs 1:5–53) is presupposed as the first enthronement here, and consequently is led to understand that, presupposing the first one, the present work describes the second enthronement, which is performed in a secure situation and in the context of temple-building preparation.

Summing up, reading through the genealogies, the account of Saul, that of David, and the emergence of Solomon as the temple builder in the account of David, the reader can become familiar with *omission, allu-sion*, and *new information*,[28] as characteristics of Chronicles, as the second

27. Selman also recognizes the hint (Selman, *1 Chronicles*, 196–97). Selman thinks that the Chronicler is aware of David's adultery but "wishes to stress Samuel's conclud-ing emphasis in the Uriah/Bathsheba tragedy on repentance, forgiveness and restora-tion" (2 Sam 12:13, 24–25; cf. Ps 51:13–19 [ET 11–17]); "awkward transition between verses 1 and 2, but a more evocative allusion is preserved in the enigmatic phrase, *but David remained in Jerusalem* (v. 1; cf. 2 Sa. 11:1)" [Selman's emphasis] (Selman, *1 Chronicles*, 196–97).

28. A case of increased nuance or complexity as a characteristic of Chronicles is observed in the account of David's census (1 Chr 21), as shown in chapter 4. However,

history. The reader can also see the increased emphasis on the temple building, cultic affairs, and observation of the law in the work, when compared to the first history. The reader can also clearly notice that the serious sin of David is omitted, but with a significant trace or hint of it. Now the reader, who also has a prior knowledge of the Pentateuch (and at least some parts of Joshua as well) with its stipulations, is ready to turn to the Solomon account.

3. SOLOMON'S CHARIOTS AND HORSES IMPORTED FROM EGYPT (2 CHR 1:14, 16–17; 9:25, 28)

Most scholars consider the passages about Solomon's horses and chariots from Egypt in Chronicles have nothing to do with Solomon's faults, but as part of a description of Solomon's wealth and God's blessing upon him. It is also argued that Solomon's wealth is shown in the form of military power and precious materials, and that the latter is presented as the basic source for the temple building,[29] while the former is presented not only as a source of wealth, but also as an instrument to secure peace for the building project. This understanding goes well with the perspective which views the Solomon portrayed in Chronicles as idealized, blameless, and faultless. Even McConville, who insists that Deuteronomy was written at a very early stage of Israel's history,[30] does not interpret the passages through the lens of the Deuteronomic law (i.e., the king's law which bans accumulation of many horses and importation of Egyptian horses (Deut 17:16)).[31] This shows how strongly the view of an ideal, blameless Solomon in Chronicles affects the interpretation of the passages. Further, when it is considered that there are some commentators who think that Solomon's importation of Egyptian horses and chariots should be construed as his

---

it is hard to propose that the reader is accustomed to the characteristics of the work, for the increased nuance or complexity of the kings' presentations is, at the present stage, not yet sufficiently evident to the reader.

29. It is generally alleged that Solomon's wealth in 2 Chr 1:14–17 is at the same time the fulfillment of God's promise before, and the preparatory source for the temple building (Williamson, *1 and 2 Chronicles*, 196; Selman, *2 Chronicles*, 295; Jarick, *2 Chronicles*, 34–35).

30. McConville, "Deuteronomy"; McConville, *Deuteronomy*, 33–40. McConville does not see any problem in 2 Chr 1:14–17, but only sees "riches . . . "given by God as a reward for Solomon's selflessness" (McConville, *Chronicles*, 112), and again in 2 Chr 9:13–28 simply "his wealth . . . inextricably linked with his wisdom to the end" (McConville, *Chronicles*, 148).

31. McConville, *Chronicles*, 109–10, 112–13.

prosperity under God's blessing, even in the Solomon narrative in Kings[32] (i.e., even in the Deuteronomistic history, the Deuteronomic stipulation of "Egyptian horses importation" is not considered), it is not surprising that the commentators on Chronicles do not consider the stipulation of Deut 17 in their interpretation. However, on the grounds that "the Egyptian horse importation" has been the material which shows Solomon's corruption in Kings, it is reasonable and worthwhile to explore whether the same material has been re-used by the Chronicler in order to allude to Solomon's faults, for it is presumed, in this study, that exploiting the reader's prior knowledge is one characteristic of the author's writing style.

It should be pointed out, first of all, that Solomon's importation of Egyptian horses and chariots appears twice (2 Chr 1:14–17; 9:25–28), each instance including the mention of Jerusalem's wealth (2 Chr 1:15; 9:27), at the beginning and end of the Solomon account in Chronicles. While repetitive description of similar subjects appears in the Solomon narrative in Kings in order to imply progressive and subtle change through Solomon's reign (as seen in chapter 3), the importation of Egyptian horses and chariots is one of very few subjects which appear repeatedly in Chronicles.[33] What matters is that the conspicuous repetition of the subject, in Chronicles, makes an impression upon the reader that this matter has significance in Solomon's reign. The explanation that the Chronicler retained the double appearance of Solomon's horses simply because the matter appears twice in the *Vorlage* cannot be satisfactory. When it is considered that the work has the tendency of bold omission or abridgement, the repetitive appearance of the subject of the Egyptian horses should be regarded as a marker that betrays a strong intention of the author to allude to some-

---

32. Japhet presumes that only in 1 Kgs 1–2, 11, do Solomon's faults appear (Japhet, *I & II Chronicles*, 646). However, our stance is that Solomon's importation of Egyptian horses and intermarriage with Pharaoh's daughter, which appear outside the chapters in Kings, constitute the prime of Solomon's faults. It seems that a stance such as Japhet's on the Solomon narrative in Kings, affects interpretation of the Solomon account in Chronicles. Hence, the application of the king's stipulation that bans importation of Egyptian horses seems to be pre-excluded by many commentators on the account in Chronicles.

33. The two descriptions of the levy system (2 Chr 2:16–17 [ET 2:17–18]; 8:7–9), of silver and gold with its sycamore trees in Jerusalem which is inserted in the materials of horses and chariots matters (2 Chr 1:15 and 9:27), of importation of gold (and other treasures and exotic animals) from abroad with ship and the help of Hiram's subjects (2 Chr 8:17–18 and 9:21). Being compared to the case of Kings where that the main structure of the whole account is a chiastic structure shows, most subjects or elements appear twice having the building of the temple as its symmetrical centre, the few subjects which appears twice in Chronicles have much more significance.

thing significant. In other words, that these passages are "bookends" to the Solomon account may give an impression that this is a characteristic of Solomon's reign from start to finish.

Additionally, it is plain that the double appearance of the matter in Chronicles is not simple a copying or retaining of its *Vorlage*, but one that plainly shows the Chronicler's strong touch. The two passages about Solomon's horses in Kings are as follows. In Chronicles, the modification of the two passages is plain, as follows.

Kings	Chronicles
Solomon also had forty thousand stalls of horses for his chariots, and twelve thousand horsemen (1 Kgs 5:6 [ET 4:26]).	Solomon gathered together chariots and horses; he had fourteen hundred chariots and twelve thousand horses, which he stationed in the chariot cities and with the king in Jerusalem. . . . Solomon's horses were imported from Egypt in collection; the king's traders received them in collection[A] at the prevailing price. They imported from Egypt, and then exported, a chariot for six hundred shekels of silver, and a horse for one hundred fifty; so through them these were exported to all the kings of Hittites and the kings of Aram (2 Chr 1:14, 16–17) [my translation].
Solomon gathered together chariots and horses; he had fourteen hundred chariots and twelve thousand horses, which he stationed in the chariots cities and with the king in Jerusalem. . . . Solomon's horses were imported from Egypt in collection,[B] the king's traders received them in collection at a price. They imported from Egypt, and then exported, a chariot for six hundred shekels of silver, and a horse for one hundred fifty; so through them (i.e., king's traders[C]) these were exported to all the kings of the Hittites and the kings of Aram (1 Kgs 10:26, 28–29) [my translation].	Solomon had four thousand stalls for horses and chariots, and twelve thousand horses, which he stationed in the chariot cities and with the king in Jerusalem. . . . Horses were imported for Solomon from Egypt and from all lands (2 Chr 9:25, 28).

A. The present study prefers "in collection" to "from Kue" for the translation of מִקְוֵה (Kings) and מִקְוֵא (Chronicles). The reading of it is so complicatedly related to other issues that Curtis humbly confesses that "The question of the true reading must remain *sub lite*." While NRSV, NIV, and most others' reading, which translates מִקְוֵה as "from Kue," is supported by LXX and Vulgate and a majority of scholars, RV translates it as 'in drove.' The former reading is not natural and smooth in terms of syntax because it makes the sentence unbalanced in that the king's traders are mentioned only in relation to horse importation from Kue, leaving the horse importation from Egypt without any mention of agent. Furthermore, according to the reading, the detailed price of horse and chariot is only described concerning Egypt, without any mention of it concerning Kue. Moreover, in Chronicles when the phrase "from Egypt and from all lands" in 2 Chr 9:28 is considered, it is more likely that מִקְוֵה does not mean a region which has equal status with Egypt as the source of horse importation (for related issues, see Dillard, *2 Chronicles*, 1987, 9, 13–14). The "from Kue" reading is even absurd when the geographical relationship between the places is considered. That is, it is unlikely that Israel could be a channel between Cilicia (Kue) which is far north from Israel, and Aram which is near north of Israel. Furthermore, it should be pointed out that מִקְוֵה is used as "gathering" in Gen 1:10 and some other places in OT, which supports the RV translation. Having said this, even if the majority translation "from Kue" is accepted, it does not seriously affect our argument.

B. See footnote A.

C. Literally, "by their hands."

From comparison of the two pairs of passages, several points can be made. Firstly, the second passage in Kings reappears not in the second place, but in the first place in Chronicles. Secondly, although the second passage in Chronicles has elements in common with the first passage in Kings, there is a significant addition. It is plain that the Chronicler did not simply move the first to the second, and the second to the first. With this observation, a question can be raised: why did the Chronicler use the second passage in Kings first in his work? Was it simply his accidental dislocating of the two passages? The additional information in the second case in Chronicles strongly suggests that this is not the case. The additional information "Horses were imported for Solomon from Egypt and from all lands," has a kind of climactic atmosphere as a final stage of his horse importation: the second case in Chronicles is far different from the first case in Kings where the mere number of horses and chariots appears. The second case in Chronicles has not only the climactic addition, but also restates Solomon's keeping the chariot and horse forces in chariot cities and Jerusalem, which does not appear in the first case in Kings. The overall consideration can lead us to the conclusion that the Chronicler had a specific intention in this change. However, most scholars do not try to explain the significance of the repeated appearance of the same materials, not to mention the intention of the alterations of the two passages in Chronicles from that of its *Vorlage*. Rather commentators simply engage themselves with the geographical, botanic (i.e., of sycamore, 2 Chr 1:15;

9:27), and textual transmission issues,[34] while some admit the literary conspicuousness of the repetition.[35] However, at the very least, it is plain that the Chronicler tried to make an unusually significant impression upon his reader's mind regarding these matters.

3.1. The Reason for and Effect of the Rearrangement of the Material about the Horses in Chronicles

It is interesting to notice that in a reversal from Kings, in Chronicles the more detailed description of the importation of Egyptian horses appears in the first instance (i.e., 2 Chr 1:14–17). In Kings, only horses and chariots are mentioned in the first instance without any mention of their Egyptian origin (1 Kgs 5:6 [ET 4:26]), and a more detailed description of Solomon's horses and chariots appears in the second instance with clear mention of their Egyptian origin (1 Kgs 10:26–29). In Chronicles, a more detailed description of Solomon's horses and chariots with clear mention of their Egyptian origin appears in the first instance (2 Chr 1:14–17), Then a slightly abridged form of the same description with additional information (of Solomon's territory in 2 Chr 9:26, and his horse importation from all nations along with Egypt in 9:28), appears in the second instance (2 Chr 9:25–28), with the recurring reference to the Egyptian origin of some horses. That means that it is easier for the reader to perceive, from the start of the Solomon account in Chronicles, the Egyptian element or connection which is prohibited in the king's law (Deut 17:16), in contrast to Kings.

Additionally, there is something in the first case in Chronicles that directly reminds the reader of the king's law; "the king's traders" (2 Chr 1:16),[36] who import Egyptian horses, corresponds to the phrase of the law "he must not . . . return *the people* to Egypt in order to acquire more horses" (since the Lord has said to you, "You must never return that way again") (Deut 17:16b). Even the order of the horse matters in Chronicles

34. For example, see Dillard, *2 Chronicles*, 74; Selman, *2 Chronicles*, 357.

35. Johnstone calls the reappearance "a part of . . . 'ring-construction' on Solomon's reign" (Johnstone, *1 Chronicles 1–2 Chronicles 9*, 303), but does not provide a satisfactory explanation of the reason for the existence of the structure, except that the second passage is simply "rounding off" Solomon's account (Johnstone, *1 Chronicles 1–2 Chronicles 9*, 374). The second passage is even not treated as itself, as some commentators suggest referring their comments on the first passage for the second passage. On 9:28, for example, Dillard, *2 Chronicles*, 74.

36. It (סֹחֲרֵי הַמֶּלֶךְ) appears in 1 Kgs 10:28, as well.

corresponds to the order of the law about horses in Deut 17:16. That is, the first point of the law is to ban the king's acquiring many horses, and the second point is to ban the king's sending people to Egypt to acquire horses in Deut 17:16.[37] The description of the matter of Solomon's horses appears in the same order, a large number of horses (with chariots) in 2 Chr 1:14, then Egyptian horse importation through the king's traders in 2 Chr 1:16.[38]

The law that bans Israel's king's importation of Egyptian horses is a conspicuous one in the Deuteronomic law, and in the king's stipulation (Deut 17) as well. In the passage of Kings, the matter of "the Egyptian horses" could and should be a trap for the reader, for the climactic atmosphere which contains the matter (in 1 Kgs 10), could easily blind the reader to Solomon's transgression of it. However, here in Chronicles the setting of the first appearance of Egyptian horses is far different from that of Kings. The reign of Solomon has just started, and in this setting, the reader can more easily detect the problematic nature of the matter (Additionally, it is possible that this is highlighted in David's hamstringing of the acquired chariot horses (1 Chr 18:4), another conspicuous event that has reminded the reader that not only importation of Egyptian horses but also king's maintaining many horses is prohibited. Although the event has its parallel in 2 Sam 8:4, the effect of the mention of the event in Chronicles is more effective and consequently memorable, for the description of David's reign is simpler than that in Samuel-Kings).

In summing up, while the first instance in Kings tries to hide the Egyptian element or connection, the first instance in Chronicles makes it clear that Solomon's horses and chariots have an Egyptian origin, which transgresses the conspicuous stipulation on the king. The difference between the two instances can be easily explained. In Kings, in order to highlight the insidious progress of sin, the clear marker should be concealed until the last stage. In Chronicles, however, the clear marker should be proposed from the start in order to emphasize the grace of God which is

---

37. "Even so, he must not acquire many horses for himself, or return the people to Egypt in order to acquire more horses, since the Lord has said to you, 'You must never return that way again.'"

38. It is the same with the second case of Kings' presentation (1 Kgs 10:26–29) and the second case in Chronicles (2 Chr 9:25, 28) as well. That is, the exact correspondence appears in all cases, except the first in Kings' presentation (1 Kgs 5:6 [ET 4:26]) where the Egyptian element is regarded as being hidden on purpose, as has been shown in chapter 3.

given to its beneficiary in spite of his shortcomings, which is an essential theme of the work as shown in the chapter on the purpose of Chronicles.[39]

3.2. The Reader's Prior Knowledge and a Brief Reconstruction of the Reading Experience of the Passages

As has been presupposed and explored so far, the reader's prior knowledge does include the law of the king in Deut 17 and a full understanding of the Solomon narrative in Kings, as has been shown in chapter 3. If the reader is well aware of the nature of the *Vorlage* of the Solomon account (as explored in chapter 3), which naturally includes the awareness of the king's law (Deut 17:14–20), then he or she cannot but perceive that Solomon's Egyptian horse importation, along with his acquiring many horses (2 Chr 1:14–17), which appears right after God promises abundant wealth and wisdom (2 Chr 1:11–12), constitutes a kind of tension in contrast with God's special blessing in favor of the king. Therefore, when the reader sees, in the following passages, that wealth and wisdom is given to the kings and that the project of the building of the temple is done smoothly or rather in an increasingly glorious mood, it becomes clear to the reader that the prosperity and success of the king is given to him as God promised, in spite of his faults or shortcomings. In other words, the reader can see that Solomon's shortcomings appear from the very start of his reign and that most of Solomon's reign is under God's grace that is given in spite of the fault of its beneficiary.[40]

---

39. It is interesting to observe that God's blessing that is given to a beneficiary even after the beneficiary's fault appears in the case of David too. That is, David enjoys God's blessing (as victory over Philistines (1 Chr 14:8–17. Cf. see also the anachronistic description of the building his palace, progeny in 1 Chr 14:1–2, 3–7) even after his failure in his first attempt of ark bringing (1 Chr 13:1–14). Kelly rightly points out that the case shows that God grants blessing to one "in spite of" one's failure concerning God (Kelly, *Retribution and Eschatology*, 76). Kelly proposes the case as one that supports his main view that the retribution in Chronicles is not a "strict recompense for actions" (Kelly, *Retribution and Eschatology*, 79). Kelly's view is a contrast to a classical view (i.e., the view which tries to interpret the work as a whole by "retribution theology") (Mosis, *Untersuchungen*, 55–61; Im, *Davidbild*, 80–81, 180–81) that God grants blessing upon David for David's attempt at ark bringing is a pious one as his first action as king. The classical view is not convincing, for in the case of Chronicles the faults of David are more emphasized than in Kings' presentation. For example, in Chronicles "divine initiative to the venture" appears (1 Chr 13:2) while it is absent in the *Vorlage*, and the law breaking on the first occasion is more clearly admitted (1 Chr 15:13) than in its *Vorlage*.

40. Rudolph, "Problems."

When the reader reaches the second case in 2 Chr 9:25–28, he or she becomes aware of the importance of this matter: the first and second cases constitute a framing of the narrative. It becomes clearer that all the success and prosperity described so far has been thanks to God's grace in spite of Solomon's faults or shortcomings, at least in terms of his acquiring many horses and importing horses from Egypt.[41] In particular, the description that horses were imported not only "from Egypt," but also "from all lands," which contains a sense of exaggeration, stimulates the reader to realize Solomon's excess. Also the reader becomes mentally prepared to accept the following passage where Solomon's more serious fault is revealed in the description of the ensuing events.

3.3. The Technique of Allusion and Its Dual Purpose

The reappearance of the Egyptian horses in the second case (2 Chr 9:25–28) gives the reader the impression that this is a significant matter in the reign of Solomon. When the reader is reminded by this of Solomon's strong connection to Egypt (Pharaoh's daughter, 2 Chr 8:11), it is not a sudden surprise to see the people's complaint of Solomon's heavy burden upon them, in the directly following passage (2 Chr 10). In that sense, the reader does not see any theological dilemma when he or she reaches 2 Chr 10. Moreover, the end part of the second case has a subtle similarity to the description of Solomon's excessive intermarriages in 1 Kgs 11. The statement that "Horses were imported for Solomon from Egypt and from all the lands" (2 Chr 9:28) resembles the description of Solomon's intermarriage in 1 Kgs 11:1, where the criticism is explicitly made that Solomon loved many foreign women along with the daughter of Pharaoh.[42] While the exaggerated expression, "(and) from all the lands" (וּמִכָּל־הָאֲרָצוֹת) in 2 Chr 9:28 does not appear in any place in its *Vorlage* in regard to Solomon's horses, it is more likely that the expression is more easily linked with Solomon's wives who cover a variety of nations as well as Egypt. As the reader has been reminded of the problem of Solomon's intermarriage already in 2 Chr 8:11,[43] Solomon's importation of the horses from all lands

41. Solomon's intermarriage is another issue in the same direction, which the following section will explore.

42. See the case of the technique of allusion by conflation as proposed in the chapter on literary characteristics of Chronicles. In the case of David's census, in Chronicles, elements of his adultery and its punishment (i.e., punishing "sword," "four sons") are subtly assimilated through the technique of allusion.

43. This matter will be discussed in the following section.

may remind the reader of his intermarriages with an enormous number of foreign women (1 Kgs 11:1–3), for there is a common impression of self-indulgence both in Solomon's importation of horses "from Egypt and from all the lands" (2 Chr 9:28) and in Solomon's intermarriage starting from the Egyptian princess to 1,000 wives (seven hundred princesses and three hundred concubines) including many foreign women (Moabites, Ammonite, Edomite, Sidonian, and Hittite women) (1 Kgs 11:1–3).[44]

Further, it can be said that with a minimum of devices, the Chronicler captures the nature of Solomon's corruption in the cases of his importation of Egyptian horses. Firstly, as both cases show, Solomon's disobedience toward the king's law is placed in the context of God's blessing (for example, God's promise of blessing (2 Chr 1:12), and Solomon's income due to God-given wisdom (2 Chr 9:23) are very near to the passages). This shows that Solomon's fault is in the presence or middle of God's blessing. Secondly, the two cases show the nature of the increasing sin of Solomon. In the first case, Solomon's horses are imported from Egypt only (2 Chr 1:16), while in the second case, the horses are imported not only from Egypt but also from all the lands (2 Chr 9:28). The two points are coherent with the reader's prior knowledge of the first history concerning Solomon's corruption as insidiously increasing, as has been explored in chapter 3.[45]

Further, it can be considered what will happen if the reader fails to notice the problematic nature of Solomon's Egyptian horse importation in 2 Chr 1:14–17, through carelessness in reading the text or even ignorance of the old tradition. He or she has another chance to become aware of it in 2 Chr 9:25–28 where the Egyptian designation clearly appears once more, although with less detail than the first one. (As explained above, the main function of the second case is to make a strong impression upon the reader of Solomon's Egyptian connection, which is against the law of the king, so that the reader may be reminded of the first case and realize the significance of the matter of the horses.) It is possible that the reader who has missed the significance of the importation of the Egyptian horses in the first passage could miss the significance again in the second. However, the author does not fail in his primary intention even if his reader fails to notice the hints provided. At least, the reader cannot miss the major point of the author that Solomon's reign over the united kingdom was a glorious era, as God had promised and fulfilled (most scholars' understanding of

44. Cf. see 3.3.5. "Allusion by Conflation" in chapter 5.

45. Recently, J. J. Kang's study (Kang, *The Persuasive Portrayal*) reaches the same conclusion.

the Solomon account at the moment grasps this point at least). In other words, the reader's perceiving Solomon's fault in the passages is not the primary intention of the author, but a secondary one.

Additionally, it can be admitted that even in the very faults of Solomon, the aura of God-promised blessing is present. Without God-given wisdom and prosperity, his accumulation of many horses and importation of Egyptian horses would have been impossible. In other words, the motif is ambiguous, denoting both divine blessing and human disobedience. In that sense, even when the reader overlooks some negative connotations of the passages and only sees the positive aspects, it cannot be said that he or she totally misses the implication of the passages. A similar situation is found, although from another work of the Hebrew Bible, in Josh 9. While it is pointed out as a fault of the Israelite leaders (including Joshua) not to ask direction from the Lord when the cunning Gibeonites tried to deceive and be guaranteed their lives by a treaty with Israelites, the episode still shows how much the fame of Israelis strength with its accompanying God intimidated the Canaanite tribes (Josh 9:24, cf. 2:11; 5:1). A positive aura is present even in the passage that plainly admits a fault of the leadership of Israel.

What matters is that at any rate the reader can not escape the author's intention in the end and is confronted with the solemn description of Solomon's heavy burden upon the people (2 Chr 10:4, 9, 11, 14) and the direct mention of Ahijah's prophecy (2 Chr 10:15) with the following significant prophecy of Shemaiah (2 Chr 11:2–4). If the reader has prior knowledge of the old tradition, he or she cannot but be reminded of it. If the reader does not have prior knowledge of the old tradition, he or she cannot understand those allusions until referring to the old tradition (in which case he or she is in a sense disqualified as a reader of Chronicles anyway, for the work is full of omissions and allusions). However, it is important that even when the reader cannot understand the allusion, owing to his or her ignorance of the old tradition, the glorious aspect of the united kingdom together with the Jerusalem temple, which is the prime intention of the author for his reader, will make an immense impression on the reader's mind.

3.4. The Need for the Technique of Allusion for Dual Purpose in the Passage

The Solomon account is the very part in which the most important themes of Chronicles reveal themselves in a significant way according to the nature of the account. As the builder of the temple specially chosen by God, Solomon is the king whose reign is presented as the climax of the kingdom, which shows the glory of the united kingdom along with the temple building. At the same time, as the one responsible for the division of the kingdom through his faults, as clearly shown in the *Vorlage*, he provides an exemplary case in which God shows his grace given in spite of the faults of his beneficiary, and this grace is the hope of the post-exilic community.

In the case of Kings' presentation of Solomon, the thematic background of the account (i.e., the law of the king (Deut 17:16)) and the material of "Egyptian horse importation" have the same direction, to present Solomon's faults implicitly. The thematic background and the material were combined together in the form of a retroactive re-evaluation, in order to convey most effectively the message or lesson of the account, "the insidious progress of sin." In contrast to Kings, the Chronicler's general thematic focus is laid on "glory, hope, and grace," as shown in chapter 4, in spite of the presence of Solomon's faults. Hence, it becomes clear that the Chronicler's motive is significantly different from that of the author of Kings. The Chronicler had to present Solomon's faults in as mild a way as possible (for it is impossible to omit them completely in the flow of the history), in order to keep the reader's attention on the main theme of the glory of the kingdom and temple. On the other hand, the author might have hoped, in the account, to present the grace of God that is given in spite of the faults of its beneficiary, which is also an important theme of the work.

3.5. The Reason for the Absence of Explicit Criticism of the Matter of the Horses in the Account of Solomon in Chronicles

One may raise a question about the absence of clear criticism of Solomon's importation of Egyptian horses, for it is generally acknowledged that it is a characteristic of the Chronicler's writing style to give a clear evaluation of other kings. It is clear in the cases of the following kings that the Chronicler is more concerned with giving evaluative comments in as many places as possible. Does the Chronicler's silence on the Egyptian horse importation mean that he ignored the stipulation on the king and intended only to glorify Solomon's prosperity and power in the presence of the Egyptian military devices? First of all, it should be recognized that the portrayal of David and Solomon, as a pair, is somewhat different from that of the following kings. While the following kings' misdeeds have been evaluated explicitly, David's have been described more or less implicitly (his adultery and murder are only hinted in 1 Chr 20:1b, and accordingly, are not explicitly criticized). The Chronicler's intention in this is explained by the fact that the two kings' reign should be presented as the most glorious period of Israel as a united kingdom, when the temple building is prepared and achieved successfully.[46]

Secondly, Solomon's reign is presented in an exceptional way in that a summing-up evaluation statement is absent, the parallel of which is found only in the interesting case of King Abijah. It is plain that both kings find special favor from God according to the grace of God upon David (Abijah, 1 Kgs 15:4; Solomon, 2 Sam 7:14–15 / 1 Chr 17:13), and both kings' faults which are very clear in the *Vorlage* are not presented explicitly in Chronicles, although alluded to in implicit ways (e.g., in the case of Abijah, 2 Chr 14:2–4 [ET 14:3–5]; in the case of Solomon, 2 Chr 10).[47] This can be understood in that the faults of the kings who enjoy God's blessing in spite of those faults (which are evident in its *Vorlage*) are not presented explicitly in Chronicles, and it is a very practical way of reflecting the situation that God blessed them in virtue of David, overlooking their faults (through the implicit way of mentioning or hint or allusion), as if God does not pay full attention to the faults, which are only alluded to.[48]

---

46. Johnstone's observation that מעל does not appear in the reign of David and Solomon possibly reflects the same point, while it should be admitted that other terms that imply "sin" still appear in the description of the same reign (i.e., 1 Chr 15:13; 21:8, 17; 2 Chr 6: 21, 36).

47. Furthermore, Abijah's prayer and any good evaluation of him are conspicuously absent. This matter has already been explored in chapter 2.

48. Selman points out a similar view, saying that "a more evocative allusion is preserved in the enigmatic phrase, *but David remained in Jerusalem* (v. 1; *cf.* 2 Sa. 11:1). Two purposes may be discerned in the Chronicler's version, both based on elements already found in Samuel. Firstly, although the Chronicler is not unaware that David is guilty of great sin (*cf.* 21:8), he wishes to stress Samuel's concluding emphasis in the Uriah/Bathsheba tragedy on repentance, forgiveness and restoration (2 Sa. 12:13, 24–25; *cf.* Ps. 51:13–19). Guilt because of sin did not disqualify a person from playing a leading role in God's kingdom, as both post-exilic and New Testament believers continued to need reminding (*cf.* Zc. 3:1–10; 5:1–11; 1 Cor. 6:9)."

3.6. Chronicler's View of Military Power throughout the Work

It is also important to scrutinize how the Chronicler presents military power in Chronicles, in order to make sure that our interpretation of Solomon's horses and chariots so far is in line with the Chronicler's general stance on military matters. Issues related to military power have been discussed among scholars under various themes, including the building of fortifications, army notices, military victories and defeats, war and peace,[49] and alliance either with a foreign country or northern Israel.[50] Usually, these themes have been observed in the bigger picture of "reward and punishment" or "retribution theology" in the work.[51] The question of authenticity of the military information in the work has also attracted scholarly attention as an important issue.[52] While some think that the military information in the work is more or less the Chronicler's own composition, i.e., "fabrication," in order to meet the author's intention,[53] others propose that although the Chronicler's own language and style is evident, the information is generally based on earlier sources.[54]

While it is most scholars' view that strong military power is presented as God's blessing upon good kings in the system of retribution principle,[55]

49. Welten, *Geschichte und Geschichtsdarstellung*, 79–114; Kelly, *Retribution and Eschatology*, 115–26, 204–11.

50. Kelly, *Retribution and Eschatology*, 204–11; Knoppers, "Yhwh Is Not."

51. Kelly, *Retribution and Eschatology*, 115–26, 129–31; 190–96; "Most of the Chronicler's references to war have an obvious function within his schema of reward and punishment" (190).

52. Kelly's discussion on the matter of military information, which criticizes Welten's proposal, is largely focused on maintaining that the information has an authentic basis (ibid., 118–26).

53. For example, de Wette (1806), Wellhausen (1885), Welten (1973), and Strübind (1991).

54. Noth, Rudolph (1955), Myers (1965), Johnson (1969), Williamson (1982), Deboys (1990), Schniedewind (1991), and Kelly show positive evaluation of the material on military issues in Chronicles (Kelly, *Retribution and Eschatology*, 111–31).

55. For example, Duke states that "Blessing took a variety of forms: victory in battle, rest from one's enemies, united support of the people, prosperity, wisdom, healing, the ability to execute building projects or to *strengthen one's army and fortifications*. Cursing or retribution took the opposite forms: military defeat, illness or death, rebellion of the people and so on" [my emphasis] (Duke, "A Rhetorical Approach," 117. the list of referential works that contain the indications of blessing and cursing in Chronicles, see Duke, "A Rhetorical Approach," 117 n. 55). McKenzie also states that "The rewards that become characteristic of the Chronicler's account of history include 'rest' and 'quiet,' building activity, *military strength*, a large family, wealth, international refutation, and respect from subjects" [my emphasis] (McKenzie, *1–2 Chronicles*, 52).

a close reading of Chronicles reveals that the point of the Chronicler is elsewhere. In this regard, military strength and military success should be distinguished in Chronicles,[56] a point that seems to have been neglected. While military strength itself does not necessarily imply God's blessing, military success proves God's favor or blessing. The following list, which comprehensively covers military occasions in Chronicles, will show this.

1. The Reubenites, the Gadites, and the half-tribe of Manasseh (total 44,760) were victorious over the Hagrites, Jetur, Naphish, and Nodab, although the latter were surely larger in number than the Israelites (from the fact that only the number of them in captivity was 100,000 (1 Chr 5:21b)) because the Israelites cried to God in the battle and God granted their entreaty (1 Chr 5:18–22).

2. The captivity of the Reubenites, the Gadites, and the half-tribe of Manasseh to the kings of Assyria in the end was described as solely due to their transgression against the God of their ancestors, and to God stirring up the spirits of foreign kings, without any mention of the military situation (1 Chr 5:25–26). It is noteworthy that just before the explanation of the Transjordan tribes' fall, the numerousness and powerfulness of the half-tribe of Manasseh is introduced (1 Chr 5: 23–24).

3. King Saul's defeat and death do not come from his lack of military power, but from his unfaithfulness to the Lord and his commandment (1 Chr 10:13–14a).

4. David's growing power is the result of God's being with him rather than his getting more military strength (1 Chr 11:9).

5. David owes his victory over the Philistines to God's instruction and help rather than to his own military power (1 Chr 14).

6. David himself rejected the opportunity to increase his military power by hamstringing all the chariot horses that he had taken through the victory over King Hadadezer of Zobah. David left only one hundred

---

Williamson states, following Welten, that "he [the Chronicler] uses certain motifs, such as building, in stereotyped ways as a means of passing a theological verdict on the reign being described." [my insertion] (Williamson, *1 and 2 Chronicles*, 23).

56. Braun is cautious in stating that the sign of God's blessing is victory in war rather than military strength: "the reigns of faithful kings are frequently associated with building operations, family, and *victory in war* (cf. 2 Chr 26:1–15)." [my emphasis] (Braun, *1 Chronicles*, 178).

horses from one thousand chariots and seven thousand cavalry (1 Chr 18:4).

7. It is plainly stated that it was "the Lord" that "gave victory to David wherever he went" (1 Chr 18:6b), after David rejected increasing his military power, by the hamstringing.[57]

8. Although Hanun and the Ammonites hire thirty-two thousand chariots and cavalry from Mesopotamia, from Arammaacah, and from Zobah, paying a thousand talents of silver (1 Chr 19:6b–7a), they are defeated by the Israelite army, which is most likely non-chariot and non-cavalry troops, led by Joab (19:8–15). It is interesting to observe that in its *Vorlage* there is no mention of cavalry or chariots of the enemy army.[58]

9. Again, most probably with the same army with few horses, David defeats the Aramean army, killing seven thousand Aramean charioteers, forty thousand foot soldiers, and Shophach the commander of their army (1 Chr 19:18).[59]

10. That David's census—which seems to have a military purpose, for it counts the number of men who drew swords (1 Chr 21:5) and is conducted by Joab, the chief commander of Israelis army (21:2–6, cf. 11:6)—causes the wrath of God (21:7–30, cf. 21:3), seems to imply that God is not pleased that David considers his military power or

57. The same sequence appears in the *Vorlage*, i.e., in 2 Sam 8:4, 6, although the details of what David took from King Hadadezer differ. That is, "David took from him *one thousand seven hundred horsemen,* and twenty thousand foot soldiers. David hamstrung all the chariot horses, but left *enough for a hundred chariots*" (2 Sam 8:4) and "David took from him *one thousand chariots, seven thousand cavalry,* and twenty thousand foot soldiers. David hamstrung all the chariot horses, but left *one hundred of them*" (1 Chr 18:4). Having observed this difference between the Chronicler's work and its *Vorlage*, further exploring the difference or change is beyond the concern of the present study.

58. "Hanun and the Ammonites sent *a thousand talents of silver* to hire *chariots and cavalry* from Mesopotamia, from Aramaacah and from Zobah. They hired *thirty-two thousand chariots* and the king of Maacah with his army" (1 Chr 19:6b–7a), and "the Ammonites sent and hired the Arameans of Bethrehob and the Arameans of Zobah, *twenty thousand foot soldiers,* as well as the king of Maacah, *one thousand men,* and the men of Tob, *twelve thousand men*" (2 Sam 10:6b–7).

59. There are differences in details between the description in the Chronicler's work and its *Vorlage*. "David killed of the Arameans *seven hundred chariot teams,* and *forty thousand horsemen* (NRSV footnote: some Gk Mss read *foot soldiers*)" (2 Sam 10:18), and "David killed *seven thousand Aramean charioteers* and *forty thousand foot soldiers*" (1 Chr 19:18). To explore the differences is not crucial for the present discussion, and is beyond the concern of the present study.

potential rather than God himself, as his strength.[60] It is noteworthy that the very event becomes the trigger of building of the temple
through which God's forgiveness is given.

11. Rehoboam's fortifying of cities and making the fortresses strong (2
Chr 11:5–12) is not described as God's blessing in the context, but is
a mere factual description, for no previous obedience or faithfulness
of Rehohoam is referred to.[61] Further, in the following passages, it
becomes clear that the fortresses and fortified cities cannot protect
the kingdom from Shishak's invasion (2 Chr 12:2–9).

12. Although Abijah's army (400,000) is half the size of Jeroboam's
(800,000) (2 Chr 13:3) and is even put into a crisis by a tactic of the
northern army, Abijah's army defeats Jeroboam's in the end because
the Lord helps them when they cry out to him (2 Chr 13:14–15).

13. King Asa's comparatively massive army—"three hundred thousand[62]
from Judah, armed with large shields and spears, and two hundred
eighty thousand troops from Benjamin who carried shields and drew
bows; all these were mighty warriors" (2 Chr 14:7 [ET 14:8])—ironically turns out to be weak, and Asa had to cry to the Lord for help
(2 Chr 14:10 [ET 14:11]), when an even greater army invades Israel;
"Zerah the Ethiopian came out against them with an army of a million men and three hundred chariots" (2 Chr 14:8 [ET 14:9]).

14. It was "the Lord" that "defeated the Ethiopians before Asa and before
Judah" (2 Chr 14:11 [ET 14:12]). Further, it is noteworthy that it is
said that it was "the Lord" that gave him (Asa) and Judah peace (2
Chr 14:5 [ET 14:6]; 15:15).

15. Asa's relying on the king of Aram in the military alliance is criticized
by the seer (2 Chr 16:1–9), who represents God, and is described as
"doing foolishly" (2 Chr 16:9b), while it is stated that "For the eyes

60. "[It] was apparently for military purpose (cf. vv. 2, 5), and betrayed lack of trust
in Yahweh who had so far acted as Israel's commander in war" (Kelly, *Retribution and
Eschatology*, 81).

61. It is unlikely that Rehoboam's simply giving up his expedition to the northern
Israel deserves such a blessing or result. Moreover, there is no explicit indication which
connects his obedience to the word of God and his fortification of the cities and im-
provement of military strength.

62. Scholars such as McConville suggest that "the thousand" (אֶלֶף) might mean
something other (a military unit) than a literal thousand (McConville, *Chronicles*, 3).
For a more detailed discussion, see Mendenhall, "The Census Lists," 52–66; Wenham,
"Large Numbers," 19–53; Klein, "How Many?," 270–82.

of the Lord range throughout the entire earth, to strengthen those whose heart is true to him" (2 Chr 16:9a).

16. Ironically, even though Jehoshaphat has a massive army—"Of Judah, the commanders of the thousand: Adnah the commander, with three hundred thousand mighty warriors, and next to him Jehohanan the commander, with two hundred eighty thousand, and next to him Amasiah son of Zichri, a volunteer for the service of the Lord, with two hundred thousand mighty warriors. Of Benjamin: Eliada, a mighty warrior, with two hundred thousand armed with bow and shield, and next to him Jehozabad with one hundred eighty thousand armed for war" (2 Chr 17:14b–19a)—totaling 1,116,000 warriors plus those whom the king had placed in the fortified cities throughout all Judah (2 Chr 17:19b), his life was seriously threatened by the Aramean captains of the chariots in a battle, and he made a narrow escape only because "the Lord helped him"; "God drew them away from him" after "Jehoshaphat cried out" (2 Chr 18:31b), while Ahab, the king of Israel, Jehoshaphat's ally died in the battle (2 Chr 18:33–34).

17. Again, when the allied army of Moabites, Ammonites, and some of the Meunites invades Israel, ironically Jehoshaphat and his army turn out to be "powerless against this great multitude that is coming against" them and they "do not know what to do" (2 Chr 20:12b). The victory over the enemies is won by God rather than Jehoshaphat's military power, as it is stated "the battle is not yours but God's," "see the victory of the Lord," "the Lord set an ambush," "the Lord had fought against the enemies of Israel" (2 Chr 20:15b, 17, 22, 29), after the prayer and fast of Jehoshaphat and all Judah (2 Chr 20:3). It is also noteworthy that it was "God" that "gave him (Jehoshaphat) rest" (2 Chr 20:30).

18. Jehoram, the king of Judah, fails to subdue the revolt of Edom, even with all his chariots and commanders, for he has forsaken the Lord, the God of his ancestors (2 Chr 21:8–10).

19. The army of Aram, with a few men, could defeat the Judahite king Joash's very great army (2 Chr 24:23–24), for the Judahite people had abandoned the Lord (24:17–19), King Joash had killed the prophet Zechariah son of the priest Jehoiada (24:20–22) who had shown kindness to him, and God used the army of Aram to execute judgment on them.

20. King Amaziah's hiring an Israelite army for the battle against Seir or the Edomites (2 Chr 25:6) is criticized by a man of God, and Amaziah is told that it is "God" that "has power to help or to overthrow" (2 Chr 25:8b). That is, the man of God says that victory or defeat comes not from military power but from God. Not only the appellation "man of God" (25:7, 9), but also the result of following God's command, i.e., the Judahite army's victory over Seir or the Edomites without the help of the northern army (25:11–12, 14a), prove that the statement is true which reflects the Chronicler's stance.

21. God made King Uzziah successful and "prosper as long as he sought the Lord" (2 Chr 26:5b, 7, 15b) in several areas, including his international status (26:6–8), agricultural projects (26:10). As well, his strong military power is most conspicuous (26:7, 11–15), yet it is described in the following passage that "when he became strong, he grew proud and false to the Lord his God" (2 Chr 26:16). Therefore, it seems that Uzziah's pride in his military power is the main cause of his tragic downfall.

22. When King Sennacherib of Assyria invaded Judah, the deliverance of Judah did not come from Hezekiah's military power but from an angel sent by the Lord after Hezekiah and the prophet Isaiah's prayer (2 Chr 32:20–22), while Hezekiah's military preparation is described and not criticized (2 Chr 32:3–8). Even in Hezekiah's encouraging speech to his army, it is plainly confessed that Judah's hope is not in military power but their God (32:7–8): "for there is one greater with us than with him (the king of Assyria). With him is an arm of flesh; but with us is the Lord our God, to help us and to fight our battles" (32:7b–8).

23. King Ahab's chariot could not help him survive the battle (2 Chr 18:34), even when he had disguised himself (2 Chr 18:29).

24. In his chariot, King Josiah is shot, and carried to Jerusalem in the chariot of his deputy (or his second chariot), but dies (2 Chr 35:23–24a).

From the observations above, it appears that, in Chronicles, military power is not present as a reliable resource against enemies, and is even ridiculed on some crucial occasions, as with Asa's and Jehoshaphat's. This observation does not deny that God's blessing appears in the form of military strengthening in some cases (e.g., 1 Chr 11:9ff; 2 Chr 26:15b). Nevertheless, in the Chronicler's view, only the Lord God is the real and reliable strength of a king and his people.[63] In fact, it is observed that in some cases, military strength has nothing to do with God's blessing (e.g., 2 Chr 11:5–12).[64] Moreover, the Chronicler shows not only that a king's relying on his or an alliance's military power is not acceptable to God,[65] but also that having strong military power might lead a king to dangerous arrogance. Therefore, if it is right that we read Solomon's military power described in 2 Chr 1:14–17 and 9:25–27 in this light, it can be said that the interpretation of the passages (of Solomon's horses and chariots force) which sees only God's blessing there fails to understand the author's theological intention. That is, if military power itself cannot be construed as positive, and a military alliance is construed as totally negative, should Solomon's Egyptian horses and chariots, originally introduced from a foreign nation, then be interpreted as positive?[66]

63. That military power (especially horse and chariot) is not the reliable source for victory is a coherent stance of the Hebrew Bible both in pre-exilic and post-exilic period. E.g., Ps 20:8 [ET 20:7]; 33:16–17; Prov 21:31; Hos 1:7; Hag 2:22 (in the case of enemy). Furthermore, the danger of arrogance in having them appears, for example in Isa 2:7ff. Isa 31:1, especially of relying on Egyptian horse and chariot forces (cf. Ezek 17:15, of relying on Egyptian horse and army).

64. It is noteworthy that there is no mention of Rehoboam's obedience or loyalty to God, or God's rewarding favor on him, which precedes Rehoboam's military strengthening (building many defense cities and making the fortresses strong, etc.) in 2 Chr 11:5–12. It is true that Rehoboam and all Israel in Judah and Benjamin obeyed the word of God given through Shemaiah (11:4). However, their giving up starting a war does not seem to be such a substantial obedience that the military strengthening in 11:5–12 is given by God as a reward.

Welten proposes that "building notices," "army notices," and "military victories" are a verdict on the reign (or part of it) that is evaluated positively. For another example, Welten regards the notice of Amaziah's vast army in 2 Chr 25:5, as a positive verdict on the king (Welten, *Geschichte und Geschichtsdarstellung*, 1973, 92–93, 95). However, it should not be overlooked that his employing of mercenaries of the northern Israel kingdom immediately follows the notice of his own army (25:6), and the two armies are, in fact, a kind of allies for the attack on Edom. In this regard, it is hard to maintain that the notice of the vast army in 25:5 is intended as a positive verdict for Amaziah, for his employing the mercenaries is described as very negative (25:7–9, 13). One may point out that Amaziah's obedience to the law (25:3–4) is described just before the notice of his own army. However, it is also true that the evaluation in 25:2 does not deserve the vast size of army, as God's reward. Most of all, it should be pointed out that there is no apparent link shown between 25:4 and 25:5 as cause and effect. Therefore, these examples at least show that Welten's thesis that the notice of fortification and vast army is given as a positive theological verdict on a king, needs reconsideration.

65. The point is thoroughly explored by Kelly and Knoppers almost at the same time (Kelly, *Retribution and Eschatology*, 204–11; Knoppers, "Yhwh Is Not").

66. While it is plain that Solomon sells Egyptian horses and chariots at a profit (2 Chr 1:16–17), it is also true that his chariotry and cavalry is composed of those

3.7. Additional Observations of the Context of Solomon's Military Strength

There are still more points which can be uncovered in a more complex way, which support indirectly a negative interpretation of the passages of Solomon's military power with Egyptian horses and chariots in Chronicles.

Firstly, when looking at the presentation of David and Solomon, we can see a strong contrast in the way they accumulated their armies. In the case of David, it is quite evident that his military forces are accumulated through God's help or guidance. At least five occasions show this:

1. The statement that "David became greater and greater, for the Lord of hosts was with him" (1 Chr 11:9) and the following list (or combination of list and episodes) of David's mighty warriors and army (1 Chr 11:11—12:41 [ET 11:11—12:40]) show that David's warriors and army have been accumulated by the help or guidance of God. The introduction of the list, "Now these are the chiefs of David's warriors, who gave him strong support in his kingdom, together with all Israel, to make him king, *according to the word of the Lord* concerning Israel" (1 Chr 11:10), makes it clearer: the gathering of the military forces is the means of achieving God's will.

2. Among the combination of list and episodes of David's mighty warriors and army, the account of Amasai's confession of loyalty to and blessing David by the spirit of God (1 Chr 12:19 [ET 12:18]) plainly shows that it is God's doing that the mighty warriors are gathered to be David's great army. The content of Anasazi's confession also shows this: "We are yours, O David; and with you, O son of Jesse! . . . For your God is the one who helps you."

3. Again, among the combination of list and episodes, the likening of David's forces to "an army of God" (1 Chr 12:23b [ET 12:22b]) can be construed as implying that the formation of the force is God's work.

4. The phrase "according to the word of the Lord" in the context of the introduction of "the numbers of the divisions of the armed troops who came to David in Hebron to turn the kingdom of Saul over to

---

imported ones (2 Chr 1:14; 9:25). In the second passage of his matter of horses, his selling them for profit is not mentioned (2 Chr 9:25, 28). Additionally, it is noteworthy that the law which bans importation of Egyptian horses is not only against a king's accumulation of many horses (Deut 17:16a), but also against a contact with or returning to Egypt (Deut 17:16b). In that sense, even Solomon's trading of horses for profit is against the law.

him" (1 Chr 12:24 [ET 12:23]), also implies that David's army is the instrument of God, gathered according to God's will. In other words, the great gathering of the army according to each tribe is fundamentally God's work.

5. In the process of making David king, the loyalty or "single mind" of his warriors as well as all the rest of Israel (1 Chr 12:39 [ET 12:38] cf. 12:34 [ET 12:33] "to help (David) with singleness of purpose"[67]), and people's willing devotion to offer food and drink for the occasion (12:40–41a [ET 12:39–40a]) and the joy with them (12:41b [ET 12:40b]), all imply that God provides the great army for David as well as their loyalty to him. What matters is that, in contrast to the army of David which is full of a positive and divine aura, Solomon's force lacks the same thing,[68] rather Solomon's Egyptian horses are plainly against God's law, especially the stipulation on the king (Deut 17:16).

Secondly, a contrast can be observed between Solomon's military force and David's in terms of "peace." While David secures the peace (1 Chr 22:18) around the nation with few horses so that the project of building of the temple becomes possible (1 Chr 22:19), Solomon who has been given God's promise of peace in his days (1 Chr 22:9) accumulates a large number of horses, especially Egyptian ones (2 Chr 1:14, 16–17; 9:25, 28). However, while the peace obtained by David continues in his successor's reign, the peace Solomon tried to maintain with many horses fails to last after his death (which only proves that military force with many horses cannot secure the peace of the nation).

Thirdly, it should not be overlooked that the case of David's hamstringing of the horses acquired through battle (case 6; 1 Chr 18:4) has special significance in terms of the interpretation of the Solomon account. When it is considered that David and Solomon are paired in many ways in Chronicles, the contrast in the case of horses should be taken all the more seriously.[69] Further, it should be admitted that this occasion is conspicu-

---

67. The Hebrew Bible lacks "David" while the LXX has "David." However, it is clear from the context that it is no one other than David that the warriors of Zebulun came to help.

68. It cannot be denied that in the case of Solomon's enthronement a similar atmosphere to David's appears in the Solomon account (1 Chr 29:22), but not with his army.

69. While some scholars are aware of the contrast between David's hamstringing of acquired horses and Solomon's maintaining great number of horses, especially Egyptian horses, they do not consider the contrast against the stipulation on the king in Deut 17:16 (Japhet, *I & II Chronicles*, 533; Johnstone, *1 Chronicles 1–2 Chronicles 9*, 303).

ous and the fact that the same account appears in the *Vorlage* (2 Sam 8:4) cannot reduce the significance of its reappearance in Chronicles. Rather the reappearance, not being omitted according to the tendency of the Chronicler, should be taken as meaningful. As has been explored in the previous chapter, the Chronicler presupposed not only the Pentateuch, but also Joshua, as the reader's prior knowledge (i.e., in the parallel case of the succession between David and Solomon following that between Moses and Joshua, as well demonstrated by Williamson), and the account is possibly intended to remind the reader of a parallel account in Joshua. The account in Josh 11:1–15 contains not only God's direct command to Joshua to "hamstring their horses, and burn their chariots with fire" (11:6), promising victory over the great allied army led by King Jabin of Hazor (11:1–4), but also Joshua's faithful execution of God's command (11:9). The significance of both accounts of David and Joshua lies not only in that the accounts are in contrast to the description of Solomon's enormous number of horses and chariots (2 Chr 1:14; 9:25 and its Egyptian origin in 2 Chr 1:17; 9:28), but also in that the actions of David and Joshua most probably reflects the stipulation of the king (not to mention of its corresponding to God's command directly given to Joshua (Josh 11:6)), which bans the Israel king's excessive possession of horses (Deut 17:16a), especially Egyptian horses (Deut 17:16b), while Solomon's acts are plainly and squarely against it.

B. Halpern thinks that David's hamstringing of enemy's horses in 2 Sam 8:4 reveals that David may have known the law of the king. Further, Halpern provides a noteworthy observation, in regards to the law of the king (Deut 17:17b), that the following text 2 Sam 8:7–12 shows David's accumulating "vast quantities of silver, gold, and bronze," not for himself, unlike Solomon, but for consecrating to God.[70]

Fourthly, it is significant that David's successive victories against his enemies or neighboring countries are described in the passage that follows the conspicuous event of hamstringing his acquired horses. The main part of the account of David's campaign covers from right after David's receiving God's covenant up to the point immediately before his significant remaining in Jerusalem (1 Chr 18:1—19:19; the present study supposes that the sin of David with Bathsheba is implied here in the expression "David remained at Jerusalem" (1 Chr 20:1b)). To demonstrate this point, it is necessary to observe the overall military affairs in the reign of David.

---

70. Halpern, *Constitution*, 231.

Military affairs including war or battles in the reign of David appear in several distinctive passages in Chronicles: (1) David's capture of Jerusalem right after his becoming king of Israel (1 Chr 11:4-7), (2) the battle episodes of his warriors that are inserted in the list of his warriors (1 Chr 11:11-23), (3) the forming of his mighty army (1 Chr 12:1-39 [ET 12:1-38]), (4) his two battles with the Philistines just after becoming king of Israel (1 Chr 14:8-17), (5) David's war and battles against several neighboring countries after transporting the ark into Jerusalem and receiving God's promise, i.e., the so-called Davidic covenant (1 Chr 18:1—19:19), (6) David's exploiting Rabbah and other Ammonite cities (1 Chr 20:1-3),[71] (7) several anecdotes about David's warriors who killed Philistine giants (1 Chr 20:4-8).

On the passages about David's military affairs in Chronicles, two points can be made. Firstly, when compared to their *Vorlage*, the passages about David's military affairs are more neatly clustered in Chronicles. While the passages about David's military affairs in Samuel are very widely dispersed, in Chronicles, the seven passages are clustered within 1 Chr 11:4—20:8 only interrupted by some crucial accounts of the moving of the ark and the following ceremony (1 Chr 13:1-14; 15:1—16:43), of the building of his palace and list of his offspring (1 Chr 14:1-7), and of the Davidic covenant (1 Chr 17:1-27). Secondly, among the seven passages of David's military affairs in Chronicles, the most significant in its location and size is the fifth one, David's war and battles against several neighboring countries, which is the longest account and immediately follows his transporting the ark into Jerusalem and receiving god's promise, i.e., the so-called Davidic covenant (1 Chr 18:1—19:19).

Among the seven passages mentioned above, probably the most significant is the fifth one, i.e., 1 Chr 18:1—19:19. From the context, that seems to refer to the greatest period of David, and it is very much involved with David's war or battles against the horse and chariot forces of his enemies. What matters is that the account nearly opens with the conspicuous description of his hamstringing of the captured horses. In this part (1 Chr 18:1—19:19) David or his army are engaged wars or battles with neighboring countries which have a horse and chariot army. Firstly, David defeated Hadadezer the king of Zobah who had at least 1,000 chariots and 7,000 cavalry (NIV: charioteers) (besides 20,000 foot

---

71. In contrast to its *Vorlage*, the capture of Rabbah is described as done by Joab in Chronicles (1 Chr 20:1b), who is the actual achiever of it. In its *Vorlage*, it is stated that Joab called David at the end of the siege so that the glory of the capture of the city could be attributed to David (2 Sam 12:26-29).

soldiers) (1 Chr 18:3–4). Secondly, Joab and the entire army of warriors sent by David defeated the Ammonites army with 32,000 hired chariots and cavalry (NIV: charioteers) from Mesopotamia (NIV: Aram Naharaim), Aram Maacah and Zobah at the cost of 1,000 talents of silver (besides the king of Maacah with his troops) (1 Chr 19:6–15). Thirdly, David defeated and killed Hadadezer's Aramean army led by Shophach the commander of the army including 7,000 charioteers[72] (as well as 40,000 foot soldiers) (1 Chr 19:16–18). The frequent mention of Hadadezer in the first and the end parts of the account (1 Chr 18:3, 5, 7, 8, 9, 10 (twice), 19:16, 19 cf. 19:6 "Zobah") is significant, for it is Hadadezer the king of Zobah whose horse and chariot force David defeated, and whose horses David hamstrung conspicuously and significantly. In that sense, David's hamstringing of the horses captured from Hadadezer is symbolic. The symbolic meaning is clear: his victory against his enemies or neighboring countries does not come from his military force but from God the helper (18:6b "The Lord gave victory to David everywhere he went," 18:13b "The Lord gave David victory everywhere he went," cf. 19:13b "Be strong and let us fight bravely for our people and the cities of our God. The Lord will do what is good in his sight").

Fifthly, an irony is observed in regard to Solomon's Egyptian war-horses and chariots on the occasion of the Egyptian king's invasion in the reign of Solomon's successor (2 Chr 12:2–9). Although it should be considered that this occurs not in the reign of Solomon, but of his successor, and the war is brought about as a punishment of God toward Rehoboam, the successor of Solomon, for his infidelity to God's law (2 Chr 12:1), it can still be construed as an intended irony implanted by the author that King Rehoboam, the son of Solomon, is unable to defend Jerusalem when the Egyptian king Shishak attacks Jerusalem with twelve hundred chariots and sixty thousand cavalry together with the allied army of Libyans, Sukkiim, and Ethiopians (2 Chr 12:3–4, 9). It is explicitly said that it is only early in Rehoboam's reign, in the fifth year of his reign (2 Chr 12:2), and it is not an unreasonable expectation that Solomon's Egyptian chariots and horses are still in use, although it is not clear from the text. His father Solomon's great Egyptian war horses and chariots do not seem to work effectively against an attack from the king of Egypt where the horses and chariots came from. (Alternatively, if the reader supposes that Solomon's Egyptian war horses and chariots could not be maintained even for such a short time, and have disappeared, the uselessness of the force in a crisis such

---

72. The change of the number from the *Vorlage* implies something.

as this is implied.[73]) Since Solomon's Egyptian war horses and chariots appear in 2 Chr 9:25, 27 for the last time, which is not far from the passage of Shishak's attack against Rehoboam the son of Solomon, the contrast or irony can easily be captured (in the perspective of the reader-sensitive approach). Also, it can be pointed out that the comparison of the numbers of the Egyptian chariots and horses between Solomon's forces (thus possibly Rehoboam's) and Shishak's is meaningful. It is plainly stated that Shishak attacks with 60,000 cavalry, while Solomon's cavalry was comparatively small, numbering 12,000 (as for chariots, it is impossible to compare exactly, for while the number of Shishak's chariots comes to 1,200, in 2 Chr 9 only the number of Solomon's 4,000 stalls for horses and chariots is mentioned. It is possible that the placement of the number of the Solomon's chariots, 1,400 in 2 Chr 1, i.e., far from the present event, is intentional for drastic comparison of the cavalry numbers between Shishak's (2 Chr 12:3) and Solomon's (2 Chr 9:25)). In short, Solomon's Egyptian war horses and chariots turn out to be useless and powerless in front of the greater Egyptian military force.[74]

Considering that the Egyptian chariots and cavalry with which Shishak attacks Jerusalem do not appear in its *Vorlage*, but are introduced by the Chronicler, the probability increases that the author intended a comparison. As the cases of King Asa and King Jehoshaphat show in an ironic touch, the Chronicler tries to show that however much military power an Israelite king has, whether it is from Egypt or not, it is no longer great, and even useless, when an even greater foreign military power attacks against Israel. Therefore, it can be strongly suggested that the same irony in Asa's and Jehoshaphat's cases is intended here against Rehoboam's military force in the presence of Shishak's military force. It is significant that the wealth which King Solomon has accumulated partly through the

73. "And the highly professional chariot army may have simply melted away in a succession of missed paydays before Shishak's army appeared in the land of Israel" (Hauer, "The Economics," 69–70).

74. Hauer's concluding statement summarizes well the inefficiency of Solomon's horse and chariot military force in contrast to the efficiency of David's infantry troops (Hauer's study treats both Kings' and Chronicles' portrayal of Solomon together). "One must observe that when his son Rehoboam confronted the dual threat of internal rebellion and external invasion, the splendid chariot army and the formidable fortress cities did not deter revolution. The chariots were not well suited for internal security work in the Israelite highlands – David's infantry would have done much better there. . . . At any rate, one may supposes that Pharaoh Shishak died a happier man for never having met David, Joab, Abishai and the mighty men in a dark valley of their choosing" (ibid., 69–70).

trade of Egyptian horses and chariots (2 Chr 1:16–17 cf. 9:28) is so simply and thoroughly taken away by the Egyptian king Shishak who, with Egyptian chariots and cavalry (2 Chr 12:9), attacks Jerusalem. The description "he took everything. He also took away the shields of gold that Solomon had made" (12:9b), not only emphasizes the intense irony of the event, but also highlights an ironic link between Shishak and Solomon. Solomon's chariots and horses imported from Egypt were unable to guard Solomon's wealth, partly earned through the trade in Egyptian horses and chariots, from the attack by a king of Egypt.

Sixthly, another observation can be added to strengthen the fifth point mentioned above. It can be said that in the text there is an element that supports the contrast, or the irony that the contrast highlights. A close reading reveals a contrast between David's army with its few horses and Solomon's army with its many horses in terms of their resulting wealth (1 Chr 18:3–14 / 2 Chr 1:14–17, 9:25–28, 12:9–11). While David acquires plenty of wealth (1 Chr 18:6, 7, 8, 10 cf. 18:11) after he rejects the opportunity to acquire and maintain many horses (1 Chr 18:4), through subduing enemies and receiving contributions (18:7, 8, 10), Solomon's horses and chariots fail to protect his wealth in the period of his son's reign (2 Chr 12:9).[75] It is very interesting, in the context, to observe that in each case silver and gold are involved and especially the golden shields (1 Chr 18:7, 11; 2 Chr 12:9). After David's success in accommodating the ark of the covenant in Jerusalem (1 Chr 15 16) and God's establishing the so-called Davidic covenant (1 Chr 17:10b–14), the first detailed report of David's campaign against neighboring countries is that of Hadadezer king of Zobah (1 Chr 18:3–11). Within the report, the conspicuous account of David hamstringing all but a hundred of the chariot horses of Hadadezer appears (18:4). Rejecting the opportunity to maintain many horses or a huge chariot force, David's ongoing victory against his enemies is given to him by the Lord, as it is clearly described: "The Lord gave David victory everywhere he went" (1 Chr 18:6b). Then the significant comment that "David took the gold shields that were carried by the servants of Hadadezer and brought them to Jerusalem" (18:7) follows. In contrast to Solomon's gold

---

75. Hauer shows the same view. "One must observe that when his son Rehoboam confronted the dual threat of internal rebellion and external invasion, the splendid chariot army and the formidable fortress cities apparently did him little good. The splendid fortress cities did not deter revolution. The chariots were not well suited for internal security work in the Israelite highlands—David's infantry would have done much better there" (ibid., 69).

shields taken by Shishak king of Egypt, David's gaining the gold shields has been achieved without any horses or chariot forces.

The following account of David's gaining "a great quantity of bronze" "from Tibhath and from Cun, cities of Hadadezer" (1 Chr 18:8a, it is noteworthy that Solomon's use of the bronze (1 Chr 18:8b) does not appear in the same context of the *Vorlage*, while David's gaining of the bronze does (2 Sam 8:8, 10b)) seems to be simple and fragmentary information that is only involved with David's accumulation of materials for temple building. The following description that Solomon used the bronze to make "the bronze Sea and the pillars and the vessels of bronze" (1 Chr 18:8) shows that the case is linked to the temple building. However, the account has more than that. It has also something to do with the account of Solomon's "shields of gold" being taken away and the "shields of bronze" that substitute them, in the fifth year of Rehoboam, the successor of Solomon (2 Chr 12:9–11).

Rehoboam's many chariots and horses could not protect his gold shields, and they are replaced with other shields made of bronze. Then where did the bronze come from? There is no mention of Solomon's gaining bronze in the period of his reign, while there are two occasions mentioned in the account of David. And the accounts of David that refer to his gaining bronze appear in the wider context of his victory over Hadadezer the king of Zobah's army (1 Chr 18:8, 10b–11), which was heavily equipped with chariots and horses. Therefore, it is most probable that the bronze with which Rehoboam made his bronze shields to replace the gold ones came from David's plunder. It should be noticed that the account of David's gaining not only gold shields but also bronze material follows his hamstringing of chariot horses (whatever the real sequence of the history might be, that is the literary arrangement), which he could have saved in order to form his own chariotry or cavalry. Without the military power of horses and chariots, and following the law of the king of a ban on horses (Deut 17), David could obtain victory by the help of God (1 Chr 18:6b, 13b), while Solomon's chariots and horses cannot protect his gold shields. Even the bronze shields, which were substituted for the gold ones, had come from David's heritage that had been acquired without horses but with God's help.

It can be added here that the materials for the temple building and its treasure (i.e., gold, silver, and bronze, 1 Chr 18:7, 8, 10b, 11 cf. 1 Chr 22:14 "With great pains I have provided for the house of the Lord one hundred thousand talents of gold, one million talents of silver, and bronze and iron beyond weighing, for there is so much of it; timber and stone too I have provided. To these you must add more"), are acquired more by David than by Solomon. Additionally, it can be pointed out again that while David had a military force with few horses and yet acquired those materials, Solomon's military force with a huge number of horses cannot keep the treasure (including the gold and silver) of the temple along with his gold shields.

Finally, one more point can be added concerning the sole military action of Solomon in Chronicles (2 Chr 8:3–4). The passage seems to show Solomon's military success in the region. However, Hauer proposes well that while "Hamath had voluntarily submitted to David" (1 Chr 18:9–10), Solomon's capturing of it is "at most the recovery of a straying subject."[76] If this is the case, it can be said that the superiority of David (who acquires voluntary submission with God's help) over Solomon (who has to do battle with his horse and chariot troops, after losing control of the region somehow) is implied even here, in the single description of Solomon's successful military action.

4. SOLOMON'S EGYPTIAN WIFE, THE DAUGHTER OF PHARAOH (2 CHR 8:11)

Solomon's intermarriage with many foreign women is presented in the narrative flow of the first work of history (1 Kgs 11:1–13) as the most direct cause of his apostasy and, consequently, of the division of the kingdom. Moreover, it is plain that Solomon's "foreign marriages" were regarded as his crucial fault by the post-exilic community at least for a certain period, as clearly shown in Neh 13:26.[77] However, in the wake of the view

76. Hauer, "The Economics," 68.

77. In spite of this plain information of the post-exilic community's view of Solomon's intermarriage, the negative evaluation has been excluded from interpreting Solomon's intermarriage in 2 Chr 8:11. One of the reasons for this, is that most scholars think that the "ideology" (including the attitude toward intermarriage) of Ezra–Nehemiah is quite different from (or even contradicts) that of Chronicles. Since the long sustained view of the common authorship of the two works (originally proposed by Zunz) has been challenged by S. Japhet (Japhet, "Authorship of Chronicles and Ezra-Nehemiah"), which is strongly followed and supported by H. G. H. Williamson (Williamson, *Israel*, 5–70), the view of different ideology between the two works became the majority view. The most comprehensive list of the issues is provided by Williamson (Williamson, *Israel*, 60–69) in order to support his stance of different authorship of Ezra–Nehemiah and Chronicles.

In fact, the near consensus view (with a few opponents such as Blenkinsopp

of the idealized or impeccable Solomon in the Chronicler's presentation, the small but crucial allusion to the problem of Solomon's intermarriage in the work (2 Chr 8:11) has not generally been construed as retaining the negative connotation that is clearly shown in the first history.[78] Further, the probable prior knowledge of the reader has not been taken seriously, although some scholars admit that the reader's prior knowledge of Solomon's intermarriage which appears in Kings is presupposed in the passage.[79] Rather, the passage has been construed by some simply or only as an indication of Solomon's piety, in that Solomon is careful not to transgress the holiness of the place.[80]

In contrast to frequent mentions of Solomon's intermarriage with Pharaoh's daughter in the *Vorlage* (i.e., 1 Kgs 3:1; 7:8; 9:16, 24; 11:1), the Chronicler mentions the fact only once, in 2 Chr 8:11, in the context of the

---

(Blenkinsopp, *Ezra-Nehemiah*, 53–54)) seems to contribute, to some extent, to the idealized Solomon (in Chronicles) view, and vice versa. Even Selman and Kelly, who think that Solomon in Chronicles is not presented as flawless, accept the view, and do not see any negative sense in Solomon's intermarriage with Pharaoh's daughter in 2 Chr 8:11. Though Kelly thinks that "The Chronicler's work should be understood as presupposing and building upon the account in Ezra-Nehemiah" (Kelly, *Retribution and Eschatology*, 232), he follows Williamson's view which sees a different attitude toward intermarriage (24–25). Selman also puts the issue of "mixed marriage" on the list which is alleged to show that Chronicles and Ezra-Nehemiah "deal with the same themes in contrasting ways" (Selman, *1 Chronicles*, 68).

Unfortunately, the present work does not have space to discuss the issue, but two points can be made here. Firstly, the different settings of the works should be considered. That is, while Chronicles covers primarily the period of united and separate kingdom(s), Ezra-Nehemiah describes the restoration events of the post-exile period. Hence, different theological emphases can be taken as natural without presuming that the two works are based upon contrasting or contradictory theological stances. Secondly, simple "difference" and "contradiction" should be distinguished concerning the "contrast" which is observed between the two works. Two works can have a theologically different appearance, while they maintain reconcilable and not contradictory stances. Ackroyd detected the problem of conceptual confusion of "difference" and "contrast" (contradiction) in the discussion of the relationship of Chronicles and Ezra-Nehemiah: "it is more difficult to detect how far the differences are to be understood in terms of a contrast between two sharply divergent attitudes . . ." (Ackroyd, *His Age*, 355).

78. Most commentators like Japhet observe that Solomon's marriage to the daughter of Pharaoh in Kings (1 Kgs 3:1; 9:16, 24; 11:1) is "a special indication of Solomon's greatness" (Japhet, *I & II Chronicles*, 625). Recently, Jarick also observes only "an example of Solomon's grandeur" here (Jarick, *2 Chronicles*, 55).

79. Williamson, *1 and 2 Chronicles*, 231; Dillard, *2 Chronicles*, 65, 62.

80. For example, McKenzie, *1–2 Chronicles*, 254; Johnstone, *2 Chronicles 10–36*, 24: "the utmost propriety."

description of his building her palace away from the city of David that has become holy due to the presence of the ark.

> Solomon brought Pharaoh's daughter from the city of David to the house that he had built for her, for he said, 'My wife shall not live in the house of King David of Israel,[81] for the places to which the ark of the Lord has come are holy' (2 Chr 8:11).

With the background knowledge of the first history, the passage can easily be construed as having a negative a connotation, but most commentators on Chronicles who see an impeccable Solomon in the work neglect or suppress the negative connotation. It seems that the idea of the impeccable Solomon leads the commentators to explain that the cause of Solomon's removing his wife, the daughter of Pharaoh, is not her ethnicity but her gender. Further, this interpretation is in tune with the view that the Chronicler has an inclusive attitude toward foreigners, which even implies that the Chronicler's stance on intermarriage is positive.[82]

For example, W. Johnstone observes that the Chronicler shows an international outlook from the beginning of the work;[83] descriptions of Solomon's Egyptian connection are intended simply to show positively the high international status of Solomon,[84] and here in 2 Chr 8:11 the interpre-

---

81. Japhet thinks that no connection between "the house of David" and "the tent of the ark" can be observed from 2 Sam 6:17; 1 Kgs 3:15; 1 Chr 15:1. Japhet states that it is the reason why commentators prefer the LXX reading "my wife shall not live in the *city* of David" (Japhet, *I & II Chronicles*, 626). However, in 1 Chr 15:1, 3, "David built houses for himself in the city of David, and he prepared a place for the ark of God and pitched a tent for it. . . . David assembled all Israel in Jerusalem to bring up the ark of the Lord to its place, which he had prepared for it," although it is not very clear it can be said that it is implied that the palace (David's houses) and the place of the tent is closely related. Hence, if we think that while "the city of David" (עִיר דָּוִיד) (cf. 1 Chr 11:4–5, 7) is part of Jerusalem, the "palace of David King of Israel" (בֵּית דָּוִיד מֶלֶךְ־יִשְׂרָאֵל) contains the place of the tent for the ark as a kind of palace and temple complex, then her question can be reasonably answered. Her additional question "If the queen's living in proximity to the ark in the city of David constituted a transgression, why is this never mentioned in reference to Solomon's initial decision to bring her 'into the city of David until he had finished building his own house . . . (I Kings 3.1)?," is not hard to answer. Firstly, it can be said that because the only place the queen may reside in the city of David, is the house(s) of David, her moving from the city of David actually means her moving from David's houses. Further, it should be pointed out that Solomon's initially letting her live in "the city of David" is implied even in 2 Chr 8:11. It means that Solomon allowed the transgression until finishing the building of her palace, being aware of the transgression.

82. For example, Japhet, *Ideology*, 346–51.

83. Johnstone, *1 Chronicles 1–2 Chronicles 9*, 10, 12, 24ff.

84. Ibid., 365. Johnstone sees that "Solomon's marriage to the daughter of Pharaoh

tation of Kings which disapproves of Solomon's intermarriages "must not be allowed to print through."[85] According to Johnstone, understandably, the issue at stake in 2 Chr 8:11 is only the gender of Solomon's wife.[86] Likewise S. Japhet, who sees a different ideology between Ezra-Nehemiah and Chronicles,[87] observing that the Chronicler sees intermarriage positively,[88] firmly maintains that Solomon's building the palace for the daughter of Pharaoh is not due to her ethnicity, but her gender.[89]

For those who advocate that the issue is to do with gender rather than ethnicity, the wording "no wife of mine" in the text is the most direct evidence.[90] However, this explanation causes difficulty, for it is most unlikely that a king's palace would operate without any females, i.e., queens or maid-servants. Furthermore, as Siedlecki points out, "we have no biblical evidence to support the idea that gender rather than ethnicity was the main issue in 2 Chron. 8:11."[91] Moreover, the "question of ethnicity" can be strongly supported by Selman's observation that the context of 2 Chr 8:11, i.e., the passage 2 Chr 8:7–11 of foreigners in Israel, should be taken seriously.[92] It is beyond question that the preceding passage to 8:11 is of "slave labor force taken from the descendants of the pre-Israelite inhabitants of Canaan" (8:7–8). However, Selman's observation seems to be a bit stretched in that he puts all three of "the Canaanites' slave labor" (8:7–8), "Israelites' distinctive status from those slaves" (8:9–10), and "Solomon's Egyptian wife" (8:11) under one title "Foreigners in Solomon's kingdom," while the second part is evidently not about foreigners, and his title does not fit the contents of 8:7–11 very well. Nevertheless, Selman's observation is helpful to indicate that the whole passage of 8:7–11 shows a distinc-

---

is thus testimony to the recognition which he has secured even among the traditionally most threatening of Israel's neighbours, and to the positive relations that can prevail when the nations are in harmony through that recognition."

85. Ibid., 365.

86. Ibid., 366.

87. Williamson also has a similar stance to Japhet, on the ideology between Chronicles and Ezra-Nehemiah (Williamson, *Israel*, 60–70).

88. Japhet, *Ideology*, 346–51

89. Japhet, *I & II Chronicles*, 626; Japhet, *Ideology*, 350 n. 296 (Japhet introduces Rudolph, *Chronik*, 220).

90. Dillard, *2 Chronicles*, 65; Japhet, *Ideology*, 350 n. 296. Japhet states that "the Chronicler's note of reservation focuses on the queen's identity as a woman, not as a foreigner: 'No wife of mine shall live in the house of David king of Israel' (see Rudolph, *Chronik*, 220). Her foreign origins are not considered noteworthy."

91. Siedlecki, "Foreigners," 252.

92. Selman, *2 Chronicles*, 348, 347.

tion between Israelites and foreigners, that is, a distinction between native Israelites and foreigners concerning forced labor (7–10) and holiness (11).

In his comment on 2 Chr 8:11 Williamson cautiously suggests that the reason why Solomon brought Pharaoh's daughter from the city of David to the house that he had built for her is both her ethnicity and her gender.[93] Williamson acknowledges that in Chronicles the fact that Solomon's wife is a foreigner can be regarded as a source of cultic impurity. Williamson suggests that the Chronicler attempted to modify the exclusivist attitude of the post-exilic community that appears in Ezra-Nehemiah, and consequently the attitude of the Chronicler is different from that of the author of Ezra-Nehemiah towards intermarriage. It is noteworthy that while Williamson suggests that the Chronicler's attitude towards intermarriage is different from that of Ezra-Nehemiah, he is cautious not to put it in contradiction to that of Ezra-Nehemiah.[94]

The interesting and problematic thing, however, is that while some commentators like Williamson and Dillard admit that in 2 Chr 8:11 the reader's prior knowledge of Solomon's problematic intermarriages is presupposed,[95] they do not ask how the reader's prior knowledge should be reflected in the interpretation of the passage.

4.1. Reconstruction of the Reader's Prior Knowledge and Reading Experience of the Passage

The reader has the prior knowledge of Solomon's intermarriage and its tragic result not only through the first history or the old tradition, but also through common knowledge of the history among the post-exilic

---

93. Williamson, *1 and 2 Chronicles*, 231. Williamson thinks that "as a gentile and as a woman she should not be allowed contact with the *holy*" (Williamson's emphasis).

94. Williamson, *Israel*, 61. According to Williamson, "it seems hard to believe that the Chronicler condemned mixed marriages with the same vigour as Ezr.-Neh."

95. Williamson, *1 and 2 Chronicles*, 231. "the present verse, based on I Kg. 9:24, can hardly be understood without knowledge of the earlier account"; Dillard, *2 Chronicles*, 65, 62. "The Chronicler presumes that his audience is already familiar with the diplomatic marriage of Solomon and Pharaoh's daughter" (65), "The Chronicler frequently assumes the audience's knowledge of the parallel account; in this context he relies on the reader's prior familiarity with the earlier history in connection with Solomon's otherwise unmentioned marriage to Pharaoh's daughter (8:11; 1 Kgs 3:1; 7:8; 9:16, 24; 11:1)" (62) In discussion of the problematic passage of 2 Chr 8:1–2, Dillard uses the case of 8:11 to show "the reader's prior familiarity with the earlier history," for Solomon's marriage with the Pharaoh's daughter is suddenly introduced in the Chronicler's work (62).

community (Neh 13:26). Solomon's corruption regarding his excessively numerous intermarriages is so conspicuous that it is hard for the matter to escape the reader's prior knowledge.

When the prior knowledge of the reader is presupposed, his or her reading experience of the passage can be reconstructed as follows. Before reaching 2 Chr 8:11, the reader has already read 2 Chr 1:16–17, where the explicit description of Solomon's horses and chariots imported from Egypt has caught his or her attention, and reminded him or her of Solomon's problematic connection to Egypt, including his excessive intermarriage which, most probably, started with the daughter of Pharaoh. The earlier revelation of the identity of Solomon's horses and chariots (i.e., Egyptian) has helped the reader to detect or notice Solomon's problem more easily than in the case of its *Vorlage* where the identity of Solomon's horses and chariots is revealed only in the later stages (1 Kgs 10:29), immediately before the explicit criticism of Solomon begins. Therefore, the reader has perceived that Solomon's prosperity was not given because Solomon was perfect before God, but rather it was given him through God's faithful fulfillment of his promise or God's grace which was given in spite of the faults of its beneficiary. When the reader reads 2 Chr 8:11, it is plain from the text that Solomon himself was aware of the problematic nature of his intermarriage. For the reader who knows the problem of Solomon's intermarriage well, it is plain that the issue at stake is that of his wife's ethnicity rather than gender. The negative image of Solomon's intermarriage is immediately recalled for the reader, for Solomon himself confesses that his wife cannot stay in holy premises.

What Solomon thought of his intermarriage does not appear in the first history, and this new information about Solomon's own understanding of his intermarriage is very conspicuous to the reader of the second history. Through Solomon's words here it becomes clear that although he has married for the first time a foreign woman who would be followed by many other foreign women, he was still maintaining his piety to some extent, and so was trying to avoid serious transgression against the cultic purity or dignity of the holy place. In other words, the reader observes Solomon, although he began to enter a most tragic course of corruption, maintaining his consciousness of holiness, and even making an effort to maintain his pious stance. The co-existence of his pious awareness and the reality of his impious intermarriage is very significant to the reader, if he or she perceives it sensitively.

Therefore, the reader learns from the text a lesson on the nature of Solomon's corruption. Solomon's loss of his piety did not happen in a moment. The insidious nature of the progress of Solomon's corruption has been presented already in the Solomon account in Kings. Now an additional deeper aspect of the corruption is introduced. At least in the first or early stage of his excessive intermarriages the king maintained or tried to maintain his piety. However, it is very plain to the reader, from his or her prior knowledge of the following result (i.e., as shown or alluded in 2 Chr 10:15, cf. 11:4), that the compromise did not work for Solomon in the end.

Nevertheless, it is true that here in Chronicles the matter of Solomon's intermarriage requires less of the reader's attention than it does in Kings, with the reduced frequency of its appearance or references to it. It is also true that the piety that Solomon still shows here also reduces the degree of the reader's attention to the problematic nature of his intermarriage.

However, it is plain that even if the reader fails to catch sufficiently the advanced message of the work through 2 Chr 8:11, Solomon's intermarriage cannot remain uncriticized in the work. The reader cannot escape the unchangeable historical truth of Solomon's corruption in connection with his excessive intermarriage, for in the end the reader should be reminded of that basic truth when he or she reaches the passage of the fulfillment of Ahijah's prophecy in 2 Chr 10:15 (furthermore, the mention of Ahijah's book in 9:29, and Shemaiah's prophecy in 11:2). Therefore, it can be said that from the reconstruction of the reader's prior knowledge and his or her reading experience of the passage, there is no theological dilemma at 2 Chr 10 (especially 10:15b which mentions the fulfillment of Ahijah's prophecy), but only a natural confirmation of the reader's prior knowledge.

4.2. The Need for the Technique of Allusion for the Dual Purpose about Solomon

It is understandable that the Chronicler faced a tricky situation in writing the Solomon account. On the one hand, the problem of Solomon's intermarriage should not distract the reader's attention from the glory of the united kingdom along with the temple built on the God-chosen place by the chosen temple builder. On the other hand, Solomon's fault regarding his intermarriage has to be mentioned either explicitly or implicitly, for it is inevitable in order to unfold the flow of the history. Moreover, the reader's prior knowledge of the cause of the division does not allow any deviation from it. In that sense, the Chronicler was required to employ extreme subtlety, which could solve the dilemma (or the dual tasks) that he faced. By showing Solomon's sensitivity to holiness and his effort to maintain it, the author succeeds in portraying the king as positively as possible, which is evidently one of his concerns in the work, while at the same time a certain degree of negative connotation, which is plainly included in the fact that Solomon's wife is an unacceptable person to Israelis holiness, is also perceived by the reader. Through the subtle passage in 2 Chr 8:11, Solomon's excessive intermarriages with foreign women can be slightly recalled by the reader who is supposed to have a prior knowledge of the content in the *Vorlage*. It consequently prepares the reader to accept the destructive consequence of Solomon's excessive intermarriages (which is symbolized in what is probably his first or prime intermarriage with the daughter of Pharaoh), i.e., the division of the kingdom along with the statement of the fulfillment of Ahijah's prophecy which inevitably appears later. Therefore, it can be said that a dilemma does not exist in the account, but existed in the Chronicler's situation, and the author succeeded in solving it with the subtlety of allusion.

4.3. The Suitability of the Device in Chronicles

This interpretation fits in well with the reader's prior knowledge. It also fits in well with the following disclosure of Solomon's fault in 2 Chr 10, especially the mention of the fulfillment of Ahijah's prophecy. Moreover, the interpretation fits in well with the literary characteristics of the work, the greater complexity and allusion technique, which have already been shown in chapter 5. That is, as the second history, the author could increase the nuance or complexity of his account, revealing a more nuanced or complex reality that had not been shown in the first history. Further, as author of the second history, he could exploit his reader's prior knowledge of the first history, and allude to the contents that he omitted, with small hints or allusions. Therefore the interpretation that has been suggested here is well matched with the hypothetical fact (i.e., working hypothesis) that Chronicles is the second history, which is aware of and exploits the first one.

Solomon's own awareness or perception of his intermarriage as problematic is something that does not appear in its *Vorlage*. In the account of Kings only Solomon's conduct of intermarriage is described; here in Chronicles, as the second history, his own thoughts on the matter are revealed. This advanced disclosure of the reality of Solomon's intermarriage is possible here in the second history on the basis of the reader's basic prior knowledge of the problem. In other words, it can be proposed here that the author expected that the two-sidedness of Solomon's piety and impiety at the same time is something that could and should be revealed in his work, as the second history that presupposes the facts known through the first one.

When the close relationship between the presentations of David and Solomon, and the unity of the two kings' reign, is considered, the interpretation involving a negative connotation of Solomon's intermarriage has more ground. The conflict between the ark and an unholy or disqualified person appears in the accounts of both David and Solomon in Chronicles. The case of the death of Uzzah on the threshing floor of Chidon when he put out his hand to hold the ark as the oxen shook it (1 Chr 13:9–10) has its parallel here in 2 Chr 8:11. It is admitted that in 2 Chr 8:11 no conflict between an holy thing and an unholy or disqualified person actually happens. Nevertheless, a similar idea exists behind both cases, the conflict between holy and unholy things, as Williamson rightly observes.[96] Moreover, that both cases are involved with exactly the same material, i.e., the ark, supports the observation that they are paired anyway. The disqualified person's wrong treatment of the holy object caused a tragic result. It should be noticed that this point is made clear in Chronicles (1 Chr 15:11–15), while in its *Vorlage* it is not mentioned as clearly.[97] By removing his wife from the city of David which has become holy due to the ark, Solomon is admitting that his wife is a disqualified person before the holiness of God.[98]

96. Williamson, *1 and 2 Chronicles*, 231. "Since the Chronicler had earlier stressed the importance of the right personnel to carry the ark (I Chr. 15:2), he extended the principle to more remote contact, and so understood that Solomon's action was motivated by concern for his *wife's* safety" (Williamson's emphasis).

97. "David summoned the priests Zadok and Abiathar, and the Levites Uriel, Asaiah, Joel, Shemaiah, Eliel, and Amminadab. He said to them, 'You are the heads of families of the Levites; sanctify yourselves, you and your kindred, so that you may bring up the ark of the Lord, the God of Israel, to the place that I have prepared for it. Because you did not carry it the first time, the Lord our God burst out against us, because we did not give it proper care.' So the priests and the Levites sanctified themselves to bring up the ark of the Lord, the God of Israel. And the Levites carried the ark of God on their shoulders with the poles, as Moses had commanded according to the word of the Lord" (1 Chr 15:11–15). In 2 Sam 6, the passage does not appear, while only the changed way of carrying the ark is mentioned in the phrase, "when those who bore the ark of the Lord had gone six paces" (2 Sam 6:13).

98. Wilcock suggests the issue at stake might be simply being an "unauthorized" person (like Uzzah) as well as being a woman or gentile (Wilcock, "1 and 2 Chronicles,"

The correspondence of the two cases does not appear in the *Vorlage*, where the possible conflict between the ark and Solomon's foreign wife is not referred to. In this light, Solomon's moving his Egyptian wife from the holy place has more significance. In Chronicles, in the second attempt to move the ark of covenant after Uzzah's tragic death, the fundamental problem of the first attempt is explained explicitly through David's mouth (1 Chr 15:13–15), which does not occur in the *Vorlage*. Likewise, the problem of Solomon's intermarriage is stated indirectly through the mouth of Solomon himself (2 Chr 8:11). That means that in Chronicles consciousness and emphasis on a legal stipulation appear more clearly than in its *Vorlage*. In line with this, it can be proposed that in Chronicles the wife of Solomon is presented as a foreigner who cannot live with God's holiness (which appears through his holy object), and consequently causes Solomon's eventual apostasy, and there is an allusion that the intermarriage is against the spirit of the legal stipulation (Deut 7:1–4) which can be applied to Solomon's case (while there is no mention of Solomon's worshipping an Egyptian god or goddess, the intermarriage with the daughter of Pharaoh began the excessive intermarriages of Solomon, which eventually leads him into apostasy). In other words, when it is considered that Chronicles is a law-sensitive or stipulation-sensitive history, it is highly probable that a negative connotation is intended in 2 Chr 8:11 to some extent.

Additionally, it can be pointed out that the general stance of the Chronicler is that foreign alliances are not advisable in the sense that it is a betrayal against the God of Israel (as apparently shown, for example, in 2 Chr 16:7–9; 28:16, 20–23), which does not allow Solomon's diplomatic intermarriage with Pharaoh's daughter to be read as positive.[99]

---

405). P. Hooker points out 2 Chr 6:32–33 where "the openness of the Temple to the prayers of devout foreigners" is apparent. He suggests that Pharaoh's daughter's continuing worship practice for her Egyptian deities was the problem (Hooker, *First and Second Chronicles*, 152). If it is the case, the image of Solomon's apostasy through intermarriage becomes stronger here.

99. Dillard states, in his comment on 2 Chr 8:1–2, that "the Chronicler is uniformly opposed to foreign alliances in the remainder of his history" (Dillard, *2 Chronicles*, 63). A substantial study of Judah's alliances with foreign powers and the northern kingdom is done by Knoppers. He proposes that alliance is one of Chronicler's patterns or *topoi*, and concludes that all alliances are presented as negative in Chronicles (Knoppers, "Yhwh Is Not"). Discussing in terms of Judean alliance, Knoppers proposes that "The affiliated interests of Chronicles and of Ezra-Nehemiah in preserving Judaean integrity suggest that the opposition between them has been overdrawn" (Knoppers, "Yhwh Is Not," 624), which is in tune with the position of this dissertation. The same issue is treated by Kelly almost at the same time with similar conclusion (Kelly, *Retribution and Eschatology*, 204–11). Kelly adds an interesting observation that Hezekiah's

Lastly, it can be proposed that the present observation that 2 Chr 8:11 contains a negative connotation fits with the observations discussed in chapter 2 that strongly suggest that Solomon is not regarded as flawless in his reign. For example, while King David confessed his sin in particular cases (1 Chr 21:8, 21a),[100] Solomon confesses human fragility without exception before God in keeping his law (2 Chr 6:36, "there is no one who does not sin") with his own mouth, and there is no clear positive evaluation statement for Solomon as there is in the cases of most good kings.

4.4. The Chronicler's View of Intermarriage: A Refutation of Japhet's View

One of the most comprehensive explorations of the Chronicler's view of intermarriage has been produced by S. Japhet. Her view of the Chronicler's view of intermarriage is proposed as part of her discussion of the Chronicler's view of foreigners.[101] Her basic view is that the Chronicler has a pro-intermarriage stance, in contradiction to the Deuteronomistic history.[102] A brief outline of her view and her grounds for it, and a refutation against it, is as follows.

---

recourse to Egypt for help under Assyrian attack in the *Vorlage* (2 Kgs 18:21, 24), which is criticized in Isa 30:1–5; 31:1–3, is suppressed in Chronicles (Kelly, *Retribution and Eschatology*, 206). Furthermore, considering the positive relationship of David and Solomon's kingdom with Hiram and the queen of Sheba, Kelly rightly concludes that "the Chronicler's objection is not to alliances *per se*, but rather to those associations that express disloyalty to Yahweh and foster religious corruption in his covenant people"(Kelly, *Retribution and Eschatology*, 209). In this light, it is more likely that Solomon's intermarriage which results in "disloyalty to Yahweh and fostering religious corruption" cannot, with the reader's prior knowledge, escape a negative implication in Chronicles.

100. Selman points out that in David's confession his sin in Chronicles is expressed as weightier than that of Kings.

101. Japhet, *Ideology*, 334–51. Japhet's view of the Chronicler's view of intermarriage is stated in her book pp. 346–51 as a part of the section titled "Foreigners and Aliens" (334).

102. Knoppers proposes a similar view to Japhet's (Knoppers, "Intermarriage, Social Complexity, and Ethnic Diversity in the Genealogy of Judah," 15–30). He, after examining genealogy of Judah, concludes that "in Chronicles the phenomenon of mixed marriages is one means by which Judah expands and develops within the land" (30). He maintains that "if the genealogist found the mixed marriages highly objectionable or reprehensible, he could have criticized them" (19), however we do not agree with his statement, the reason for which will be explained.

Japhet's view that the Chronicler has a pro-intermarriage stance is based upon three observations. Firstly, in several cases in the genealogy in 1 Chr 1–9, foreigners are included in the Israel community in a significant way, occupying important places (i.e., 1 Chr 2:3; 2:17; 2:34–35; 4:18; 7:14).[103]

a. "The sons of Judah: Er, Onan, and Shelah; these three the *Canaanite woman* Bath-shua bore to him" (1 Chr 2:3a).

b. "Abigail bore Amasa, and the father of Amasa was Jether *the Ishmaelite*" (1 Chr 2:17).

c. "Now Sheshan had no sons, only daughters; but Sheshan had an *Egyptian slave*, whose name was Jarha. So Sheshan gave his daughter in marriage to his slave Jarha; and she bore him Attai" (1 Chr 2:34–35).

d. "These are the sons of Bithiah, *daughter of Pharaoh*, whom Mered married" (1 Chr 4:18[104]).

e. "The sons of Manasseh: Asriel, whom his *Aramean concubine* bore" (1 Chr 7:14a).

Secondly, the Chronicler mentions more cases of intermarriage (1 Chr 3:2; 2 Chr 2:12–13 [ET 2:13–14]; 12:13) without any criticism, including Solomon's intermarriage with the daughter of Pharaoh.[105] Thirdly, of the subjects of Joash who killed the king and were treated or punished according to the law (2 Chr 25:3–4),[106] the Chronicler made it clear that they had foreign mothers (2 Chr 24:26),[107] while the names of the Israelite fathers of the killers appear in its *Vorlage* (cf 2 Kgs 12:22 [ET 12:21]).[108] Japhet suggests that the revelation of the mothers' identity as foreigners, and the fact that they were punished according to the Israelite law, show that

103. Ibid., 346–50.

104. NRSV puts this verse in 4:17.

105. Ibid., 350.

106. "As soon as the royal power was firmly in his hand he killed his servants who had murdered his father the king. But he did not put their children to death, according to what is written in the law, in the book of Moses, where the Lord commanded, 'The parents shall not be put to death for the children, or the children be put to death for the parents; but all shall be put to death for their own sins'" (2 Chr 25:3–4).

107. "Those who conspired against him were Zabad, son of Shimeath an Ammonite woman (הָעַמּוֹנִית) and Jehozahad, son of Shimrith the Moabite woman (הַמּוֹאָבִית)" (NIV, 2 Chr 24:26). NRSV does not make it clear that Shimeath and Shimrith are female.

108. "His servants arose, devised a conspiracy, and killed Joash in the house of Millo, on the way that goes down to Silla. It was Jozacar son of Shimeath and Jehozabad son of Shomer, his servants, who struck him down, so that he died" (2 Kgs 12:21–22a [ET 12:20–21a]).

although the subjects were the sons of foreign women, they were treated as true members of Israel. Therefore, according to Japhet, the descendants through intermarriage are also regarded as true Israelites, and no negative connotation of intermarriage is shown in Chronicles.[109] This argument can be refuted as follows.

Firstly, it should be pointed out that a genealogy which includes some foreigners without any explicit criticism of the intermarriage does not necessarily mean that the author intended to advocate intermarriage. While the presence of some foreigners' names in the genealogy evidently shows that the author took the existence of foreigners in the genealogy as significant information, the foreigners' names may have been included only because they were simply conspicuous historical facts. The absence of any criticism of the intermarriage is not hard to explain, even presuming that the Chronicler regarded it as negative; criticism of intermarriage is not his focal concern or interest, especially in the genealogy. A similar case can be seen in Samuel-Kings, if we can see them as a unity. That is, while Solomon's intermarriage is explicitly criticized at the end of the Solomon narrative (1 Kgs 11:1–8), David's foreign wife is introduced without any criticism in the same work (2 Sam 3:2–5). While other explanations are possible, it can be proposed that the reason why David's intermarriage is not criticized is simply that it is not the interest of the author in the passage. Likewise, the absence of criticism of the intermarriage in the genealogy does not necessarily mean the author did not regard intermarriage as negative, especially that of Solomon, but it can simply mean that intermarriage is not his concern or interest at this point.

Japhet states that "The family tree is a long and detailed one that reveals that the dynasty was founded by an Egyptian slave . . . what is striking about the biblical text is its emphasis on an Egyptian as founder of a dynasty," in her comment on 1 Chr 2:34.[110] However it is not clear why she thinks that Sheshan's Egyptian slave Jarha is in the family tree of the dynasty, for Sheshan's line comes from Jerahmeel son of Hezron (2:9, 25), while David's line comes from Ram son of Hezron (2:9). Japhet's confusion that Jarha, an Egyptian slave is the founder of the Davidic dynasty seems to be caused by the fact that the name of Jerahmeel's firstborn, is Ram, which is the same as the name of a direct ancestor of David, Ram son of Hezron (2:9 and 2:25, 27). However even the Ram in 2:25, 27 is not a

---

109. Japhet, *Ideology*, 350–51.

110. Ibid., 349.

direct ancestor of Sheshan, for Sheshan is a descendant of Onam, another son of Jerahmeel (2:26, 28ff.).

Secondly, an anti-intermarriage stance for the reason of avoiding religious corruption is compatible with the stance that accommodates foreigners into the Israelite community of faith within the distinctive biblical literatures. For example, in Deuteronomy, while intermarriage that might lead Israelites into apostasy is apparently prohibited (Deut 7:1–4), some foreigners can be included in the community after an appropriate delay condition (Deut 23:8–9 [ET 23:7–8]).[111] The same is true in Ezra-Nehemiah. While intermarriage is severely condemned in several places (Ezra 9–10; Neh 10:29, 31 [ET 10:28, 30]; 13:23–29 cf. 13:26),[112] those of foreign origin are included as prominent members of the community (cases in which Israelites are in danger of losing their identity under the influence of gentiles: Ezra 2:43, 58, 70; 7:7; 8:17, 20(x2); Neh 3:26; 7:46, 7:72 [ET 7:73]; 10:29 [ET 10:28]; 11:21),[113] even in cultic ceremony, i.e., Passover (Ezra 6:21)[114]. Therefore, it can be said that the fact that some foreigners are included in the genealogy of Israel in Chronicles cannot be any proof that the Chronicler approves or even welcomes intermarriage, especially that of Solomon which eventually leads him into apostasy.[115]

Thirdly, it is evident that in analyzing the crucial verse in 2 Chr 24:26 Japhet ignores the negative connotation of the verse, which not a few

111. Furthermore, it is noteworthy that the ban of Israelite king's possessing many wives in Deut 17:16 is not simply the matter of many women, but "political alliance with a foreign entity" or "political power achieved through international treaties sealed by marriage" that "each wife represents." Christensen exemplifies Solomon's case for the law (Christensen, *Deuteronomy 1:1–21:9*, 381, 384).

112. The meaning of Neh 9:2 is not clear.

113. NRSV interprets *the Nethinim* (הַנְּתִינִים) as "the temple servants" according to their function.

114. NRSV "all who had joined them and separated themselves from the pollutions of the nations of the land to worship the Lord, the God of Israel."

115. While the anti-intermarriage law in Deut 7:1–5, which concerns consequent apostasy, does not include Egypt in the list, 1 Kgs 11:8 ("He [Solomon] did the same for *all* his foreign wives, who offered incense and sacrificed to their gods") implies that the daughter of Pharaoh (1 Kgs 11:1) also leads Solomon to apostasy.

Additionally, the fact that Oeming, who has studied the genealogy in a most comprehensive way, maintains that the Chronicler has an anti-intermarriage stance also supports our view. Scholars who think that the Chronicler has an anti-intermarriage stance are Blenkinsopp (1988), Oeming (1990), and Mason (1990). All of these scholars also think that the work has anti-Samaritan stance, which we do not agree with. Kelly himself thinks that on the intermarriage issue, the Chronicler and the author of Ezra-Nehemiah have different stances (Kelly, *Retribution and Eschatology*, 232, 22).

scholars observe.[116] In contrast to Japhet's view, when the context of the passage is considered, the opposite conclusion can be drawn; the Chronicler's alteration of the identities of the parents of the assassins of King Joash from Israelites fathers to an Ammonite mother and a Moabite mother can be construed not as an inclusive attitude towards foreigners, but as antipathy to the Ammonites and Moabites. M. P. Graham suggests that the alteration by the Chronicler has a twofold aim. Firstly, "further degradation for the wicked Joash (not only was he assassinated, but his murderers were men of mixed ancestry, descendants of two peoples with ignoble origins)," secondly, "further disparagement for the practice of interracial marriage."[117] It is more likely that the revealing of the assassins' parents' foreign origin was intended more to convey a negative connotation than a positive one, when the context of the verse is considered. In Kings, Joash's faults are not presented as seriously as in Chronicles. In Kings, the only faults described are his allowing high places while he is estimated as doing "what was right in the sight of the Lord" (2 Kgs 12:3–4 [ET 12:2–3]), and his giving away all the votive gifts and gold from the treasuries of the temple, and gold from his house to appease King Hazael of Aram and avoid the attack of Aramean army against Jerusalem (2 Kgs 12:18–19 [ET 12:17–18]). By contrast, in Chronicles, his idolatry after Jehoiada's death and rejecting of the prophets' word (2 Chr 24:17–19), especially his killing of Zechariah the son of Jehoiada who was moved by the spirit of God and delivered the word of God (2 Chr 24:20–21), are presented. Moreover, in Chronicles, the narrator's statements that Joash killed Zechariah in spite of his father's grace upon him,[118] and that the attack of the Aramean army

116. Geiger's view of the issue is expressed well in his statement that "Nur Söhne solcher Mütter können eine solche Unthat vollführen!" (Geiger, *Urschrift*, 49 n. 3). Torrey expresses well the majority view of the problematic alteration. Torrey states that "The zeal of the Chronicler for the pure blood of Judah and Benjamin – as well as of the House of Levi – was always, and must of necessity have been, a leading motive in his work. The true stock of Israel must keep itself separate from 'the heathen of the land' . . . The Chronicler's aversion to the marriage of Hebrews with foreigners shows itself in many places. Perhaps the most striking single instance is found in the passage II Chron. 24:26, which is his own improved version of II Kings 12:21. . . . In the story as he tells it, the one of the two conspirators (impious wretches in his eyes, even though the king had deserved his fate) was 'the son of שׁמעת the Ammonitess,' and the other was 'the son of שׁמרית the Moabitess.' The alteration here made is one of the most instructive in all the Chronicler's work" (Torrey, *Ezra Studies*, 212–13).

117. Graham, "Connection," 258.

118. Furthermore, the description of the Jehoiadah's acts to provide two wives for Joash, as if a father does for his son (2 Chr 24:3) and the high respect toward Jehoiadah up to burying him in king's tomb (2 Chr 24:15–16), also makes Joash's killing

is God's punishment upon Joash, paint Joash in a much more negative tone than in Kings. In this light, we can justifiably construe the alteration of the assassins' parents' origin to foreigners as being intended to further degrade the wicked Joash. It should therefore be admitted that this case presupposes an antipathy to those foreigners and to intermarriage with them as well.[119]

Furthermore it should be pointed out that Japhet's argument lacks persuasive power in the following aspect. Although Japhet, ignoring the context linking the verse to 2 Chr 25:3–4, insists that the verse shows that even those who have foreign origins are treated as members of Israel, it is highly questionable whether this is the best or even a suitable example to show the author's stance that those of foreign origin are also true members of Israel. Clearly it is doubtful whether putting somebody in an assassin's role to kill a king of Judah and to be punished according to the law is an appropriate way to stress his status as a true member of Israel. Moreover, it should be remembered that in the Deuteronomic law condemning intermarriage is compatible with treating foreigners in the same way as Israelites. In other words, in the case of Deuteronomy, treating foreigners according to the law which is basically applied to Israelites (e.g., Deut 31:12[120] cf. 24:14, 17, 19),[121] does not eliminate condemning intermarriage which can lead to apostasy (Deut 7:1–4).

Fourthly, if the Chronicler had really wanted to propose a pro-intermarriage stance through the genealogy in 1 Chr 1–9, it is questionable why he did not make it clear that Tamar, Judah's daughter-in-law, was a Canaanite woman.[122] Because Tamar was the mother of Perez, a direct ancestor of David, if there had been any slight mention or notice in the genealogy that Tamar was a Canaanite, it would possibly have been a strong and effective device to advocate a "pro-intermarriage" stance. However,

Zechariah the son of Jehoiada more wicked.

119. It should be reminded that the antipathy against Ammonites and Moabites is presented also in Deut 23:4–7 [ET 23:3–6].

120. "Assemble the people—men, women, and children, as well as the aliens residing in your towns – so that they may hear and learn to fear the Lord your God and to observe diligently all the words of this law . . . "

121. In the Deuteronomic law, it is observed that in some cases, foreigner are supposed to be treated the same as Israelites (e.g., Deut 24:20; 29:10 [29:11]), and in other cases not the same as Israelites (e.g., Deut 14:21; 15:3; 23:21 [ET 23:20]), and the transition of the foreigner's status appears (Deut 23:8–9 [ET 23:7–8]).

122. Japhet herself states that "Genesis 38 does not state that Tamar was Canaanite, but the story would seem to indicate that she was" (Japhet, *Ideology*, 347 n. 284), in her analysis of 1 Chr 2:3, and observes that Tamar was "apparently" Canaanite (ibid, 347).

this was not the case, and although Judah's wife Bath-shua's being a Canaanite woman is clearly mentioned (1 Chr 2:3a), she did not produce any direct ancestors of the dynasty.

Fifthly, it can be pointed out that in any case Solomon's intermarriage is not described positively but rather in a negative tone. His foreign wife is regarded as someone who should not be in Israel's holy places, although it can be admitted that Solomon's sensitivity to avoid any conflict between his foreign wife and Israel's holiness implies his piety to some extent.

Sixthly, it can be pointed out that there are some cases in Chronicles which evidently show that there were negative consequences, especially in religious matters, from some undesirable marriages: (1) in 2 Chr 21:6, of Jehoram, "He walked in the way of the kings of Israel, as the house of Ahab had done; for the daughter of Ahab was his wife. He did what was evil in the sight of the Lord," and (2) in 2 Chr 22:2–3, of Ahaziah, "His mother's name was Athaliah, a granddaughter of Omri. He also walked in the ways of the house of Ahab, for his mother was his counselor in doing wickedly." Athaliah, the daughter of Ahab, granddaughter of Omri, wife of Jehoram, and mother of Ahaziah is not a total foreigner. While it is true that only her mother Jezebel is a foreign woman, wickedly devoted to idolatry (1 Kgs 16:31), it can be said that Athaliah is a semi-foreigner in blood and full foreigner in spirit.[123] Athaliah, as her mother does, causes a tragic consequence in the Judahite kingdom after she enters the dynasty through marriage (2 Chr 21 22). Hence it can be said that in his work the Chronicler shows his awareness of the danger of inappropriate marriage.

Japhet's view of the Chronicler's stance regarding foreigners is basically that the Chronicler had such an inclusive attitude towards foreigners that there is no foreigner in the territory of Israel, in the sense that foreigners in the land have been assimilated into the Israel community. Thus, Japhet proposes that it is more likely that "a *ger*, . . . who has joined the people of Israel, adopted their religion, . . . lost his foreign identity," while she cautiously admits that "it is possible to understand '*ger*' in the book of Chronicles as we find it in Priestly literature—a sociological term for an alien who could participate in the religious life of the Israelite community."[124] However, her proposition is not convincing for several reasons. Firstly, her view is contradictory to the description of Solomon's special burden

123. Although Athaliah's mother being a foreigner, Jezebel daughter of King Ethbaal of the Sidonians, is not mentioned in Chronicles, it is reasonable that the identity of the famous woman, who affects not only the northern kingdom, but also the southern kingdom in terms of severe apostasy, cannot escape the reader's prior knowledge.

124. Japhet, *Ideology*, 346.

of levy for the construction of the temple put upon the remnants of the Canaanites in the land. It is noteworthy that in Chronicles the discrimination of the people is more conspicuous (2 Chr 2:16–17 [ET 2:17–18]; 7:7–9) than in Kings, by the omission of the levy put upon Israelites which appears in the *Vorlage* (1 Kgs 5:27–28 [ET 5:13–14] cf. 9:20–22). Japhet's view cannot be sustained without ignoring the passage that plainly shows the discrimination between Israelites and the foreigners which is stated as sustained "until today" (2 Chr 8:8). Secondly, her view cannot explain why the term *ger* was still used to denote those foreigners if they had really been assimilated into the Israelite community.

4.5. Gender and Ethnicity in Terms of Cultic Purity and Impurity in Old Tradition

Japhet's view that the issue at stake in 2 Chr 8:11 is the gender rather than the ethnicity of Solomon's wife, the daughter of Pharaoh, does not have any support from the Hebrew Bible, as mentioned already.[125] Here additional observations can be proposed to refute her view. Many passages of the old tradition show that a woman (or women) is allowed to approach cultic items.

1. The stipulation of women's purification after childbirth (Lev 12:2–5) ironically reveals that a woman was allowed to "touch anything sacred or go to the sanctuary" (Lev 12:4) in her normal state. The purity stipulation commands that it takes thirty-three days for the mother to be purified from her bleeding after childbirth in the case of a son (Lev 12:4), and sixty-six days in the case of a daughter (Lev 12:5), and that "she must not touch anything sacred or go to the sanctuary until the days of her purification are over." The implication of the stipulation is clear. After a thirty-three or a sixty-six day purification period, a woman was allowed to touch anything sacred or even go to the sanctuary, whatever that exactly means. When the close relationship

---

125. Japhet introduces Qumran documents and late Rabbinic literature to defend her view (while Targum also supports her view), but cannot base her view upon biblical grounds as Siedlecki points out. In fact, her effort to secure evidence for her argumentation from outside biblical material, itself betrays the difficulty of finding a biblical basis for her view. Moreover, the later rabbinic document that Japhet uses for her case does not concern gender, but sexual intercourse as the source of cultic impurity – "No man shall lie with a woman in the city of the Sanctuary, to defile the city of the Sanctuary" (Japhet, *I & II Chronicles*, 626).

between the Pentateuchal law, especially the so-called P document,[126] and Chronicles is considered, it is hard to believe that the Chronicler regarded gender as the fundamental problem in 2 Chr 8:11 that Japhet (and Johnstone) suggests.[127]

2. Exod 38:8 shows that women served at the entrance to the tent of meeting, the very center of Israel's cult. They reappear in 1 Sam 2:22, in the context of the scandalous report that Eli's sons slept with the women who served at the entrance of the tent of meeting. If it is true that women's service was necessary in the tent of meeting, there is no reason that we should not suppose that women's service was necessary in the temple, which has succeeded the function of the tent of meeting among the same people. Although no explicit stipulation in the Pentateuch mentions women's service in cultic matters, it is evident and understandable that some duties (or chores) that are related to the cult but are not articulated in the stipulations are carried out by women from the first stage of Israel's cultic tradition.[128]

126. Referring to "P document" does not mean that this study presupposes the J, E, D, P documents hypothesis; the usage of the terms is only for convenience.

127. If it is accepted that the Chronicler is a faithful successor of the old tradition as Kelly suggests in the last chapter of his work (Kelly, *Retribution and Eschatology*), the issue in 2 Chr 8:11 cannot be gender, but ethnicity. Furthermore, Ezek 44:7, 9 are a source that reveals a negative post-exilic attitude toward foreigners in terms of temple purity.

128. Another fact can be pointed out here, though it is not directly related to the present point. It is evident that without women some cultic material or items could not even exist. As well as the existence of women in the service at the entrance of the tent of meeting, Exod 38:8 also shows that the bronze basin and its bronze stand were made from the mirrors of the women who served at the place. Among the materials that were offered for the construction of the tent of meeting and sacred garments (Exod 35:21), a variety of colorful yarns and fine linen, and material from goat hair, had been made by skilled women (Exod 35:25–26). Furthermore, it is explicitly described that "men and women" alike offered their "gold jewellery of all kinds: broaches, ear-rings, rings and ornaments" for the construction of the tent of meeting (Exod 35:22, 29; cf. 36:6). The anointing of the tabernacle and all furniture that is in it with oil, which consecrates them (Exod 40:9–11), does not seem to mean that those are regarded as previously unclean because of women. The following passage of anointing of Aaron and his sons (40:12–15) supports this. It is plain that Aaron and his sons do not need the anointing because they are regarded as previously unclean. Rather, the anointing means that they are now separated for the holy service of the Lord. The same meaning can be implied in the case of the tabernacle and all furniture in it, which are made of the materials offered by Israelite men and women. Moreover, it is odd to think that the tabernacle and all furniture in it need the anointing only because there are some materials offered or made by women, among them. Rather, Exod 35:25–26 highlights the role of women in making the tabernacle in a positive light.

Considering these cases, it is hard to think that the "uncleanness" issue in 2 Chr 8:11 is about gender. The issue is better understood as that of ethnicity.

5. SOLOMON'S HEAVY BURDEN UPON ISRAELITES (2 CHR 10:4, 10, 11, 14)

Second Chr 10 describes how Rehoboam, the son of Solomon, refuses to accept the people's request to lighten the burden laid by Solomon upon their shoulders, and why this foolish decision was made by Rehoboam, on two levels. Superficially, it was caused by Rehoboam's foolishly choosing the wrong advice provided by his young subjects (10:8–14) on the matter of the northern tribes' request about Solomon's heavy burden but, fundamentally, it was caused by God who would fulfill the prophecy through Ahijah in order to punish Solomon's apostasy (10:15).

Second Chr 10 plainly shows through two negative elements that Solomon's reign is not flawless.[129] Firstly, the text plainly means or reveals that under Solomon's reign, most probably in the latter period,[130] the Israelites could not enjoy their lives because of the heavy burden laid upon their shoulders by him (2 Chr 10:4, 10, 11, 14). It should be noticed that all parties in 2 Chr 10 acknowledge this. While the northern tribes complain of the heavy burden, Rehoboam the successor of Solomon, his old subjects, and his young subjects all admit it, and do not deny the heavy burden laid by Solomon upon the northern tribes. Secondly, the mention of the fulfillment of Ahijah's prophecy in 10:15 (along with the word of God through the mouth of Shemaiah the man of God in 11:2–4), reminds the reader of Solomon's apostasy that is the fundamental cause of the division of the united kingdom according to the first history. It is interesting to observe that two negative elements of Solomon's reign are linked together smoothly here in 2 Chr 10. That is, in the process of God's punishment

129. In Hebrew narrative, it is observed that the issues around a person's or a king's life are not necessarily confined to the span of his lifetime or reign. For example, David's merit has continual influence or power on his successors. Furthermore, the fourfold punishment concerning David's adultery and murder is executed beyond his lifetime, and Adonijah, the fourth sheep paid, is killed in the reign of Solomon (discussed in chapter 4). Therefore it is not strange that significant information of Solomon's reign appears in the account of his successor's reign.

130. As shown in chapter 3, in the presentation of Solomon in the first history, at least, Israelites' enjoying their life is mentioned in the early stage of the reign (1 Kgs 4:20; 5:5 [ET 4:25]) while it is lacking in latter part of Solomon's reign.

against Solomon's apostasy, Solomon's other fault or shortcoming (i.e., putting an excessive burden on his people) acts as a trigger.

Dillard suggests that "the biblical text alludes to the sociopolitical ills that attended the splendor of the Solomon empire" while the Chronicler intended to describe Solomon as flawless.[131] However, it is doubtful that the text conveys unintended information to the reader. Rather, if it is admitted that the Chronicler is a historian with high literary ability, it should be acknowledged that he intentionally provides the information for the reader, in order to constitute the whole picture of the history in terms of Solomon's reign. As for the fulfillment of Ahijah's prophecy, it should be admitted that if the reader's prior knowledge of the division of the united kingdom as it appears in the first history were not presupposed here, the mention of Ahijah's prophecy would be totally absurd, and the account of the division of the kingdom would be made cryptic by the mention of it.

Overlooking the significance of the reference in 10:15,[132] most commentators attribute the division of the kingdom to causes other than Solomon. However, as has been discussed already in chapter 2, no attempt to remove the responsibility for the division of the united kingdom from Solomon to any other party is successful. Those attempts cannot be made without overlooking or distorting the plain sense of the text (i.e., chapter 10), especially the statement that the event happened as the fulfillment of Ahijah's prophecy (10:15).

---

131. Dillard, *2 Chronicles*, 88. Dillard observes that the blame for the division of the kingdom goes to both "Jeroboam's lust for power" and "Rehoboam's folly" rather than Solomon whose reign is presented as "blameless" (89).

132. Jarick suggests that 10:15 seems to remind the reader of Exod 9:12 and 11:9 where God hardens Pharaoh's heart in order to demonstrate his wonders and power in the land of Egypt, while he does not consider 10:15's function to remind the reader of its *Vorlage* (Jarick, *2 Chronicles*, 92–93). It is interesting to observe that he himself seems to be reminded of the content of the *Vorlage* by 10:15 when he describes Jeroboam as "a man who had apparently received a prophetic word that he would be successful in a revolt . . . ," while the text (10:15) itself does not tell what the contents of Ahijah's prophecy were (ibid., 94). He states again that "the words which Yahweh 'had spoken by Ahijah the Shilonite to Jeroboam' (10.15) . . . had presumably led Jeroboam to think that he would be successful in rebelling against Rehoboam" (104).

Although Kalimi does not treat the 2 Chr 10:15 as a significant allusion case, he mentions the verse in terms of "promise vs. fulfilment" (Verheißung vs. Erfüllung) (as a subcategory of "Harmonization" (chapter 7) and admits the reader's prior knowledge of Ahijah's prophecy in the *Vorlage* (1 Kgs 11:29–39) is presumed here. He states that "Gelegentlich bringt der Chronist aus seiner Vorlage auch nur die Erfüllung, so daß der Leser die Verheißung aus seiner Erinnerung an den Text in Könige oder aus dem Kontext erschließen muß" (Kalimi, *Zur Geschichtsschreibung*, 144).

It is understandable that interpreters who believe or presuppose that Solomon is presented as flawless in the passage about his reign in Chronicles find it uncomfortable to accept the text as it is. Hence, S. Japhet sees a "theological dilemma" in 2 Chr 10,[133] for she cannot but admit that the text reveals Solomon's fault or shortcoming while she, with many other scholars, cannot see any fault presented in the portrayal of Solomon in previous passages.

If the Chronicler truly had wanted to conceal Solomon's faults in terms of the division of the kingdom, he could have simply omitted the mention of Ahijah's prophecy along with Shemaiah's. It would not have been difficult for the author to omit those crucial passages, and still create a smooth narrative flow, if he had wanted to. The account would have made sense without the mention of Ahijah's prophecy and Shemiah's words do not necessarily need to include the problematic "this thing is from me" (11:4). The whole episode (11:1–4) could even have been omitted. However, this is not the case. Was the Chronicler such an incompetent editor that he was unable to polish his work to erase a clumsy editorial trace? The high quality of the work that has been increasingly discovered so far does not allow such a view.

5.1. The Reconstruction of the Reader's Prior Knowledge and Reading Experience of the Passage

In terms of Solomon's corruption, the reader is supposed to have prior knowledge in the following aspects. From the first history, the reader understands that Solomon's excessive intermarriages led him to apostasy, which resulted in the division of the kingdom as God's punishment after his death. The problematic nature of Solomon's intermarriage is well acknowledged in the post-exilic Judahite community (Neh 13:26 cf. Ezra 9–10; Neh 13:23–28), to which, most probably, the first readers of the text belonged. Also, the ideal reader is supposed to understand, from the first

---

133. Japhet, *I & II Chronicles*, 657. McKenzie, in a similar sense, states that "it causes problems in Chronicles" (McKenzie, *1–2 Chronicles*, 263). Recently, Hooker facing this dilemma and concluding that the dilemma cannot be resolved, suggests that "On the human level it is sin [of the northern party] . . . on the divine level, it is God's will, perhaps in consequence to the sin of Rehoboam" [my reference] (Hooker, *First and Second Chronicles*, 168–69). His solution is not convincing, for the first three years of Rehoboam's reign is described positively. He seems to admit the reader's prior knowledge of 1 Kgs 11:26–40 in terms of Jeroboam's exile in Egypt (2 Chr 10:2) (165), but does not apply it to his interpretation.

history, that the nature of Solomon's corruption is "returning to Egypt," with three key elements (Solomon's intermarriage with Pharaoh's daughter, his importation of Egyptian horses, and his heavy burden upon the Israelites as an Egyptian way of rule) as explored in chapter 3.

So far, the reader has read the account of Solomon quite tightly focused on the temple building issue. In fact, the issue has been the centre of the work since the latter part of the account of David (e.g., 1 Chr 22, 28, 29). The reader has also noticed Solomon's importing of Egyptian horses (2 Chr 1:16–17) in the early stages of his reign, which is more conspicuously presented there than in Kings. If the reader is sensitive enough, he or she is reminded of the problematic nature of Solomon's importation of Egyptian horses, and would have been impressed by the abundance of God's grace and blessing in spite of the presence of Solomon's shortcomings in the succeeding accounts. Then, the reader reads the passage of Solomon's intermarriage with Pharaoh's daughter (8:11). The problematic nature of this marriage is recalled by the reader, who has prior knowledge of it. However, Solomon's piety that accompanies him even in his problematic intermarriage dilutes the negative connotation. The negative connotations of those two references (to Egyptian horses and Pharaoh's daughter) do not distract the reader's attention strongly from the flow of the account that is focused on the successful temple building and splendid glory of the united kingdom. At last, when the reader reaches the final description of Solomon's reign in 9:28, it is significant that the last sentence of the description is of his importation of horses from all nations, including Egypt. In other words, the second mention of Solomon's importation of the Egyptian horses, which is explicitly against the law of the king in Deut 17, reminds the reader of the significance of the case, and the excessiveness of the horse importation also reminds the reader of Solomon's excessive intermarriage (and his following fault of apostasy).

If the reader has been careless and missed the allusions and hints of the negative connotations, and the glory and blessing of the united kingdom under Solomon's reign is solely impressed upon the reader's mind, it means that the main purpose of the account is still achieved. If the reader has caught the slight hints or allusions to Solomon's misconduct, he or she can still perceive the abundance, generosity and sincerity of God's blessing along with the glory of the united kingdom.

In any case, when the reader reaches the account of Solomon's heavy burden in 2 Chr 10, the negative aspects of Solomon's reign come into direct light. With the prior knowledge of the Solomon narrative in Kings, it is not hard for the reader to accept and understand the account. Although the Israelites' conscription for levy does not appear in the Chronicler's account (2 Chr 2:16–17 [ET 2:17–18]; 8:7–9), and the crucial passage about the northern tribes' forced labor (1 Kgs 11:28) is also omitted, and the glorious dimension of the united kingdom is more emphasized, the reader's prior knowledge allows him or her to accept the present passage (2 Chr 10) without difficulty. Moreover, if the reader understands "the heavy burden" (originally, the hard service and heavy yoke in 10:4) as not only forced labor but also taxation, the luxurious lifestyle of the king described in the preceding passage (2 Chr 9:13–21) provides the reason for "the heavy burden." Hence, without any mention of a levy on Israelites in the preceding passages, the reader can accept "the heavy burden" in 2 Chr 10.

In a sense, 2 Chr 10 functions as 1 Kgs 11:1 does in the Solomon account in Kings. 2 Chr 10 makes it clear that Solomon's faults have been hinted at or alluded to in the preceding part of the account. In other words, Solomon's overall misdeeds are confirmed in 2 Chr 10, just as the problem of his intermarriage with Pharaoh's daughter in the preceding passages (1 Kgs 3:1; 7:8; 9:16, 24) is confirmed at last in 1 Kgs 11:1, which functions also as a trigger to make the reader realize Solomon's other faults.

Finally, the mention of the fulfillment of Ahijah's prophecy (2 Chr 10:15) that concludes the heavy burden account decisively puts a seal on the reader's prior knowledge of Solomon's faults. Because the reader is already familiar with the work's literary tendency of bold omission and allusion, the mention is sufficiently significant. Moreover, the following account in which God states that "this thing is from me," through Shemaiah the man of God (2 Chr 11:2–4), confirms the reader's prior knowledge once more.[134]

---

134. Furthermore, as Kelly points out, the mention of the "prophecy of Abijah" which records "the rest of Solomon's acts . . . from first to last" (2 Chr 9:29b, no parallel) is also significant (Kelly, *Retribution and Eschatology*, 90–91). Kelly also adds an interesting observation that God's offering to Solomon a long life conditional on his obedience to Yahweh's statutes and commandments (1 Kgs 3:14) is omitted in Chronicles, while the mention of Solomon's forty-year reign (2 Chr 9:30/1 Kgs 11:42) is retained. Kelly suspects that "the omission may . . . reflect a recognition of Solomon's failings." He adds that "the motif of a long life is not common in Chronicles, but it is used of David (1 Chron. 29.28) and Jehoiada (2 Chron. 24.15), possibly as an indication of reward" (Kelly, *Retribution and Eschatology*, 91 n. 54).

5.2. The Nuance (or Complexity) and Necessity of the Account in 2 Chr 10

Although 2 Chr 10 is an almost literal reusing of its *Vorlage* as it is,[135] it should be recognized that this is because the Chronicler's own intention can be reflected as it is. Analysis of 2 Chr 10, can explain why the account in the *Vorlage* is used in this way, as follows.

Firstly, the account in its *Vorlage* is nuanced or complex enough already, and consequently well matched with the general characteristic of Chronicles. On the one hand, the passage plainly shows that at least the end part of Solomon's reign was not ideal for the Israelites. Solomon is described, in 2 Chr 10, as a kind of tyrant who forced heavy burdens on his people with oppressive power. It is evidently something that a king of Israel is prohibited to be or to do (it is against the king's stipulation "not to exalt his heart above his brothers [my translation]" (Deut 17:20a)). On the other hand, the passage shows that the old subjects, who had served Solomon from his early reign, were wise. That the old subjects' advice, if it had been taken by the young king, could have saved the united kingdom from splitting, betrays implicitly the excellency of the wisdom of Solomon's early days.[136] It is interesting to see that even the passage that decidedly reveals a fault or shortcoming of Solomon has an aura or trace of the wisdom of his days. In that sense, the passage contains a positive element which praises Solomon's old days, although at the same time it plainly reveals Solomon's shortcomings or faults, in terms of the heavy burden. In that sense, the nuance or complexity that is a characteristic of the work's portrayal of kings exists already in its *Vorlage*.

It can also be suggested that the plain contrast between the wisdom of the old subjects who have served Solomon from the early days and the audacious and oppressive attitude of the young subjects who were, undoubtedly, raised in the latter period of Solomon's reign,[137] implies

135. Some minor alterations are observed. Considering the fact together with the presumption that the Chronicler's *Vorlage* was the present text of Kings, the minor alterations mean that the Chronicler did not re-use the contents thoughtlessly, but with his own intention, although it should be admitted that there is a possibility that the Chronicler's text of Kings already had the alterations, as Lemke argues (Lemke, "The Synoptic Problem").

136. Cf. 2 Chr 9:7. Notice that the old advisers are plainly denoted as "the old men who had attended his father Solomon while he was still alive" (2 Chr 10:6b).

137. When it is considered that Rehoboam was "forty-one years old when he began to reign" (2 Chr 12:13) and Solomon's reign had lasted for "forty years" (2 Chr 9:30), it is plain that Rehoboam and his young subjects "who had grown up with him" (2 Chr

or reflects the transition of wise Solomon into an oppressive ruler in his latter days. The oppressive attitude of the young subjects may reflect the atmosphere of Solomon's court in his latter days, in which they were raised with Rehoboam (2 Chr 10:8, 10), while the old subjects' wisdom reflects Solomon's wisdom in his early days (cf. 2 Chr 9:7). In that sense, the contrast effectively and economically displays the transition of Solomon from a wise king into an oppressor.[138]

Secondly, the account is, in an overall view of the Chronicles, an important (acceptable and not contradictory to his view, of course), and essential part to describe the process of the division of the united kingdom, and the Chronicler chose to include the part intentionally, as a faithful historian.

5.3. The Suitability of the Passage in Chronicles and the Identity of the Heavy Burden in the Solomon Account

Contrary to S. Japhet's view that there is a theological dilemma in 2 Chr 10, the present study, which presupposes that the author assumed the reader's prior knowledge of the old tradition (i.e., Deuteronomic law and the first history), does not see any kind of dilemma there. Rather, it is proposed that this part of the account plainly confirms that Chronicles firmly follows the previous tradition and presupposes the reader's prior knowledge of it. As previously shown, the small hints or allusions which indicate Solomon's faults (i.e., his Egyptian horse importation, and his intermarriage with the Egyptian princess, as misdeeds against God's law), prepares the ideal reader, who understands the hints or allusions, to accept the present passage which plainly acknowledges Solomon's faults during his reign, even though they are not explicitly described or evaluated in the preceding passage.

In fact, even the seemingly sudden introduction of Solomon's shortcomings or faults in 2 Chr 10 (i.e., the heavy burden, and his apostasy that is indirectly revealed in the mention of Ahijah's prophecy) is well matched with both the purpose of the Solomon account (or the whole of Chronicles), and the literary features of the work. As for the purpose of the account or the work, the emphasis on the subject of the temple

---

10:8, 10), were in their twenties and thirties in the latter period of Solomon's reign.

138. The same point can be applied to the Solomon narrative in Kings. The point is in line with the interpretation of the transition of the atmosphere of the Solomon's court or his ruling style, which is a main point of our interpretation of the narrative.

building requires a temple-building focused presentation. The emphasis should not be distracted by other themes such as Solomon's shortcomings or faults. Hence, it is necessary or appropriate to reveal Solomon's short-comings or faults openly only after his reign has ended. As for the features of the work, the sudden introduction of Solomon's shortcomings or faults is not unusual when compared to the preceding sudden introductions of Saul's death (1 Chr 10), and David's emergence as the king of Israel (1 Chr 11–12), which are only understandable with the reader's prior knowledge of the contexts.

Additionally, the suitability of the introduction of Solomon's heavy burden in 2 Chr 10 is supported by observing the nature of the heavy burden. If the heavy burden is understood in a wider sense (of the Solomon narrative in Kings, as shown in chapter 3), it can be said that there are clues that hint at or allude to the reason for it in the preceding passages in Chronicles, as there are in Kings. Here, the wide sense of the heavy burden means not only the service of forced labor (and military duty), but also the heavy tax charged upon the Israelites as an obligation.[139] Solomon's luxurious lifestyle is evident from the text, and it is natural that a heavy tax should be required for the king to afford such a luxurious lifestyle.

It is noteworthy that the four subjects that appear twice in Chronicler's Solomon account can all be significantly related to the people's complaint in 2 Chr 10. The four subjects are (1) Solomon's many horses and chariot forces with his importation of Egyptian horses (2 Chr 1:14, 16–17; 9:25, 28), (2) Solomon's importation of luxurious treasures or exotic animals through sea trade with the help of Huram's subjects (2 Chr 8:17–18; 9:10–11), (3) Solomon's levy system which includes Israelites' service in the later stages (2 Chr 2:16–17 [ET 2:17–18]; 8:7–10), (4) the excessive wealth in Jerusalem with sycamore trees, and gold and silver (2 Chr 1:15; 9:27).[140]

It is not difficult to see that the four subjects can be clues that explain the consequences (i.e., the people's complaint) in 2 Chr 10. (1) It is well known that maintaining many horses and chariot forces is expensive, as Hauer shows.[141] (2) It is not too hard to imagine that the importation

---

139. Dillard thinks that "The issues were heavy taxation and forced labor . . ." (Dillard, 2 *Chronicles*, 86), and "the hated corvée and heavy taxation are undoubted factors that fanned the dissatisfaction in the North" (Dillard, 2 *Chronicles*, 88).

140. "Silver and gold" (2 Chr 1:15), "silver" (2 Chr 9:27).

141. Hauer, "The Economics." Hauer contrasts David's economical and effective infantry troops and Solomon's expensive and less useful chariot troops in the mountainous territory of Israel.

of treasuries and exotic animal from abroad costs not a little money. (3) Although Israelites were not treated in the same way as the remnant of Canaanites who served as forced slave labor, it is plain that Israelites could not be free from various forms of national duty in Solomon's day, and it is quite possible that the weight of the burden of duty increased in the course of time.[142] (4) The excessive wealth in Jerusalem, but not in the whole nation, can imply that there was a kind of exploitation of the other parts of the nation.[143] In fact, the northerners' complaint of their heavy burden in chapter 10 contrasts with the wealth of Jerusalem. If the heavy burden is understood in a wider sense, as not only forced labor but also a heavy tax to support Solomon's luxurious lifestyle, the account in 2 Chr 10 is not surprising, but rather a natural consequence.[144]

Lastly, the explicit introduction of Solomon's shortcomings and faults in 2 Chr 10 is well matched with the significant fact that there is no positive evaluative comment on him, and Solomon's own confession that there is no one who does not sin (2 Chr 6:36).[145]

6. CONCLUSION

In this chapter, it was shown how three Egyptian elements in Chronicles function to present Solomon in realistic terms, reflecting his faults, but at the same time not strongly attracting the reader's attention to them. His faults have to be hinted at, because they provide clues in unfolding the plot of this history, but they should not attract the reader's attention

142. 1 Kgs 11:28 reveals that at a certain point of Solomon's reign, most probably at a later point in time, at least the Joseph tribes had the burden of levy (סֵבֶל) under the supervision of Jeroboam.

143. Solomon's discriminatory policies have been noticed in the first history. For example, Bimson points out that Judah and Israel are referred to as separate entities in 1 Kgs 4:20, and Judah is not included in the administrative regions which pay taxes to supply the needs of the royal household, in his comment on 1 Kgs 4 (Bimson, "1 and 2 Kings," 343). He also observes that Hiram's evaluation of the twenty cities in Galilee, which Solomon transfers to Hiram to pay for Hiram's help in building projects, as "the land of good-for-nothing" implies that "the immense prosperity enjoyed in Jerusalem did not extend to the northern parts of the kingdom" (Bimson, "1 and 2 Kings," 349). For another example, see also Walsh, "Solomon in First King 1–5," 492; Kang, *The Persuasive Portrayal*, 232 (1 Kgs 4:7–19), 234 (1 Kgs 5:27–32 [ET 5:13–18]).

144. The omission of the Israelites' forced labor in the Chronicler's Solomon account may give the reader the impression that the heavy yoke is mainly heavy taxation.

145. Additional observations are possible. For example, as pointed out in chapter 2, the significant mention of seventy years' land Sabbath (2 Chr 36:21) implicitly supports this view.

too directly, because if they did so the author's intention to put the main focus on the glorious aspect of the golden age would be undermined. This chapter showed how the three Egyptian elements are presented in order to achieve the intention of the Chronicler, according to the perspective of the reader's reading process and prior knowledge. It was also shown that each case of new interpretation is in tune with the Chronicler's theological stance on the related issue and the literary features of the work.

8

Conclusion

1.SUMMARY

WHILE CHRONICLES CONTAINS SEVERAL implicit indications that Solomon was not flawless or impeccable, and 2 Chr 10 even reveals explicit evidence of Solomon's faults, the view of an idealized, impeccable Solomon in Chronicles has been very dominant and suppressed a fair interpretation of the portrayal of Solomon in Chronicles. This view relies heavily on the false assumption that Solomon's faults that appear in Kings are omitted in Chronicles. Furthermore, the form-critically or rhetorically orientated approach (which assumes that speeches in the work precisely reflect the author's view) to Abijah's speech (like other royal speeches in the work) has suppressed the observation of the clear disparity between the description of political schism in 2 Chr 10 and Abijah's distorted description of the situation in 2 Chr 13:7. However, through a careful reading, the falsity of Abijah's description of the division was pointed out.

The consensus observation that the Chronicler presupposed the reader's prior knowledge of the first history or old traditions encouraged us to apply a reader-sensitive approach to the Solomon account. This approach was showed to be effective primarily in its application to the Solomon narrative in Kings, which showed that three Egyptian elements (Egyptian horse and chariot importation, intermarriage with Pharaoh's daughter, Egyptian-style rule) were Solomon's prime faults in Kings. Interestingly, the three elements reappear in Chronicles concerning Solomon.

Along with the working hypothesis that the Chronicler was conscious of writing a second work of history which depends upon the authority of the first one, and that one of the major purposes of the work is to provide hope for the restoration of the Davidic monarchy, some features of Chronicles were explored. It was shown that generally Chronicles provides a more complex portrayal of each king than the first history, and that a technique of allusion is employed frequently, exploiting the reader's prior knowledge of the old traditions. Further, the close connection between Chronicles and the Deuteronomic law was shown to imply that it is natural that the law of the king in Deut 17:16–20, which condemns Solomon's deeds, should be applied to the Solomon account.

Finally, a reader-sensitive approach was applied to the three Egyptian elements in the Solomon account. In the Solomon narrative in Kings, the reader's reading process was taken as another important hermeneutical element, calculated by the author for the maximum effect upon the reader's mind. In the Solomon account in Chronicles, however, it was shown that the prior knowledge of the reader which, the author assumed, was the prime hermeneutical element intended by the author. In other words, the two major elements in constructing the meaning of the text of Chronicles are pre-knowledge which the author supposes the reader to have and certain allusions that presupposes the reader's prior knowledge. The work of two elements was in the intention of the author. Additionally, it was shown that the new interpretations are supported by the Chronicler's theology and well matched with literary features of Chronicles on the issues related to the Egyptian elements.

2. THE READER-SENSITIVE APPROACH TO THE SOLOMON ACCOUNTS IN KINGS AND CHRONICLES

When compared to the Solomon narrative in Kings, which is concerned with a dramatic change[1] of Solomon's attitude towards his God, from a

---

1. Many scholars, including most recently J. J. Kang and E. A. Seibert who treat the Solomon narrative in their monographs, observe that Solomon's corruption appears from an early stage of his reign in Kings' presentation. The present study agrees with them in that Solomon's corruption does start in an early stage of his reign. However, the present study does not agree with them in that the reader can perceive Solomon's corruption in the early stage of Solomon's reign from his or her first reading. As has been shown in chapter 3, the retroactive re-evaluation technique is employed to make

pious king to an apostate, the account in Chronicles presents a rather fixed portrayal of the king. In the Solomon narrative in Kings, the king's dramatic change has immense significance in terms of the intended message or lesson, and consequently investigation of the subtle literary technique (i.e., retroactive re-evaluation technique), which is much more involved with the reader's reading process than the reader's prior knowledge, was crucial. The technique is employed in order to maximize the effect of the message of the narrative.

However, the concerns of the Chronicler are different, because of the different nature and intention of the account from that in Kings. The Chronicler wanted to highlight the glory of the united kingdom under the grace of the God of Israel, and the building of the Jerusalem temple is the focus of that presentation. Writing a second history, when not only the author but also his readers already know the authorized history, and are aware that the tradition provides a ground for the present work, the author is confronted by a dilemma. He needs as far as possible to present the period of the united kingdom as a glorious era, so that the reader may have hope for the restoration of the kingdom on the grounds that the restoration of the temple had already been achieved. But the flow of events in the account of the first history does not allow the author to present King Solomon as an impeccable king, for the division of the kingdom is ultimately caused by his faults. Moreover, the presence of the first history, the common knowledge of the old tradition or history of the nation (as revealed in Neh 13:26), and the plain presence of the Torah in his (post-exilic) community or his reader's mind, would not have allowed any presentation that contradicted the first authorized one. Hence the author of Chronicles had to solve his dilemma by presenting the reign of David and Solomon through his own subtle literary technique.

Our study shows how the author tried to solve the dilemma. While reconstruction of the reading process was the most vital point in analyzing the Solomon narrative in Kings, the main focus of the study of the Solomon account in Chronicles was the author's use of techniques to exploit his reader's prior knowledge in order to achieve the intention of the work on one hand, and to solve the dilemma between the old tradition (or his reader's prior knowledge) and his intention to glorify the period of the united kingdom on the other. Although the main points or concerns

---

the reader realize insidious progress of corruption of Solomon only in his or her latter stage of the reading. It means that, in the reader's point of view, Solomon's change from a God-loving king (1 Kgs 3:3) to a foreign-women-loving apostate (1 Kgs 11:1–10) is striking and even dramatic in his or her first reading.

through which the two accounts are analyzed are different, it is plain that consideration both of the reading process and of the reader's prior knowledge are reader-sensitive approaches. It should be remembered that even in the analysis of the Solomon narrative in Kings, it has been proved that the reader's prior knowledge of the law of the king (Deut 17:14–20) functions as an essential element in order to introduce the intended meaning of the text. Likewise, the reading process of the reader could not be ignored in the investigation of the Chronicler's technique for his own purpose in the Solomon account.

As shown in the case of the narrative in Kings, the Egyptian elements (i.e., Solomon's Egyptian horses, Egyptian princess, and "Egyptian" rule) provide the key material for revealing Solomon's faults. On the assumption that the author of Chronicles had to follow the old tradition in locating the responsibility for the division of the kingdom (i.e., upon Solomon's shoulders), it was most likely that this material provides the clearest evidence. Hence the present study has tried to explore the passages of "Egyptian" elements in Chronicles, and has shown that these were re-employed in Chronicles to allude to Solomon's faults or at least shortcomings.

To sum up, the author of Kings was concerned with the progress of Solomon's corruption and employed a retroactive re-evaluation technique, in order to achieve his intention. The author of Chronicles, however, set forth a concern for the glory of the united kingdom of Israel and the grace of God in spite of Solomon's shortcomings, and did not point out Solomon's faults directly, at least during the portrayal of his reign. To achieve his intention to minimize the impression of the Solomon's faults in order not to attract the full attention of his reader to them, in spite of the necessity of their very presence there, the author of the Chronicles employed the technique of allusion.

If our conclusion is applied to the historical setting that this thesis presupposes, it can be said that the Chronicler intended to emphasize the grace of God, as the ultimate hope, in spite of the limits of the reformation of Ezra and Nehemiah, in order to encourage his first readers to hold their stance in this hope.

3. THE JUSTIFICATION AND MERITS
OF THE NEW INTERPRETATION

Although each chapter has already sought to justify the new interpretation of the Solomon account in Chronicles, the new interpretation's justification or merits can be summed up as follows.

1. The new interpretation can solve the so-called theological "dilemma" in 2 Chr 10, where the blameworthiness of Solomon's heavy burden upon the Israelites and the fulfillment of Ahijah's prophecy plainly appear. A few interpreters have maintained that the view of the "flawless Solomon" presentation in Chronicles cannot be sustained because of this passage, but they have not been able to propose specific passages which are intended to show Solomon's faults other than the contents of 2 Chr 10. The new interpretation explains how the seemingly sudden and abrupt appearance of the negative elements of Solomon's reign can be accepted by the reader, pointing out the specific passages which allude to Solomon's faults. The new interpretation also shows how the mechanism of the allusion technique works through the reader's mind.

2. The new interpretation is well matched with the literary nature of the Chronicles, i.e. the increased complexity and the allusion technique of the work. In the light of the increased nuance or greater complexity of the portrayals of the kings, the alleged flawless presentation of Solomon is not probable. Being aware of the allusion technique, we are able to observe the presence of allusions to Solomon's faults within the scope of his reign.

3. The new interpretation is well matched with our understanding of the purposes of the work. When it is considered that a prime purpose of the work may have been to give the reader hope for the restoration of the Israelite kingdom or the Davidic dynasty, which is closely linked to the building of the temple, it can be said that the account of Solomon has weighty significance, for he establishes the Davidic monarchy by his succession and building the house of God. Hence, the account has to be presented as a most glorious period of the dynasty and the kingdom, and consequently the need arises to blur the king's faults, although they cannot be thoroughly deleted for several

reasons.[2] In that sense, the new interpretation is coherent with the purpose of the whole work.

4. The new interpretation is well matched with the probable atmosphere of the post-exilic community in terms of the application of the Torah to the life of individual and nation. If the present form of Deuteronomy, at least, was an authoritative document in the community, and consequently the law of the king in Deut 17:14–20 is part of the reader's prior knowledge together with the contents of the first history, Solomon's faults in the present account cannot escape the reader's notice.

5. The new interpretation is well matched with the consensus view that the reigns of David and Solomon are presented as a pair which constitutes the golden age of Israel. If this view is correct, it is natural to expect that the evaluations of the two kings should be balanced.[3] It is very plain that King David is not presented as flawless, and his faults are presented both explicitly (i.e., in the first attempt at moving the ark, and the census) and implicitly (the adultery). If Solomon should be presented as flawless, it would be a point of strong contrast, which would break the unity of the two kings' reigns. Solomon's faults are also described explicitly (heavy yoke) and implicitly (intermarriage, Egyptian horses importation, luxurious life), according to our interpretation. As the builder of the temple, which has enormous significance and is a focal point throughout the work, Solomon's faults need be presented in a more allusive way than David's, in order not to distract the reader's attention from the focus.

6. The new interpretation is well matched with the implications of several observations concerning Solomon's alleged flawlessness. For example, (1) Solomon's own confession that there is nobody who does not commit sin (2 Chr 6:36a), (2) the seventy years' land Sabbath after the destruction of the kingdom (2 Chr 36:21), which implies

---

2. That is, for example, the historical authenticity of the events, and the emphasis of the abundance of the God's grace in spite of the beneficiary's shortcomings.

3. Contra Japhet, who thinks that "the images of the two kings are equated in certain respects when the Chronicler transfers some of David's qualities to Solomon and some of Solomon's achievements to David;" however she adds "The image of Solomon (unlike that of David) becomes that of flawless king" (Japhet's own parenthesis) (Japhet, *Ideology*, 1997, 488). It is noteworthy that while David is presented as the standard of subsequent kings several times in general evaluation of their reign (2 Chr 17:3; 28:1; 29:2; 34:2), Solomon is presented as an exemplary only in cultic matters (2 Chr 30:26. cf. 35:4). The context of 2 Chr 11:17 is also cultic as shown already in chapter 2.

that the law of land Sabbath has never been observed throughout the dynasty and therefore that there has never existed a perfect observance of the Torah, (3) the presentation of King Josiah whose impeccable image in the *Vorlage* has been modified (2 Chr 35:21–22) (since a king who is presented as perfect in its *Vorlage* is now presented as having faults, it is more likely that Solomon is presented as not perfect), and (4) the absence of any praise of Solomon. It is plain that the new interpretation of the Solomon account is coherent with the implications of these interesting observations.

4. A PAINTING ANALOGY OF THE SOLOMON ACCOUNT[4]

The subtlety of the Solomon account in Chronicles can be understood by analogy with a painting. In a painting, even dark colored objects near to a bright light (e.g., a flame, lamp, or the sun) are painted in bright or shining colors because the objects reflect the strong light. The painter does not intend the viewer of the painting to think that the objects are really bright or shining, but that they are depicted that way because they are near the light. The fact that the objects near to the light are painted not with their original dark colors, but in bright colors, highlights the intensity of the light. Likewise, while the author knows that Solomon's "Egyptian" elements really have a negative implication (are in "dark colors"), and also expects the reader to know this, the light which radiates from the "temple" (or "temple building" which is the most significant focus of the whole work) covers or overwhelms the dark colors of Solomon's faults. Hence, no explicit criticism of the negative elements appears in the account. Rather, it is painted as if even those elements radiate a similar light. However, in places far from the light objects recover their own colors. Solomon's heavy burden upon his people (2 Chr 10:4, 10, 11, 14), "the fulfillment of the prophecy of Abijah" (10:15) and the word of the Lord through Shemaiah

---

4. V. Philips Long uses a painting analogy to explain the nature of biblical history-writing (Long, *The Art of Biblical History*, 1994, 63ff., 76–86). He states that "the Chronicler presents a *second* painting of Israel's monarchical history, not an *over*painting of Samuel-Kings," thinking that "the Chronicler's aim was to recast and supplement, not repress or supplant the earlier history" (82). Duke also uses a painting analogy to describe the nature of Chronicles. He states, comparing "the Deuteronomistic History" and "Chronicler's History," "An analogy to this process is how two skilled painters can paint two different but equally accurate portraits of the same person" (Duke, "Chronicles," 2005, 162).

the man of God that the division is from God (11:2–4), reveal what the objects' original colors were.

5. THE IMPLICATIONS OF THE NEW INTERPRETATION

When a paradigm cannot explain one or more phenomena, a new paradigm is required, so that the overall phenomena can be explained in a more reliable and coherent system. It is called a "paradigm shift."[5] Alter's fresh suggestion[6] which proposes that biblical narratives can be more reasonably understood in terms of literary technique and their literary nature rather than source or redaction criticism, can, in that sense, be seen as a call for a paradigm shift in the field of biblical study. Since that time, a number of scholars have contributed to the progress in understanding the literary nature and technique of the biblical narratives, and its function in terms of the interpretation of the text.[7] On the other hand, the importance of the role of the reader in the interpretation of the biblical text has also been noticed.[8] In some cases, the emphasis on the reader's role in deciding the meaning of the text goes beyond the point where the author's intention is no longer regarded as the prime concern.[9] However,

5. For a discussion of the implication of Thomas Kuhn's theory to biblical studies or interpretation, see Poythress, "Science and Hermeneutics," 1996, especially chapter 4 under the title "Implications of Kuhn's Theory for Biblical Interpretation" (461–68). T. Longman III mentions "paradigm shift" in the biblical interpretation (99), and provides other scholars who proposes the same view (J. D. Crossan and M. Fishbane) in his article "Literary Approaches to Biblical Interpretation," (99 n. 3).

6. Alter, *Art*, 1981. In fact, the literary features and techniques of the OT narrative (and poetry as well) had been recognized long before Alter's work. For example, see Sands, *Literary Genius of the OT*, 1924. Sands proposes four characteristics of OT narratives as follows, (1) "Perfection of simplicity and vivid picturesqueness," (2) "Homely realism and concreteness," (3) "Absence of elaboration and of descriptive details of character, scenery, dress, etc," (4) "Dramatic power, due to their rapidity, use of dialogue, climaxes."

7. Most notably, Bar-Efrat, *Narrative Art*, 1989; Berlin, *Poetics*, 1983; Sternberg, *The Poetics of Biblical Narrative*, 1985; Gunn and Fewell, *Narrative in the Hebrew Bible*, 1993.

8. As recent biblical study has been indebted to modern secular literary criticisms for its ideas and approaches, the insight and understanding of the importance of reader's role to meaning of a text was introduced into the biblical studies from the secular literary criticism. For modern secular literary criticism which discovers and emphasizes the role of the reader, see, for example, Tompkins (ed.), *Reader-Response Criticism*, 1980; Freund, *The Return of the Reader*, 1987; Bennett (ed.), *Readers and Reading*, 1995; Scholes, *The Crafty Reader*, 2001.

9. It can be said that one extreme of it is Derrida's deconstructionism.

generally the close relationship between the literary technique of the text, employed by the author to deliver his own message, and the role of the reader, has been noticed. In fact, the relationship is unquestionable, for literary technique can function only through the reader's mind. In other words, consciously or unconsciously, the role of the reader is an intrinsic and integral part when any literary technique is employed in a text. Therefore, detecting literary technique in a text and the function of the technique in the reader's mind should be an important concern of interpreters of biblical narrative. The present study, which includes the interpretation of the Solomon accounts in Kings and Chronicles, can be an example of this. The two interpretations suggest that the authors of the biblical narrative are so sensitive to the reader's mind that their literary technique is designed with consideration, at least, of the reader's prior knowledge and reading process. In other words, the biblical authors are reader-sensitive. The application of the approach has solved the difficulty of deciding the starting point of Solomon's corruption in Kings, and the theological dilemma in the Solomon account in Chronicles, which can be a proof of the credulity or effectiveness of the approach as an effective paradigm for the interpretation of the biblical narrative.

The present study has explored some literary characteristics of Chronicles in detail, and proposed a case that supports the argument that the Chronicler presupposed and exploited the reader's prior knowledge of the very detailed parts. Usually, the Solomon account has been regarded as a typical example to show that Chronicles has a far different and even contradictory presentation of kings from their portrayal in its *Vorlage*. However, our study has shown that in fact the very account is construed as substantially presupposing and exploiting the reader's prior knowledge. It can be significant evidence to show that the Chronicler was following the old tradition faithfully and took it as his own foundation.[10] While Solomon's faults and failings are not a central concern of the work, these are not intentionally concealed. Rather Solomon's faults are hinted at through the technique of allusion. The prime concern of the account is the glory of the temple building and the united kingdom era. Nevertheless, the present study encourages a further study of the nature of Chronicles in terms of its relationship with the old tradition or its *Vorlage*, and also shows the effectiveness of the reader-sensitive approach to the narrative of the Hebrew Bible.

10. Contra Wellhausen, "complete transformation of the ancient tradition," Wellhausen, *Prolegomena*, 1958 (1885), 224.

Bibliography

Ackroyd, Peter R. *I & II Chronicles, Ezra, Nehemiah.* TBC. London: SCM, 1973.

———. "The Chronicler as Exegete." *JSOT* 2 (1977) 2–32.

———. *The Chronicler in His Age.* JSOTSup 101. Sheffield, UK: JSOT, 1991.

———. "History and Theology in the Writings of the Chronicler." *CTM* 38 (1967) 501–15.

———. *The Second Book of Samuel.* CBC. Cambridge: Cambridge University Press, 1979.

———. "The Theology of the Chronicler." *LTQ* 8 (1973) 101–16. Reprint, In *The Chronicler in His Age.* JSOT Sup 101, 273–89. Sheffield, UK: JSOT, 1991.

Albright, W. F. "The Date and Personality of the Chronicler." *JBL* 40 (1921) 104–24.

Allen, L. C. *1, 2 Chronicles .* CC. Waco, TX: Word, 1987.

———. "Kerygmatic Units in 1 & 2 Chronicles." *JSOT* 41 (1988) 21–36.

Alter, Robert. *The Art of Biblical Narrative.* New York: Basic, 1981.

Anderson, A. A. *2 Samuel.* WBC. Dallas, TX: Word, 1989.

Auld, A. Graeme. *Kings.* DSB. Edinburgh: Saint Andrew, 1984.

———. *Kings without Privilege.* Edinburgh: T. & T. Clark, 1994.

Bar-Efrat, Shimon. *Narrative Art in the Bible.* BLS 17. Sheffield, UK: Almond, 1989.

Barker, Philip C. *II. Chronicles.* PC. London: Kegan Paul, Trench, Trübner, 1890.

Barnes, W. E. *The Books of Chronicles.* CBSC. Cambridge: Cambridge University Press, 1899.

———. "Chronicles as Targum." *ExpTim* 8 (1896–7) 316–19.

Begg, C. "'Seeking Yahweh' and the purpose of Chronicles." *LS* 9 (1982) 128–41.

Bennett, Andrew, editor. *Readers and Reading.* London: Longman, 1995.

Berlin, Adele. *Poetics and Interpretation of Biblical Narrative.* BLS. Sheffield, UK: Almond, 1983.

Bickerman, E. J. *From Ezra to the Last of the Maccabees: Foundations of Post-Biblical Judaism.* New York: Schocken, 1962.

Bimson, John J. "1 and 2 Kings." In *New Bible Commentary,* edited by D. Carson et al., 334–87. Leicester, UK: InterVarsity, 1994.

Blenkinsopp, Joseph. *Ezra-Nehemiah: A Commentary.* OTL. London: SCM, 1989.

Braun, Roddy. *1 Chronicles.* WBC. Waco, Texas: Word, 1986.

———. "Chronicles, Ezra and Nehemiah: Theology and Literary History." In *Studies in the Historical Books of the Old Testament,* edited by J. Emerton, 52–64. Leiden: Brill, 1979.

———. "Chronicles, Ezra and Nehemiah: Theology and Literary History." In *Studies in the Historical Books of the Old Testament*, edited by J. Emerton, 52–64. Leiden: Brill, 1979.

———. "A Reconsideration of the Chronicler's Attitude toward the North." *JBL 96* (1977) 59–62.

———. "Solomon, the Chosen Temple Builder: The Significance of 1 Chronicles 22, 28, and 29 for the Theology of Chronicles." *JBL 95* (1976) 581–90.

———. "Solomonic Apologetic in Chronicles." *JBL 92* (1973) 501–16.

Breasted, James Henry. *A History of the Ancient Egyptians*. New York: Charles Scribner's Sons, 1908.

Brettler, M. "The Structure of 1 Kings 1–11." *JSOT 49* (1991) 87–97.

Bright, John. *A History of Israel*. 3rd ed. Philadelphia: Westminster, 1981.

Bruce, F. F. *The Canon of Scripture*. Glasgow: Chapter House, 1988.

Brueggemann, W. *1 and 2 Kings*. SHC. Macon, GA: Smyth & Helwys, 2000.

———. *First and Second Samuel*. Interpretation. Louisville: John Knox, 1990.

———. *The Land*. OBT. London: SPCK, 1978.

Burns, John Barclay. "Solomon's Egyptian Horse and Exotic Wives." *FFF 7* (1991) 29–44.

Caquot, A. "Peut-on parler de messianisme dans l'oeuvre du Chroniste?" *RTP 16* (1966) 110–20.

Childs, B. S. *Introduction to the Old Testament as Scripture*. Philadelphia: Fortress, 1979.

Christensen, Duane L. *Deuteronomy 1:1—21:9*. Rev. ed. WBC. Nashville, TN: Thomas Nelson, 2001.

Clements, R. E. *Deuteronomy*. 1989. Reprint, OTG. Sheffield, UK: Sheffield Academic Press, 1997.

Clines, David J. A. "The Ancestor in Danger: But Not the Same Danger" In *What Does Eve Do to Help?*, 67–84. JSOPSup 94. Sheffield, UK: JSOT, 1990.

Cogan, Mordechai. *Kings*. AB. London: Doubleday, 2000.

Coggins, R. "Theology and Hermeneutics in the Books of Chronicles" In *In Search of True Wisdom: Essays in Old Testament Interpretation in Honour of Ronald E. Clements*, edited by Edward Ball, 263–78. JSOTSup 300. Sheffield, UK: Sheffield Academic Press, 1999.

Cohen, Shaye J. D. "Solomon and the Daughter of Pharaoh: Intermarriage, Conversion, and the Impurity of Women." *JANES 16–17* (1984–85) 23–37.

Cross, F. M. "A Reconstruction of the Judean Restoration." *JBL 94* (1975) 4–18.

Cultis, E. L., and A. A. Madsen. *The Books of Chronicles*. ICC. New York: Scribner's Sons, 1910.

Davies, Margaret "Reader-Response Criticism" In *Dictionary of Biblical Interpretation*, edited by R. J. Coggins et al., 578–80. London: SCM, 1990.

Deboys, David G. "History and Theology in the Chronicler's Portrayal of Abijah." *Biblica 71* (1990) 48–62.

De Vries, S. J. *1 and 2 Chronicles*. FOTL. Grand Rapids: Eerdmans, 1989.

———. "The Land's Sabbath in 2 Chr 36:21." *PEGLMBS 6* (1986) 96–103.

De Wette, W. M. L. *Beiträge zur Einleitung in das Alte Testament*. Halle: Schimmelpfennig, 1806–1807.

Dillard, Raymond B. *2 Chronicles*. WBC. Waco, TX: Word, 1987.

———. "The Chronicler's Jehoshaphat." *TJ 7* (1986) 17–22.

———. "The Chronicler's Solomon." *WTJ 43* (1980) 289–300.

———. "The Literary Structure of the Chronicler's Solomon Narrative." *JSOT 30* (1984) 85–93.

———. "The Reign of Asa (2 Chronicles 14–16): An Example of the Chronicler's Theological Method." *JETS 23* (1980) 207–18.

———. "Reward and Punishment in Chronicles: The Theology of Immediate Retribution." *WTJ 46* (1984) 164–72.

Dirksen, Peter B. *1 Chronicles*. HCOT. Leuven: Peeters, 2005.

Driver, S. R. *An Introduction to the Literature of the Old Testament*. 9th ed. Edinburgh: T. & T. Clark, 1913.

———. "The Speeches in Chronicles." *The Expositor 5th series vol. 1* (1895) 241–56.

Duke, Rodney K. "Chronicles, Books of." In *Dictionary of the Old Testament Historical Books*, edited by Bill T. Arnold et al., 161–81. Leicester, UK: InterVarsity, 2005.

———. "The Ethical Appeal of the Chronicler." In *Rhetoric, Ethic, and Moral Persuasion in Biblical Discourse: Essays from the 2002 Heidelberg Conference*, Thomas. H. Olbricht et al., 33–51. ESEC 11. London: T. & T. Clark, 2005.

———. "A Model for a Theology of Biblical Historical Narratives Proposed and Demonstrated with the Books of Chronicles." In *History and Interpretation: Essays in Honour of John H. Hayes*, edited by M. Patrick Graham et al., 65–77. Sheffield, UK: Sheffield Academic Press, 1993.

———. *The Persuasive Appeal of the Chronicler: A Rhetorical Analysis*. Sheffield, UK: Almond, 1990.

———. "A Rhetorical Approach to Appreciating the Books of Chronicles." In *The Chronicler as Author*, edited by M. Patrick Graham et al., 100–35. Sheffield, UK: Sheffield Academic Press, 1999.

Eissfeldt, O. *The Old Testament: An Introduction*. Translated by Peter R. Ackroyd. Oxford: Blackwell, 1965.

Elmslie, W. A. L. *The Books of Chronicles*. CBSC. Cambridge: Cambridge University Press, 1916.

Enns, Peter. "Law of God." In *New International Dictionary of Old Testament Theology and Exegesis*, edited by Willem A. VanGemeren, 893–900. Grand Rapids: Zondervan, 1997.

Eskenazi, Tamara C. "A Literary Approach to Chronicles' Ark Narrative in 1 Chronicles 13–16." In *Fortunate the Eyes that See: Essays in Honor of David Noel Freedman in Celebration of His Seventieth Birthday*, edited by A. B. Beck et al., 258–74. Grand Rapids: Eerdmans, 1995.

Eslinger, Lyle. "Chapter 5: King Solomon's Prayers." In *Into the Hands of the Living God*, 123–81. JSOTSup 84. Sheffield, UK: Almond, 1989.

Evans, Mary J. *1 and 2 Samuel*. NIBC. Peabody, MA: Hendrickson, 2000.

Fewell, D. N. "Sennacherib's Defeat: Words at War in 2 Kings 18.13—19.37." *JSOT 34* (1986) 79–90.

Fishbane, Michael. *Biblical Interpretation in Ancient Israel*. Oxford: Clarendon, 1985.

Fitzmeyer, Joseph A. *The Gospel according to Luke I–LX*. AB. Garden City, NY: Doubleday, 1981.

Fokkelman, J. P. *Narrative Art and Poetry in the Books of Samuel. Vol. 2: The Crossing Fates*. Assen/Maastricht, The Netherlands: Van Gorcum, 1986.

Freedman, D. N. "The Chronicler's Purpose." *CBQ 23* (1961) 436–42.

Fretheim, T. E. *First and Second Kings*. WeBC. Westminster: John Knox, 1999.

Frisch, A. "The Exodus Motif in 1 Kgs1–14." *JSOT 87* (2000) 3–21.

————. "Structure and its Significance: The Narrative of Solomon's Reign (1 Kings 1–12:24)." *JSOT 51* (1991) 3–14.

Freund, Elizabeth, editor. *The Return of the Reader: Reader-Response Criticism.* New York: Methuen, 1987.

Galling, K. *Die Bücher der Chronik, Esra, Nehemia.* ATD 12. Göttingen: Vandenhoeck & Ruprecht, 1954.

Geiger, A. *Urschrift und Übersetzungen der Bibel in ihrer Abhängigkeit von der Inneren Entwicklung des Judentums.* 1857. 2nd ed. Frankfurt am Main: Madda, 1928.

Gordon, Robert P. *1 & 2 Samuel.* Exeter, UK: Paternoster, 1986.

Graham, M. Patrick. "Aspects of the Structure and Rhetoric of 2 Chronicles 25." In *History and Interpretation: Essays in Honour of John H. Hayes,* edited by M. Patrick Graham et al., 78–89. Sheffield, UK: Sheffield Academic Press, 1993.

————. "A Connection Proposed between II Chr 24, 26 and Ezra 9–10." *ZAW 97* (1985) 256–58.

Gray, J. *1 & 2 Kings: A Commentary.* OTL. London: SCM, 1964.

Green, Joel B. *The Gospel of Luke.* NICNT. Grand Rapid: Eerdmans, 1997.

Greenberg, M. "Some Postulates of Biblical Criminal Law," In *Yehezkel Kaufmann Jubilee Volume,* edited by M. Haran, 5–28. Jerusalem: Magnes, 1960.

Gunn, David. "In Security: The David of Biblical Narrative." In *Signs and Wonders: Biblical Texts in Literary Focus,* edited by J. C. Exum, 134–51. Atlanta: Scholars, 1989.

Gunn, David, and D. N. Fewell. *Narrative in the Hebrew Bible.* OBS. Oxford: Oxford University Press, 1993.

Hamilton, Victor P. *Handbook on the Historical Books.* Grand Rapids: Baker Academic, 2001.

Halpern, Baruch. *The Constitution of the Monarchy in Israel.* Chico, CA: Scholars, 1981.

Harrison, R. K. *Introduction to the Old Testament.* London: Tyndale, 1969.

Hauer Jr., Chris. "The Economics of National Security in Solomonic Israel." *JSOT 18* (1980) 63–73.

Hays, J. Daniel. "Has the Narrator Come to Praise Solomon or to Bury Him?: Narrative Subtlety in 1 Kings 1–11." *JSOT 28* (2003) 149–74.

Heaton, E. W. *Solomon's New Man: The Emergence of Ancient Israel as a Nation State.* New York: Pica, 1974.

Hooker, Paul K. *First and Second Chronicles.* WeBC. Louisville, KY: Westminster John Knox, 2001.

Hyman, R. T. "The Rabshakeh's Speech (II Kg. 18–25): A Study of Rhetorical Intimidation." *JBQ 23* (1995) 213–20.

Im, T. S. *Das Davidbild in den Chronikbüchern: David als Idealbild des theokratischen Messianismus für den Chronisten.* Frankfurt: Lang, 1985.

Japhet, Sara. "The Supposed Common Authorship of Chronicles and Ezra-Nehemiah Investigated Anew." *VT 18* (1968) 330–71.

Japhet, Sara. *I & II Chronicles.* OTL. Louisville, KY: Westminster/John Knox, 1993.

————. "Chronicles, Book of." In *EncJud* vol. 5, 517–34. 1971.

————. *The Ideology of the Book of Chronicles and Its Place in Biblical Thought.* Frankfurt: Lang, 1997.

————. "The Relationship between Chronicles and Ezra-Nehemiah." In *Congress Volume: Leuven 1989,* edited by J. A. Emerton , 298–313. VTSup 43 Leiden: Brill, 1991.

————. "Sheshbazzar and Zerubbabel—Against the Background of the Religious and Historical Tendencies of Ezra-Nehemiah." *ZAW 94* (1982) 66–98.

Jarick, John. *1 Chronicles.* RNBC. Sheffield, UK: Sheffield Academic Press, 2002.

————. *2 Chronicles.* RNBC. Sheffield, UK: Sheffield Phoenix, 2007.

Jobling, David. "'Forced Labor': Solomon's Golden Age and the Question of Literary Representation." *Semeia 54* (1992) 57–76.

John C. Endres, S.J. "The Spiritual Vision of Chronicles: Wholehearted, Joy-filled Worship of God." *CBQ 69* (2007) 1–21.

Johnson, M. D. *The Purpose of the Biblical Genealogies.* Cambridge: Cambridge University Press, 1969.

Johnstone, William. *1 and 2 Chronicles: 1 Chronicles 1–2 Chronicles 9. Israel's Place among the Nations.* Vol. 1. JSOTSup. Sheffield, UK: Sheffield Academic Press, 1997.

————. *1 and 2 Chronicles: 2 Chronicles 10–36. Guilt and Atonement.* Vol. 2. JSOTSup. Sheffield, UK: Sheffield Academic Press, 1997

————. "Guilt and Atonement: The Theme of 1 and 2 Chronicles." In *A Word in Season: Essays in Honour of William MaKane,* James D. Martin et al., 113–38. Sheffield, UK: JSOT, 1986.

————. "Reactivating the Chronicles Analogy in Pentateuchal Studies, with Special Reference to the Sinai Pericope in Exodus." *ZAW 99* (1987) 16–37.

Jones, G. H. *1 and 2 Kings Volume I.* NCBC. Grand Rapid: Eerdmans, 1985.

————. *1 & 2 Chronicles.* OTG. Sheffield, UK: Sheffield Academic Press, 1999.

Kaiser, Otto. *Introduction to the Old Testament.* Oxford: Blackwell, 1975.

Kalimi, Isaac. "The Contribution of the Literary Study of Chronicles to the Solution of its Textual Problems." *BibInt 3* (1995) 190–212.

————. "Paronomasia in the Book of Chronicles." *JSOT 67* (1995) 27–41.

————. *Zur Geschichtsschreibung des Chronisten: Literarisch-historiographische Abweichungen der Chronik von ihren Paralleltexten in den Samuel- und Königsbüchern.* BZAW 226. Berlin: de Gruyter, 1995.

Kalimi, Isaac. "Was the Chronicler a Historian?" In *The Chronicler as Historian,* edited by M. P. Graham et al., 73–89. JSOTSup 238. Sheffield, UK: Sheffield Academic Press, 1997.

Kang, Jung Ju. *The Persuasive Portrayal of Solomon in 1 Kings 1–11.* Bern: Lang, 2003.

Keil, C. F. *I & II Kings, I & II Chronicles, Ezra, Nehemiah, Esther.* Translated by Andrew Harper. COTTV 3. Grand Rapid: Eerdmans, 1973.

Kellerman, M. "*sabal.*" In *TDOT vol. 10,* 139–44. Reprint. Grand Rapids: Eerdmans 1999.

Kelly, Brian E. "Messianic Elements in the Chronicler's Work." In *The Lord's Anointed: Interpretation of Old Testament Messianic Text,* edited by P. E. Satterthwaite et al., 249–64. Grand Rapid: Baker, 1996.

————. *Retribution and Eschatology in Chronicles.* JSOTSup 211. Sheffield, UK: Sheffield Academic Press, 1996.

————. "'Retribution' Revisited: Covenant, Grace, and Restoration." In *The Chronicler as Theologian: Essays in Honour of Ralph W. Klein,* edited by M. P. Graham et al., 206–27. JSOTSup 371. London: T. & T. Clark, 2003.

Kidner, Derek. *Ezra and Nehemiah.* TOTC. 1979. Reprint. Leicester, UK: InterVarsity, 2003.

Kissling, Paul J. *Reliable Characters in the Primary History: Profiles of Moses, Joshua, Elijah and Elisha.* JSOTSup 224. Sheffield, UK: Sheffield Academic Press, 1996.

Klein, Ralph W. *1 Chronicles*. Hermeneia. Minneapolis: Fortress, 2006.

———. "The God of the Chronicler." In *And God Saw That It Was Good: Essays on Creation and God in Honor of Terence E. Fretheim*, edited by F. J. Gaiser et al., 120–27. WWSup 5. St. Paul, MN: Word & World, Luther Seminar, 2006.

———. "How Many in A Thousand?" In *The Chronicler as Historian*, edited by M. P. Graham et al., 270–82. JSOTSup 238. Sheffield, UK: Sheffield Academic Press, 1997.

Kleinig, J. W. "The Divine Institution: the Lord's Song in Chronicles." *JSOT* 55 (1992) 75–83.

———. "Recent Research in Chronicles." *CRBS* 2 (1994) 43–76.

Knoppers, Gary N. "The Deuteronomist and the Deuteronomic Law of the King: A Reexamination of a Relationship." *ZAW* 108 (1996) 329–46.

———. "Intermarriage, Social Complexity, and Ethnic Diversity in the Genealogy of Judah." *JBL* 120 (2001) 15–30.

———. "Jehoshaphat's Judiciary and 'The Scroll of YHWH's Torah.'" *JBL* 113 (1994) 59–80.

———. "Rehoboam in Chronicles: Villain or Victim?" *JBL* 109 (1990) 423–40.

———. "Solomon's Fall and Deuteronomy." In *The Age of Solomon: Scholarship at the Turn of the Millennium*, edited by L. Handy, 392–410. Leiden: Brill, 1997.

———. *Two Nations under God: The Deuteronomistic History of Solomon and the Dual Monarchies. Volume 1: The Reign of Solomon and the Rise of Jeroboam*. HSM 52. Atlanta: Scholars, 1993.

———. "'Yhwh Is Not with Israel': Alliances as a Topos in Chronicles." *CBQ* 58 (1996) 601–26.

Lemke, W. E. "The Synoptic Problem in the Chronicler's History." *HTR* 58 (1965) 349–63.

Lohfink, Norbert "Die deuteronomistische Darstellung des Übergangs der Führung Israels von Moses auf Josue. " *Scholastik* 37 (1962) 32–44.

Long, Burke O. *1 Kings with an Introduction to Historical Literature*. FOTL 9. Grand Rapid, Michigan: William B. Eerdmans Publishing Company.

Long, V. Philips. *The Art of Biblical History*. FCI 5. Leicester, UK: Apollos, 1994.

Longman III, Tremper. "Literary Approaches to Biblical Interpretation." (1987), In *Foundations of Contemporary Interpretation*, edited by M. Silva, 91–192. Grand Rapids: Zondervan, 1996.

Mendenhall, G. E. "The Census Lists of Numbers 1 and 26." *JBL* 77 (1958) 52–66.

Mason, R. "Some Echoes of the Preaching in the Second Temple?" *ZAW* 96 (1984) 221–35.

———. *Preaching the Tradition: Homily and Hermeneutics after the Exile*. Cambridge: Cambridge University Press, 1990.

Mathias, D. "'Levitische Predigt' und Deuteronomismus." *ZAW* 96 (1984) 23–49.

McCarter, Jr., P. Kyle. *II Samuel*. AB. Garden City, NY: Doubleday, 1984.

McCarthy, D. J. "An Installation Genre?" *JBL* 90 (1971) 31–41.

McConville, J. G. *Chronicles*. DSB. Edinburgh: St Andrew, 1984.

———. "Deuteronomy." In *NBC*, 21st Century Edition, edited by D. Carson et al., 198–232. Leicester, UK: InterVarsity, 1994.

———. *Deuteronomy*. ApOTC. Leicester: Apollos, 2002.

———. "Narrative and Meaning in the Book of Kings." *Biblica* 70 (1989) 31–48.

McKenzie, Steven L. *1–2 Chronicles*. AbOTC. Nashville: Abingdon, 2004.

―――. *The Chronicler's Use of the Deuteronomistic History.* HSM 33. Atlanta: Scholars, 1985.

Mendenhall, George E. "The Census Lists of Numbers 1 and 26." *JBL 77* (1958) 52–66.

Mendelsohn, I. "On Corvée Labor in Ancient Canaan and Israel." *BASOR 167* (1962) 31–35.

Mettinger, Tryggve N. D. *Solomonic State Officials: A Study of the Civil Government Officials of the Israelite Monarch.* ConBOT 5. Lund: Skanska Centraltryckeriet, 1971.

Milgrom, Jacob. *Studies in Levitical Terminology I.* NES 14. Berkeley: University of California Press, 1970.

Mitchell, Christine. "The Ironic Death of Josiah in 2 Chronicles." *CBQ 68* (2006) 421–35.

Mosis, R. *Untersuchungen zur Theologie des chronistischen Geschichtswerkes.* FTS 92. Freiberg: Herder, 1973.

Muilenburg, James. "Form Criticism and Beyond." *JBL 88* (1969) 1–18.

Murray, Donald F. "Retribution and Revival: Theological Theory, Religious Praxis, and the Future in Chronicles." *JSOT 88* (2000) 77–99.

Myers, J. M. *I Chronicles.* AB. Garden City, NY: Doubleday, 1965.

―――. *II Chronicles.* AB. Garden City, NY: Doubleday, 1965.

Newsome, James D. "Toward a New Understanding of the Chronicler and His Purposes." *JBL 94* (1975) 201–17.

Nelson, Richard D. *First and Second Kings.* Interpretation. Louisville: John Knox, 1987.

Nolland, John. *Luke 1—9:20.* WBC. Dallas, TX: Word, 1989.

North, R. "The Chronicler: 1–2 Chronicles, Ezra, Nehemiah." In *The Jerome Biblical Commentary,* edited by R. E. Brown et al., 402–38. Englewood Cliffs, NJ: Prentice-Hall, 1968.

Noth, Martin. *The Chronicler's History.* JSOTSup 50. Translated by H. G. M. Williamson. Sheffield, UK: JSOT, 1987.

―――. *The Deuteronomistic History.* JSOTSup 15. Translated by Jane Doull. 1981. Reprint. Sheffield, UK: JSOT, 1991.

Oblath, M. "Pharaohs and Kings—Whence the Exodus?" *JSOT 87* (2000) 23–42.

Oeming, M. *Das wahre Israel: Die genealogische 'Vorhalle' 1 Chronik 1–9.* Stuttgart: Kohlhammer, 1990.

Olley, John W. "Pharaoh's Daughter, Solomon's Palace, and the Temple: Another Look at the Structure of 1 Kings 1–11." *JSOT 27* (2003) 355–69.

Parker, K. I. "Repetition as a Structuring Device in 1 Kings 1–11." *JSOT 42* (1988) 19–27.

―――. "Solomon as Philosopher King?: The Nexus of Law and Wisdom in 1 King 1–11." *JSOT 53* (1992) 75–91.

Payne, D. F. "The Purpose and Methods of the Chronicler." *FT 93* (1963) 64–73.

―――. *Samuel.* DSB. Edinburgh: Saint Andrew, 1982.

Pfeiffer, Robert H. "The Books of Chronicles." In *Introduction to the Old Testament,* 782–812. London: Adam and Charles Black, 1953.

Plöger, Otto. "Reden und Gebete im deuteronomistischen und chronistischen Geschichtswerk." In *Festschrift für Günther Dehn: zum 75. Geburtstag am 18. April 1957 dargebracht von der Evangelisch-Theologischen Fakultät der Rheinischen Friedrich Wilhelms-Universität zu Bonn,* edited by W. Schneemelcher, 35–49. Neukirchen: Moers, 1957.

————. *Theocracy and Eschatology*. Translated by S. Rudman. Oxford: Blackwell, 1968.

Polzin, Robert. *Late Biblical Hebrew: Toward an Historical Typology of Biblical Hebrew Prose*. HSM 12. Missoula, MT: Scholars, 1976.

Porten, B. "The Structure and Theme of the Solomon Narrative (1 Kgs 3–11)." *HUCA 38* (1966) 93–128.

Porter, J. R. "The Succession of Joshua." In *Proclamation and Presence: Old Testament Essays in Honour of Gwynne Henton Davies*, edited by J. I. Durham and J. R. Porter, 102–32. London: SCM Press, 1970.

Poythress, Vern S. "Science and Hermeneutics: Implications of Scientific Method for Biblical Interpretation." (1988) In *Foundations of Contemporary Interpretation*, edited by M. Silva, 431–531. Grand Rapid: Zondervan, 1996.

Provan, Iain W. *1 and 2 Kings*. NIBC. Peabody, MA: Hendrickson, 1995.

Pucci, Joseph. *The Full-Knowing Reader: Allusion and the Power of the Reader in the Western Literary Tradition*. New Haven: Yale University Press, 1998.

Reinhartz, A. "Anonymous Women and the Collapse of the Monarch: A Study in Narrative Technique." In *Feminist Companion to Samuel and Kings*, edited by A. Brenner, 43–67. FCB 5. Sheffield, UK: Sheffield Academic Press, 1994.

Rigsby, R. O. "The Historiography of Speeches and Prayers in the Books of Chronicles." ThD diss., Southern Baptist Theological Seminary, 1973.

Riley, William. *King and Cultus in Chronicles*. JSOTSup 160. Sheffield, UK: JSOT, 1993.

Rothstein, J. W. and Hänel, J. *Das erste Buch der Chronik*. KAT 18/2. Leipzig: Scholl, 1927.

Robbins, Vernon K. *Jesus the Teacher: A Socio-Rhetorical Interpretation of Mark*. Philadelphia: Fortress, 1984.

Rudolph, W. *Chronikbücher*. HAT 21. Tübingen: Mohr, 1955.

————. *Esra und Nehemia*. Tübingen: Mohr, 1949.

————. "Problems in the Book of Chronicles." *VT 4* (1954) 401–9.

Sands, P. C. *Literary Genius of the Old Testament*. Oxford: Clarendon, 1924.

Sarvan, G. "1 and 2 Kings." In *The Literary Guide to the Bible*, edited by R. Alter et al., 146–64. London: Collins, 1987.

Satterthwaite, Philip, and J. G. McConville. *Exploring the Old Testament, Volume 2: The Histories*. London: SPCK, 2007.

Schaefer, G. E. "The Significance of Seeking God in the Purpose of the Chronicler." ThD. diss., Southern Baptist Theological Seminary, 1972.

Schearing, Linda S. "Wealth of Women: Looking behind, within, and beyond Solomon's Story." In *The Age of Solomon: Scholarship at the Turn of the Millennium*, edited by L. Handy, 428–56. Leiden: Brill, 1997.

Schniedewind, William M. *The Word of God in Transition: From Prophet to Exegete in the Second Temple Period*. JSOTSup 197. Sheffield, UK: Sheffield Academic Press, 1995.

Scholes, Robert. *The Crafty Reader*. New Haven: Yale University Press, 2001.

Seibert, Eric A. *Subversive Scribes and the Solomonic Narrative: A Reading of 1 Kings 1–11*. LBS 436. London: T. & T. Clark, 2006.

Selman, Martin J. *1 Chronicles: An Introduction and Commentary*. TOTC. Leicester, UK: InterVarsity, 1994.

————. *2 Chronicles: A Commentary*. TOTC. Leicester, UK: InterVarsity, 1994.

————. "The Kingdom of God in the Old Testament." *TynBul 40* (1989) 162–83.

Shaver, Judson R. *Torah and the Chronicler's History Work: An Inquiry into the Chronicler's Reference to Laws, Festivals, and Cultic Institutions in Relationship to Pentateuch Legislation.* BJS 196. Atlanta: Scholars, 1989.

Siedlecki, Armin. "Foreigners, Warfare and Judahite Identity in Chronicles." In *The Chronicler as Author: Studies in Text and Texture,* edited by Steven L. McKenzie, 229–66. Sheffield, UK: Sheffield Academic Press, 1999.

Silva, M. "Old Testament in Paul." In *Dictionary of Paul and His Letters,* edited by Gerald F. Hawthorne et al., 630–42. Leicester, UK: InterVarsity, 1993.

Slotki, I. W. *Chronicles.* SBB. London: Soncino, 1952.

Smith, Henry Preserved. *Critical and Exegetical Commentary on the Books of Samuel.* ICC. Edinburgh: T. & T. Clark, 1912.

Snaith, Norman H. "The Historical Books." In *The Old Testament and Modern Study,* edited by H. H. Rowley, 84–114. Oxford: Clarendon, 1955.

Snyman, Gerrie. "'Tis a Vice to Know Him': Readers' Response-Ability and Responsibility in 2 Chronicles 14–16" *Semeia 77* (1997) 91–113.

Solomon, Anne M. "The Structure of the Chronicler's History: A Key to the Organization of the Pentateuch." *Semeia 46* (1989) 51–64.

Sommer, Benjamin D. "Exegesis, Allusion and Intertextuality in the Hebrew Bible: A Response to Lyle Eslinger." *VT 46* (1996) 479–89.

Staley, Jeffrey Lloyd. *The Print's First Kiss: A Rhetorical Investigation of the Implied Reader in the Fourth Gospel.* SBLDS 82. Atlanta: Scholars, 1988.

Strübind, K. *Tradition als Interpretation in der Chronik: König Josaphat als Paradigma chronistischer Hermeneutik und Theologie.* BZAW 201. Berlin: de Gruyter, 1991.

Sternberg, Meir. *The Poetics of Biblical Narrative: Ideological Literature and the Drama of Reading, Indiana Studies in Biblical Literature.* Bloomington, IN: Indiana University Press, 1985.

Stinespring, W. F. "Eschatology in Chronicles." *JBL 80* (1961) 209–19.

Sugimoto, Tomotoshi. "Chronicles as Independent Literature." *JSOT 55* (1992) 61–74.

Talshir, D. "A Reinvestigation of the Linguistic Relationship between Chronicles and Ezra-Nehemiah." *VT 38* (1988) 165–93.

Talshir, Zipora. "Several Canon-Related Concepts Originating in Chronicles." *ZAW 113* (2001) 386–403.

Tate, W. Randolph *Biblical Interpretation: An Integrated Approach.* Rev. ed. Peabody, MA: Hendrickson, 1997.

Thompson, J. A. *1, 2 Chronicles.* NAC. Nashville: Broadman & Holman, 1994.

Throntveit, Mark A. "The Idealization of Solomon as the Glorification of God in the Chronicler's Royal Speeches and Royal Prayers." In *The Age of Solomon: Scholarship at the Turn of the Millennium,* edited by L. Handy, 411–27. Leiden: Brill, 1997.

———. "Linguistic Analysis and the Question of Authorship in Chronicles, Ezra and Nehemiah." *VT 32* (1982) 201–16.

———. *When Kings Speak: Royal Speech and Royal Prayer in Chronicles.* SBLDS 93. Atlanta: Scholars, 1987.

Tompkins, Jane P., editor. *Reader-Response Criticism.* Baltimore: Johns Hopkins University Press, 1980.

Torrey, C. C. "Chronicler as Editor and as Independent Narrator." *AJSL XXV* (1908–9) 157–73, 88–217.

———. *Ezra Studies.* Chicago: University of Chicago Press, 1910.

Trotter, James M. "Reading, Readers and Reading Readers Reading the Account of Saul's Death in 1 Chronicles 10." In *The Chronicler as Author: Studies in Text and Texture*, edited by M. Patrick Graham, 294–310. Sheffield, UK: Sheffield Academic Press, 1999.

Tuell, Steven S. *First and Second Chronicles*. Interpretation. Louisville, KY: John Knox, 1996.

Van Seters, John. "The Chronicler's Account of Solomon's Temple Building: A Continuity Theme." In *The Chronicler as Historian*, edited by M. P. Graham et al., 283–300. JSOTSup 238. Sheffield, UK: Sheffield Academic Press, 1997.

Viviano, P. "Glory Lost: The Reign of Solomon in the Deuteronomistic History." In *The Age of Solomon: Scholarship at the Turn of the Millennium*, edited by L. Handy, 336–47. Leiden: Brill, 1997.

Von Rad, G. *Das Geschichtsbild des Chronistischen Werkes*. Stuttgart: Kohlhammer, 1930.

———. "The Levitical Sermon in I and II Chronicles." (1934) In *The Problem of the Hexateuch and Other Essays*, 267–80. Edinburgh: Oliver & Boyd, 1966.

———. *Old Testament Theology, I*. London: SCM, 1962.

Walsh, J. "The Characterization of Solomon in First King 1–5." *CBQ 57* (1995) 471–93.

———. "Symmetry and the Sin of Solomon." *Shofar 12* (1993) 11–27.

Weinfeld, Moshe. *Deuteronomy and the Deuteronomic School*. Oxford: Clarendon, 1972.

Weitzman, Steven. "Allusion, Artifice, and Exile in the Hymn of Tobit." *JBL 115* (1996) 49–61.

Welch, Adam C. *Post-Exilic Judaism*. Edinburgh: Blackwood & Sons, 1935.

———. *The Work of the Chronicler: Its Purpose and its Date*. London: Oxford University Press, 1939.

Wellhausen, J. *Prolegomena to the History of Ancient Israel*. Translated by J. S. Black and A. Menzies. Edinburgh: T. & T. Clark, 1958.

Welten, P. *Geschichte und Geschichtsdarstellung in den Chronikbüchern*. WMANT 42. Neukirchen: Neukirchener Verlage, 1973.

Wenham, Gordon. *Exploring the Old Testament Volume 1: The Pentateuch*. London: SPCK, 2003.

Wenham, J. W. "Large Numbers in the Old Testament." *TynBul 18*, (1967) 19–53

Whybray, R. Norman. *The Good Life in the Old Testament*. London: T. & T. Clark, 2002.

Wilcock, Michael. "1 and 2 Chronicles." In *New Bible Commentary*, edited by G. Wenham et al., 388–419. Leicester, UK: InterVarsity, 1994.

———. *The Message of Chronicles*. BST. Leicester, UK: InterVarsity, 1987.

Wilda, G. "Das Königsbild des chronistischen Geschichtswerkes." PhD diss., Rheinische Friedrich-Wilhelms Universität, 1959.

Willi, T. *Die Chronik als Auslegung: Untersuchungen zur literarischen Gestaltung der historischen Überlieferung Israels*. FRLANT 106. Göttingen: Vandenhoeck & Ruprecht, 1972.

Williams, D. "Once Again: The Structure of the Narrative of Solomon's Reign." *JSOT 86* (1999) 49–66.

Williamson, H. G. M. *1 and 2 Chronicles*. NCBC. London: Marshall, Morgan & Scott, 1982.

———. "The Accession of Solomon in the Books of Chronicles." *VT 26* (1976) 351–61.

———. "Eschatology in Chronicles." *TynBul 28* (1977) 115–54.

———. *Ezra, Nehemiah*. WBC. Nashville, TN: Thomas Nelson, 1985.

─────. *Ezra and Nehemiah*. OTG. 1987. Reprint. Sheffield, UK: Sheffield Academic Press, 1996.

─────. *Israel in the Books of Chronicles*. Cambridge: Cambridge University Press, 1977.

Wiseman, D. J. *1 and 2 Kings: An Introduction and Commentary*. TOTC. Leicester, UK: InterVarsity, 1993.

Younger, Jr., K. Lawson. "The Figurative Aspect and the Contextual Method in the Evaluation of the Solomonic Empire (1 Kings 1–11)." In *The Bible in Three Dimensions: Essays in Celebration of Forty Years of Biblical Studies in the University of Sheffield*, edited by David J. A. Clines, 157–75. Sheffield, UK: JSOT, 1990.

Zimmerli, Walther. *Old Testament Theology in Outline*. Translated by David E. Green. Edinburgh: T. & T. Clark, 1978.

Zöckler, Otto. "Chronicles." In *A Commentary on The Holy Scriptures: Chronicles, Ezra, Esther*, 1–278. Grand Rapids: Zondervan, 1976.

Zunz, L. *Die gottesdienstlichen Vorträge der Juden historisch entwickelt*. 1832. Reprint. Darmstadt: Wissenschaftliche Buchgesellschaft, 1966.

Index of Authors

Index of Authors

Fishbane, Michael, 99, 277
Fitzmeyer, Joseph A., 183
Fokkelman, J. P., 52
Frisch, A., 9, 60–61, 71, 73, 75, 83, 87
Freedman, D. N., 117
Fretheim, T. E., 78
Freund, Elizabeth, 277

Galling, K., 116
Geiger, A., 255
Gordon, Robert P., 52
Graham, M. Patrick, 103, 255
Gray, J., 62, 63, 89
Green, Joel B., 183
Gunn, David., 107
Gunn, D. and Fewell, D., 63, 145, 146, 277

Hamilton, Victor P., 106
Halpern, B., 235
Harrison, R. K., 110, 111, 115
Hauer, Jr. Chris, 74, 238, 239, 241, 267
Hays, J. Daniel, 63, 65, 71, 74, 76, 78, 81
Heaton, E. W., 74
Hooker, Paul K., 44, 117, 250, 262
Hyman, R. T., 55

Im, T. S., 1, 17, 117–18

Japhet, Sara, 1, 4–5, 7, 9, 16, 17, 22, 25, 27, 29, 30, 32, 40, 48, 58, 99, 102, 104, 105, 106, 108, 109, 112, 114, 116, 117, 118, 119, 124, 126–27, 128, 161, 163, 164–65, 168, 173, 175, 177, 178–80, 181, 184, 185, 186, 187, 188, 190, 192, 198, 199, 200, 201, 202, 204–5, 215, 234, 241, 242, 243, 244, 251–60, 262, 266, 275
Jarick, John, 16, 26, 214, 242, 261
Jobling, David, 9
John C. Endres, S. J., 117
Johnson, M. D., 109, 226
Johnstone, William, 25, 26, 37, 38, 39, 99, 108, 109, 123, 143, 147, 201, 218, 225, 242, 243, 244

Jones, G. H., 9, 17, 28, 42, 62, 89, 99, 100, 117, 118, 191, 201

Kaiser, Otto., 19, 177
Kalimi, Isaac, 99, 103, 127, 143, 145–46, 261
Kang, Jung Ju, 9, 10, 59, 63, 66–67, 76, 91, 222, 268, 271
Keil, C. F., 21, 44, 52, 120
Kellerman, M., 90
Kelly, Brian E., 5–7, 8, 11, 12, 20, 24, 27, 105, 108, 109, 111, 113, 119, 121, 126, 128, 163, 220, 226, 229, 232, 242, 250–51, 254, 259, 264
Kidner, Derek, 106, 114, 175, 176
Kissling, Paul J., 43–44, 136
Klein, Ralph W., 100, 117, 119, 229
Kleinig, J. W., 103, 187
Knoppers, Gary N., 8, 18, 25, 32, 33, 34, 35, 36- 37, 38, 39, 62, 65, 81, 82, 122, 134, 142, 149, 150–51, 226, 232, 250, 251

Lemke, W. E., 6, 183, 265
Lohfink, Norbert, 156, 189
Long, Burke O., 86
Long, V. Philips, 276
Longman III, Tremper, 277

Mason, R., 21, 22, 40, 41, 47, 123, 135, 254
Mathias, D., 40
McCarter, Jr. P. Kyle., 52
McCarthy, D. J., 189
McConville, J. G., 10, 26, 36, 38, 55, 62, 75, 76, 79, 119, 162, 196, 198, 214, 229
McKenzie, Steven L., 5, 6, 17, 28, 29, 31, 32, 37, 39, 99, 104, 117, 118, 119, 121, 184, 200, 226, 242, 262
Mendenhall, George E., 229
Mendelsohn, I., 89
Mettinger, Tryggve N. D., 89
Milgrom, J., 161
Mitchell, Christine, 142, 201
Mosis, R., 1, 2, 3–4, 118, 119, 142, 210, 220
Muilenburg, James, 42, 43

Index of Authors

Wilda, G., 120, 163, 201

Willi, T., 99, 100, 105, 142, 153, 161, 162, 189

Williams, D., 61

Williamson, H. G. H., 4, 7, 9, 16, 17, 18, 20, 22, 24, 25, 26, 28, 29, 32–36, 37, 38, 39, 40, 42, 43, 44, 48–50, 55, 99, 100, 101, 102, 104, 105, 106, 107, 108, 109–10, 111, 112, 114, 116, 117, 118, 120, 122, 126, 128, 136, 143, 147, 148, 149, 150, 153, 155, 156, 157–58, 163, 170, 173, 180, 183, 184, 185, 188, 189, 190–91, 197, 199, 200, 201, 206, 208, 214, 226, 227, 241, 242, 244, 245, 249

Wiseman, D. J., 62, 63, 89

Younger, Jr., K. Lawson, 80

Zimmerli, Walther, 200

Zöckler, Otto., 21

Zunz, L., 99, 105, 106, 241

Index of References

1 KINGS

1 CHRONICLES